LIEDER LINE BY LINE

LIEDER
LINE BY LINE
and word for word

REVISED EDITION

Lois Phillips

CLARENDON PRESS · OXFORD
1996

Oxford University Press, Great Clarendon Street, Oxford OX2 6DP

Oxford New York

Athens Auckland Bangkok Bogota Bombay
Buenos Aires Calcutta Cape Town Dar es Salaam
Delhi Florence Hong Kong Istanbul Karachi
Kuala Lumpur Madras Madrid Melbourne
Mexico City Nairobi Paris Singapore
Taipei Tokyo Toronto Warsaw

and associated companies in
Berlin Ibadan

Oxford is a trade mark of Oxford University Press

Published in the United States by
Oxford University Press Inc., New York

First edition published by
George Duckworth & Co. Ltd 1979
Revised edition 1996

British Library Cataloguing in Publication Data
Data available

Library of Congress Cataloging in Publication Data
Phillips, Lois.
Lieder line by line, and word for word / Lois Phillips.
—Rev. ed.
p. cm.
1. Songs—Texts. I. Title.
ML54.6.P55L5 1996 <Case> 782.42168'0268—dc20 95-42311
ISBN 0-19-879017-1

3 5 7 9 10 8 6 4 2

Printed in Great Britain
on acid-free paper by
J. W. Arrowsmith Ltd
Bristol, Avon

Contents

Preface

'Of course what young singers really need when they are studying *Lieder* is a word-for-word translation, with the equivalent English word printed under each German word,' said Roy Henderson during a conversation with Sir Anthony Lewis, Principal of the Royal Academy of Music in 1969.

Shortly afterwards I too happened to be discussing the study and performance of *Lieder* with Sir Anthony, and he repeated what Roy Henderson had said. I was very interested; such translations would indeed be extremely useful, printed together with a version in good, clear prose, which would be essential to disentangle the often unintelligible series of words resulting from a literal word-for-word translation. After some further discussion I was invited by Sir Anthony Lewis to undertake a series of translations for the singing students of the Royal Academy, with a view to eventual publication to enable them to be much more widely used.

Singing in a foreign language presents many problems. Apart from correct pronunciation and emphasis, it is of the utmost importance for the singer to know what the song is about, not merely in the general sense, but in every detail, if a real interpretation is to be achieved. Nowhere in song literature is this more necessary than in German *Lieder*, where at its most demanding, as for instance in any song of Hugo Wolf, the singer – and also the pianist – must understand every word and phrase, so close do the words lie to the music flowing from them.

It is the aim of this book to help the performer to a better and more complete knowledge of the language, and of the poems themselves. It is certainly not intended to save him the trouble of searching out all he can for himself, or even of learning German at all! But most young singers when they begin to study *Lieder* are ill-equipped to deal with the formidable problems that they are likely to encounter in the poems: those of grammar, including the considerable difference in the order of words in German from that used in English; the use of obsolete words and expressions, and of dialect; the often far from easy language of poetry itself, with its special use of words and hidden depths of meaning. No translation is 'the answer'; it can, however, be a valuable starting point for further search and research.

I would like to thank most warmly for their invaluable help: Miss Susannah Finzi for her collaboration in the initial stages of preparing the first manuscript; to Miss Ilse Wolf, Dr. Irene Marinoff, and Dr. Eva Schiff for their expert help in preparing the first edition; and finally to Dame Janet Baker and Mr Roy Henderson for their interest and encouragement, and to Sir Anthony Lewis for his always ready advice and support.

L.P.

Bamford College
South Hill Avenue
Harrow Hill
Middlesex

Dear Miss Phillips,
It is difficult to put my enthusiasm for your translations into adequate words. This is exactly what students desperately need, an accurate *word* for *word* detail, without which a Lied cannot be coloured vocally. Of course, they should all sit down and do this for themselves, but I'm afraid they never do.

Your project is urgently needed, it is a wonderful idea and I shall be among the very first to buy copies as soon as you have published.

Yours sincerely
Janet Baker

1979

Notes on
Word-for-Word Translations

To help the clarity of these:

1. Brackets have been used round:

(a) reflexive pronouns, where they would be omitted in English.

> e.g. *Drum   sehn' ich mich   nach ihr*
> therefore long I (myself) for her

(b) (little), where a diminutive ending means something like 'dear little', in an affectionate sense.

> e.g. *Geistlein*
> (little) ghost

(c) (it) in impersonal expressions.

> e.g. *Es sass ein Salamander*
> (it) sat a   salamander

(d) words in certain common expressions, where the meaning would be unnecessarily misleading if the single words were literally translated.

> e.g. *es   gibt* rather than: *es gibt*
> (there is)   it gives

(e) a word that is understood, but not actually there.

> e.g. *Meine alte Katze tanzt wahrscheinlich mit*
> my   old cat   dances probably   with (us)

(f) certain words which are unnecessary in English.

2. A dash – has been used in inseparable verbs, where the prefix has no clear meaning apart from the rest of the verb.

> e.g. *stellt . . . ein*
> presents –

3. Words are written between – and –, where the German words belong together as an expression.

> e.g. *heute Nacht*
> – tonight –

Ludwig van Beethoven
(1770–1827)

1. *ADELAIDE*
ADELAIDE (also set by Schubert)

Friedrich Matthisson

Einsam wandelt dein Freund im   Frühlingsgarten,
solitary wanders your friend in the spring-garden

Mild vom   lieblichen Zauberlicht umflossen,
gently by the lovely   magic-light encircled

Das durch   wankende Blütenzweige   zittert,
that through wavering blossoming-twigs trembles

Adelaide!
Adelaide!

In der spiegelnden Flut,   im   Schnee der   Alpen,
in the sparkling   torrent in the snow   of the Alps,

In des   sinkenden Tages Goldgewölken,
in of the declining day   gold-mass of clouds

Im   Gefilde der   Sterne strahlt dein Bildnis,
in the domain of the stars   shines your image

Adelaide!
Adelaide!

Abendlüfte   im   zarten   Laube flüstern,
evening breezes in the delicate foliage whisper

Silberglöckchen des   Mais im   Grase säuseln,
little silver bells of the May in the grass rustle

Wellen rauschen und Nachtigallen flöten:
waves murmur and nightingales flute

Adelaide!
Adelaide!

Einst, o Wunder! entblüht   auf meinem Grabe
once O miracle springs into flower on my   grave

Eine Blume der   Asche meines Herzens;
a   flower (from) the ash   of my heart

Deutlich schimmert auf jedem Purpurblättchen:
clearly   shimmers on each crimson-(little) petal

Adelaide!
Adelaide!

1. ADELAIDE

Lonely your friend wanders in the spring garden, wrapped in a soft, enchanted light, that trembles through swaying blossoms, Adelaide!

In the mirroring waves, in the snow of the Alps, in the golden clouds of declining day, in the firmament of stars your image shines, Adelaide!

Evening breezes whisper in the delicate foliage; little silver bells of May stir in the grass; waves murmur and nightingales call: Adelaide!

One day, O miracle! – on my grave will bloom a flower from the ashes of my heart; and on each crimson petal will shimmer so clear: Adelaide!

2. *SECHS LIEDER*
SIX   SONGS

2. SIX SONGS

Christian Fürchtegott Gellert

i. Bitten
   prayer

i. Prayer

Gott, deine Güte   reicht   so weit,
God your goodness extends so far

O God, Your goodness extends as far as the clouds above. You exalt us with Your mercy, and are quick to succour us. Lord, my stronghold, my refuge, my rock – hear my supplication! Listen to my words, for I would pray to You!

So weit die Wolken gehen;
as far the clouds go

Du krönst uns mit Barmherzigkeit,
you exalt us   with mercy

Und eilst,   uns beizustehen.
and hasten us to succour

Herr! meine Burg,   mein Fels, mein Hort,
Lord my   stronghold my rock my   refuge

Vernimm mein Flehn,   merk   auf mein Wort;
hear   my supplication give heed to my   word

Denn ich will   vor   dir beten!
For I   want before you to pray

ii. Die Liebe des   Nächsten
   the love of the neighbour

ii. Love of thy neighbour

So jemand   spricht: Ich liebe Gott!
if someone says   I   love God

If someone says, I love my God! and yet he hates his brothers, he makes a mockery of God's truth and drags it in the dust. God is Love, and desires that I love my neighbour as I love myself.

Und hasst doch seine Brüder,
and hates yet   his   brothers,

Der treibt mit Gottes Wahrheit Spott,
he makes with God's truth   mockery

Und reisst sie ganz   darnieder.
and drags her wholly down

Gott ist die Lieb', und will,   dass ich
God is the love   and wants that I

Den Nächsten   liebe, gleich als mich.
the neighbour love same as myself

iii. *Vom Tode*
of the death

iii. On death

Meine Lebenszeit verstreicht,
my   life-span slips by

My span of life slips by, I hasten
hourly to the grave. What is it that
perhaps I still must do? Think, O
man, of your death! Do not delay,
for this one thing you must do.

Stündlich eil   ich zu dem Grabe;
hourly   hasten I   to the grave

Und was ist's, das ich vielleicht,
and what is it that I   perhaps

Das ich noch zu leben habe?
that I still to live have

Denk, o Mensch, an deinen Tod!
think O man   on your death

Säume nicht, denn Eins   ist not.
defer not   for one thing is needful

iv. *Die Ehre Gottes aus   der Natur*
the praise of God from the nature

iv. Praise of God by Nature

Die Himmel rühmen des   Ewigen Ehre,
the Heavens praise of the eternal glory

The heavens praise the glory of the
Eternal; they sound forth His
name far and wide! The whole
earth praises Him, the oceans
praise Him! Hear, O man, their
divine word!

Ihr Schall pflanzt seinen Namen fort.
their sound spreads His   name   forth

Ihn rühmt der Erdkreis, ihn preisen die Meere;
Him praises the earth   Him praise the oceans

Vernimm, o Mensch, ihr   göttlich Wort!
hear   O man   their divine word

Wer trägt   der   Himmel unzählbare Sterne?
who sustains of the heavens countless stars

Who sustains the countless stars in
the firmament? Who leads the sun
from its tabernacle – the sun that
comes and – shines and laughs at
us from afar, and runs its course,
like a hero?

Wer führt die Sonn' aus ihrem Zelt?
who leads the sun   from her   tabernacle

Sie kommt und leuchtet und lacht uns von ferne,
she comes and shines and laughs to us from afar

Und läuft den Weg, gleich als ein Held!
and goes the way like   as a hero

v. *Gottes Macht und Vorsehung*
God's might and providence

v. God's might and providence

Gott ist mein Lied!
God is my   song

God is my song! He is the God of
might! Exalted is His name, and
great are His works; all the
Heavens are His domain.

Er ist der Gott der   Stärke;
He is the God of the strength

Hehr   ist sein Nam',
exalted is His name

Und gross sind seine Werke,
and great are His works

Und alle Himmel sein Gebiet.
and all   heavens His domain

    vi. Busslied   vi. Song of repentance
      repentance-song

An dir   allein, an dir hab' ich gesündigt,   Before You alone have I sinned;
to you alone to you have I   sinned   often have I done wrong before
                                                  You. You see my sin, that
Und Übel   oft   vor   dir getan.   proclaims to me how cursed I am.
and wrong often before you done   Behold me, God, in my misery.

Du siehst die Schuld, die   mir   den Fluch verkündigt;
you see   the sin   that to me the curse proclaims

Sieh, Gott, auch meinen Jammer an.
look God also my   misery at

Dir   ist mein Flehn,   mein Seufzen nicht verborgen,   From You my prayers and sighs
to you is my   supplication my sighing not   concealed   are not hidden; my tears are there
                                                                 before You. O God, my God, how
Und meine Tränen sind vor   dir.   long must I endure my woes; how
and my   tears   are before you   long will You withhold Your
                                                                 being?
Ach Gott, mein Gott, wie lange soll   ich sorgen?
oh God my   God how long shall I   be anxious

Wie lang entfernst du dich   von mir?
how long absent   you yourself from me

Herr, handle nicht mit mir nach   meinen Sünden,   God, do not deal with me
Lord deal   not with me according to my   sins   according to my sin; do not punish
                                                             me for my iniquity! I seek You, let
Vergilt   mir nicht nach meiner Schuld.   me see Your countenance, O God
pay back me not for   my   guilt   of mercy and forbearance.

Ich suche dich; lass mich dein Antlitz   finden,
I   seek you let me   your countenance find

Du Gott der   Langmut   und Geduld.
You God of the forbearance and endurance.

Früh wollst du mich mit deiner Gnade füllen,   Fill me soon with Your grace,
soon may you me with your grace fill   Lord and Father of mercy. Let me
                                                   rejoice in You, for Your name's
Gott, Vater der   Barmherzigkeit.   sake; You are the One who readily
God Father of the mercy   brings comfort.

Erfreue   mich um deines Namens willen;
let rejoice (me) for your   Name's sake

Du bist ein Gott, der gern   erfreut.
you are one God who readily comforts

Lass deinen Weg mich wieder freudig wallen,
let   your   way me   again joyfully travel

Und lehre mich dein heilig Recht,
and teach me   your divine law

Mich täglich tun   nach   deinem Wohlgefallen;
me   daily   to do according to your   pleasure

Du bist mein Gott, ich bin dein Knecht.
you are my   God   I   am your servant

Herr, eile   du, mein Schutz, mir beizustehen,
Lord make haste you my   refuge   me to succour

Und leite mich auf ebner Bahn.
and lead me   on level path

Er hört   mein Schrei'n, der Herr erhört mein Flehen,
He hears my   cry   the Lord hears my   supplication

Und nimmt   sich   meiner Seelen an.
and takes care (Himself) of my soul   –

Let me follow Your path again with joy, and teach me Your Holy Law, to act each day according to Your will; for you are my God, and I your servant.

O Lord, my refuge, make haste to help me, and lead me on to paths of righteousness! He hears my cry, the Lord accepts my supplication, and receives my soul.

3. MAILIED
MAY-SONG

Johann Wolfgang van Goethe

Wie herrlich   leuchtet
how gloriously shines

Mir   die Natur!
to me the Nature

Wie glänzt die Sonne,
how gleams the sun

Wie lacht   die Flur!
how laughs the meadow

Es dringen   Blüten
(it) break out blossoms

Aus jedem Zweig
from every twig

Und tausend   Stimmen
and thousand voices

Aus dem Gesträuch,
from the bushes

3. SONG IN MAY

How gloriously does nature shine! How the sun gleams, and how the meadows laugh!

Blossoms burst forth on every twig, a thousand voices from every tree,

Und Freud und Wonne
and joy   and bliss

Aus jeder Brust:
from every breast

O Erd, o Sonne,
O earth O sun

O Glück,   o Lust!
O happiness O delight

O Lieb, o Liebe,
O love O love

So golden schön,
so golden fair

Wie Morgenwolken
like morning-clouds

Auf jenen Höhn!
on those heights

Du segnest herrlich
you bless   gloriously

Das frische Feld,
the fresh field

Im   Blütendampfe
in the blossom-mist

Die volle   Welt.
the whole world

O Mädchen, Mädchen,
O maiden   maiden

Wie lieb ich dich!
how love I   you

Wie blickt   dein Auge,
how glances your eye

Wie liebst du   mich!
how love you me

So liebt die Lerche
so loves the lark

Gesang und Luft,
song   and air

And joy and ecstasy from every
heart. O earth! O sun! O
happiness! O bliss!

O love, so golden, and fair as
morning clouds on mountain
peaks!

Gloriously you bless the green
fields – the whole world in its sea
of flowers.

O maiden, maiden how I love you!
The look in your eyes – how you
love me!

As the lark loves singing in the air,
and a morning flower the
fragrance of the heavens,

Und Morgenblumen
and morning-flowers

Den Himmelsduft,
the heaven's-fragrance

Wie ich dich liebe
how I you love

so passionately do I love you –
you, who give me youth, and joy
and spirit

Mit warmem Blut,
with warm blood

Die du mir Jugend
that you to me youth

Und Freud und Mut
and joy and spirit

Zu neuen Liedern
to new songs

for new dances and new songs! Be
for ever joyful in your love for me!

Und Tänzen gibst.
and dances give

Sei ewig glücklich,
be for ever happy

Wie du mich liebst!
as you me love

4. *FLOHLIED DES MEPHISTO* FLEA-SONG OF THE MEPHISTOPHELES

4. SONG OF THE FLEA BY MEPHISTOPHELES

Johann Wolfgang van Goethe
(from *Faust* Part I)

Es war einmal ein König,
there was once a king

Der hatt' einen grossen Floh,
who had a great flea

Den liebt er gar nicht wenig:
whom loved he at all not little

Als wie seinen eignen Sohn.
like as his own son.

Da rief er seinen Schneider,
then called he his tailor

There was once a king, who had a
great flea, for whom his love was
far from small; he loved him as his
only son. He called for his tailor,
and the tailor came: 'Measure the
young nobleman for jacket and
trousers!'

Der Schneider kam   heran:
the tailor   came nigh

'Da, miss   dem Junker   Kleider,
there measure to the young nobleman garments

Und miss   ihm   Hosen an!'
and measure to him trousers –

In Sammet und in Seide
in velvet   and in silk

War er nun angetan,
was he now clad

Hatte Bänder auf dem Kleide,
had   ribbons on the attire

Hatt' auch ein Kreuz daran,
had   also a   cross on it

Und war sogleich Minister
and was at once minister

Und hatt' einen grossen Stern.
and had a   great star

Da   wurden seine Geschwister
then became his   brothers and sisters

Bei Hof   auch grosse Herrn.
at   court also great gentlemen.

Now he was dressed in velvet and silk, he had ribbons on his clothes, and a cross, and at once he was made a minister and given a Star of Honour. Then all his brothers and sisters became nobles at court as well.

Und Herrn   und Fraun am   Hofe,
and gentlemen and ladies at the court

Die waren sehr geplagt,
they were   very plagued

Die Königin und die Zofe
the queen   and the lady-in-waiting

Gestochen und genagt,
bitten   and nibbled

Und durften   sie nicht knicken,
and were allowed they not to squash

Und weg sie jucken   nicht.
and away them to scratch not

Wir knicken und ersticken
we squash and smother

Doch gleich, wenn einer sticht!
yet   at once when one bites

The ladies and gentlemen of the court were all greatly distressed; the queen and her lady-in-waiting, they were nibbled and bitten – but were not permitted to squash them to get rid of the itch – though when we are bitten, we smother and squash them at once!

5. *WONNE DER WEHMUT*
JOY OF THE MELANCHOLY

Johann Wolfgang von Goethe

Trocknet nicht, trocknet nicht,
dry not dry not

Tränen der ewigen Liebe!
tears of the eternal love

Ach, nur dem halbgetrockneten Auge
oh only to the half-dried eye

Wie öde, wie tot die Welt ihm erscheint!
how desolate how dead the world to it seems

Trocknet nicht, trocknet nicht,
dry not dry not

Tränen unglucklïcher Liebe!
tears of unrequited love

5. JOY IN MELANCHOLY

Never cease, never cease, O tears of eternal love! Only to eyes half-dry does the world seem desolate and dead! Never cease, never cease, O tears of hapless love.

6. *AN DIE FERNE GELIEBTE*
TO THE DISTANT BELOVED

Alois Jeitteles

i.

Auf dem Hügel sitz ich spähend
on the hill sit I gazing

In das blaue Nebelland,
into the blue mist-land

Nach den fernen Triften sehend,
towards the distant pastures looking

Wo ich dich, Geliebte, fand.
where I you beloved found

Weit bin ich von dir geschieden,
far am I from you separated

Trennend liegen Berg und Tal
dividing lie mountain and valley

6. TO THE DISTANT BELOVED

i.

I sit on the hillside gazing into a hazy blue land, at the distant pastures where I found you, my love.

So far am I from you – mountain and valley lie between us, dividing us and our tranquillity, our happiness and pain.

Zwischen uns und unserm Frieden,
between us and our tranquillity

Unserm Glück und unsrer Qual.
our happiness and our pain.

Ach, den Blick kannst du nicht sehen,
ah the look can you not see

Der zu dir so glühend eilt,
which to you so glowing hastens

Und die Seufzer, sie verwehen
and the sighs they scatter

In dem Raume, der uns teilt.
In the space which us divides

Ah, you cannot see the look I send you in glowing haste, and in the space dividing us, my tears are lost.

Will denn nichts mehr zu dir dringen,
will then nothing more to you penetrate

Nichts der Liebe Bote sein?
nothing of the love messenger be

Singen will ich, Lieder singen,
sing will I songs sing

Die dir klagen meine Pein!
which to you lament my pain

Can nothing further reach you – can there be no messenger of love? I will sing for you songs that lament my pain!

Denn vor Liedesklang entweichet
for before song's-sound vanishes

Jeder Raum und jede Zeit,
each space and each time

Und ein liebend Herz erreichet
and a loving heart reaches

Was ein liebend Herz geweiht!
what a loving heart blessed

Before their strains all space and time can vanish, and a devoted heart can reach the heart it has truly blessed!

ii.

Wo die Berge so blau
where the mountains so blue

Aus dem nebligen Grau
out of the misty grey

Schauen herein,
look in here

Wo die Sonne verglüht,
where the sun ceases glowing

ii.

Where the blue mountains peer from a misty grey, where the sun's rays fade, and clouds float by – there should I like to be!

Wo   die Wolke umzieht,
where the cloud moves by

Möchte   ich sein!
should like I   to be

Dort im   ruhigen Tal
there in the quiet   valley

Schweigen Schmerzen und Qual.
are silent sorrows   and pain

Wo   im   Gestein
where in the rock

Still die Primel   dort sinnt,
still the primrose there reflects

Weht so leise   der Wind,
blows so gently the wind

Möchte   ich sein!
should like I   to be

Hin   zum sinnigen Wald
thither to the brooding wood

Drängt mich Liebesgewalt,
urges   me   love's-violence

Innere Pein.
inner pain

Ach, mich zög's   nicht von hier,
ah   me   draws it not   from here

Könnt ich, Traute, bei dir
could I   dear one with you

Ewiglich sein!
for ever be

Where in the quiet valley sorrow
and pain are still, where the silent
primrose muses in the rocks, and
the breeze so gently blows – there
should I like to be!

I am driven to the brooding wood
by the violence of my love and
inner torment. But nothing would
draw me from here, my love, if
you were ever at my side!

iii.

Leichte Segler in den Höhen,
light   sailers in the heights

Und du, Bächlein   klein und schmal,
and you little brook small and narrow

Könnt mein Liebchen   ihr erspähen,
could my   sweetheart you espy

Grüsst sie mir   viel tausendmal.
greet   her to me many thousand-times

iii.

O you, light clouds, sailing on
high, and you, little brook, so
narrow and small – if you espy my
sweetheart, bring her a thousand
greetings!

Seht, ihr Wolken, sie   dann gehen
see   you clouds they then go

Sinnend in dem stillen Tal,
musing in the still valley

Lasst mein Bild   vor   ihr entstehen
let   my image before her arise

In dem luftgen Himmelssaal.
in the airy   heaven's-hall

Wird sie an den Büschen stehen,
will she by the bushes stand

Die   nun herbstlich   falb   und kahl,
which now autumnally pale yellow and bare

Klagt ihr,   wie mir   ist geschehen,
lament to her how to me is happened

Klagt ihr, Vöglein,   meine Qual.
lament to her little birds my   anguish

Stille Weste,   bringt im   Wehen
calm west wind bring in the blowing

Hin   zu meiner Herzenswahl
thither to my   heart's-choice

Meine Seufzer, die   vergehen
my   sighs   which vanish

Wie der   Sonne letzter Strahl.
like of the sun   last   ray

Flüstr' ihr   zu mein Liebesflehen,
whisper to her to my love's-beseeching

Lass sie, Bächlein,   klein und schmal,
let   her little brook small and narrow

Treu in deinen Wogen sehen
truly in your   waves see

Meine Tränen ohne   Zahl!
my   tears   without number

Then, o clouds, if you should see her, walking pensive in the quiet valley – let my image rise before her in the lofty dome of heaven!

And if you should see her beneath the trees, that now in autumn are pale and bare – tell her of my fate, little birds, lament to her my anguish!

On your drifting breezes, calm west wind, carry to my heart's desire the sighs that vanish like the sun's last ray.

Little brook, so narrow and small, whisper to her of my beseeching love, and in your ripples truly let her see my countless tears!

iv.

Diese Wolken in den Höhen,
these clouds in the heights

Dieser Vöglein   muntrer Zug,
of these little birds merry flock

iv.

These clouds on high, this merry flock of birds – they will see my gracious one! O take me on your airy flight!

Werden dich, o Huldin, sehen.
will you O gracious one see

Nehmt mich mit im leichten Flug!
take me with (you) in the light flight

Diese Weste werden spielen
these west winds will play

These west winds will lightly play about your cheeks and breast, and stir your silken locks. Could I but share such joy!

Scherzend dir um Wang und Brust,
jestingly to you about cheek and breast

In den seidnen Locken wühlen.
into the silky locks burrow

Teilt ich mit euch diese Lust!
shared I with you this joy

Hin zu dir von jenen Hügeln
thither to you from those hills

The little brook busily hastens to you from the hills. If you should reflect her image – then flow back without delay!

Emsig dieses Bächlein eilt.
busily this little brook hastens

Wird ihr Bild sich in dir spiegeln,
will her image itself in you reflect

Fliess zurück dann unverweilt!
flow back then without delay

v.

Es kehret der Maien, es blühet die Au.
it returns (the) May it blooms the meadow

May is returning, the meadows are in flower, the breezes blow so gentle and mild, and the babbling brooks now flow.

Die Lüfte, sie wehen so milde, so lau.
the breezes they blow so gently so mildly

Geschwätzig die Bäche nun rinnen.
babbling the brooks now flow

Die Schwalbe, die kehret zum wirtlichen Dach,
the swallow who returns to the hospitable roof

The swallow returns to the hospitable roof, and eagerly builds her bridal chamber, for love shall dwell within.

Sie baut sich so emsig ihr bräutlich Gemach,
she builds herself so eagerly her bridal chamber

Die Liebe soll wohnen da drinnen.
the love shall live there within

Sie bringt sich geschäftig von kreuz und von quer
she brings herself busily from criss- and from -cross

From far and wide she busily brings soft scraps for her bridal bed, and to warm her little ones.

Manch weicheres Stück zu dem Brautbett hieher,
some softer piece to the bridal-bed hither

Manch wärmendes Stück für die Kleinen.
some warming piece for the little ones

Nun wohnen die Gatten beisammen so treu,
now live   the mates together   so faithfully

Was Winter geschieden, verband nun der Mai,
what winter divided   joined   now the May

Was liebet, das weiss er zu einen.
what loves that knows he to unite

Now the pair dwells faithfully together; what winter divided, May has joined, uniting all who love!

Es kehret der Maien, es blühet die Au.
it returns (the) May   it blooms the meadow

Die Lüfte, sie wehen so milde, so lau.
the breezes they blow so gently so mildly

May is returning, the meadows are in flower, breezes blow so gentle and mild, but I cannot stir from here.

Nur ich kann nicht ziehen von hinnen.
only I can not move from here

Wenn alles, was liebet, der Frühling vereint,
when everything that loves the spring unites

Nur unserer Liebe kein Frühling erscheint,
only to our love no spring appears

While spring is joining all who love, our love alone knows no spring, and tears are its only reward.

Und Tränen sind all ihr Gewinnen.
and tears are all her gain

vi.

Nimm sie hin denn, diese Lieder,
take them – then these songs

Die ich dir, Geliebte, sang,
which I to you love   sang

Singe sie dann abends wieder
sing them then in the evening again

Zu der Laute süssem Klang!
to of the Lute sweet sound

Now take these songs, my love, which I have sung to you – sing them again in the evening to the sweet sound of the lute.

Wenn das Dämmrungsrot dann ziehet
when the twilight-red then moves

Nach dem stillen blauen See,
towards the still blue lake

Und sein letzter Strahl verglühet
and its last ray ceases glowing

Hinter jener Bergeshöh;
behind that mountain-top

And when the twilight glows on the still blue lake, and the last ray fades behind the mountain-tops;

Und du singst, was ich gesungen,
and you sing what I sung

Was mir aus der vollen Brust
what to me out of the full breast

and you sing what I have sung, that flowed from a full and simple heart that knows only longing –

Ohne   Kunstgepräng erklungen,
without artifice   sounded

Nur der Sehnsucht sich   bewusst:
only the longing   itself is conscious of

Dann vor   diesen Liedern weichet,
then   before these songs   yields

then will that which divides us
yield before these songs. For a
devoted heart can reach the one it
truly loves!

Was geschieden uns so weit,
what separated us so widely

Und ein liebend Herz erreichet,
and a   loving heart reaches

Was ein liebend Herz geweiht!
what a   loving heart blessed

7. DER KUSSE
   THE KISS

7. THE KISS

Christian Felix Weisse

Ich war bei   Chloen ganz allein,
I   was with Chloe quite alone

I was alone with Chloe, and
wanted to kiss her. But she said it
would be in vain, for she would
scream.

Und küssen wollt'   ich sie:
and to kiss wanted I   her

Jedoch sie   sprach,
yet   she said

Sie würde schrein,
she would scream

Es sei vergebne Müh.
it be vain   labour

Ich wagt' es doch   und küsste sie,
I   dared it however and kissed her

But I dared to kiss her although
she did protest. And did she
scream? Oh yes, she screamed –
but a long time afterwards!

Trotz   ihrer Gegenwehr.
in spite of her   resistance

Und schrie   sie nicht?
and screamed she not

Jawohl,   sie schrie,
yes indeed she screamed

Doch lange hinterher,
but   long afterwards

Doch, ja doch!
indeed yes indeed

Ja lange hinterher!
yes long afterwards

8. *DAS GEHEIMNIS*
   THE SECRET

I.H.K. von Wessenberg

Wo blüht das Blümchen, das nie verblüht?
where blooms the (little) flower that never fades

Wo strahlt das Sternlein, das ewig glüht?
where shines the (little) star that for ever glows

Dein Mund, o Muse! dein heil'ger Mund
your mouth O Muse your hallowed mouth

Tu mir das Blümchen und Sternlein kund.
make to me the (little) flower and (little) star known

'Verkünden kann es dir nicht mein Mund,
make known can it to you not my mouth

Macht es dein Innerstes dir nicht kund.
makes it your innermost soul to you not known

Im Innersten glühet und blüht es zart,
in the innermost soul glows and blooms it tenderly

Wohl jedem, der es getreu bewahrt!'
happy to each who it true keeps

8. THE SECRET

Where blooms the little flower that never fades? Where shines the little star that gleams for ever? Your lips, O Muse, your hallowed lips tell me of this little flower and star.

'My lips can tell you nothing that you know not in your heart. A star gleams, a flower blooms in every heart – happy is he who truly tends it there.'

9. *ICH LIEBE DICH*
   I   LOVE YOU

K.F. Herrosee

Ich liebe dich, so wie du mich,
I love you thus as you me

Am Abend und am Morgen,
in the evening and in the morning

9. I LOVE YOU

I love you, as you love me, in the morning and at night; no day passed when you and I did not share our griefs.

Noch war kein Tag, wo   du und ich
yet   was no   day where you and I

Nicht teilten   unsre Sorgen.
not   shared our   sorrows

Auch waren sie   für dich und mich
also   were they for you and me

Geteilt leicht zu ertragen;
shared easy to bear

Du tröstetest   im   Kummer mich,
you comforted in the sorrow   me

Ich weint in deine Klagen.
I   wept in your lamenting

Drum   Gottes Segen   über dir,
therefore God's blessing on   you

Du meines Lebens Freude,
you my   life's   joy

Gott schütze dich, erhalt dich mir,
God protect you   keep you (for) me

Schütz und erhalt uns beide!
protect and keep us both

Shared, they were easy to bear for us both; in my sorrow you gave me comfort; in your distress I wept.

And so I send you God's blessing – you, the joy of my life. For me, may God protect you: protect and shield us both!

Franz Schubert
(1797–1828)

1. *GRETCHEN AM* GRETCHEN AT THE *SPINNRADE* SPINNING-WHEEL

1. GRETCHEN AT THE SPINNING-WHEEL

Johann Wolfgang von Goethe
(also set by Spohr)

Meine Ruh   ist hin,
my   peace is gone

Mein Herz ist schwer;
my   heart is heavy

Ich finde sie   nimmer
I   find her never

Und nimmermehr.
and never more

My heart is heavy, my peace is gone; never, never shall I find it again.

Wo   ich ihn nicht hab,
where I   him not have

Ist mir   das Grab,
is to me the grave

Die ganze Welt
the whole world

Ist mir   vergällt.
is to me become bitter

Where he is not with me, to me is a grave; the whole world seems bitter as gall.

Mein armer Kopf
my   poor head

Ist mir   verrückt,
is to me mad

Mein armer Sinn
my   poor mind

Ist mir   zerstückt.
is to me cut into pieces

My poor head is in a frenzy, my poor mind shattered.

Nach ihm nur schau ich
for   him only look I

I seek only him as I peer from my
window; to seek only him do I
leave the house.

Zum Fenster hinaus,
to the window out

Nach ihm nur geh ich
for   him only go I

Aus   dem Haus.
out of the house

Sein hoher Gang,
his   proud carriage

His proud bearing, his noble
figure, his smiling lips, and
compelling eyes,

Sein' edle   Gestalt,
his   noble figure

Seines Mundes Lächeln,
his   mouth's smile

Seiner Augen Gewalt,
of his eyes   power

Und seiner Rede
and of his speech

the magic of his speech, the touch
of his hand, and ah, his kiss!

Zauberfluss,
magic-flow

Sein Händedruck,
his hand's-shake

Und ach, sein Kuss!
and ah   his kiss

Mein Busen drängt
my   bosom presses

My heart yearns for him. Oh, I
could but embrace him and hold
him,

Sich   nach   ihm hin.
(himself) towards him (towards)

Ach, dürft ich fassen
oh   might I   clasp

Und halten ihn!
and hold   him

and kiss him as I would – from his
kisses would I perish!

Und küssen ihn,
and kiss   him

So wie ich wollt,
so as I   wanted

An seinen Küssen
on his   kisses

Vergehen sollt!
perish   should

2. *SCHÄFERS   KLAGELIED*
SHEPHERD'S LAMENTATION

2. SHEPHERD'S
LAMENT

Johann Wolfgang von Goethe

Da   droben auf jenem Berge
there above on that   hill

Da   steh   ich tausendmal,
there stand I   thousand times

An meinem Stabe hingebogen
on my   staff bent over

Und schaue hinab in   das Tal.
and look   down into the valley

High on the hill there, I have
stood a thousand times, leaning on
my staff, looking down into the
valley.

Dann folg   ich der weidenden Herde,
then follow I   the grazing   flock

Mein Hündchen bewahret mir   sie;
my   (little) dog protects (to) me her

Ich bin herunter gekommen,
I   am down   come

Und weiss doch selber   nicht wie.
and know yet   myself not   how

I have followed the grazing flock,
my dog keeping watch. I have
come here below – but I cannot
say how.

Da   stehet von schönen Blumen
there is   of   lovely flowers

Die ganze Wiese   so voll;
the whole meadow so full

Ich breche sie,   ohne   zu wissen,
I   gather them without – knowing –

Wem   ich sie   geben   soll.
to whom I   them to give shall

The meadow is full of beautiful
flowers. I gather them, not
knowing to whom I shall give
them.

Und Regen, Sturm und Gewitter
and rain   storm and thunderstorm

Verpass ich unter   dem Baum.
miss   I   beneath the tree

I shelter beneath the trees from
the rain and thundery storms. Her
door there remains closed – alas, it
is all a dream.

Die Türe dort bleibet verschlossen;
the door there remains closed

Doch alles ist leider ein Traum.
but all is alas a dream

Es stehet ein Regenbogen
(it) stands a rainbow

There is a rainbow over her house, but she has gone far across the land.

Wohl über jenem Haus!
indeed over that house

Sie aber ist fortgezogen
she but is moved away

Und weit in das Land hinaus,
and far into the land away

Hinaus in das Land und weiter,
away into the land and further

Across the land, and further on across the sea! It is ended, you sheep, all ended! And your shepherd's heart is full of grief.

Vielleicht gar über die See.
perhaps even over the sea

Vorüber, ihr Schafe, nur vorüber!
over you sheep just over

Dem Schäfer ist gar so weh.
to the shepherd is very so sad

3. *NÄHE DES GELIEBTEN* NEARNESS OF THE BELOVED

3. THE BELOVED IS NEAR

Johann Wolfgang von Goethe

Ich denke dein, wenn mir der Sonne Schimmer
I think of you when to me of the sun shimmer

I think of you, when the shimmer of the sun gleams on the sea; I think of you, when the glimmer of the moon is reflected in spring water.

Vom Meere strahlt;
from the sea shines

Ich denke dein, wenn sich des Mondes Flimmer
I think of you when (itself) of the moon glimmer

In Quellen malt.
in springs reflects

Ich sehe dich, wenn auf dem fernen Wege
I see you when on the distant paths

I see you, when the dust rises on distant paths; in deepest night, when the traveller crosses the narrow bridge.

Der Staub sich hebt;
the dust (itself) rises

In tiefer Nacht, wenn auf dem schmalen Stege
In deep night   when on the narrow   bridge

Der Wandrer bebt.
the wanderer trembles

Ich höre dich, wenn dort   mit   dumpfen Rauschen
I   hear you when there with dull   rushing

I hear you, when waters surge with a dull roar; in the quiet wood I go to listen, when all is still.

Die Welle steigt,
the wave rises

Im   stillen Haine geh ich oft   zu lauschen,
in the quiet wood go I   often to listen

Wenn alles schweigt.
when all   is silent

Ich bin bei   dir, du seist auch noch so ferne,
I   am with you you be   even still so far away

I am with you; however far you are, to me you are near! The sun is sinking, soon the stars will light my way. O that you were here!

Du bist mir   nah!
you are to me near

Die Sonne sinkt,   bald leuchten mir   die Sterne.
the sun   is sinking soon shine   to me the stars

O wärst du da!
O were you there

4. DES   MÄDCHENS KLAGE
OF THE MAIDEN   LAMENT

4. THE MAIDEN'S LAMENT

Friedrich Schiller

Der Eichwald braust, die Wolken ziehn,
the oak-wood blusters the clouds move

The oak trees bluster in the wood, the clouds are racing. The young maiden sits on a green bank, where waves break with all their might. She sighs into the darkness, her eyes clouded with weeping.

Das Mägdlein sitzt an Ufers   Grün,
the maiden   sits on bank's green

Es bricht sich   die Welle mit Macht, mit Macht,
(it) breaks (itself) the wave with might with might

Und sie seufzt hinaus in   die finstre Nacht,
and she sighs out   into the dark night

Das Auge vom   Weinen getrübet.
the eye   from the weeping clouded

'Das Herz ist gestorben, die Welt ist leer,
the heart is dead   the world is empty

'My heart is dead, the world is empty; no longer can it fulfil my desire. O holy saint, call your child home! I have tasted earthly joys – I have lived and loved!'

Und weiter gibt sie dem Wunsche nichts   mehr.
and further gives she to the desire   nothing more

Du Heilige, rufe dein Kind zurück,
you holy one call your child back

Ich habe genossen das irdische Glück,
I   have enjoyed the earthly happiness

Ich habe gelebt und geliebet!'
I   have lived and loved

Es rinnet der   Tränen vergeblicher Lauf,
(it) runs of the tears   useless   course

Die Klage, sie wecket die Toten nicht auf;
the lament she wakes the dead not up

Doch nenne, was tröstet   und heilet die Brust
but   name what comforts and heals the breast

Nach der   süssen Liebe verschwundener Lust,
after of the sweet love   vanished   delight

Ich, die Himmlische, will's nicht versagen.
I   the heavenly one will it not   deny

'Lass rinnen der   Tränen vergeblichen Lauf,
let   run   of the tears   useless   course

Es wecke die Klage den Toten nicht auf,
(it) wakes the lament the dead not up

Das süsseste Glück   für die trauernde Brust,
the sweetest happiness for the mourning breast

Nach der   schönen Liebe verschwundener Lust,
after of the beautiful love vanished   delight

Sind der   Liebe Schmerzen und Klagen.'
are of the love griefs   and laments

Her tears run their useless course, but laments cannot waken the dead. 'Tell me, what comforts and heals the heart when the delights of sweet love have vanished – I, your saint, will not deny it you.'

'Let my tears run their useless course – laments cannot waken the dead. But when the delights of sweet love have vanished, love's grief and lamenting is the sweetest joy to a mourning heart.

5. *AN DEN MOND*
TO THE MOON

Ludwig Hölty

Geuss, lieber Mond, geuss deine Silberflimmer
shed   dear moon shed your silver-glimmer

Durch   dieses Buchengrün,
through this   beeches-green

Wo   Phantasien und Traumgestalten immer
where fantasies   and dream-shapes always

5. TO THE MOON

Dear moon, shed your silvery gleam through the green beeches, where phantoms and dream-like shapes pass before my eyes! Draw back your veil, that I may find the place where my love so often sat, forgetting the golden town in the

Vor   mir vorüber flieh'n!
before me past   flee

Enthülle dich,   dass ich die Stätte finde,
unveil   yourself that I   the place find

Wo   oft   mein Mädchen sass,
where often my girl   sat

Und oft   im   Weh'n   des   Buchbaums und der
and often in the fluttering of the beech-tree and of the

    Linde
    linden-tree

Der   gold'nen Stadt vergass!
of the golden   town forgot

Enthülle dich,   dass ich des   Strauchs mich   freue,
unveil   yourself that I   of the bush   (myself) delight

Der Kühlung ihr gerauscht,
that coolness her charmed

Und einen Kranz   auf jeden Anger   streue,
and a   garland on every meadow strew

Wo   sie den Bach belauscht!
where she the brook listened to

Dann, lieber Mond, dann nimm den Schleier wieder,
then   dear moon then take the veil   again

Und trau'   um deinen Freund,
and mourn for your   friend

Und weine durch   den Wolkenflor hernieder,
and weep through the cloud-veil down

Wie dein Verlassner   weint!
as   your forsaken-one weeps

fluttering of the beeches and the linden tree. Draw back your veil, that I may delight in their cool foliage, and strew flowers in every meadow where she listened by the stream. Then, dear moon, draw your veil again, and mourn for your beloved, weeping through this misty veil of clouds, as the one you have forsaken weeps.

6. WANDERERS NACHTLIED
WANDERER'S NIGHT-SONG

Johann Wolfgang von Goethe
(also set by Liszt and Wolf)

Der du   von dem Himmel bist,
who you of the heaven are

Alles Leid und Schmerzen stillst,
all   pain and griefs   assuage

Den, der doppelt elend   ist,
him who twofold wretched is

6. WANDERER'S
NIGHT SONG

Thou, who art in Heaven, assuage all pain and grief. He who suffers twofold, Thou fillest twofold with joy. Ah, how weary I am of life's strivings! To what end, all this joy and sorrow? Come, sweet peace, O come into my heart!

Doppelt mit Entzücken füllst,
twofold with delight   fill

Ach, ich bin des   Treibens müde!
ah I   am of the bustle weary

Was soll   all der Schmerz und Lust?
what means all the grief   and joy

Süsser Friede,
sweet peace

Komm', ach komm' in   meine Brust!
come ah come into my   breast

7. DER FISCHER
THE FISHERMAN

Johann Wolfgang von Goethe
(also set by Richard Strauss)

Das Wasser rauscht', das Wasser schwoll,
the water rushed the water rose

Ein Fischer   sass daran,
a   fisherman sat thereby

Sah   nach der Angel ruhevoll,
looked at   the angle quietly

Kühl bis ans   Herz hinan.
cool – up to the heart upwards –

Und wie er sitzt, und wie er lauscht,
and as he sits and as he listens

Teilt sich   die Flut   empor;
divides (herself) the torrent upwards

Aus   dem bewegten Wasser rauscht
out of the moved   water rushes

Ein feuchtes Weib   hervor.
a   damp   woman forth

Sie sang zu ihm, sie sprach zu ihm,
she sang to him, she spoke to him

'Was lockst du meine Brut
why entice you my   brood

Mit Menschenwitz und Menschenlist
with human-wit   and human-cunning

Hinauf in   Todesglut?
upwards into death's-fire

7. THE FISHERMAN

The water rushed, the water rose,
a fisherman sat quietly watching
his rod, his very heart cool. And as
he sat and listened, the surging
waters parted, and from the
swirling stream rose a woman's
form.

She sang to him, she spoke to him,
'Why do you entice my brood with
human wit and cunning, up to
their parching death? If you but
knew how content are the fishes
here below, you would come down
as you are, and be for the first time
whole.

Ach wüsstest du, wie's   Fischlein ist
ah knew   you how the little fish is

So wohlig   auf dem Grund,
so content on the bottom

Du stiegst   herunter, wie du bist,
you would climb down   as you are

Und würdest   erst   gesund.
and would be (only then) well

Labt   sich   die liebe Sonne nicht,
refreshes herself the dear sun   not

Der Mond sich   nicht im   Meer?
the moon himself not   in the ocean

Kehrt   wellenatmend   ihr Gesicht
returns waves-breathing her face

Nicht doppelt schöner   her?
not   twice   more fair back

Lockt   dich der tiefe Himmel nicht,
tempts you the deep sky   not

Das feuchtverklärte Blau?
the moist-radiant blue

Lockt   dich dein eigen Angesicht
tempts you your own face

Nicht her   in ew'gen Tau?'
not   here in eternal dew

Is not the moon refreshed in the ocean? And the sun – is her wave-washed face not twice as fair? Does the sky not tempt you with its radiant blue? Or your own face into eternal waters?'

Das Wasser rauscht', das Wasser schwoll,
the water   rushed   the water rose

Netzt'   ihm   den nackten Fuss;
moistened to him the naked   foot

Sein Herz wuchs ihm   so sehnsuchtsvoll,
his   heart grew   to him so full of longing

Wie bei der   Liebsten Gruss.
as   at of the beloved greeting

Sie sprach zu ihm, sie sang zu ihm;
she spoke to him she sang to him

Da   war's um ihn gescheh'n:
then was it to him happened

Halb zog   sie ihn, halb sank er hin,
half drew she him half sank he there

Und ward nicht mehr gesehen.
and was   not   more seen

The water rushed, the water rose, his feet were lapped by the waves; his heart filled with longing, as from the kiss of the beloved. She spoke to him, she sang to him, and he was lost for ever – half dragged by her, half sinking down, he was never seen again.

8. *ERSTER VERLUST*
   FIRST   LOSS

Johann Wolfgang von Goethe
(also set by Mendelssohn)

Ach! wer bringt die schönen Tage,
ah   who brings the fair   days

Jene Tage der   ersten Liebe,
those days of the first   love

Ach! wer bringt nur eine Stunde
ah   who brings only one hour

Jener   holden Zeit zurück!
of that sweet time back

Einsam nähr' ich meine Wunde,
alone   nurse I   my   wound

Und mit   stets erneuter Klage
and with ever renewed lament

Traur' ich um's   verlor'ne Glück.
mourn I   for the lost   happiness

Ach, wer bringt die schönen Tage,
ah   who brings the fair   days

Wer jene holde Zeit zurück!
who that sweet time back

9. *LIEBE SCHWÄRMT AUF ALLEN*
   LOVE SWARMS   ON   ALL
   WEGEN
   PATHS

Johann Wolfgang von Goethe
(from *Claudine von Villa Bella*)

Liebe schwärmt auf allen Wegen,
love swarms on all   paths

Treue   wohnt für sich   allein;
fidelity lives for itself alone

Liebe kommt euch rasch   entgegen,
love comes you swiftly towards

Aufgesucht will   Treue sein.
sought out requires fidelity to be

8. FIRST LOSS

Oh, who can bring back those fair
days, those days of my first love!
Oh, who can bring back just one
hour of that sweet time! Alone I
nurse my wounds, and with ever-
renewed lament, I mourn my lost
happiness.

Oh, who can bring back those fair
days, who can bring back that
sweet time!

9. LOVE ABOUNDS
   ON EVERY PATH

Love abounds on every path,
fidelity lives for itself alone; love
comes swiftly to meet you, but you
must seek after fidelity.

10. *HIN   UND WIEDER*
THERE AND BACK AGAIN
FLIEGEN PFEILE
FLY   ARROWS

10. ARROWS FLY HITHER AND THITHER

Johann Wolfgang von Goethe
(from *Claudine von Villa Bella*)

Hin und wieder   fliegen Pfeile,
there and back again fly   arrows

Amors   leichte Pfeile   fliegen
Cupid's light   arrows fly

Von dem schlanken goldnen Bogen,
from the slender   golden bow

Mädchen seid ihr nicht getroffen?
maidens are you not   struck

Es ist Glück, es ist nur Glück.
it is fate   it is only fate

Arrows fly hither and thither; light arrows fly from Cupid's fine golden bow. Have you young maidens not yet been struck? It is fate, only fate!

Warum fliegt er so in Eile?
why   flies he so in haste

Jene   dort will   er besiegen;
that one there wants he to vanquish

Schon ist er vorbei geflogen,
already is he past   flown

Sorglos bleibt   der Busen offen.
carefree remains the bosom open

Gebet Acht! er kommt   zurück!
give   heed he is coming back

Why does he fly in such haste? He seeks to vanquish that maid there. Already he has flown past; her heart is still free. Take care, for he is coming back!

11. *HEIDENRÖSLEIN*
LITTLE BRIAR-ROSE

11. WILD ROSE

Johann Wolfgang von Goethe
(also set by Brahms)

Sah ein Knab ein Röslein   stehn,
saw a boy a little rose standing

Röslein   auf der Heiden,
little rose on the heath

War so jung   und morgenschön,
was so young and morning-fair

A boy saw a wild rose growing on the heath, as fresh and lovely as the day. Quickly he ran up to see it, looked at it with great delight. Little rose, little rose, little red rose upon the heath.

Lief er schnell, es nah zu sehn,
ran he quickly it near to see

Sah's mit vielen Freuden.
saw it with much delight

Röslein, Röslein, Röslein rot,
little rose little rose little rose red

Röslein auf der Heiden.
little rose on the heath

Knabe sprach: ich breche dich,
boy said I gather you

Röslein auf der Heiden!
little rose on the heath

Röslein sprach: ich steche dich,
little rose said I prick you

Dass du ewig denkst an mich,
that you for ever think of me

Und ich will's nicht leiden.
and I will it not suffer

Röslein, Röslein etc.

Und der wilde Knabe brach
and the unruly boy plucked

s'Röslein auf der Heiden;
the little rose on the heath

Röslein wehrte sich und stach,
little rose defended itself and pricked

Half ihm doch kein Weh und Ach,
helped him but no (oh) and ah

Musst' es eben leiden.
had to it just suffer

Röslein, Röslein etc.

The boy said, I'll pluck you, little rose upon the heath! The rose said, I'll prick you, so you'll never forget me – for I'll not suffer it!

But the wilful boy plucked the little rose upon the heath. She defended herself and pricked him, but her cries were in vain – and she just had to suffer it.

12. AN DEN MOND
TO THE MOON

Johann Wolfgang von Goethe

Füllest wieder Busch und Tal
fill again bush and valley

Still mit Nebelglanz,
silently with mist-splendour

12. TO THE MOON

Silently you fill once more each wood and valley with your misty splendour; at last my soul is wholly free.

Lösest   endlich auch einmal
set free at last also once

Meine Seele ganz;
my   soul wholly

Breitest über mein Gefild'
spread over my   domain   Your gentle gaze reaches out over
                                                 the countryside, like the kindly eye
Lindernd deinen Blick,   of a friend over my destiny.
soothing your   glance

Wie des   Freundes Auge mild
as   of the friend   eye   kindly

Über mein Geschick.
over my   destiny

Jeden Nachklang fühlt mein Herz
each echo   feels my   heart   My heart feels each echo of glad
                                                 and troubled times. I wander in
Froh' und trüber   Zeit,   solitude between sorrow and joy.
glad   and of melancholy time

Wandle zwischen Freud' und Schmerz
wander between joy   and sorrow

In der Einsamkeit.
in the solitude

Fliesse, fliesse, lieber Fluss!
flow   flow   dear river   Flow on, dear river, flow on!
                                                 Never can I be glad; for thus did
Nimmer werd'   ich froh,   laughter and love pass away, and
never   become I   glad   thus fidelity.

So   verrauschte   Scherz und Kuss,
thus passed away jest   and kiss

Und die Treue   so.
and the fidelity thus

Selig,   wer sich   vor der Welt
blissful who himself from the world   Blessed is he, who can turn from
                                                 the world without hate, who can
Ohne   Hass verschliesst,   hold a friend close to his heart,
without hate shuts away   and share with him,

Einen Freund am   Busen hält
a   friend to the bosom holds

Und mit   dem geniesst,
and with him enjoys

Was, von Menschen nicht gewusst
what of men not known

Oder nicht bedacht,
or not considered

Durch das Labyrinth der Brust
through the labyrinth of the breast

Wandelt in der Nacht.
wanders in the night

that which unknown and
unheeded by men meanders at
night in the labyrinth of the breast.

13. *LIEBHABER IN ALLEN* LOVER IN ALL *GESTALTEN* FORMS

13. LOVER IN MANY FORMS

Johann Wolfgang von Goethe

Ich wollt' ich wär' ein Fisch,
I (would) wish I were a fish

So hurtig und frisch;
so nimble and cool

Und kämst du zu angeln,
and came you to angle

Ich würde nicht mangeln.
I would not be wanting

Ich wollt' ich wär' ein Fisch,
I would I were a fish

So hurtig und frisch.
so nimble and cool

I wish I were a fish, so nimble and
cool; if you came to catch me, I'd
be there. I wish I were a fish, so
nimble and cool!

Ich wollt' ich wäre Gold,
I would I were gold

Dir immer im Sold;
to you ever in the pay

Und tät'st du was kaufen
and did you something buy

Käm' ich gelaufen.
would come I running

I wish I were a gold piece ever in
your pay; so if you wished to buy
something, I'd go running off to
get it. I wish I were a gold piece
ever in your pay.

Ich wollt' ich wäre Gold,
I   would I   were gold

Dir   immer im   Sold.
to you always in the pay

Doch bin ich, wie ich bin,
but   am I   as I   am

Und nimm mich nur hin,
and take   me   just –

Willst bess're   besitzen,
want better one to possess

So lass dir   sie schnitzen.
so   let (for) you her cut

Ich bin nun wie ich bin;
I   am now as I   am

So nimm mich nur hin!
so accept me   just –

I am, however, as I am, and you'll
have to take me thus; and should
you want someone better, then let
her be made to measure. I am,
however, as I am, and you'll have
to take me thus!

14. DAS ROSENBAND
THE ROSES-RIBBON

Friedrich Gottlieb Klopstock
(also set by Richard Strauss)

Im   Frühlingsschatten fand ich sie;
in the spring's-shadow found I   her

Da band ich sie mit Rosenbändern:
then bound I   her with rose-ribbons

Sie fühlt' es nicht und schlummerte.
she felt   it not   and slumbered

Ich sah   sie an; mein Leben hing
I   looked her at   my   life   hung

Mit diesem Blick   an ihrem Leben;
with that   glance on her   life

Ich fühlt' es wohl   und wusst' es nicht.
I   felt   it indeed and knew it not

Doch lispelt'   ich ihr   sprachlos zu
yet murmured I   to her speechless –

Und rauschte mit den Rosenbändern:
and rustled with the rose-ribbons

Da wachte sie vom   Schlummer auf.
then woke   she from the slumber   up

14. THE GARLAND OF
ROSES

I found her in spring-shadows,
and bound her with rosy ribbons:
But she did not feel them, and
slumbered on.

I looked at her, and in that glance,
my life was caught in hers. This I
felt full well, but did not know.

But I murmured to her wordless,
and rustled the rosy ribbons, and
she awoke from her sleep.

Sie sah   mich an; ihr Leben hing
she looked me   at   her life   hung

Mit diesem Blick   an meinem Leben:
with that   glance on my   life

Und um   uns ward Elysium.
and about us was Elysium

And looked at me, and in that glance, her life was caught in mine, and all around us was Elysium.

15. *DEM   UNENDLICHEN* TO THE INFINITE

15. TO THE INFINITE

Friedrich Gottlieb Klopstock

Wie erhebt sich   das Herz, wenn es dich,
how lifts   (itself) the heart when it you

Unendlicher, denkt!   Wie sinkt es,
Infinite One considers how sinks it

Wenn es auf sich   herunterschaut!
when it at   itself looks down

Elend   schaut's wehklagend dann und Nacht und Tod!
wretched looks it lamenting then and night and death

How my heart lifts up when I think of You, the Infinite! When it sees itself, how it is cast down! Wretched and lamenting, it sees then but night and death.

Allein du rufst mich aus   meiner Nacht, der im
alone you call me   from my   night who in the
   Elend, der im   Tode hilft!
   misery who in the death helps

Dann denk' ich es ganz, dass du ewig   mich schufst,
then think I   it wholly that you for ever me   created

Herrlicher,   den   kein Preis, unten am   Grab,
Glorious One whom no   praise below in the grave
   oben am   Thron,
   above at the throne

Herr Gott, den, dankend entflammt, kein Jubel
Lord God who thanking kindled   no jubilation
   genug besingt!
   enough praises

You alone recall me from my darkness; You who help in times of trouble and in death! Then I know with my whole being, that You, O God of glory, created me, that I might live for ever. Whether I praise You from my grave, or at Your throne in Heaven, no praise is great enough. O Lord, You kindle in me eternal praise.

Weht, Bäume des   Lebens, in's   Harfengetön!
blow trees of (the) life   into the harps'-tones

Rausche mit ihnen in's   Harfengetön, kristallner
murmur with them into the harps'-tones crystal
   Strom!
   stream

O tree of life, blow to the strains of the harp; let your murmuring unite with its tones, O crystal stream! You may whisper and murmur, harps, but your music will never suffice, for it is God Himself whom you praise!

Ihr lispelt und rauscht, und, Harfen, ihr tönt
you lisp　and murmur and harps　you sound

Nie　es ganz! Gott ist es, den　ihr preist!
never it wholly God is it　whom you praise

Welten donnert, im　feierlichen Gang, in der
worlds thunder in the solemn　course in of the
　　Posaunen Chor!
　　trumpets chorus

Tönt,　all' ihr Sonnen auf der Strasse voll Glanz,
resound all　you suns　on the way　full splendour

In der　Posaunen Chor!
in of the trumpets chorus

Ihr Welten, ihr donnert,
you worlds　you thunder

Du, der Posaunen Chor, hallest　nie　es ganz
you the trumpets chorus resound never it wholly

Gott, Gott ist es, den　ihr preist!
God　God is it　whom you praise

Ring out your trumpets, all you
peoples of the earth! All you suns
in your radiant course, join the
chorus of trumpets!

But you peoples of the world with
your trumpet chorus will never
suffice. It is God, God Himself
whom you praise!

16. *KENNST DU　DAS LAND . . .*
KNOW　YOU THE LAND
(*Mignons Gesang*)

16. DO YOU KNOW
THE LAND . . .
(Mignon's Song)

Johann Wolfgang von Goethe
(from *Wilhelm Meister*)
(also set by Beethoven, Schumann, Liszt and Wolf)

Kennst du　das Land, wo　die Zitronen blühn,
know　you the land　where the lemons　blossom

Im　dunklen Laub　die Gold-Orangen glühn,
in the dark　foliage the gold-oranges　glow

Ein sanfter Wind vom　blauen Himmel weht,
a　gentle wind from the blue　sky　blows

Die Myrte still　und hoch der Lorbeer steht,
the myrtle silent and high the laurel　stands

Kennst du　es wohl?
know　you it perhaps

Dahin! Dahin
thither thither

Möcht'　ich mit dir, o mein Geliebter, ziehn.
would like I　with you O my　love　to go

Do you know the land where the
lemon-trees blossom, and oranges
glow golden in dark foliage; where
a soft breeze blows from a blue
sky, and high laurels and silent
myrtles grow? Do you know it? O
there would I go with you,
beloved, there!

Kennst du   das Haus? Auf Säulen ruht sein Dach,
know   you the house on pillars rests its   roof

Es glänzt   der Saal, es   schimmert das Gemach,
(it) gleams the hall   (it) shimmers the room

Und Marmorbilder   stehn und sehn mich an:
and marble-statues stand and look me   at

Was hat man dir,   du armes Kind, getan?
what has one to you you poor child done

Kennst du   es wohl?
know   you it perhaps

Dahin! Dahin
thither thither

Möcht"   ich mit dir, o mein Beschützer, ziehn.
should like I   with you O my   protector   to go

Kennst du   den Berg   und seinen Wolkensteg?
know   you the mountain and his   cloud-path

Das Maultier sucht im   Nebel seinen Weg;
the mule   seeks in the mist its   way

In Höhlen wohnt der   Drachen alte   Brut;
in caves   lives of the dragons ancient brood

Es stürzt   der Fels und über ihn die Flut.
(it) plunges the rock and over it   the torrent

Kennst du   ihn wohl?
know   you it   perhaps

Dahin! Dahin
thither thither

Geht unser Weg! o Vater, lass uns ziehn!
goes our   way O father let us go

Do you know a house – its roof rests on pillars; there's a gleaming hall, and shimmering rooms, and marble statues look at me and say, 'What have they done to you, poor child?' Do you know it? O there would I go with you, my protector, there!

Do you know a mountain with a path veiled in clouds? The mule seeks its way in the mist; in caves dwell an ancient dragon's brood, and the torrent sweeps over a plunging rock. Do you know it? There lies our way, O father, let us go there!

17. RASTLOSE LIEBE
RESTLESS LOVE

17. RESTLESS LOVE

Johann Wolfgang von Goethe

Dem Schnee, dem Regen,
the snow   the rain

Dem Wind entgegen,
the wind against

In the face of the snow, the rain and the wind, through damp, dim ravines and drifting mists – keep on! Keep on, without rest or peace!

Im   Dampf der   Klüfte,
in the steam of the ravines

Durch   Nebeldüfte
through mist-vapours

Immer zu! Immer zu!
ever   on ever   on

Ohne   Rast und Ruh!
without rest and peace

Lieber durch   Leiden
rather through suffering

I had rather make my way through suffering, than endure so much of life's joy.

Möcht'   ich mich   schlagen,
would like I   myself to cast

Als   so viel   Freuden
than so much joy

Des   Lebens ertragen.
of the life   endure

Alle das Neigen
all   the drawing

In the drawing together of heart to heart, oh, how strange are the workings of grief!

Von Herzen zu Herzen,
of   heart   to heart

Ach, wie so eigen
ah   how so strangely

Schaffet das Schmerzen!
works   the grief

Wie soll   ich flieh'n?
how shall I   flee

Shall I then flee into the woods? In vain, in vain! Crown of life, joy without peace – you are Love!

Wälderwärts zieh'n?
forestwards go

Alles, alles vergebens!
all   all in vain

Krone des   Lebens,
crown of the life

Glück   ohne   Ruh,
happiness without peace

Liebe, bist du!
love   are you

18. ERLKÖNIG
ERL-KING

Johann Wolfgang von Goethe

Wer reitet so spät durch   Nacht und Wind?
who rides so late through night and wind

Es ist der Vater mit seinem Kind;
it is the father with his   child

Er hat den Knaben wohl   in dem Arm,
he has the boy   indeed in the arm

Er fasst ihn sicher, er hält   ihn warm.
he holds him safe   he holds him warm

'Mein Sohn, was birgst du so bang   dein Gesicht?'
my   son   why hide you so fearfully your face

'Siehst, Vater, du den Erlkönig nicht?
see   father you the Erl-King not

Der Erlenkönig mit Kron   und Schweif?'
the Erl-King   with crown and train

'Mein Sohn, es ist ein Nebelstreif.'
my   son   it is a mist-streak

'Du liebes Kind, komm, geh mit mir!
you dear child come   go with me

Gar schöne Spiele spiel ich mit dir;
very lovely games play I   with you

Manch bunte   Blumen sind an dem Strand,
many gaily-coloured flowers are on the shore

Meine Mutter hat manch gülden Gewand.'
my   mother has many a golden robe

'Mein Vater, mein Vater, und hörest du nicht,
my   father my   father and hear you not

Was Erlenkönig mir   leise   verspricht?'
what Erl-King   to me softly promises

'Sei ruhig, bleibe ruhig, mein Kind:
be quiet stay   quiet my   child

In dürren   Blättern säuselt der Wind.'
in withered leaves   rustles the wind

'Willst, feiner Knabe, du mit mir gehn?
want fine   boy   you with me to go

Meine Töchter   sollen dich warten schön;
my   daughters shall you serve   well

Who rides so late through the wind and the night? It is a father with his child; in his arms he clasps the boy, holds him safe, keeps him warm.

'My son, why do you hide your face in fear?' 'O father, do you not see the Erl-King, the Erl-King with his crown and train?' 'My son, it is only a swirl of mist.'

'Sweet child, come, come away with me! I will play fine games with you. There are many bright flowers by the shore, and my mother has golden robes.'

'O father, father, do you not hear the Erl-King's soft promises?' 'Be still, be still, my child! The wind is rustling the withered leaves.'

'You beautiful boy, will you not come with me? My daughters would serve you well; they lead the nightly dance, and would rock

Meine Töchter   führen den nächtlichen Reihn
my   daughters lead   the nightly   dance

Und wiegen und tanzen und singen dich ein.'
and rock   and dance and sing   you (to sleep)

you, and dance for you, and sing you to sleep.'

'Mein Vater, mein Vater, und siehst du   nicht dort
my   father my   father and see   you not   there

Erlkönigs Töchter   am   düstern Ort?'
Erl-King's daughters in the dark   place

'O father, father, do you not see the Erl-King's daughters in that dark, dismal place?' 'My son, my son, I see them clearly; it is only the glimmer of old willow trees.'

'Mein Sohn, mein Sohn, ich seh es genau:
my   son   my son   I   see it exactly

Es   scheinen die alten Weiden so grau.'
(it) gleam   the old   willows so grey

'Ich liebe dich, mich reizt   deine schöne Gestalt;
I   love you me   allures your lovely form

'I love you, and am stirred by your beauty; if you do not come willingly, I must use force.' 'O father, father, he is seizing me now! The Erl-King has wounded me!'

Und bist du   nicht willig, so brauch ich Gewalt.'
and are you not   willing so need   I   force

'Mein Vater, mein Vater, jetzt fasst   er mich an!
my   father my   father now seizes he me   –

Erlkönig   hat mir ein Leids getan!'
Erl-King has me a   harm done

Dem   Vater grauset's,   er reitet geschwind,
(to) the father shudders (it) he rides fast

The father shudders, swiftly he rides, holding the moaning child in his arms. He reaches the court-yard in anguished haste, but in his arms the child is dead.

Er hält   in Armen das ächzende Kind,
he holds in arms   the moaning child

Erreicht den Hof   mit Müh und Not:
reaches the court-yard with toil   and distress

In seinen Armen das Kind war tot.
in his   arms   the child was dead

19. *SELIGKEIT*
ECSTASY

19. ECSTASY

Ludwig Hölty

Freuden sonder   Zahl
joys   without number

Blüh'n   im   Himmelssaal
blossom in the heaven's-hall

Engeln und Verklärten,
angels and (the) blessèd

Countless joys abound in the halls of Heaven – angels and the blessèd, so the elders say. O would that I were there, rejoicing for ever and ever!

Wie die Väter   lehrten,
as   the forefathers taught

O da   möcht'   ich sein
O there would like I   to be

Und mich   ewig   freun!
and myself for ever rejoice

Jedem   lächelt traut
to each smiles intimately

Eine Himmelsbraut;
a   heaven's-bride

Harf' und Psalter klinget,
harp and psalter resound(s)

Und man tanzt   und singet.
and one dances and sings

O da   möcht'   ich sein
O there would like I   to be

Und mich   ewig   freun!
and myself for ever rejoice

A heavenly bride smiles at each
one, harp and psalter resound, and
they all dance and sing. O would
that I were there, rejoicing for ever
and ever!

Lieber bleib' ich hier,
rather stay I   here

Lächelt Laura mir
smiles Laura to me

Einen Blick, der saget,
a   glance that says

Dass ich ausgeklaget.
that I   finished lamenting

Selig   dann mit ihr,
blissful then with her

Bleib' ich ewig   hier!
stay I   for ever here

Laura smiles at me, and her glance
says I need lament no more. For
blissful then with her, I'll stay for
ever here!

20. *GOTT IM   FRÜHLING*
GOD IN THE SPRING

Johann Peter Uz

In seinem schimmernden Gewand
in his   shimmering   robe

Hast du   den Frühling uns   gesandt,
have you the spring   to us sent

Und Rosen um   sein Haupt gewunden.
and roses about his head   wound

20. GOD IN
SPRINGTIME

You have sent us the spring,
twining his head about with roses.
Already he is here, smiling
sweetly, and each hour, dear God,
leads him nearer to his flowery
throne.

Holdlächelnd   kommt er schon!
sweetly-smiling comes he already

Es führen ihn die Stunden,
(it) lead   him the hours

O Gott, auf   seinen Blumenthron.
O God upon his   flower-throne

Er geht in   Büschen und sie   blühn;
he goes into bushes and they blossom

Den   Fluren   kommt ihr   frisches Grün,
to the meadows comes their fresh   green

Und Wäldern wächst ihr   Schatten wieder,
and woods   grow   their shadows again

Der West,   liebkosend, schwingt sein tausendes
the west (wind) caressing flourishes his thousand
   Gefieder,
   feathers

Und jeder frohe Vogel singt.
and each glad bird sings

He walks amongst the bushes and they blossom; a fresh green comes to the meadows, and in the woods shadows grow again. The west wind caresses with his thousand wings, and every bird sings merrily.

Mit eurer Lieder süssem Klang,
with your songs sweet sound

Ihr Vögel, soll   auch mein Gesang
you birds shall also my   song

Zum Vater der   Natur sich   schwingen.
to the father of the nature (himself) soar

Entzückung reisst   mich hin!
delight   transports me –

Ich will dem   Herrn lobsingen,
I   will to the Lord sing praises

Durch den   ich wurde, was ich bin!
through whom I became what I   am

You birds, I will join my song with your sweet strains, as they rise to the Father of all nature. I am filled with delight – and will praise the Lord, in whom I have my being!

21. *GESÄNGE DES   HARFNERS*
SONGS   OF THE HARPER

21. THE HARPER'S SONGS

Johann Wolfgang von Goethe

  i. (also set by Schumann and Wolf)

i.

Wer   sich   der   Einsamkeit ergibt,
he who himself to the solitude   yields

Ach! der ist bald allein;
ah   he is soon alone

He who succumbs to solitude, ah, he is soon alone; others live, others love, and leave him to his torment.

Ein jeder lebt, ein jeder liebt
everyone lives everyone loves

Und lässt   ihn seiner Pein.
and leaves him to his pain

Ja! lasst mich meiner Qual!   Yes, leave me to my anguish! Can
yes leave me   to my anguish   I but once feel loneliness, I will be
                                                  no longer alone.
Und kann ich nur einmal
and can I   but once

Recht einsam sein,
quite alone be

Dann bin ich nicht allein.
then am I not alone

Es schleicht ein Liebender lauschend sacht,   Does a lover steal up softly to find
(it) steals   a   loving one listening softly   if his love is alone? Thus each day
                                                  and night anguish and torment
Ob seine Freundin allein?   steal into my solitude.
if his   friend   alone

So überschleicht bei Tag und Nacht
so steals over by day and night

Mich Einsamen   die Pein,
me   solitary one the pain

Mich Einsamen   die Qual.
me   solitary one the anguish

Ach, werd' ich erst einmal   Alas, only when I lie within my
alas will I   just once   solitary grave will they truly leave
                                                  me alone.
Einsam im   Grabe sein,
solitary in the grave be

Da lässt sie mich allein!
then leaves she me   alone

   ii. (also set by Schumann, Liszt and Wolf)   ii.

                                                  He whose bread was never moist
Wer   nie   sein Brot mit Tränen ass,   with tears, who never lay weeping
he who never his bread with tears   ate   the miserable nights away – he
                                                  cannot know you, heavenly
Wer   nie   die kummervollen Nächte   powers!
he who never the sorrowful   nights

Auf seinem Bette weinend sass,
on his   bed weeping sat

Der kennt euch nicht, ihr himmlischen Mächte!
he knows you not   you heavenly   powers

Ihr führt ins   Leben uns hinein,
you lead into the life   us thither

Ihr lässt den Armen   schuldig werden,
you let the poor wretch guilty   become

Dann überlasst ihr ihn der   Pein;
then abandon you him to the pain

Denn alle Schuld rächt   sich auf Erden.
for   all guilt   revenges itself on earth

You bring us into life, you let man in his misery transgress, then you leave him in his torment; on earth all guilt brings its own retribution.

iii. (also set by Schumann and Wolf)

An die Türen will ich schleichen,
to the doors will I   steal

Still   und sittsam will ich stehn;
silent and modest will I   stand

Fromme Hand wird Nahrung   reichen,
pious   hand will sustenance give

Und ich werde weiter gehn.
and I   will   on   go

Jeder wird sich   glücklich scheinen,
each will himself happy   seem

Wenn mein Bild   vor   ihm erscheint;
when my   image before him appears

Eine Träne wird er weinen,
a   tear   will he weep

Und ich weiss nicht, was er weint.
and I   know not   what he weeps

iii.

I will steal from door to door, and stand there humble and still. Charitable hands will give me sustenance, and I will go my way. Each man will think how happy he is, when I but appear before him; he will shed a tear, and I will not know for what he weeps.

22. *JÄGERS   ABENDLIED*
HUNTER'S EVENING-SONG

Johann Wolfgang von Goethe

Im   Felde schleich ich still   und wild,
in the field steal   I   silent and savage

Gespannt mein Feuerrohr,
cocked   my   rifle

Da   schwebt so licht   dein liebes Bild,
then hovers so lightly your dear image

Dein süsses Bild   mir vor.
your sweet image me in front of

22. HUNTER'S
EVENING SONG

I prowl through the fields, savage and silent, my rifle cocked and ready. And your dear image, your sweet image hovers lightly before me.

Du wandelst jetzt wohl   still   und mild
you go   now perhaps silent and gentle

Durch   Feld und liebes Tal,
through field and dear valley

Und ach, mein schnell verrauschend Bild,
and ah my   quickly dying away   image

Stellt   sich   dir's   nicht einmal?
appears (itself) to you it not   once

Mir   ist es, denk' ich nur an dich,
to me is it think I only of you

Als in den Mond zu sehn;
as in the moon to see

Ein stiller Friede kommt auf   mich,
a   quiet peace comes upon me

Weiss nicht, wie mir   geschehn.
know not   how to me happened

Perhaps you go now, gentle and silent, through the fields and the well-loved valley. Oh, does my quickly fading image not appear even once before you?

It seems I see you in the moonlight as I think only of you; over me steals a quiet peace, and I cannot say what has befallen me.

23. *AN SCHWAGER   KRONOS*
TO 'POSTILLION' TIME

23. TO TIME, THE
COACHMAN

Johann Wolfgang von Goethe

Spute   dich,   Kronos!
make haste yourself Time

Fort, den rasselnden Trott!
away the rattling   trot

Bergab   gleitet der Weg,
downhill glides the path

Ekles   Schwindeln zögert
disagreeable giddiness   lingers

Mir   vor   die Stirne dein Zaudern.
to me before the brow your dallying

Frisch, holpert es gleich,
briskly jolts   it at once

Über Stock und Steine den Trott
over stick and stone the trot

Rasch ins   Leben hinein!
swiftly into the life   thither

Make haste, O Time – away at a rattlng trot! The path runs smoothly down the hill; your tarrying brings a galling giddiness to my brow. Briskly we jolt over sticks and stones, trotting swiftly into life!

Nun schon   wieder Den eratmenden Schritt
now already again the gasping   step

Mühsam   Berg hinauf!
laboriously hill   up

Auf denn, nicht träge   denn,
up then not sluggishly then

Strebend und hoffend hinan!
striving and hoping upwards

Weit, hoch, herrlich Rings   den Blick
far   high glorious around the glimpse

ins   Leben hinein,
into the life   thither

Vom   Gebirg   zum Gebirg
from the mountains to the mountains

Schwebet der ewige   Geist,
soars   the eternal spirit

Ewigen   Lebens ahndevoll.
of eternal life   portentous

Seitwärts des   Überdachs Schatten
sideways of the roof   shadow

Zieht dich an,
draws you –

Und ein Frischung verheissender Blick
and a   renewal of promising glimpse

Auf der Schwelle des   Mädchens da.
on the threshold of the girl   there

Labe dich!   Mir auch, Mädchen,
refresh yourself to me also girl

Diesen schäumenden Trank,
this   sparkling   drink

Diesen frischen Gesundheitsblick!
this   fresh   health's glance

Ab   denn, rascher hinab!
down then swifter down

Sieh, die Sonne sinkt!
see   the sun   is sinking

Eh' sie sinkt, eh'   mich Greisen
before she sinks before me   old man

Now once more the breathless
pace, labouring up the hill! Up
then, not sluggish – striving
hopefully upwards!

Wide and high, a glimpse into Life
itself; from peak to peak the
eternal spirit soars, portent of
eternal life.

Sideways, drawn by the shadow of
a roof, and a promising glimpse of
a girl on the step. Refresh
yourself! For me too, maiden, this
sparkling drink, this health-giving
glance!

Down again, still faster – see, the
sun is sinking – Before it sinks,
before the moorland mists encircle
me, an old man, with chattering
toothless jaws and trembling
limbs!

Ergreift im   Moore Nebelduft,
seizes   in the moor misty-fragrance

Entzahnte Kiefer schnattern
toothless jaws   chatter

Und das schlotternde Gebein.
and the trembling   bones

Trunk'nen vom   letzten Strahl
drunk   from the last   ray

Reiss' mich, ein Feuermeer
seize me   a fire-sea

Mir   im   schäumenden Aug'
to me in the sparkling   eye

Mich geblendeten Taumelnden
me   dazzled   reeling one

In der Hölle nächtliches Tor.
in the hell   of nightly gateway

Seize me, drunk from the last rays
of the sun, a sea of fire blinding
my sight, that dazzled, I reel into
Hell's nocturnal gateway.

Töne, Schwager, ins   Horn,
blow coachman into the horn

Rassle den schallenden Trab,
rattle the echoing   trot

Dass der Orkus vernehme: wir kommen,
that the Orcus may hear we are coming

Dass gleich   an der Tür
that at once at the door

Der Wirt   uns freundlich empfange.
the inn-keeper us cheerfully may receive.

Coachman, sound the horn – on
at a rattling trot! That Orcus hears
we are coming, and the innkeeper
waits at the door, to welcome us!

24. DER WANDERER
THE WANDERER

24. THE WANDERER

Georg Philipp Schmidt von Lübeck

Ich komme vom   Gebirge   her,
I   come from the mountains (from)

Es dampft das Tal,   es braust das Meer,
(it) steams the valley (it) rages the ocean

I come from the mountains. Mists
rise in the valley, the ocean rages.
Silently I wander, seldom happy,
always asking in my sighs,
'Where?' always, 'Where?'

Ich wandle still,   bin wenig froh,
I   wander silently am little happy

Und immer fragt der Seufzer: wo?
and always asks the sigh   where

Immer: wo?
always where

Die Sonne dünkt mich   hier so kalt,
the sun   seems (to) me here so cold

Here the sun seems so cold, the flowers faded, life old. The chatter of men is an empty sound; I am a stranger everywhere.

Die Blüte   welk, das Leben alt,
the blossom faded the life   old

Und was sie reden, leerer Schall,
and what they talk   empty sound

Ich bin ein Fremdling überall.
I   am a stranger everywhere

Wo   bist du, mein geliebtes Land?
where are you my beloved land

Where are you my beloved land? I have sought you, dreamt of you, but never found you! A land so green with hope, the land where my roses bloom,

Gesucht, geahnt,   und nie   gekannt!
sought imagined and never known

Das Land, das Land, so hoffnungsgrün,
the land the land so hope's-green

Das Land, wo   meine Rosen blühn,
the land where my   roses bloom

Wo   meine Freunde wandelnd gehn,
where my   friends wandering go

where my friends roam, where my dead come to life; the land where they speak my tongue – O land, where are you?

Wo   meine Toten auferstehn,
where my   dead rise

Das land, das meine Sprache spricht,
the land that my   language speaks

O Land, wo   bist du?
O land   where are you

Ich wandle still,   bin wenig froh,
I   wander silently am little happy

Silently I wander, seldom glad; always asking in my sighs, 'Where?' always 'Where?' A ghostly whisper echoes back, 'There, where you are not, there is bliss.'

Und immer fragt der Seufzer: wo?
and always asks the sigh   where

Immer: wo?
always where

Im   Geisterhauch tönt's   mir   zurück:
in the ghost-breath sounds it to me back

Dort, wo   du nicht bist, dort ist das Glück!
there where you not   are   there is the happiness

25. *LIED   EINES SCHIFFERS AN*
SONG OF A   SAILOR   TO
DIE DIOSKUREN
THE DIOSCURI

25. SAILOR'S SONG
TO CASTOR AND
POLLUX

Johann Mayrhofer

Dioskuren, Zwillingssterne,
Dioscuri twin-stars

O Castor and Pollux, twin stars,
you light my little boat, and calm
me on the sea with your gentle
watching.

Die ihr leuchtet meinem Nachen,
who you light   my   boat

Mich beruhigt auf dem Meere
me   calm   on the sea

Eure Milde,   euer Wachen.
your gentleness your watching

Wer auch fest   in sich   begründet,
who-ever strong in himself proves

Whoever proves his strength by
meeting storms undaunted, in
your light feels twice as bold and
blessed.

Unverzagt dem Sturm begegnet,
undaunted the storm meets

Fühlt sich   doch   in euren Strahlen
feels himself indeed in your rays

Doppelt mutig und gesegnet.
twice   bold and blessed

Dieses Ruder, das ich schwinge,
this   oar   that I wield

These oars I wield to part the
ocean waves; when I reach safety I
will hang them on the pillars of
your temple, O Castor and Pollux,
twin stars!

Meeresfluten zu zerteilen,
ocean-waves to divide

Hänge ich, so ich geborgen,
hang   I   so I in safety (am)

Auf an eures   Tempels Säulen,
on to of your temple pillars

Dioskuren, Zwillingssterne.
Dioscuri   twin-stars

26. AM   GRABE ANSELMOS
AT THE GRAVE ANSELMO'S

26. AT ANSELMO'S GRAVE

Matthias Claudius

Dass ich dich verloren habe,
that I you lost have

Dass du nicht mehr bist,
that you no more are

Ach! dass hier in diesem Grabe
ah that here in this grave

Mein Anselmo ist,
my Anselmo is

Das ist mein Schmerz!
that is my grief

Seht, wie liebten uns wir beide,
see how loved ourselves we both

Und so lang' ich bin, kommt Freude
and so long I am comes joy

Niemals wieder in mein Herz.
never again into my heart

I have lost you, you are no more. Ah, here in this grave my Anselmo lies – that is my grief. How we loved each other! Never again, as long as I live, can joy enter my heart.

27. AN DIE NACHTIGALL
TO THE NIGHTINGALE

27. TO THE NIGHTINGALE

Matthias Claudius

Er liegt und schläft an meinem Herzen,
he lies and sleeps on my heart

Mein guter Schutzgeist sang ihn ein;
my good guardian-spirit sang to sleep him –

Und ich kann fröhlich sein und scherzen,
and I can marry be and jest

Kann jeder Blum und jedes Blatts mich freun.
can of every flower and of every leaf myself rejoice

Nachtigall, ach! Nachtigall, ach!
nightingale ah nightingale ah

Sing mir den Amor nicht wach!
sing to me the Cupid not awake

He lies sleeping on my breast; my guardian spirit sang him to sleep. I can be merry and jest, rejoice in every leaf and flower. Nightingale, O nightingale – do not wake my Cupid with your song!

28. *WIEGENLIED*
CRADLE-SONG

Matthias Claudius

Schlafe, schlafe, holder, süsser Knabe,
sleep   sleep   lovely sweet boy

Leise wiegt dich deiner Mutter Hand;
softly rocks you of your mother hand

Sanfte Ruhe, milde Labe
gentle sleep tender comfort

Bringt dir   schwebend dieses Wiegenband.
brings to you hovering this   cradle-ribbon

Schlafe, schlafe in dem süssen Grabe,
sleep   sleep in the sweet grave

Noch beschützt dich deiner Mutter Arm;
still   shelters you of your mother arm

Alle Wünsche, alle Habe
all desires   all possession

Fasst sie liebend, alle liebewarm.
holds she lovingly all love-warm

Schlafe, schlafe, in der   Flaumen Schosse,
sleep   sleep   in of the down   lap

Noch umtönt   dich lauter Liebeston;
still surrounds you pure love's-sound

Eine Lilie, eine Rose,
a   lily a   rose

Nach dem Schlafe werd' sie   dir zum   Lohn.
after the sleep   get   they you as the reward

29. *AN DIE LAUTE*
TO THE LUTE

Friedrich Rochlitz

Leiser, leiser, kleine Laute,
softer softer little lute

Flüstre, was ich dir   vertraute,
whisper what I   to you entrusted

28. CRADLE SONG

Sleep, sleep, my fine sweet boy,
your mother's hand softly rocks
you. The swaying of the cradle
brings you tender comfort, gentle
sleep.

Sleep, sleep in the sweet sheltering
hollow of your mother's arm; all
she has, all she desires, she holds
in the warmth of her love.

Sleep, sleep, cradled in down, with
the pure strains of love echoing
around you. When you awake,
she'll give you a lily, and a rose.

29. TO THE LUTE

Softer, softer, little lute! Whisper
my secret message up there to that
window. Send it to my mistress,
like a gently billowing breeze, like

Dort zu jenem Fenster hin!
there to that   window thither

Wie die Wellen sanfter Lüfte,
like the waves of gentle breezes

Mondenglanz und Blumendüfte,
moonlight   and flower-scents

Send' es der Gebieterin!
send it to the mistress

Neidisch sind des Nachbars Söhne,
jealous are of the neighbour sons

Und im Fenster jener Schöne
and in the window of that fair one

Flimmert noch ein einsam Licht.
glimmers still a solitary light

Drum noch leiser, kleine Laute:
therefore still softer little lute

Dich vernehme die Vertraute,
you hear   the entrusted one

Nachbarn aber Nachbarn nicht!
neighbours but neighbours not

moonlight and the scent of flowers.

The neighbours' sons are jealous – a solitary light glimmers in the window of my fair one. So play still softer, little lute, so my beloved hears you – but not the neighbours, not the neighbours!

30. *LOB DER TRÄNEN* PRAISE OF THE TEARS

30. IN PRAISE OF TEARS

August Wilhelm von Schlegel

Laue Lüfte,
warm breezes

Blumendüfte,
flower-scents

Alle Lenz- und Jugendlust;
all spring- and youth-joy

Frischer Lippen
of cool lips

Küsse nippen,
kisses sip

Sanft gewiegt an zarter Brust;
softly rocked on tender breast

Warm breezes, scent of flowers, all the joys of spring and youth; cool lips touched by kisses, softly rocked on tender breast; grapes stolen nectar, dancing and merry-making: all the senses' pleasures – O can they ever fulfil the heart?

Dann der Trauben
then of the grapes

Nektar rauben;
nectar steal

Reihentanz und Spiel und Scherz;
dance and play and jest

Was die Sinnen
what the senses

Nur gewinnen:
only gain

Ach, erfüllt es je das Herz?
ah fulfils it ever the heart

Wenn die feuchten
when the moist

Augen leuchten
eyes shine

Von der Wehmut lindem Tau,
of the melancholy gentle dew

Dann entsiegelt,
then unseals

Drin gespiegelt,
therein mirrored

Sich dem Blick die Himmelsau.
(herself) to the glance the Heaven's pasture

Wie erquicklich
how refreshingly

Augenblicklich
instantly

Löscht es jede wilde Glut!
quenches it each wild passion

Wie vom Regen
as by the rain

Blumen pflegen,
flowers tend

Hebet sich der matte Mut.
raises itself the faint spirit

When our moist eyes shine with the gentle dew of melancholy, there unveiled and mirrored is a glimpse of Heaven's meads. In a moment is each passion quenched, and so as flowers refreshed by rain, do the faint of heart revive.

Nicht mit süssen
not with sweet

Wasserflüssen
water-rivers

Zwang Prometheus unsern Leim:*
mastered Prometheus our (size)

Nein, mit Tränen;
no with tears

Drum im Sehnen
therefore in the yearning

Und im Schmerz sind wir daheim.
and in the grief are we at home

Bitter schwellen
bitter rise

Diese Quellen
these springs

Für den erdumfangnen Sinn.
for the earth-encircled sense

Doch sie drängen
yet they press

Aus den Engen
from the narrowness

In das Meer der Liebe hin.
into the ocean of the love thither

Ew'ges Sehnen
eternal longing

Floss in Tränen
flowed in tears

Und umgab die starre Welt,
and surrounded the benumbed world

Die in Armen
which in arms

Sein Erbarmen
his mercy

Immerdar umflutend hält.
ever washed around holds

    * =*Lehm* (poetic licence) clay

Not with sweet river water did Prometheus mould our clay, but with tears; thus yearning and grief are part of our being. These springs rise bitter to our earthly senses, yet from narrow straits they strive towards Love's ocean.

God's eternal longing flowed in tears about a world benumbed, which, held in His arms, was encompassed like waves by His mercy. If then you would be free of earth's dust, the tears you weep must unite with the waters of the Eternal womb.

Soll   dein   Wesen
shall your being

Denn genesen
then recover

Von   dem Erdenstaube los,
from the earth-dust free

Musst im   Weinen
must in the weeping

Dich   vereinen
yourself unite

Jener   Wasser heilgem Schoss.
of those waters to holy womb

31. *DER TOD   UND DAS*
THE DEATH AND THE
MÄDCHEN
MAIDEN

31. DEATH AND THE
MAIDEN

Matthias Claudius

(Das Mädchen)
  the maiden

(The maiden)

'Vorüber, ach, vorüber!
 by   ah by

'Pass by, oh, pass by, cruel Death!
I am still young – go, kind Death,
and do not touch me!'

Geh, wilder Knochenmann!
pass savage Death (as a skeleton)

Ich bin noch jung,   geh, Lieber!
I   am still young go   dear fellow

Und rühre mich nicht an.'
and touch me   not –

(Der Tod)
  the death

(Death)

'Gib deine Hand, du schön und zart   Gebild,
 give your hand you fair   and gentle creature

'Give me your hand, you fair,
gentle creature. I am your friend,
and come not to judge you
harshly. Be of good courage! I am

Bin Freund und komme nicht zu strafen.
am friend and come not to punish

Sei gutes   Muts!   Ich bin nicht wild,
be of good courage I   am not   savage

not cruel – you shall sleep gently
in my arms.'

Sollst sanft   in meinen Armen schlafen.'
shall gently in my   arms   sleep

32. GANYMED
   GANYMED

32. GANYMEDE

Johann Wolfgang von Goethe
(also set by Wolf)

Wie im   Morgenglanze
how in the morning-splendour

How you glow around me in your
morning splendour, beloved
Spring! In a thousandfold ecstasy
of love, the divine sense of your
eternal warmth presses against my
heart, infinite beauty!

Du rings   mich anglühst,
you around me   glow at

Frühling, Geliebter!
spring   beloved

Mit tausendfacher Liebeswonne
with thousandfold love's-ecstasy

Sich   an mein Herz drängt
herself on my   heart presses

Deiner ewigen Wärme
your   eternal warmth

Heilig Gefühl,
divine sensation

Unendliche Schöne!
infinite   beauty

Dass ich dich fassen möcht
that I   you hold might

Could I but hold you in my arms!

In diesen Arm!
in these arm(s)

Ach, an deinem Busen
ah   on your   bosom

Ah, I lie languishing at your
breast, and your flowers and your
grasses press against my heart.
You cool the burning thirst within
my breast, sweet morning breeze!
The nightingale calls lovingly to
me from the misty valley.

Lieg ich und schmachte,
lie I   and languish

Und deine Blumen, dein Gras
and your flowers your grass

Drängen sich   an   mein Herz.
press   (themselves) against my   heart

Du kühlst den brennenden
you cool   the burning

Durst meines Busens,
thirst of my bosom

Lieblicher Morgenwind!
lovely   morning-breeze

Ruft drein   die Nachtigall
calls thereto the nightingale

Liebend nach mir aus   dem Nebeltal.
lovingly to   me from the misty-valley

Ich komm,   ich komme!
I   am coming I   am coming

I am coming, I am coming!
Whither, O whither?

Wohin? Ach, wohin?
whither oh   whither

Hinauf! Hinauf strebt's.
upwards upwards strives it

Upwards, striving upwards!
Clouds float downwards, reaching
towards my yearning love; to me,
to me! In your lap, now upwards –
embracing, embraced! Upwards to
your breast, all-loving Father!

Es schweben die Wolken
(it) float   the clouds

Abwärts,   die Wolken
downwards the clouds

Neigen   sich   der   sehnenden Liebe.
bow down (themselves) to the yearning love

Mir! Mir!
to me to me

In eurem Schosse
in your lap

Aufwärts!
upwards

Umfangend umfangen!
embracing embraced

Aufwärts an deinen Busen,
upwards on your   bosom

Alliebender Vater!
all-loving father

33. *DER JÜNGLING UND DER* THE YOUTH AND THE *TOD* DEATH

33. THE YOUTH AND DEATH

Josef von Spaun

(Der Jüngling)
  the youth

(The youth)

Die Sonne sinkt,
the sun   is sinking

O könnt' ich mit ihr scheiden
O could I   with her depart

Mit ihrem letzten Strahl entfliehn!
with her   last   ray   flee away

Ach diese namenlosen Qualen   meiden
ah these nameless   torments avoid

Und weit in schön're Welten zieh'n!
and far in fairer   world go

The sun is sinking – O, if I could
but flee away for ever with her last
ray, and leave these nameless
torments to go into a fairer world!

O komme, Tod!
O come   death

Und löse   diese Bande!
and loosen these bonds

Ich lächle dir,   o Knochenmann,
I   smile to you O skeleton

Entführe   mich leicht in   geträumte Lande!
lead away me   lightly into dreamed of land

O komm und rühre mich doch an,
O come and touch me   do   –

O komm!
O come

Come, O Death, and loosen these
bonds! I smile at you, Death. O
lead me gently away to the land of
which I dream. Come, lay your
hands on me! O come!

(Der Tod)
  the death

(Death)

Es ruht sich kühl   und sanft in meinen Armen,
it rests itself coolly and gently in my   arms

Du rufst, ich will mich   deiner Qual   erbarmen.
you call I   will (myself) of your torment have mercy

You may rest gently in my cool
arms. You call! I will have mercy
on you in your torment.

34. *AN DIE MUSIK*
TO THE MUSIC

Franz von Schober

Du holde   Kunst, in wieviel   grauen Stunden,
you gracious art   in how many grey   hours

Wo   mich des   Lebens wilder   Kreis umstrickt,
when me   of the life   turbulent circle ensnared

Hast du mein Herz zu warmer Lieb entzunden,
have you my   heart to warm   love kindled

Hast mich in   eine bessre Welt   entrückt!
have me   into a   better world carried off

Oft   hat ein Seufzer, deiner   Harf entflossen,
often has a   sigh   (of) your harp flowed from

Ein süsser, heiliger Akkord von   dir
a   sweet divine chord   from you

Den Himmel bessrer   Zeiten mir   erschlossen,
the heaven of better times to me unlocked

Du holde   Kunst, ich danke dir dafür!
you gracious art   I   thank you for it

34. TO MUSIC

O gracious art, how often in dark
hours, when caught in life's
tumultuous round, you have
kindled warm love in my heart,
and carried me into a better world!

How often a sigh flowing from
your harp, a sweet, divine chord,
has unlocked for me a heaven of
fairer moments. O gracious art, for
this I thank you!

35. *DIE FORELLE*
THE TROUT

Christian Friedrich Daniel Schubart

In einem Bächlein   helle,
in a   little brook bright

Da   schoss in froher Eil
there darted in glad   haste

Die launische Forelle
the moody   trout

Vorüber wie ein Pfeil.
past   like an arrow

35. THE TROUT

In a sparkling little brook, a
playful trout darted gaily past me
like an arrow. I stood on the bank
in quiet content, watching the
little fish bathing in the clear
brook.

Ich stand an dem Gestade
I   stood on the bank

Und sah   in süsser Ruh
and watched in sweet quiet

Des   muntern Fischleins Bade
of the lively   little fish bath

Im   klaren Bächlein   zu.
in the clear   little brook –

Ein Fischer mit   der Rute
an   angler with the rod

Wohl   an dem Ufer stand,
indeed on the bank stood

An angler on the bank with his
rod, was coldly watching the little
fish darting about. So long as the
water is clear, I thought, he'll not
catch the trout with his line.

Und sah's mit   kaltem Blute,
and saw it with cold   blood

Wie sich   das Fischlein wand.
how (itself) the little fish turned about

So lang' dem   Wasser Helle,
so long to the water   clearness

So dacht   ich, nicht gebricht,
so thought I   not   is wanting

So fängt   er die Forelle
so catches he the trout

Mit seiner Angel   nicht.
with his   fishing-rod not

Doch   endlich ward dem   Diebe
however at last was to the thief

Die Zeit zu lang. Er macht'
the time too long he made

But at last the thief was impatient,
and slyly he muddied the stream,
and with a jerk of the rod, the
trout was struggling there – and as
I looked at the cheated little fish,
my blood rose.

Das Bächlein   tückisch trübe,
the little brook artfully muddy

Und eh   ich es gedacht,
and before I   it thought

So zuckte seine Rute,
so jerked his   rod

Das Fischlein zappelt dran,
the little fish writhed on it

Und ich mit regem Blute
and I with roused blood

Sah die Betrogne an.
looked the cheated one at

36. *GRUPPE AUS DEM TARTARUS*
GROUP FROM THE TARTARUS

36. GROUP IN TARTARUS

Friedrich von Schiller

Horch – wie Murmeln des empörten Meeres,
listen like murmur of the enraged sea

Wie durch hohler Felsen Becken weint ein Bach,
as through of hollow rocks vortex weeps a brook

Stöhnt dort dumpfigtief ein schweres, leeres
groans there dankly-deep a heavy empty

Qualerpresstes Ach!
torment-extorted ah

Schmerz verzerret
grief distorts

Ihr Gesicht! Verzweiflung sperret
their face despair opens wide

Ihren Rachen fluchend auf.
their throats cursing –

Hohl sind ihre Augen, ihre Blicke
hollow are their eyes their glances

Spähen bang nach des Cocytus Brücke,
peer anxiously towards of the Cocytus bridge

Folgen tränend seinem Trauerlauf.
follow weeping his mourning-course

Fragen sich einander ängstlich leise,
ask (themselves) one another anxiously quiet

Ob noch nicht Vollendung sei?
if yet not completion be

Ewigkeit schwingt über ihnen Kreise,
eternity swings over them circles

Bricht die Sense des Saturns entzwei.
breaks the scythe of the Saturn in two

Listen – like the murmuring of an angry sea, or a brook weeping amongst hollowed rocks – listen to the deep groans wrung forth, a heavy, empty tormented wail!

Grief distorts their faces, despair twists open their mouths with cursing. Their hollow eyes peer anxiously towards the Cocytus bridge, and weeping follow its mourning course.

With low uneasy voices they ask each other if the end has not yet come! Above them circles Eternity, breaking Saturn's scythe in two.

37. *LITANEI (AUF DAS FEST LITANY ON THE FEAST 'ALLER SEELEN')* OF ALL SOULS

37. LITANY (FOR THE FEAST OF ALL SOULS)

Johann Georg Jacobi

Ruhn in Frieden alle Seelen,
rest in peace all souls

Die vollbracht ein banges Quälen,
who carried out an anxious tormenting

Die vollendet süssen Traum,
who achieved sweet dream

Lebenssatt, geboren kaum,
life-satiated born   scarcely

Aus   der Welt hinüberschieden:
out of the world over there departed

Alle Seelen ruhn in Frieden!
all souls rest in peace

All souls, rest in peace: all those in anxious torment, all those who enjoyed sweet dreams; all those tired of life, and those scarcely born – all those who left this life: all souls, rest in peace!

Liebevoller Mädchen Seelen,
of loving   maidens souls

Deren Tränen nicht zu zählen,
whose tears   not to count

Die ein falscher Freund verliess,
who a   false   friend left

Und die blinde Welt verstiess:
and the blind world rejected

Alle, die von hinnen schieden,
all   who from here   departed

Alle Seelen ruhn in Frieden!
all souls rest in peace

Loving souls of maidens, whose tears were without number, deserted by faithless lovers and rejected by a blind world – all those who left this life: all souls, rest in peace!

Und die nie   der Sonne lachten,
and those never to the sun   laughed

Unterm   Mond auf Dornen wachten,
under the moon on thorns watched

Gott, im   reinen Himmelslicht,
God in the pure heaven's-light

Einst   zu sehn von Angesicht:
one day to see by face

And those on whom the sun never smiled, who lay on thorns beneath the moon, to see one day the face of God in the pure light of Heaven; all those who left this life: all souls, rest in peace!

Alle, die von hinnen schieden,
all who from hence departed

Alle Seelen ruhn in Frieden!
all souls rest in peace

38. *Fragment aus dem Gedichte:*
Fragment from the poem
DIE GÖTTER GRIECHENLANDS
THE GODS OF GREECE

38. THE GODS OF GREECE

Friedrich Schiller

Schöne Welt, wo bist du? Kehre wieder,
lovely world where are you come back again

O lovely world, where are you?
Come back, gracious age, when
Nature bloomed! Alas, only in the
fairy-land of song does any vestige
of your myths live on. The
countryside is dead and mourning,
no deities appear before my eyes.
Ah, from that warm and living
image, only a shadow remains.

Holdes Blütenalter der Natur!
gracious blossom-epoch of the nature

Ach, nur in dem Feenland der Lieder
alas only in the fairyland of the songs

Lebt noch deine fabelhafte Spur.
lives still your mythical vestige

Ausgestorben trauert das Gefilde,
died out mourns the countryside

Keine Gottheit zeigt sich meinem Blick.
not deity appears (herself) to my glance

Ach von jenem lebenwarmen Bilde
ah from that life-warm image

Blieb der Schatten nur zurück.
stayed the shadow only back.

39. *DIE VÖGEL*
THE BIRDS

39. THE BIRDS

Friedrich von Schlegel

Wie lieblich und fröhlich,
how lovely and gay

How sweet and joyful it is to soar
and sing, and look down on the
earth from shining heights!

Zu schweben, zu singen,
to soar to sing

Von glänzender Höhe
from shining   heights

Zur   Erde zu blicken!
to the earth to look

Die Menschen sind töricht,
the men   are stupid

Sie   können nicht fliegen.
they can   not fly

Sie   jammern in Nöten,
they complain in troubles

Wir flattern gen   Himmel.
we flutter towards heaven

Der Jäger   will   töten,
the hunter wants to kill

Dem   Früchte wir pickten;
to whom fruit   we pecked

Wir müssen ihn höhnen,
we must   him mock

Und Beute gewinnen.
and booty gain

Men are foolish, for they cannot
fly! In their troubles they complain
– while we fly up to heaven.

The hunter wants to kill those who
pecked his fruit, and so we mock
him, and take our prize.

40. FRÜHLINGSGLAUBE
SPRING-FAITH

40. SPRING'S PROMISE

Ludwig Uhland

Die linden Lüfte   sind erwacht,
the soft   breezes are awakened

Sie   säuseln und wehen Tag und Nacht,
they whisper and blow day and night

Sie   schaffen an allen Enden.
they work   in all   ends

O frischer Duft, o neuer Klang!
O fresh   scent O new sound

Nun, armes Herze, sei nicht bang!
now poor heart be not anxious

Nun muss sich   alles,   alles   wenden.
now must (itself) everything everything change

Soft breezes awaken; day and
night they whisper and stir, busy
everywhere. O fresh scents, new
sounds! Be anxious no more, poor
heart – everything, everything now
must change!

Die Welt wird schöner mit jedem Tag,
the world becomes lovelier with each day

Man weiss nicht, was noch werden mag,
one knows not what yet come to be may

Das Blühen will nicht enden;
the blossoming wants not to end

Es blüht das fernste, tiefste Tal:
(it) blossoms the furthest deepest valley

Nun, armes Herz, vergiss der Qual!
now poor heart forget the torment

Nun muss sich alles, alles wenden.
now must (itself) everything everything change

The world is lovelier each day; we do not know what is yet to come, for the blossoming is never-ending – even the furthest, deepest valley flowers. Now, poor heart, forget your torment! Everything, everything now must change!

41. GEHEIMES
SECRET

41. THE SECRET

Johann Wolfgang von Goethe

Über meines Liebchens Äugeln
over my sweetheart's ogling

Stehn verwundert alle Leute;
stand astonished all people

Ich, der Wissende, dagegen,
I the one who knows on the other hand

Weiss recht gut, was das bedeute.
know very well what that may mean

Everyone wonders at my sweetheart's roving eye. But I who understand it, know full well what it means.

Denn es heisst: 'Ich liebe diesen,
for it says I love this one

Und nicht etwa den und jenen.'
and not perhaps him or that one

Lasset nur, ihr guten Leute,
leave off just you good people

Euer Wundern, euer Sehnen!
your wondering your longing

It means: 'I love this one – and not that one, or the other.' So good people, stop your wondering and desiring!

Ja, mit ungeheuren Mächten
yes with enormous power(s)

Blicket sie wohl in die Runde;
glances she indeed (in the) round

Yes, her glances are compelling as she looks around her – yet she only seeks to tell him of the next sweet hour to come.

Doch, sie sucht   nur   zu verkünden
yet   she seeks only to make known

Ihm   die nächste süsse   Stunde.
to him the next   sweet hour

42. SULEIKA I
SULEIKA

Johann Wolfgang von Goethe*
(from the *West-östlichen Divan*)
          west-east   collection of poems

Was bedeutet die Bewegung?
what means   the stirring

Bringt der Ost   mir   frohe Kunde?
brings the east (wind) to me glad tidings

Seiner Schwingen frische Regung
of his wings   fresh stirring

Kühlt des   Herzens tiefe Wunde.
cools of the heart   deep wound

Kosend   spielt er mit dem Staube,
caressing plays he with the dust

Jagt   ihn auf in leichten Wölkchen,
chases him up in light   little clouds

Treibt zur   sichern Rebenlaube
drives to the safe   vine-leaves

Der   Insekten frohes Völkchen.
of the insects glad little folk

Lindert sanft der   Sonne Glühen,
tempers gently of the sun   glowing

Kühlt auch mir   die heissen Wangen,
cools also to me the burning cheeks

Küsst die Reben noch im   Fliehen,
kisses the vines still in the fleeing

Die   auf Feld und Hügel prangen.
which on field and hill   shine

* Suleika I and II are in fact by Marianne von Willemer, although
included under Goethe's name.

42. SULEIKA I

What is stirring in the air? Is the
east wind bringing me glad
tidings? The cool rushing of its
wings soothes the deep wounds in
my heart.

It plays with the dust, raising it in
little light clouds, and chases the
joyous insect-folk to the safety of
the vines.

Gently it tempers the sun's warm
glowing, and cools my burning
cheeks. And kisses the grapes as it
hastens onward, that gleam in the
fields and hills.

Und mir   bringt sin leises Flüstern
and to me brings his quiet whispering

Von   dem Freunde tausend   Grüsse;
from the friend   thousand greetings

Eh'   noch diese Hügel düstern,
before yet   these hills   grow dusky

Grüssen mich wohl   tausend   Küsse.
greet   me   perhaps thousand kisses

Und so kannst du   weiterziehen!
and so can   you go on

Diene Freunden und Betrübten,
serve friends   and those distressed

Dort, dort, wo   hohe Mauern glühen,
there there where high walls   glow

Dort find' ich bald den Vielgeliebten.
there find I   soon the much-loved one

Ach, die wahre Herzenskunde,
ah   the   true   heart's-tidings

Liebeshauch, erfrischtes Leben,
love's-breath refreshed life

Wird mir   nur   aus   seinem Munde,
will   to me only from his   mouth

Kann mir   nur   sein Atem geben.
can   to me only his breath give

And its whispering brings a
thousand greetings from my love;
and before dusk falls on these
hills, a thousand kisses may greet
me!

So now you can go on your way,
serving friends and those in
distress. There, there where high
walls are gleaming, there will I
soon find my dearest love!

Oh, the message of a truly faithful
heart, a whisper of love and life
renewed, can only come from his
own lips; can only be given by his
breath alone.

43. *SULEIKA II*
SULEIKA

Johann Wolfgang von Goethe*
(from the *West-östlichen Divan*)
            west-east   collection of poems

Ach, um deine feuchten Schwingen,
ah   for your moist   wings

West,   wie sehr   ich dich beneide;
west (wind) how much I   you envy

43. SULEIKA II

For your wings, O moist west
wind, how I envy you! For you can
tell him how I suffer in our
separation.

   * Suleika I and II are in fact by Marianne von Willemer, although
included under Goethe's name.

Denn du kannst ihm   Kunde bringen,
for   you can   to him news   bring

Was ich in der Trennung leide!
what I   in the separation suffer

Die Bewegung deiner   Flügel
the movement of your wings

Weckt   im   Busen stilles Sehnen;
awakens in the bosom silent longing

Blumen, Auen,   Wald und Hügel
flowers meadows wood and hill

Steh'n bei deinem Hauch in Tränen.
are   by your   breath in tears

Doch dein mildes, sanftes Wehen
yet   your soft   gentle blowing

Kühlt die wunden Augenlider;
cools the sore   eye-lids

Ach, für Leid müsst' ich vergehen,
ah   for grief must I   die

Hofft' ich nicht zu seh'n ihn wieder.
hoped I   not to see   him again

Eile   denn zu meinem Lieben,
hasten then to my   loved one

Spreche sanft   zu seinem Herzen;
speak   gently to his   heart

Doch vermeid' ihn zu betrüben,
but   avoid   him to grieve

Und verbirg ihm   meine Schmerzen!
and hide   to him my   sorrows

Sag' ihm,   aber sag's bescheiden:
say   to him but say it discreetly

Seine Liebe sei mein Leben;
his   love be my   life

Freudiges Gefühl von beiden
joyful   feeling of both

Wird mir   seine Nähe   geben.
will   to me his   nearness give

Your stirring wings awaken a longing in my breast; flowers and meadows, woods and hills, are bathed in tears by your breath.

Yet your soft and gentle fluttering cools the lids of my sore eyes. Oh, I would die of grief, did I not hope to see him again!

Hasten then to my beloved, speak tenderly, and touch his heart. But see that you do not grieve him – do not tell him of my own sorrow!

Tell him, but tell him gently, that his love is my whole life; and if we both can share our feelings of joy, then this will bring him near to me.

44. DER JÜNGLING AN DER QUELLE
THE YOUTH   AT THE SPRING

Johann Gaudenz von Salis

Leise   rieselnder Quell!
gently rippling spring

Ihr wallenden flispernden Pappeln!
you fluttering whispering poplars

Euer Schlummergeräusch
your slumber-sound

Wecket die Liebe nur auf.
wakes the love only up

Linderung sucht' ich bei euch,
comfort   sought I   with you

Und sie zu vergessen, die Spröde,
and her to forget   the coy one

Ach, und Blätter und Bach
oh   and leaves and stream

Seufzen, Louise, dir nach.
sigh   Louisa you for

44. THE YOUTH AT
THE SPRING

O gentle, rippling stream, O
fluttering, whispering poplar trees,
your lullaby awakens my love. I
sought your comfort to forget her,
that coy one. Oh, the leaves and
the stream sigh for you, Louisa!

45. SEI MIR   GEGRÜSST!
BE TO ME GREETED

Friedrich Rückert

O du Entrissne   mir   und meinem Kusse,
O you torn away one to me and my   kiss

Sei mir   gegrüsst, Sei mir   geküsst!
be to me greeted be to me kissed

Erreichbar   nur meinem Sehnsuchtsgrusse,
within reach only to my   longing's-greeting

Sei mir   gegrüsst, Sei mir   geküsst!
be to me greeted be to me kissed

Du von der Hand der   Liebe diesem Herzen
you from the hand of the love to this heart

Gegebne, du von dieser
given one you from this

45. I GREET YOU!

O you, who were torn from me
and my kisses, I greet you! I kiss
you! You, that only my longing
can reach – I greet you! I kiss you!

You, who were given to my heart
by love's hand; you, who were
taken away from my breast: with
the flowing of my tears, I greet
you! I kiss you!

Brust   Genommne mir!   Mit diesem Tränengusse
breast taken one   to me with this   tears'-gushing

Sei mir   gegrüsst, Sei mir   geküsst!
be to me greeted be to me kissed

Zum Trotz   der   Ferne, die sich   feindlich
to the defiance of the distance that herself hostilely

   trennend,
   dividing

To defy the distance and all that
has come so cruelly to divide us;
to vex the envious powers of fate: I
greet you! I kiss you!

Hat zwischen mich und dich gestellt;
has between me   and you put

Dem Neid der   Schicksalsmächte zum Verdrusse
to the envy of the Fate's-powers   to the vexation

Sei mir   gegrüsst! Sei mir   geküsst!
be to me greeted be to me kissed

Wie du mir   je   im   schönsten Lenz der   Liebe
as   you to me ever in the fairest   spring of the love

Mit Gruss   und Kuss entgegenkamst,
with greeting and kiss came towards

As once you came to greet and
kiss in the fairest spring-time of
love; with the radiant outpouring
of my soul: I greet you! I kiss you!

Mit meiner Seele glühendstem   Ergusse
with of my soul most glowing effusion

Sei mir   gegrüsst! Sei mir   geküsst!
be to me greeted be to me kissed

Ein Hauch der   Liebe tilget   Räum' und Zeiten,
a   breath of the love effaces spaces and times

A breath of love can efface both
space and time; I am with you,
and you are with me. I hold you
close in my arms – and I greet you!
I kiss you!

Ich bin bei dir, du bist bei mir,
I   am with you you are with me

Ich halte dich in dieses Arms Umschlusse,
I   hold you in of this arm   embracings

Sei mir   gegrüsst, Sei mir   geküsst!
be to me greeted be to me kissed

46. *DER WACHTELSCHLAG*
    THE QUAIL-SONG

46. SONG OF THE
    QUAIL

Samuel Friedrich Sauter

Horch, wie schallt's dorten so lieblich   hervor:
listen   how sounds it yonder so delightfully forth

Fürchte Gott! fürchte Gott! ruft mir   die Wachtel
fear   God fear   God calls to me the quail

   ins   Ohr
   into the ear

Listen how sweetly it sounds forth
– 'Fear the Lord! Fear the Lord!',
the quail calls to me. Half-hidden
in the green stalks, she exhorts the
listener in the corn-field, 'Worship

Sitzend im   Grünen, von Halmen umhüllt,
sitting in the green   by stalks   covered

Mahnt sie den Horcher im   Saaten-gefild:
exhorts she the listener in the corn-fields

Liebe Gott! liebe Gott! er ist so gütig, so mild.
love God love God he is so good so gentle

Wieder bedeutet ihr hüpfender Schlag:
again   means her skipping song

Lobe Gott! lobe Gott! der dich zu lohnen vermag.
praise God praise God who you to reward is able

Siehst du die herrlichen Früchte im   Feld?
see   you the glorious fruits   in the field

Nimm es du Herzen, Bewohner der   Welt:
take   it to heart   dweller of the world

Danke Gott! danke Gott! der dich ernährt   und
thank God thank God who you nourishes and
erhält.
   preserves

Schreckt dich im   Wetter   der Herr der   Natur:
startles you in the weather the Lord of the nature

Bitte Gott! bitte Gott! ruft sie, er schonet   die Flur!
ask   God ask God calls she he cares for the field

Machen Gefahren der Krieger dir   bang':
make   perils   the warrior to you anxious

Traue Gott! traue Gott! sieh', er verziehet   nicht lang'.
trust God trust God see   he withdraws not long

the Lord! He is so gentle and good.' Again her jerky song tells us, 'Praise the Lord! Praise the Lord! He'll reward you. Do you see the glorious fruits of the field? Take it to heart, you that dwell on the earth. Thank the Lord! Thank the Lord, who feeds and keeps you.' If the Lord of nature startles you with his storms: 'Beseech the Lord, beseech the Lord!' she calls, 'for He protects the field. If the perils of the battle alarm you, trust the Lord, trust the Lord! See, not for long will He delay!'

47. NACHTVIOLEN
DAME'S VIOLETS

Johann Mayrhofer

Nachtviolen,   dunkle Augen, seelenvolle,
dame's-violets dark   eyes   soulful

Selig   ist es,
blissful is it

Sich   versenken in dem sammtnen Blau.
oneself to sink   in the velvety   blue

47. NIGHT VIOLETS

O violets of the night, dark, soulful eyes – how blissful it is to lose oneself in your velvety blue.

Grüne Blätter streben freudig euch zu helfen
green leaves strive joyfully you to help

Euch   zu schmücken;
yourselves to adorn

Doch ihr blicket ernst   und schweigend in   die laue
yet   you look   seriously and silently   into the mild
  Frühlingsluft.
  spring-air

Mit erhabnen Wehmutsstrahlen trafet   ihr mein treues
with sublime melancholy-rays touched you my   faithful
  Herz,
  heart

Und nun blüht
and now blossoms

In stummen Nächten fort die heilige Verbindung.
in silent   nights   on the sacred union

Green leaves joyfully strive to adorn you; yet solemn and silent you gaze into the mild spring air.

Gleaming with sublime melancholy you touched my faithful heart, and now on silent nights, the sacred union blossoms.

48. DIE LIEBE HAT GELOGEN
THE LOVE HAS DECEIVED

48. LOVE HAS
DECEIVED ME

August von Platen

Die Liebe hat gelogen,
the love has deceived

Die Sorge lastet   schwer,
the grief burdens heavily

Betrogen, ach! betrogen
deceived ah   deceived

Hat alles   mich umher!
has everything me   about

Es fliessen heisse Tropfen
(it) flow   hot drops

Die Wange stets   herab,
the cheek always down

Lass ab, mein Herz, zu klopfen,
leave off my   heart to throb

Du armes Herz, lass   ab!
you poor heart leave off

Love has deceived me, the burden of my grief is heavy; deceived, alas, deceived by everyone around me! Hot tears flow down my cheeks. Cease your throbbing, O my heart; poor heart, let it cease!

49. *AN DIE LEIER*
   TO THE LYRE

49. TO THE LYRE

Franz von Bruchmann
(after Anacreon)

Ich will   von Atreus' Söhnen,
I   want of Atreus' sons

I would sing of the sons of Atreus
and of Cadmus – but my strings
only send forth the strains of love.

Von Kadmus will   ich singen!
of   Cadmus want I   to sing

Doch meine Saiten   tönen
but   my   strings sound

Nur Liebe im   Erklingen.
only love in the sounding

Ich tauschte um die Saiten,
I   – changed – the strings

I have changed the strings, and
would change my lyre, for they
should resound with the might of
Alciden's conquests!

Die Leier möcht' ich   tauschen!
the lyre would like I to change

Alcidens   Siegesschreiten
Alciden's victory-marching

Sollt'   ihrer Macht entrauschen!
should of her might thunder out

Doch auch die Saiten tönen
but   even the strings sound

Yet my strings send forth only the
strains of love – so farewell, then
heroes! For my strings instead of
sounding a bold heroic song, send
forth only the sounds of love.

Nur Liebe im   Erklingen!
only love in the sounding

So lebt   denn wohl, Heroen!
so fare- then well   heroes

Denn meine Saiten   tönen
for   my   strings sound

Statt   Heldensang zu drohen,
instead of heroes' song to threaten

Nur Liebe im   Erklingen.
only love in the sounding

50. *DER MUSENSOHN* THE MUSES'-SON

50. SON OF THE MUSES

Johann Wolfgang von Goethe

Durch   Feld und Wald zu schweifen,
through field and wood to roam

Roaming through field and forest, piping my little song, I go from place to place; and everything stirs to my beat, everything moves to my rhythm.

Mein Liedchen wegzupfeifen,
my   little song pipe away

So geht's von Ort zu Ort!
so goes it from place to place

Und nach dem Takte reget
and in   (the) time moves

Und nach dem Mass   beweget
and in   the measure moves

Sich   alles   an   mir fort.
(itself) everything with me on

Ich kann sie kaum erwarten,
I   can   her hardly wait for

I can hardly wait for the first flower in the garden, the first blossom on the tree. They greet my songs, and when winter returns I still sing of this dream.

Die erste Blum im   Garten,
the first flower in the garden

Die erste Blüt   am   Baum.
the first blossom on the tree

Sie grüssen meine Lieder,
they greet   my   songs

Und kommt der Winter wieder,
and comes the winter again

Sing ich noch jenen Traum.
sing I   still that dream

Ich sing ihn in der Weite,
I   sing him in the wide expanse

I sing of it far and wide, and the length and breadth of the ice, winter blossoms fair! In its turn this vanishes, and there on ploughed slopes are new delights.

Auf Eises Läng und Breite
on ice's length and breadth

Da blüht   der Winter schön!
then blossoms the winter fair

Auch diese Blüte   schwindet,
also this blossom vanishes

Und neue Freude findet
and new delight finds

Sich   auf bebauten   Höhn.
(itself) on cultivated slopes

Denn wie   ich bei der Linde
for   when I   by the linden-tree

For when I find the young folk by the linden tree, I rouse them; the dull lads strut about, and awkward girls twirl around to my melody.

Das junge   Völkchen   finde,
the young (little) folk   find

Sogleich erreg   ich sie.
at once excite I   them

Der stumpfe Bursche bläht   sich,
the dull   lad   puffs up himself

Das steife Mädchen dreht   sich
the stiff girl   turns round herself

Nach meiner Melodie.
to   my   melody

Ihr gebt den   Sohlen Flügel,
you give to the soles   wings

You give wings to my feet, and send your favourite son over hill and dale, far from home. Dear, sweet Muses, when may I rest again on my beloved's breast?

Und treibt durch   Tal   und Hügel
and drive through valley and hill

Den Liebling weit von   Haus.
the darling far   from home

Ihr lieben, holden Musen,
you dear   kind   Muses

Wann ruh ich ihr   am   Busen
when rest I   to her on the bosom

Auch endlich wieder aus?
ever at last again —

51. *WANDERERS NACHTLIED* WANDERER'S NIGHT-SONG

51. NIGHT SONG OF THE WANDERER

Johann Wolfgang von Goethe

Über allen Gipfeln
over all   (mountain-) tops

Over all the mountain tops is peace. In all the tree-tops you hardly feel one breath; the birds are hushed in the wood. Just wait – for soon you too will rest.

Ist Ruh,
is peace

In allen Wipfeln
in all   tree-tops

Spürest du
feel   you

Kaum einen Hauch;
hardly a   breath

Die Vöglein   schweigen im   Walde.
the (little) birds are silent in the wood

Warte nur! Balde
wait   just soon

Ruhest du   auch.
rest   you too

52. *AUF DEM WASSER ZU SINGEN* ON   THE WATER TO SING

52. TO BE SUNG ON THE WATER

Friedrich Leopold Graf zu Stolberg

Mitten   im   Schimmer der   spiegelnden Wellen
in the midst in the shimmer of the sparkling   waves

Gleitet, wie Schwäne, der wankende Kahn;
glides like swans   the swaying boat

Ach, auf der   Freude sanftschimmernden Wellen
ah   on of the joy   softly-shimmering waves

Gleitet die Seele dahin wie der Kahn;
glides the soul along like the small boat

Denn von dem Himmel herab auf die Wellen
for   from the sky   down upon the waves

Tanzet das Abendrot   rund um   den Kahn.
dances the sunset glow round about the boat

Mid the shimmer of sparkling waves, the boat rocks gently like a swan; on softly shimmering waves of joy, the soul glides along like the boat, and around it the glow of the sunset sky dances on rippling waves.

Über den Wipfeln des   westlichen Haines
over the tree-tops of the westerly wood

Winket uns freundlich der rötliche Schein;
signals to us friendly   the reddish light

Unter den Zweigen des   östlichen Haines
under the boughs of the easterly wood

Säuselt   der Kalmus   im   rötlichen Schein;
murmurs the sweet-flag in the reddish light

Over the tree-tops in the westerly wood, the reddening glow warmly beckons. Beneath the boughs in the easterly wood, sweet-flag leaves rustle in the soft red glow. My soul drinks in the radiance of the sky, and the peace of the woods in the reddening light.

Freude des   Himmels und Ruhe des   Haines
joy   of the sky   and peace of the woods

Atmet   die Seel im   errötenden Schein.
breathes the soul in the reddening glow

Ach, es entschwindet mit tauigem Flügel
alas it vanishes   with dewy   wing

Mir   auf den wiegenden Wellen die Zeit.
to me on the rocking   waves the time

Morgen   entschwinde mit   schimmerndem Flügel
tomorrow let vanish with shimmering   wing

Wieder wie gestern   und heute die Zeit,
again   like yesterday and today the time

Bis   ich auf höherem strahlenden Flügel
until I   on loftier   shining   wing

Selber entschwinde der   wechselnden Zeit.
myself vanish   to the changing   time

Ah, time slips by on dewy wings, as I am gently rocked on the waves. Let tomorrow fly away like today and yesterday, until I myself vanish from the changes of Time, on loftier, shining wings.

53. *DIE SCHÖNE MÜLLERIN*
THE FAIR   MILLERESS

53. THE MILLER'S
FAIR DAUGHTER

Wilhelm Müller

  i. Das Wandern
    the wandering

i. Roving

Das Wandern ist des   Müllers Lust,
the wandering is of the miller   delight

Das Wandern!
the wandering

Roving is a miller's delight, roving! He'd be a bad miller, who never thought of roving, roving!

Das muss ein schlechter Müller sein,
that must a   bad   miller be

Dem   niemals fiel   das Wandern   ein,
to whom never   occurs the wandering –

Das Wandern.
the wandering

Vom   Wasser haben wir's gelernt,
from the water have we it learnt

We learnt it from the water, the water! It never rests by day or night, is always rushing on its way, the water!

Vom   Wasser!
from the water

Das hat nicht Rast bei Tag und Nacht,
that has not   rest by day and night

Ist stets   auf Wanderschaft bedacht,
is always on wandering   intent

Das Wasser!
the water

Das sehn wir auch den Rädern ab,
that see we also the wheels from

Den Rädern!
the wheels

Die gar   nicht gerne stille stehn,
they at all not   like   still to stand

Die sich   mein Tag nicht müde drehn,
they themselves (all) my   day not   tired to turn

Die Räder.
the wheels

Die Steine selbst,   so schwer sie   sind,
the stones themselves so heavy they are

Die Steine!
the stones

Sie   tanzen mit   den muntern Reihn
they dance with the merry   dances

Und wollen gar   noch schneller sein,
and want   even still faster   to be

Die Steine.
the stones

O Wandern, Wandern, meine Lust,
O wandering wandering my   delight

O Wandern!
O wandering

Herr Meister und Frau Meisterin,
Mr. master and Mrs. mistress

Lasst mich in Frieden weiterziehn
let   me   in peace further to go

Und wandern.
and to wander

We learn it too from the mill-wheels, the mill-wheels! They never can be still; all day they never tire of turning, the mill-wheels!

Even mill-stones, heavy as they are, the mill-stones – they join in the merry dance and would go still faster, the mill-stones!

O roving, roving, my delight, roving – O master and mistress mine, just let me go my way, roving!

ii. Wohin?
   whither

ii. Whither?

Ich hört' ein Bächlein   rauschen
I   heard a   little brook to rush

I heard a little brook rushing from
out a rocky spring, rushing down
into the valley, cool and
wondrously clear.

Wohl   aus   dem Felsenquell.
probably out of the rocks-spring

Hinab zum   Tale rauschen
down to the valley to rush

So frisch und wunderhell.
so cool and wonderfully clear

Ich weiss nicht, wie mir   wurde,
I   know not   how to me became

I do not know what compelled me,
who put it into my head; I had to
go down there too, my staff in my
hand.

Nicht, wer den Rat   mir   gab,
not   who the advice to me gave

Ich musste auch hinunter
I   had to also (go) down there

Mit meinem Wanderstab.
with my   staff

Hinunter und immer weiter,
down   and always further

Down and ever further, ever
following the brook; and ever
cooler and clearer the brook was
rushing on.

Und immer dem Bache nach,
and always the brook after

Und immer frischer rauschte
and always cooler rushed

Und immer heller   der Bach.
and always clearer the brook

Ist das denn meine Strasse?
is that then my   way

Is this then my path? O little brook
– tell me, where does it lead? With
your babbling you have quite
bewitched my mind.

O Bächlein,   sprich, wohin?
O little brook say   whither

Du hast mit deinem Rauschen
you have with your   rushing

Mir ganz berauscht   den Sinn.
me quite bewitched the mind

Was sag ich denn vom   Rauschen?
what say I   then of the rushing

Why do I speak of babbling? That
it cannot be; it must be the water-
nymphs who sing and dance there
far below.

Das kann kein Rauschen sein:
that can no rushing   be

Es singen wohl   die Nixen
(it) sing   perhaps the water-nymphs

Tief unten ihren Reihn.
deep below their dance (-tunes)

Lass singen, Gesell,   lass rauschen,
let sing   comrade let rush

Und wandre fröhlich nach!
and wander merrily after

Es gehn ja   Mühlenräder
(it) go   certainly mill-wheels

In jedem klaren Bach.
in every clear   brook

Let them sing, let the brook babble, and follow merrily, my friend – for mill-wheels surely turn in every clear brook!

  iii. Halt!
      halt

iii. Halt!

Eine Mühle seh ich blinken
a   mill   see I   gleam

Aus den Erlen heraus,
from the alders forth

Durch   Rauschen und Singen
through rushing   and singing

Bricht Rädergebraus.
breaks wheels-roaring

I see a mill gleaming through the elders; the roaring of mill-wheels breaks through the babbling and singing.

Ei willkommen, ei willkommen,
hey welcome   hey welcome

Süsser Mühlengesang!
sweet mill-song

Und das Haus, wie so traulich!
and the house how so cosy

Und die Fenster, wie blank!
and the windows how shining

Oh welcome, welcome, sweet song of the mill! How friendly the house looks! How sparkling the windows!

Und die Sonne, wie helle
and the sun   how brightly

Vom   Himmel sie scheint!
from the sky   she shines

Ei, Bächlein,   liebes Bächlein,
why little brook dear little brook

War es also gemeint?
was it thus meant

And how brightly the sun shines in the sky! Why, little brook, little brook – is this what was meant?

iv. Danksagung   an den Bach
    giving thanks to the brook

iv. Thanks to the brook

War es also gemeint,
was it thus meant

Is this what was meant, my
rushing friend? Your singing, your
babbling – is this what was meant?

Mein rauschender Freund?
my rushing   friend

Dein Singen, dein Klingen,
your singing your sounding

War es also gemeint?
was it thus meant

Zur   Müllerin   hin!
to the miller's daughter thither

To the maid of the mill! That is
what it means. Is that it, have I
grasped it? To the maid of the
mill!

So lautet der Sinn.
so ran   the sense

Gelt,   hab' ich's verstanden?
is it not so have I it understood

Zur   Müllerin   hin!
to the miller's daughter thither

Hat sie dich geschickt?
has she you sent

Was it she who sent you? Or have
you caught me in a spell? I should
so like to know – was it she who
sent you?

Oder hast mich berückt?
or   have me   charmed

Das möcht   ich noch wissen,
that should like I   still to know

Ob sie dich geschickt.
if she you sent

Nun wie 's auch mag sein,
well how it -ever may be

Well, however it may be, I'll give
in to it. I've found what I sought,
whatever that might be.

Ich gebe mich   drein:
I   give myself into it

Was ich such, ist gefunden,
what I   seek is found

Wie's immer mag sein.
how it -ever may be

Nach Arbeit ich frug,
for   work I asked

I asked to find work, and now I
have enough: for my hands, and
my heart more than enough!

Nun hab ich genug,
now have I   enough

Für die Hände, fürs   Herze
for the hands   for the heart

Vollauf   genug.
abundantly enough

v. Am   Feierabend
   in the evening rest-hour

Hätt ich tausend Arme zu rühren! had I thousand arms to move	If I had but a thousand arms to move, and could make the mill-wheels roar! And blow like the wind through the woods, and make the mill-stones turn, so the miller's fair maiden could know my true mind!

Könnt ich brausend die Räder führen!
could I   roaring the wheels drive

Könnt ich wehen durch   alle Haine!
could I   blow through all woods

Könnt ich drehen alle Steine!
could I   turn   all stones

Dass die schöne Müllerin
that the lovely miller's daughter

Merkte   meinen treuen Sinn!
perceived my   true   meaning

Ach, wie ist mein Arm so schwach!
ah   how is my arm so weak

Alas, my arm is so weak! What I can lift, and carry, and chop, and fell, so can every other miller's boy.

Was ich hebe, was ich trage,
what I lift   what I carry

Was ich schneide, was ich schlage,
what I chop   what I fell

Jeder Knappe   tut mir's   nach.
every miller's boy does (to) me it after

Und da   sitz ich in der grossen Runde,
and there sit I in the great circle

There I sit in the big family circle, in the still, cool hour when work is done. And the master says to us all, 'Your work has pleased me', and the sweet maid bids us all good-night.

In der stillen kühlen Feierstunde,
in the still cool rest-hour

Und der Meister spricht zu allen:
and the master says   to all

Euer Werk hat mir gefallen;
your work has me pleased

Und das liebe Mädchen sagt
and the dear maiden   says

Allen   eine gute Nacht.
to everyone a   good night

vi. Der Neugierige
   the curious one

Ich frage keine Blume,
I   ask   no   flower

Ich frage keiner Stern;
I   ask   no   star

Sie   können mir alle nicht sagen,
they can   me all   not say

Was ich erführ   so gern.
what I   would find out so gladly

Ich bin ja   auch kein Gärtner,
I   am indeed really no   gardener

Die Sterne stehn zu hoch;
the stars are   too high

Mein Bächlein   will ich fragen,
my   little brook will I   ask

Ob mich mein Herz belog.
if me   my   heart deceived

O Bächlein   meiner Liebe,
O little brook of my love

Wie bist du heut so stumm!
how are you today so silent

Will ja   nur eines   wissen,
want truly only one thing to know

Ein Wörtchen um   und um,
one little word round and round

Ja heisst   das eine Wörtchen,
yes is called that one little word

Das andre heisset   nein,
the other is called no

Die beiden Wörtchen   schliessen
the both   little words enclose

Die ganze Welt mir   ein.
the whole world to me –

O Bächlein   meiner Liebe,
O little brook of my love

Was bist du wunderlich!
what are you strange

vi. Curiosity

I do not ask the flowers, I do not ask the stars; none of them can tell me what I so long to know.

I am indeed no gardener, and the stars are too high; I will ask my little brook if my heart deceives me.

O little brook of my love, how silent you are today! I only want to hear one thing, one little word all around.

That one little word is 'yes' – the other is 'no'. These two little words enclose my whole world.

O little brook of my love, how strange you are! I will tell no one else – but say, little brook, does she love me?

Will's   ja   nicht weiter   sagen,
want it truly not further say

Sag, Büchlein,   liebt sie mich?
say   little brook loves she me

vii. *Ungeduld*
   impatience

vii. Impatience

Ich schnitt'   es gern   in alle Rinden ein,
I   would carve it gladly in all barks   into

I'd like to carve it on every tree, on every stone! I'd like to sow it in cress-seeds on every bed, on white scraps of paper that would all reveal: my heart is yours, and will be so for evermore!

Ich grüb   es gern   in jeden Kieselstein,
I   would engrave it gladly in every pebble

Ich möcht   es sä'n   auf jedes frische Beet
I   would like it to sow on every fresh flower-bed

Mit Kressensamen, der es schnell verrät,
with cress-seeds   that it quickly would disclose

Auf jeden weissen Zettel   möcht   ich's
on every white   scrap of paper would like I it
   schreiben:
   write

Dein ist mein Herz, und soll es ewig   bleiben.
yours is my   heart and shall it for ever remain

Ich möcht   mir   ziehen einen jungen Star,
I   would like to me to train a   young starling

I'd like to train a young starling to say like me in words pure and clear, and all my heart's passion. And then at her window to brightly sing: My heart is yours, and will be so for evermore!

Bis   dass er spräch   die Worte rein und klar,
until that he would say the words pure and clear

Bis er sie   spräch   mit meines Mundes Klang,
until he them would say with of my mouth sound

Mit meines Herzens vollem, heissem Drang;
with of my heart   full   hot   urgency

Dann säng   er hell   durch ihre Fensterscheiben:
then would sing he clearly through her window-panes

Dein ist mein Herz, und soll es ewig   bleiben.
yours is my   heart and shall it for ever remain

Den Morgenwinden möcht   ich's hauchen ein,
the morning-winds would like I it to breathe into

I'd like to whisper it into the morning breeze, and murmur it in every stirring wood. O if it but shone from every starry flower, whose fragrance could bear it to her from near and far! You ripples, can you move nothing but mill-

Ich möcht   es säuseln   durch   den regen Hain;
I   would like it to murmur through the stirring wood

O leuchtet' es aus jedem Blumenstern!
O shone   it from every flower-star

Trüg   es der Duft   zu ihr von   nah und fern!
were borne it the fragrance to her from near and far

Ihr Wogen, könnt ihr nichts   als Räder treiben?
you waves can   you nothing but wheels drive

Dein ist mein Herz, und soll   es ewig   bleiben.
yours is my   heart and shall it for ever remain

Ich meint,   es müsst in meinen Augen stehn,
I   thought it must in my   eyes be

Auf meinen Wangen müsst man's brennen sehn,
on my   cheeks must one it burn   see

Zu lesen wär's   auf meinem stummen Mund,
to read would be it on my   silent   mouth

Ein jeder Atemzug gäb's   laut   ihr   kund,
an every breath   would proclaim it loudly to her –

Und sie merkt nichts   von all dem bangen Treiben:
and she notices nothing of   all the anxious urging

Dein ist mein Herz, und soll es ewig   bleiben!
yours is my   heart and shall it for ever remain

wheels? My heart is yours, and will be so for evermore!

I thought it must be shining in my eyes, be seen on my burning cheeks. I thought it must be read on my silent lips, that each breath must betray it. Yet she saw nothing of all this anxious stirring, My heart is yours, and will be so for evermore!

viii. Morgengruss
     morning-greeting

viii. Morning greeting

Guten Morgen, schöne   Müllerin!
good morning beautiful milleress

Wo   steckst du gleich das Köpfchen hin,
whither put   you at once the little head –

Als wär dir   was   geschehen?
as were to you something happened

Verdriesst dich denn mein Gruss   so schwer?
vexes   you then my   greeting so severely

Verstört dich denn mein Blick so sehr?
troubles you then my   glance so much

So muss ich wieder gehen.
so must I   again go

O lass mich nur von ferne stehn,
O let me   only from afar stand

Nach deinem lieben Fenster sehn
at   your   dear window look

Von ferne, ganz von ferne!
from afar   quite from afar

Good morning, lovely maid of the mill! Why do you turn your face away, as if you were troubled? Does my greeting so vex you, my glances so trouble you? Then I must go away.

O let me but stand and gaze from afar at your dear window, just from afar! Fair little head, come forth! Blue morning star, in your rounded gateway come forth!

Du blondes Köpfchen, komm hervor!
you fair   little head come forth

Hervor aus   eurem runden Tor,
forth   from your   round gateway

Ihr blauen Morgensterne!
you blue   morning-stars

Ihr schlummertrunknen Äugelein,
you slumber drunk   dear eyes

Ihr taubetrübten   Blümelein,
you dew-troubled little flowers

Was scheuet   ihr die Sonne?
what shrink from you the sun

Hat es die Nacht so gut gemeint,
has it the night so well meant

Dass ihr euch   schliesst und bückt und weint
that you yourselves close   and bow and weep

Nach ihrer stillen Wonne?
for   her   silent ecstasy

You slumber-filled eyes, dew-laden flowers, why do you shrink from the sun? Was the night so good that you close, bow down, and weep for her silent ecstasy?

Nun schüttelt ab der   Träume Flor,
now shake   off of the dreams veil

Und hebt euch   frisch und frei   empor
and lift   yourselves freshly and freely upwards

In   Gottes hellen Morgen!
into God's bright morning

Die Lerche wirbelt in der Luft;
the lark   trills   in the air

Und aus   dem tiefen Herzen ruft
and from the   deep heart   cries out

Die Liebe Leid und Sorgen.
the love   pain and grief

Shake off the veil of dreams, and fresh and free, lift up your heads to God's bright morning! A lark trills high in the air, and from the depths of my heart, love declares its pain and grief.

ix. *Des   Müllers Blumen*
of the miller   flowers

ix. The miller's flowers

Am   Bach viel   kleine Blumen stehn,
by the brook many little   flowers are

Aus   hellen blauen Augen sehn;
from clear blue   eyes   look

By the brook are little flowers that look up from clear blue eyes. The brook is the miller's friend, and my sweetheart's eyes are bright blue – so they are my flowers.

Der Bach, der ist der Müllers Freund,
the brook he is the miller's friend

Und hellblau Liebchens   Auge scheint,
and light-blue sweetheart's eye   shines

Drum   sind es   meine Blumen.
therefore are they my   flowers

Dicht unter ihrem Fensterlein,
close under her   dear window

Da   will ich pflanzen die Blumen ein;
there will I   plant   the flowers –

Da   ruft ihr zu, wenn alles   schweight,
there call her to when everything is silent

Wenn sich ihr Haupt zum   Schlummer neight,
when itself her head to the slumber   bows

Ihr wisst ja,   was ich meine.
you know indeed what I   mean

Und wenn sie tät   die Äuglein   zu
and when she would close the little eyes –

Und schläft in süsser, süsser Ruh,
and sleeps in sweet sweet sleep

Dann lispelt   als ein Traumgesicht
then whisper as a   vision

Ihr zu: Vergiss, vergiss mein nicht!
her to forget   forget me not

Das ist es, was   ich meine.
that is it what I   mean

Und schliesst sie früh die Laden   auf,
and opens   she early the shutters –

Dann schaut mit Liebesblick   hinauf;
then look   with loving-glance up

Der Tau in euren Äugelein,
the dew in your (little) eyes

Das sollen meine Tränen sein,
that shall my   tears   be

Die will ich auf euch weinen.
that will I   on you weep

Close beneath her window I will plant the little flowers. And when all is silent, and her head nods off to sleep, you can call to her then, for you know what I would say.

And when her eyes are closed, and she sleeps in sweet repose, then whisper into her dreams: 'Forget, forget me not!' For that is what I would say.

And early when she opens the shutters, gaze up with looks of love, for the dew in your blue eyes will be the tears I weep on you.

x. Tränenregen
   tears-rain

x. Rain of tears

Wir sassen so traulich beisammen
we sat   so cosily   together

Im   kühlen Erlendach,
in the cool   alder-roof

We sat so close under the alder-roof; and together we looked down at the rippling brook.

Wir schauten so traulich zusammen
we looked so cosily   together

Hinab in   den rieselnden Bach.
down into the rippling brook

Der Mond war auch gekommen,
the moon was also come

Die Sternlein   hinterdrein,
the little stars afterwards

The moon had appeared, and then stars, and they too looked into the silvery mirror.

Und schauten so traulich zusammen
and looked so cosily   together

In   den silbernen Spiegel hinein.
into the silvery   mirror into

Ich sah   nach keinem Monde,
I looked at   no   moon

Nach keinem Sternenschein,
at   no   star-light

I looked at no moon, nor shining stars, but only at her image, at her eyes alone.

Ich schaute nach ihrem Bilde,
I looked at   her   image

Nach ihren Augen allein.
at   her eyes   alone

Und sahe sie   nicken und blicken
and saw them nod   and glance

Herauf aus   dem seligen Bach,
up   from the blissful brook

I saw them twinkling from the joyful brook; on the bank the blue flowers nodded, as they glanced up at her.

Die Blümlein   am   Ufer, die blauen,
the little flowers on the bank the blue ones

Sie nickten und blickten ihr nach.
they nodded and glanced her after

Und in den Bach versunken
and in the brook sunk

Der ganze Himmel schien,
the whole sky   appeared

The whole sky appeared to be deep in the brook, and seemed to draw me down into its depths.

Und wollte   mich mit   hinunter
and wanted me   with (him) downwards

In   seine Tiefe   ziehn.
into his   depths to draw

Und über   den Wolken und Sternen
and above the clouds and stars

Da   rieselte munter der Bach
there rippled merrily the brook

Und rief   mit Singen und Klingen:
and called with singing and sounding

Geselle,   Geselle,   mir nach!'
comrade comrade me after

Da   gingen die Augen mir   über,
then went the eyes   to me over

Da   ward es im   Spiegel so kraus;
then was it in the mirror so ruffled

Sie sprach: Es kommt ein Regen,
she said   it comes a   rain

Ade!   ich geh   nach Haus!
farewell I   am going – home –

Above the clouds and stars the brook rippled merrily, calling in its singing, 'Brother, brother, follow me!'

Then the tears in my eyes overflowed, and the mirror was blurred. 'It's beginning to rain,' she said, 'Goodbye, I'm going home!'

xi. Mein!
mine

Bächlein,   lass dein Rauschen sein!
little brook let your rushing be

Räder, stellt eu'r Brausen ein!
wheels cease your roaring –

All ihr muntern Waldvögelein,
all you merry   little woodland-birds

Gross und klein, endet eure Melodein!
large and small end your melodies

Durch   den Hain aus und ein
through the wood out and in

Schalle heut ein Reim allein:
sound today one rhyme alone

Die geliebte Müllerin   ist mein!
the beloved miller's daughter is mine

xi. Mine!

Little brook, stop your rushing! Mill-wheels, cease your roaring! Merry birds in the woods, great and small, hush your songs!

Today in the wood, let one refrain alone sound far and wide: the miller's beloved daughter is mine!

Frühling, sind das alle deine Blümelein?
spring   are that all your little flowers

Sonn, hast du keine hellern Schein?
sun   have you no   brighter light

Ach, so muss ich ganz allein,
ah   so must I   quite alone

Mit dem seligen Worte mein,
with the blessed word mine

Unverstanden   in der weiten Schöpfung sein!
not understood in the wide creation   be

Spring, have you no more little flowers? Sun, have you no brighter rays? Alas, I alone, in the breadth of unheeding creation proclaim this blessed word: mine!

    xii. Pause
      pause

xii. Pause

Meine Laute hab ich gehängt an die Wand,
my   lute have I   hung   on the wall

Hab sie umschlungen mit einem grünen Band –
have her wound round with a   green ribbon

Ich kann nicht mehr singen, mein Herz ist zu voll.
I   can not more sing   my heart is too full

Weiss nicht, wie ich's in Reime zwingen soll.
know not   how I it in rhyme force   shall

I have hung my lute on the wall, and twined a green ribbon round it – I can no longer sing, my heart is too full. I no longer know how to make it rhyme.

Meiner Sehnsucht allerheissesten Schmerz
of my longing   most-burning pain

Durft ich aushauchen   in Liederscherz,
needed I   to breathe out in song-jest

Und wie ich klagte   so süss   und fein,
and as I   lamented so sweet and fine

Glaubt ich doch, mein Leiden wär nicht klein.
believed I   indeed my suffering were not   small

I wanted to ease the burning pain of my longing in light-hearted song, yet in my sweet and gentle lament, I felt my suffering far from small.

Ei, wie gross ist wohl   meines Glückes   Last,
oh how great is indeed of my happiness burden

Dass kein Klang auf Erden es in sich fasst?
that no sound on earth it in itself contains

Nun, liebe Laute, ruh an dem Nagel hier!
now dear lute   rest on the nail here

Und weht ein Lüftchen   über die Saiten dir,
and blows a little breeze over the strings to you

Und streift   eine Biene mit ihren Flügeln dich,
and brushes a bee with her wings you

Oh, how great is the burden of my joy, that no sound on earth can contain it? Dear lute, now rest here on this nail! But when a gentle breeze stirs you, or a bee's wings brush over you, I am uneasy, and a shiver runs through me.

Da   wird   mir   so bange   und es durchschauert
then becomes to me so uneasy and it shudders through
    mich!
    me

Warum liess ich das Band   auch hängen so lang?
why   let I   the ribbon ever hang   so long

Oft   fliegt's um   die Saiten   mit   seufzendem Klang.
often flies it about the strings with sighing   sound

Ist es der Nachklang meiner Liebespein?
is it the echo   of my loves-pain

Soll es das Vorspiel neuer   Lieder sein?
shall it the prelude of new songs be

Why did I let the ribbon hang so
long? Often it touches the strings
with a sighing sound. Is it the echo
of love's pain? Can it be the
prelude to new songs?

   xiii. Mit dem grünen Lautenbande
     with the green lute's-ribbon

xiii. The lute's green ribbon

'Schad um   das schöne grüne Band,
pity   about the lovely green ribbon

Das es verbleicht hier an der Wand,
that it fades   here on the wall

Ich hab das grün so gern!'
I   –   the green so like

So sprachst du, Liebchen, heut zur   mir;
so said   you sweetheart today to the me

Gleich   knüpf ich's ab und send es dir:
at once unbind I it   – and send it to you

Nun hab das Grüne gern!
now –   the green like

'A pity about the fine green
ribbon, fading here on the wall.
I'm so fond of green!' That is what
you said to me today, my dear. At
once I unbind it, and send it to
you – now enjoy the green!

Ist auch dein ganzer Liebster weiss,
is even your whole dearest white

Soll Grün doch haben seinen Preis,
shall green still have   its   price

Und ich auch hab es gern.
and I   also –   it like

Weil   unsre Lieb ist immer grün,
because our love is ever green

Weil   Grün der   Hoffnung Fernen   blühn,
because green of the hope   distances to blossom

Drum   haben wir es gern.
therefore –   we it like

Even if your sweetheart is white
and pale, green still has its price,
and I like it too. Our love is
forever green, and distance
enhances the green of hope – and
that is why we are so fond of
green.

Nun schlinge in die Locken dein
now twine   in the locks   your

Das grüne Band   gefällig ein,
the   green ribbon please –

Du hast ja's   Grün so gern.
you –   indeed it green so like

Dann weiss ich, wo   die Hoffnung wohnt,
then   know I   where the hope   dwells

Dann weiss ich, wo   die Liebe thront,
then   know I   where the love   reigns

Dann hab ich's Grün erst   gern.
then   –   I the green for the first time like

Now twine the green ribbon around your locks, for you are so fond of green. Then shall I know where hope is dwelling, then shall I know where love is enthroned – only then shall I really love green.

    xiv. Der Jäger
       the huntsman

xiv. The huntsman

Was sucht denn der Jäger   am   Mühlbach hier?
what seeks then the huntsman by the mill-stream here

Bleib, trotziger Jäger,   in deinem Revier!
stay   obstinate huntsman in your   preserve

Hier gibt es   kein Wild zu jagen für dich,
here (is there) no   game to hunt for you

Hier wohnt nur ein Rehlein, ein zahmes,   für mich.
here lives   only a   little doe a   tame (one) for me

Und willst du   das zärtliche Rehlein   sehn,
and want you the tender   little doe to see

So lass   deine Büchsen im   Walde stehn,
so leave your guns   in the forest stand

Und lass   deine klaffenden Hunde zu Haus,
and leave your yelping   dogs   at home

Und lass   auf dem Horne den Saus und Braus,
and leave off on the horn   the rush and roar

Und schere vom   Kinne das struppige Haar;
and shave from the chin   the bristly   hair

Sonst   scheut sich   im   Garten das Rehlein
otherwise is afraid (itself) in the garden the little doe
    fürwahr.
     truly

What does the huntsman seek here by the mill-stream? Bold huntsman, stay in your own preserve! There's no game to hunt, but a small, tame doe, that's for me. If you would see her, then leave your gun in the wood, and your yelping hounds at home. And shave off your shaggy beard – or my doe in her garden will take fright.

Doch besser, du bliebest im Walde dazu
still better you stayed in the wood as well

Und liessest die Mühlen und Müller in Ruh.
and left the mills and millers in peace

Was taugen die Fischlein im grünen Gezweig?
what use are the (little) fishes in the green branches

Was will denn das Eichhorn im bläulichen Teich?
what wants then the squirrel in the bluish pool

Drum bleibe, du trotziger Jäger, im Hain,
therefore stay you obstinate huntsman in the wood

Und lass mich mit meinen drei Rädern allein;
and leave me with my three wheels alone

Und willst meinem Schätzchen dich machen beliebt,
and want to my little treasure yourself to make beloved

So wisse, mein Freund, was ihr Herzchen betrübt:
so know my friend what her little heart troubles

Die Eber, die kommen zu Nacht aus dem Hain
the wild boars that come at night out of the wood

Und brechen in ihren Kohlgarten ein,
and break into her cabbage-garden (in)

Und treten und wühlen herum in dem Feld;
and trample and root about in the field

Die Eber, die schiesse, du Jägerheld!
the wild boars them shoot you hunter-hero

Better still, just stay in the woods, and leave mills and millers alone. What use would fishes be in green branches, or squirrels in blue pools? Just stay in the woods, bold huntsman, and leave me alone with my three wheels. If you want to please my sweetheart, you should know, my friend, what troubles her heart: wild boars from the woods at night break into her cabbage patch, and root up her field – so just shoot those wild boars, you hunting hero!

xv. *Eifersucht und Stolz*
jealousy and pride

Wohin so schnell, so kraus und wild, mein lieber Bach?
whither so fast so ruffled and wild my dear brook

Eilst du voll Zorn dem frechen Bruder Jäger
hurry you full anger the impudent brother huntsman
    nach?
    after

Kehr um, und schilt erst deine Müllerin
turn back and scold first your miller's daughter

Für ihren leichten, losen, kleinen Flattersinn.
for her light wanton petty fickleness

Kehr um!
turn back

xv. Jealousy and pride

Whither so fast, so ruffled and wild, little brook? Are you hurrying so angrily after that impudent brother huntsman? Turn back, and first scold your miller's daughter for her light, wanton, fickleness.

Sahst du sie gestern   Abend nicht am   Tore stehn,
saw   you her yesterday evening not   at the gate stand

Mit langem Halse nach   der grossen Strasse sehn?
with long   neck towards the great   road   look

Wenn von dem Fang   der Jäger   lustig zieht
when from the capture the huntsman gaily goes
    nach Haus,
    homewards

Da   steckt kein sittsam Kind den Kopf zum   Fenster
then puts no   modest child the head to the window
    'naus.
    out

Geh, Bächlein, hin   und sag ihr   das; doch sag
go   little brook thither and say to her that but say
    ihr   nicht,
    to her not

Hörst du, kein Wort von meinem traurigen   Gesicht;
hear you no   word of   my   melancholy face

Sag ihr: Er schnitzt' bei   mir sich   eine Pfeif aus
say to her he cut   with me himself a   pipe out of
    Rohr
    reed

Und bläst den Kindern schöne Tänz   und Lieder vor.
and plays the children pretty dances and songs to.

Did you see her last night as she stood at the gate, craning her neck to see down the road? When the huntsman goes merrily home from the kill, no modest girl pokes her head out of the window!

Go, little brook, and tell her this; but no word, do you hear, of my melancholy face! Tell her, he made for himself a pipe out of reeds, and plays for the children pretty dances and songs.

    xvi. Die liebe   Farbe
      the beloved colour

In Grün will ich mich   kleiden,
in green will I   myself dress

In grüne Tränenweiden:
in green weeping-willow

Mein Schatz hat's   Grün so gern.
my   treasure – it the green so likes –

Will suchen einen Zypressenhain,
will seek a   cypress-grove

Eine Heide von grünen Rosmarein:
a   heath of green rosemary

Mein Schatz hat's   Grün so gern.
my   treasure – it the green so likes –

xvi. The beloved colour

I will dress in green, in green weeping-willow: my love is so fond of green. I will seek a cypress grove, a heath full of rosemary: my love is so fond of green.

Wohlauf zum   fröhlichen Jagen!
away   to the merry   hunting

Wohlauf durch   Heid und Hagen!
away   through heath and meadows

Mein Schatz   hat's   Jagen   so gern.
my   treasure – it the hunting so likes –

Das Wild, das ich jage, das ist der Tod;
the game that I   hunt that is the death

Die Heide, die   heiss ich die Liebesnot:
the heath that call I   the love's distress

Mein Schatz   hat's   Jagen   so gern.
my   treasure – it the hunting so likes –

Grabt mir ein Grab im   Wasen,
dig   me a   grave in the grass

Deckt mich mit   grünen Rasen:
cover me   with green turf

Mein Schatz   hat's   Grün so gern.
my   treasure – it the green so likes –

Kein Kreuzlein   schwarz, kein Blümlein
no   (little) cross black   no   (little) flower
   bunt,
   gay-coloured

Grün, alles   grün so rings und rund:
green everything green so round and round about

Mein Schatz   hat's   Grün so gern.
my   treasure – it the green so likes –

Away to the merry hunt, away
through heath and meadow! My
love is so fond of a hunt. The
game I hunt is death, the heath I
call 'love's-grief': my love is so
fond of a hunt.

Dig me a grave in the sward, and
cover me with green turf; my love
is so fond of green. No black
cross, no gay flowers – let all
around be green, green. My love is
so fond of green.

   xvii. Die böse Farbe
      the bad colour

Ich möchte   ziehn in   die Welt hinaus,
I   would like to go into the world forth

Hinaus in   die weite Welt;
forth   into the wide world

Wenn's nur so grün, so grün nicht wär
if it   only so green so green not were

Da   draussen in Wald und Feld!
there outside in forest and field

xvii. The hateful colour

I'd like to go out into the world,
out into the wide world. If only it
were not so green, so green out
there in forest and field!

Ich möchte   die grünen Blätter all
I   would like the green leaves all

Pflücken von   jedem Zweig,
to pluck from every twig

Ich möchte   die grünen Gräser all
I   would like the green grasses all

Weinen ganz totenbleich.
to weep quite deathly-pale

I'd like to pluck all the green leaves from every bough; I'd like to weep on all the green grass, till it was pale as death.

Ach Grün, du böse Farbe du,
ah   green you bad colour you

Was siehst mich immer an
what look me   always at

So stolz, so keck,   so schadenfroh,
so proud so impudent so gloating

Mich armen weissen Mann?
me   poor white man

Ah, green, you hateful colour! Why do you always look at me, so proud, so impudent, so gloating – at me, a poor, pale man?

Ich möchte   liegen vor   ihrer Tür,
I   would like to lie before her   door

In Sturm und Regen und Schnee,
in storm and rain   and snow

Und singen ganz leise   bei Tag und Nacht
and sing   quite softly by day and night

Das eine Wörtchen   ade!
the one little word farewell

I'd like to lie at her door in storm, and rain, and snow, and sing so softly, day and night, the one little word, 'farewell!'

Horch, wenn im   Wald ein Jagdhorn   schallt,
hark   when in the forest a   hunting-horn sounds

So klingt   ihr Fensterlein,
so sounds her little window

Und schaut sie auch nach mir nicht aus,
and looks she even for   me not   out

Darf ich doch schauen hinein.
may I   yet   look   in

Hark, when a hunting-horn sounds in the forest, you can hear her little window! And it is not for me she looks out, I can look in at her.

O binde   von der Stirn dir   ab
O unbind from the brow to you –

Das grüne, grüne Band;
the green green ribbon

O unwind that green, green ribbon from your brow. Farewell, farewell! And as I part, give me your hand.

Ade,   ade!   und reiche mir
farewell farewell and give   to me

Zum   Abschied deine Hand!
at the parting   your hand

xviii. *Trockne Blumen*
dry   flowers

xviii. Withered flowers

Ihr Blümlein   alle, die sie mir   gab,
you little flowers all   that she to me gave

All you flowers that she gave me
shall be laid in my grave. How
sadly you look at me – do you
know what has happened? All you
flowers, how withered you are,
how pale, and why are you so wet?

Euch soll   man legen mit mir ins   Grab.
you   shall one lay   with me in the grave

Wie seht ihr alle mich an so weh,
how look you all me   at so sadly

Als ob ihr wüsstet, wie mir   gescheh?
as if you knew   what to me would happen

Ihr Blümlein   alle, wie welk,   wie blass?
you little flowers all   how withered how pale

Ihr Blümlein   alle, wovon so nass?
you little flowers all   why   so wet

Ach, Tränen machen nicht maiengrün,
alas tears   make   not May-green

Tears, alas, cannot bring the green
of May, nor make dead love
blossom again. Spring will come,
winter will go, and flowers will
grow in the grass; and little flowers
will lie in my grave, all those that
she gave to me.

Machen tote   Liebe nicht wieder blühn,
make   dead love not again to blossom

Und Lenz   wird kommen, und Winter wird gehn,
and spring will come   and winter will go

Und Blümlein   werden im   Grase stehn,
and little flowers will   in the grass be

Und Blümlein   liegen in meinem Grab,
and little flowers lie   in my   grave

Die Blümlein   alle, die   sie mir   gab.
the little flowers all   which she to me gave

Und wenn sie wandelt am   Hügel vorbei
and when she wanders on the hill   by

And when she wanders by on the
hill, and thinks in her heart, 'His
love was true', then, all you
flowers, come forth, come forth!
For spring has come forth, and
winter is ended!

Und denkt im   Herzen: der meint' es treu!
and thinks in the heart   he meant it truly

Dann Blümlein   alle, heraus, heraus!
then little flowers all out   out

Der Mai ist kommen, der Winter ist aus.
the May is come   the winter is ended

xix. Der Müller und der Bach
   the miller and the brook

xix. The miller and the brook

(Der Müller)
  the miller

(The miller)

Wo   ein treues Herze in Liebe vergeht,
when a   true heart in love perishes

Da welken die Lilien auf jedem Beet;
then fade   the lilies in every bed

Da muss in die Wolken der Vollmond gehn,
then must in the clouds the full moon go

Damit seine Tränen die Menschen nicht sehn;
so that his tears the people   not see

Da halten   die Englein   die Augen sich
then keep shut the (little) angels the eyes   (themselves)
  zu
  —

Und schluchzen und singen die Seele zur   Ruh.
and sob   and sing   the soul to the rest

When a faithful heart dies of love, in every flower-bed the lilies fade; the full moon must hide behind clouds, that men should not see her tears; then angels cover their eyes, and with sobs sing the soul to rest.

(Der Bach)
  the brook

(The brook)

Und wenn sich   die Liebe dem   Schmerz entringt,
and when (herself) the love to the sorrow   breaks away

Ein Sternlein, ein neues,   am   Himmel erblinkt;
a   little star a   new one in the sky   twinkles

Da springen drei Rosen, halb rot und halb weiss,
then spring three roses half red and half white

Die welken nicht wieder, aus Dornenreis.
that wither not   again from thorn-sprig

Und die Engelein   schneiden die Flügel sich   ab
and the (little) angels clip   the wings themselves off

Und gehn alle Morgen   zur   Erde herab.
and go   all mornings to the earth down

And when love struggles free from its sorrow, a new star shines in the sky; three red and white roses spring from a thorny twig. And angels clip their wings, and descend each day to the earth.

(Der Müller)
  the miller

(The miller)

Ach Bächlein,   liebes Bächlein, du meinst es so gut;
ah little brook dear little brook you mean it so well

Ach Bächlein,   aber weisst du, wie Liebe tut?
ah little brook but know you how love does

Little brook, dear little brook, you mean, oh, so well – but do you know what love does? Ah, there below, is cool peace! So, little

Ach unten, da   unten die kühle Ruh!
ah   below there below the cool   peace

Ach Bächlein,   liebes Bächlein,   so singe nur zu.
ah   little brook dear little brook so sing just on

xx. *Des   Baches Wiegenlied*
    of the brook cradle-song

Gute Ruh, gute Ruh! tu   die Augen zu!
good sleep good sleep close the eyes   –

Wandrer, du müder,   du bist zu Haus.
wanderer you tired (one) you are at home

Die Treu   ist hier, sollst liegen bei mir,
the fidelity is here shall lie   with me

Bis   das Meer will trinken die Bächlein   aus.
until the ocean will drink   the little brooks empty

Will betten   dich kühl auf weichem Pfühl
will bed down you cool on soft   pillow

In dem blauen kristallenen Kämmerlein.
in the blue   crystal   little bedroom

Heran, heran, was   wiegen kann,
on   on   what rock can

Woget und wieget   den Knaben mir   ein!
billow and rock asleep the boy   to me –

Wenn ein Jagdhorn   schallt   aus dem grünen Wald,
when a   hunting-horn resounds from the green wood

Will ich sausen und brausen wohl   um   dich her.
will I   bluster and rage   indeed round you about

Blickt nicht herein, blaue Blümelein!
look   not in here blue little flowers

Ihr macht meinem Schläfer die Träume so schwer.
you make to my   sleeper the dreams so heavy

Hinweg, hinweg, von   dem Mühlensteg,
away   away   from the mill-path

Hinweg, hinweg, böses Mägdelein,
away   away   bad girl

Dass ihn dein Schatten dein Schatten nicht weckt!
that him your shadow your shadow not   wakes

brook, dear little brook, just sing on!

xx. The brook's cradle-song

Sleep well, sleep well, and close you eyes! You are home now, weary wanderer, and here you find fidelity. And with me you will find rest, until the sea swallows every stream.

For your bed I'll make a cool, soft pillow in my blue crystal chamber. Ever on, ever on, let my son be lulled to sleep!

When a hunting-horn sounds from the green woods, I'll bluster and rage all around you. Do not peep in, little flowers, for you trouble my sleeper's dreams.

Away, wicked maid, away from the mill-path, lest your shadow should wake him! And throw in your fine handkerchief, that I may cover his eyes.

Wirf   mir   herein   dein Tüchlein   fein,
throw to me in here your little kerchief fine

Dass ich die Augen ihm   halte bedeckt.
that I   the eyes   to him hold covered

Gute Nacht, gute Nacht! Bis   alles   wacht,   Good-night, good-night! Till
good night good night   until everything wakes   everything wakens, sleep away
                                                            your joy, sleep away your grief!
Schlaf aus deine Freude, schlaf aus dein Leid!   The full moon rises, and the mist
sleep out your joy   sleep out your sorrow   is clearing: how wide the sky is
                                                            there above.
Der Vollmond steigt, der Nebel weicht,
the full moon rises the mist yields

Und der Himmel da   oben, wie ist er so weit!
and the sky   there above how is he so wide

54. DU   BIST DIE RUH   ## 54. YOU ARE
YOU ARE THE TRANQUILLITY   TRANQUILLITY

Friedrich Rückert

Du bist die Ruh,   You are tranquillity, gentle peace;
you are the tranquillity   you are longing, and its assuaging.

Der Friede mild,
the peace gentle

Die Sehnsucht du,
the longing   you

Und was sie stillt.
and what she assuages

Ich weihe   dir   Full of joy and grief, I consecrate
I   consecrate to you   to you my eyes and heart for your
                                                 dwelling.
Voll Lust und Schmerz
full joy and pain

Zur   Wohnung hier
to the dwelling here

Mein Aug und Herz.
my   eye and heart

Kehr ein bei mir,   Enter this house, and quietly close
come in to me   the door behind you.

Und schliesse du
and close   you

Still   hinter   dir
quietly behind you

Die Pforte zu.
the door –

Treib andern Schmerz
drive other   grief

Aus   dieser Brust!
from this   breast

Voll sei dies Herz
full be this heart

Von deiner Lust.
of   your joy

Dies Augenzelt,
this eyes' canopy

Von deinem Glanz
from your   brightness

Allein erhellt,
alone lit up

O füll es ganz!
O fill it wholly

Drive other griefs from my breast!
May my heart be full of your joy!

Your brightness alone lights the
dwelling of my eyes – O fill it
wholly!

55. *LACHEN   UND WEINEN*
LAUGHING AND WEEPING

55. LAUGHING AND
WEEPING

Friedrich Rückert

Lachen   und Weinen zu jeglicher Stunde
laughing and weeping at each   hour

Ruht bei   der Lieb auf so mancherlei Gründe.
rests with the love on so various   causes

Morgens   lacht' ich vor Lust,
in the morning laughed I   for joy

Und warum ich nun weine
and why   I   now weep

Bei des   Abendes Scheine,
in of the evening light

Ist mir   selb' nicht bewusst.
is to me myself not   known

Laughing and weeping at any
hour, with love comes from so
many things – this morning I
laughed for joy, but why I weep
now in the evening light, I do not
know myself.

Weinen und Lachen zu jeglicher Stunde
weeping and laughing at each hour

Ruht bei der Lieb' auf so mancherlei Grunde.
rests with the love on so various causes

Abends weint' ich vor Schmerz;
in the evening wept I for grief

Und warum du erwachen
and why you waken

Kannst am Morgen mit Lachen,
can in the morning with laughing

Muss ich dich fragen, o Herz.
must I you ask O heart

Weeping and laughing at any hour, with love comes from so many things. In the evening I can weep for grief – but why I awaken in the morning filled with laughter, can I only ask you, O heart!

56. *AUFLÖSUNG*
REDEMPTION

56. REDEMPTION

Johann Mayrhofer

Verbirg dich, Sonne,
hide yourself sun

Denn die Gluten der Wonne
for the fires of the ecstasy

Versengen mein Gebein;
scorch my bones

Verstummt, ihr Töne,
be silent you sounds

Frühlingsschöne flüchte dich
spring-beauty flee (yourself)

Und lass mich allein!
and leave me alone

Hide, O sun, for the fires of ecstasy are scorching me! Hush, sweet sounds! Flee away, and leave me in peace, O beauteous spring!

Quillen doch aus allen Falten
flow but from all folds

Meiner Seele liebliche Gewalten,
of my soul sweet powers

Die mich umschlingen,
that me embrace

From every corner of my soul, sublime power flows forth, and envelopes me in divine song. Perish, world, and never more disturb this sweet ethereal harmony!

Himmlisch singen;
divinely   sing

Geh' unter, Welt, und störe
sink –   world and disturb

Nimmer, die süssen, ätherischen Chöre!
never   the sweet ethereal   choruses

57. ROMANZE
ROMANCE

Helmina von Chézy
(from the play *Rosamunde*)

Der Vollmond strahlt auf Bergeshöhn,
the full-moon shines on mountain-tops

Wie hab' ich dich vermisst!
how have I   you missed

Du süsses Herz! es ist so schön,
you sweet heart it is so beautiful

Wenn treu die Treue   küsst!
when truly the true one kisses

Was frommt des   Maien holde Zier?
what avails of the May   lovely adornment

Du warst mein Frühlingsstrahl!
you were my   spring's-ray

Licht meiner Nacht, o lächle mir
light of my night   O smile to me

Im   Tode noch einmal!
in the death again once

Sie trat hinein beim   Vollmondschein,
she went in   by the full-moon

Sie blickte himmelwärts:
she looked heavenwards

'Im   Leben fern, im   Tode dein!'
in the life   far off in the death yours

Und sanft brach Herz an Herz.
and softly broke heart on heart

57. ROMANCE

The full moon shines on the
mountain-tops – O how I have
missed you! Dear heart, how
beautiful it is when true love truly
kisses.

What avails the lovely blossoming
of May? You were my radiant
spring! Light of my darkness, O
smile at me once more from the
grave!

In the light of the full moon she
appeared, and looked towards
Heaven. 'In life apart, yours in
death!' and softly our two hearts
were broken.

58. IM ABENDROT
IN THE SUNSET

58. IN THE SUNSET

Carl Lappe

O wie schön ist deine Welt,
O how lovely is your world

Vater, wenn sie golden strahlet!
Father when she golden shines

Wenn dein Glanz herniederfällt
when your brightness falls down

Und den Staub mit Schimmer malet,
and the dust with lustre paints

Wenn das Rot, das in der Wolke blinkt,
when the red that in the cloud gleams

In mein stilles Fenster sinkt!
in my quiet window sinks

Könnt' ich klagen, könnt' ich zagen?
could I lament could I be afraid

Irre sein an dir und mir?
in error be towards Thee and me

Nein, ich will im Busen tragen
no I will in the bosom carry

Deinen Himmel schon allhier,
your heaven already here

Und dies Herz, eh' es zusammenbricht,
and this heart before it breaks down

Trinkt noch Glut und schlürft noch Licht.
drinks yet glow and sips yet light

How lovely is Thy world, O
Father, when it shines golden, and
Thy brightness falling on the earth
makes it shine; when the redness
of the glowing clouds sinks in
through my quiet window. How
can I lament? How can I be afraid?
How can I doubt Thee? No, I will
carry Thy Heaven here in my
breast, that my heart, before it
breaks, may drink in the glow and
the light.

59. DER EINSAME
THE SOLITARY ONE

59. IN SOLITUDE

Carl Lappe

Wenn meine Grillen schwirren,
when my crickets whirr

Bei Nacht, am spät erwärmten Herd,
by night by the late warmed hearth

When at night the crickets chirp, I
sit contented by my warm hearth,
and cosily gaze at the flames, light
of heart and free from care.

Dann sitz' ich, mit vernügtem Sinn,
then sit I   with contented mind

Vertraulich zu der Flamme hin,
intimately to the flame   there

So leicht, so unbeschwert.
so light so unburdened

Ein trautes stilles Stündchen
a   cosy   quiet (little) hour

At this sweet tranquil hour, we
love to gaze at the fire; stirring up
sparks when the blaze dies down;
thinking and reflecting – yet
another day.

Bleibt man noch gern   am   Feuer wach,
stays one still with pleasure by the fire   awake

Man schürt, wenn sich   die Lohe senkt,
one stirs   when (herself) the blaze sinks

Die Funken auf, und sinnt   und denkt:
the sparks up and reflects and thinks

Nun abermal   ein Tag!
now once more a   day

Was   Liebes   oder Leides
(what) pleasing (thing) or   harmful (thing)

All joys and sorrows we
encountered in its course, pass
once more through the mind; only
the bad is cast away, that it may
not trouble the night.

Sein Lauf   für uns daher gebracht,
his   course for us here brought

Es geht noch einmal durch   den Sinn,
it goes more once   through the mind

Allein das Böse wirft   man hin,
only the bad throws one away

Es störe   nicht die Nacht.
it troubles not   the night

Zu einem frohen Traume
to a   happy dream

We comfortably prepare ourselves
for pleasant dreams, and when
some fair image lightens the heart,
and longing fills the soul with
gentle pleasure, we yield to sleep.

Bereitet man gemach   sich   zu,
prepares one comfortably himself –

Wenn sorgelos ein holdes   Bild
when carefree a   pleasing image

Mit sanfter Lust   die Seele füllt,
with gentle pleasure the soul fills

Ergibt man sich   der   Ruh'.
yields one oneself to the rest

O wie ich mir   gefalle
O how I   (myself) please

O how contented I am in my quiet
rustic way! That which holds
captive the wandering heart in the

In meiner stillen Ländlichkeit!
in my   quiet rusticity

Was in dem Schwarm der   lauten Welt
that in the swarm   of the noisy world

Das irre   Herz gefesselt hält,
the bewildered heart fettered holds

Gibt nicht Zufriedenheit.
gives not   contentment

crowded noisy world brings no happiness.

Zirpt immer, liebe Heimchen,
chirp always dear crickets

In meiner Klause,   eng   und klein,
in my   hermitage narrow and small

Ich duld' euch gern: ihr stört   mich nicht,
I   suffer you gladly you disturb me   not

Wenn euer Lied das Schweigen bricht,
when your song the silence   breaks

Bin ich nicht ganz allein.
am I   not quite alone

Chirp on, dear crickets, I welcome you in my small hermitage. You do not disturb me; when your song breaks the silence, I am no longer alone.

60. *DIE JUNGE NONNE*
THE YOUNG NUN

60. THE YOUNG NUN

Johann Nickolaus Craigher de Jachelutta

Wie braust durch   die Wipfel   der heulende Sturm!
how rages through the (tree-)tops the howling storm

Es klirren die Balken, es zittert   das Haus!
(it) clatter the rafters (it) shudders the house

Es rollet   der Donner, es leuchtet der Blitz,
(it) rumbles the thunder (it) lights up the lightning

Und finster die Nacht, wie das Grab!
and dark   the night as the grave

How the raging storm howls in the tree-tops! How the rafters groan, the house shudders! How the thunder rumbles, and the lightning flashes, and the night is dark as the grave!

Immerhin, so tobt' es auch jüngst   noch in mir!
yet   so raged it also recently still in me

Es brauste   das Leben, wie jetzo der Sturm,
(it) blustered the life   as now the storm

Es bebten   die Glieder, wie jetzo das Haus,
(it) trembled the limbs   as now the house

Es flammte die Liebe, wie jetzo der Blitz,
(it) flared   the love as now the lightning

Und finster die Brust, wie das Grab.
and dark   the breast as the grave

Yet of late such storms raged in me! My life blustered as now the gale; my limbs trembled as the house; my love flared as the lightning, and my heart was dark as the grave.

Nun tobe, du   wilder gewaltger Sturm,
now rage you wild   mighty   storm

Im   Herzen ist Friede, im   Herzen ist Ruh;
in the heart   is peace in the heart   is tranquillity

Des   Bräutigams harret die liebende Braut,
(of) the bridegroom awaits the loving   bride

Gereinigt in prüfender Glut,
cleansed in testing   fire

Der   ewigen Liebe getraut.
to the eternal love wedded

Ich harre, mein Heiland, mit sehnendem Blick!
I   await my Saviour with longing   look

Komm, himmlischer Bräutigam, hole die Braut,
come   heavenly   bridegroom take the bride

Erlöse die Seele von irdischer Haft!
set free the soul from earthly confinement

Horch, friedlich   ertönet das Glöcklein vom   Turm!
listen peacefully sounds the little bell from the steeple

Es lockt   mich das süsse Getön
(it) is calling me   the sweet sound

Allmächtig   zu ewigen Höhn.
all-powerfully to eternal heights

Alleluja!
Hallelujah

Now rage, you wild and mighty storm! In my heart, is peace, in my heart tranquillity. The loving bride awaits the Bridegroom, purified in a testing fire, wedded to Eternal Love.

I await my Saviour, longing in my eyes! Come, heavenly Bridegroom, take your bride – set free my soul from its earthly prison.

Listen, how peacefully the little bell sounds in the steeple! Its sweet tones are calling me all-powerfully to the eternal heights! Hallelujah!

61. NACHT UND TRÄUME NIGHT AND DREAMS

61. NIGHT AND DREAMS

Matthäus von Collin

Heilge Nacht, du sinkest nieder;
sacred night   you sink   down

Nieder wallen auch die Träume,
down float   also the dreams

Wie dein Mondlicht durch   die Räume,
as   your moonlight through the rooms

Durch   der   Menschen stille Brust.
through of the men   still breast

Die belauschen sie   mit Lust;
they listen to   them with joy

O sacred night, gently you fall, and as your moonlight steals into each room, dreams float down and enter the still hearts of men. They receive these dreams with joy, and when day breaks, they call, 'Come back, sacred night! O lovely dreams, come back!'

Rufen, wenn der Tag erwacht:
call   when the day awakens

Kehre   wieder, heilge Nacht!
come back again   sacred night

Holde Träume, kehret   wieder!
lovely dreams come back again

62. AVE MARIA (ELLENS DRITTER HAIL MARY ELLEN'S THIRD GESANG) SONG

(from *The Lady of the Lake*)

Ave Maria!   Jungfrau mild,
hail Mary (Latin) maiden mild

Erhöre einer Jungfrau Flehen,
hear of a maiden supplication

Aus   diesem Felsen starr und wild
from this   rock rigid and wild

Soll mein Gebet zu dir hin   wehen.
shall my   prayer to you thither drift

Wir schlafen sicher bis zum Morgen,
we sleep   safely till to the morning

Ob   Menschen noch so grausam sind.
though men   still so cruel   are

O Jungfrau, sieh der   Jungfrau Sorgen,
O maiden   see of the maiden sorrows

O Mutter, hör ein bittend   Kind!
O mother hear an entreating child

Ave Maria!

Ave Maria! unbefleckt!
hail Mary   undefiled

Wenn wir auf diesen Fels hinsinken
when we on this   rock sink down

Zum Schlaf, und uns dein Schutz   bedeckt,
to the sleep   and us   your protection covers

Wird weich der harte Fels uns   dünken.
will   soft the hard rock to us seem

62. HYMN TO THE VIRGIN

Sir Walter Scott
(original text)

Ave Maria! maiden mild!
Listen to a maiden's prayer!
Thou canst hear though from the
     wild;
Thou canst save amid despair.

Safe may we sleep beneath thy
     care,
Though banished, outcast, and
     reviled;
Maiden! Hear a maiden's prayer –
Mother, hear a suppliant child!

Ave Maria! Undefiled!
The flinty couch we now must
     share
Shall seem with down of eider
     piled,
If thy protection hover there.

Du lächelst, Rosendüfte wehen
you smile   rose-scents drift

In dieser dumpfen Felsenkluft.
in this   heavy   rock-cleft

O Mutter, höre Kindes Flehen,
O mother hear child's supplication

O Jungfrau, eine Jungfrau ruft!
O maiden a   maiden calls

Ave Maria!

Ave Maria! Reine Magd!
hail Mary   pure maid

Der   Erde und der   Luft Dämonen,
of the earth and of the air   demons

Von deines Auges Huld verjagt,
by of your eye   grace driven away

Sie können hier nicht bei uns wohnen.
they can   here not with us live

Wir woll'n   uns   still dem Schicksal
we are willing (ourselves) quietly to the fate
   beugen,
   to bow

Da   uns dein heilger Trost anweht;
because us   your holy   solace wafts towards

Der Jungfrau wolle   hold   dich   neigen,
to the Virgin   be willing graciously (yourself) to bow

Dem Kind, das für den Vater fleht!
to the child, that for the father supplicates

Ave Maria!

The murky cavern's heavy air
Shall breathe of balm if thou hast
   smiled.
Then, Maiden! Hear a maiden's
   prayer,
Mother, list to a suppliant child!

Ave Maria! Stainless styled!
Foul demons of the earth and air,
From this their wonted haunt
   exiled,
Shall flee before thy presence fair.

We bow us to our lot of care,
Beneath thy guidance reconciled.
Hear for a maid a maiden's prayer
And for a father hear a child!

63. DIE ALLMACHT
THE OMNIPOTENCE

63. OMNIPOTENCE

Johann Ladislav Pyrker

Gross ist Jehova, der Herr, denn Himmel
great is Jehovah the Lord for Heaven

und Erde verkünden seine Macht.
and earth proclaim his   might

Great is the Lord Jehovah; Heaven
and earth proclaim His might.
You hear it in the raging storm,
and in the rushing of forest

Du hörst sie im   brausenden Sturm,
you hear her in the raging   storm

in des Waldstroms   laut aufrauschendem Ruf;
in the forest-streams loud uprushing   call

du hörst sie in des   grünenden Waldes Gesäusel,
you hear her in of the greening woods rustling

siehst sie in wogender Saaten Gold,
see   her in of waving corn   gold

In lieblicher Blumen glühendern Schmelz,
in of lovely flowers glowing   sweetness

im   Glanz   des   sternebesäten Himmels,
in the brilliance of the star-strewn sky

Furchtbar tönt   sie im   Donnergeroll
terrible   sounds she in the thunder-roll

und flammt in des   Blitzes   schnell hinzuckendem
and flames in of the lightning fast   jerking away
  Flug,
  flight

doch kündet   das pochende Herz dir
yet gives warning the beating heart to you
  fühlbarer   noch
  more perceptibly still

Jehovahs Macht, des   ewigen Gottes,
Jehovah's might of the eternal God

blickst du flehend   empor und hoffst auf Huld und
look   you imploringly up   and hope for grace and
  Erbarmen.
  mercy

streams. You hear it in the rustling green of spring woods; you see it in waving golden corn; in the glowing splendour of sweet flowers, in the brightness of a star-strewn sky. Terrible it sounds in rolling thunder, and terrible in lightning's jagged flashes. Yet in the beating heart you feel Jehovah's might still greater – imploring you to lift your gaze to Eternal God, and ask for His grace, and for His mercy.

64. *LIED   DER   MIGNON I*
SONG OF THE MIGNON

64. MIGNON'S SONG I

Johann Wolfgang von Goethe
(from *Wilhelm Meister*; also set by Schumann and Wolf)

Heiss' mich nicht reden,   heiss' mich schweigen,
bid   me   not to speak bid me to be silent

Denn mein Geheimnis ist mir   Pflicht;
for   my   secret   is to me duty

Do not ask me to speak, rather bid me be silent! I am bound by my secret, and long to reveal my innermost self. But fate will not allow it.

Ich möchte   dir   mein ganzes Inn're   zeigen,
I   should like to you my   whole inner self to show

Allein das Schicksal will   es nicht.
only   the fate   ordains it not

Zur   rechten Zeit vertreibt   der   Sonne Lauf
at the right   time drives away of the sun   course

The sun in its due time dispels the darkness of night: light must appear. And unyielding rock opens itself up, for the earth does not begrudge its deep hidden springs.

Die finstre Nacht, und sie muss sich   erhellen;
the dark   night   and she must herself lighten

Der harte Fels schliesst seinen Busen auf,
the hard rock opens   his   bosom –

Missgönnt der   Erde nicht die tiefverborg'nen Quellen.
begrudges to the earth not   the deeply hidden springs

Ein jeder sucht im   Arm des   Freundes Ruh',
everyone seeks in the arm of the friend   rest

Everyone seeks rest on the arm of a friend, where the heart can pour forth its lament. But an oath seals my lips, and only a god can open them again.

Dort kann die Brust in Klagen sich   ergiessen;
there can   the breast in laments (herself) pour forth

Allein ein Schwur drückt mir   die Lippen zu,
but   an oath   closes to me the lips   –

Und nur ein Gott vermag sie   aufzuschliessen.
and only a   god can   them open

65. *LIED   DER   MIGNON II*
SONG OF THE MIGNON

Johann Wolfgang von Goethe
(from *Wilhelm Meister*; also set by Beethoven, Schumann and Wolf)

Nur wer die Sehnsucht kennt,
only who the longing   knows

Only he who know longing can know how I suffer! Alone and cut off from all joy, I gaze at the heavens there beyond. Ah, the one who loves and understands me is far away. My head is spinning; my very bowels are on fire. Only he who knows longing can know how I suffer!

Weiss, was ich leide!
knows what I suffer

Allein und abgetrennt
alone and separated

Von aller Freude,
from all   joy

Seh ich ans   Firmament
look I   at the firmament

Nach   jener Seite.
towards that side

Ach!   der mich liebt und kennt,
ah   (he) who me loves and knows

Ist in der Weite.
is – far away –

Es schwindelt mir,   es brennt
it is giddy   to me it burns

Mein Eingeweide.
my   bowels

Nur wer die Sehnsucht kennt,
only who the longing   knows

Weiss, was ich leide!
knows what I   suffer

66. *LIED   DER   MIGNON III*
SONG OF THE MIGNON

| 66. MIGNON'S SONG |
| III |

Johann Wolfgang von Goethe
(from *Wilhelm Meister*; also set by Schumann and Wolf)

So lasst mich scheinen, bis   ich werde;
so let   me   appear   until I   become

So let me appear, until I am become thus – leave me in my white robe! I am hastening away from the beautiful earth down into that unyielding abode.

Zieht mir   das weisse Kleid nicht aus!
take to me the white dress not   off

Ich eile   von der schönen Erde
I   hurry from the beautiful earth

Hinab in   jenes feste Haus.
down into that firm house

Dort ruh' ich eine kleine Stille,
there rest I   a   little still (moment)

There I will rest in peace a while, until my eyes are opened anew; then I will leave behind the spotless robe, the girdle and the garland.

Dann öffnet sich   der frische Blick;
then opens (himself) the fresh glance

Ich lasse dann die reine Hülle,
I   leave then the pure raiment

Den Gürtel und den Kranz   zurück.
the girdle and the garland behind

Und jene   himmlischen Gestalten,
and those heavenly   figures

Those heavenly spirits take no heed of 'man' and 'woman', and no garments, no folds will cover my transfigured body.

Sie fragen nicht nach Mann und Weib,
they ask   not about man and woman

Und keine Kleider, keine Falten
and no   clothes no   folds

Umgeben den verklärten   Leib.
surround the transfigured body

Zwar   lebt' ich ohne   Sorg' und Mühe,
though lived I   without care and trouble

Though I have lived free from toil
and care, yet I have felt deep pain
enough; grief has aged me before
my time – O make me for ever
young again!

Doch fühlt' ich tiefen Schmerz genung!
yet felt I   deep pain   enough

Vor Kummer altert' ich zu frühe,
for grief   aged I   too early

Macht mich auf ewig wieder jung!
make me   for ever again young

67. *FISCHERWEISE*
FISHER-MELODY

67. FISHERMAN'S
SONG

Franz Xaver von Schlechta

Den Fischer   fechten Sorgen
the fisherman assail cares

No cares, no grief or sorrow
trouble the fisherman; early in the
morning he casts off his boat with
a light heart.

Und Gram und Leid   nicht an;
and grief and sorrow not –

Er löst   am   frühen Morgen
he unties in the early   morning

Mit leichtem Sinn den Kahn.
with easy   mind the boat

Da   lagert   rings   noch Friede
there lies spread around still peace

All is peace about him in the
woods and meadows and brooks.
He rouses the golden sun with his
song.

Auf Wald und Flur   und Bach,
on wood and meadow and brook

Er ruft   mit seinem Liede
he rouses with his   song

Die gold'ne Sonne wach.
the golden sun   awake

Er singt zu seinem Werke
he sings to his   work

He sings as he labours with a full
and lively heart – it gives him
strength, and strength gives joy in
living.

Aus voller frischer Brust,
from full   lively breast

Die Arbeit gibt ihm   Stärke,
the work gives to him strength

Die Stärke   Lebenslust.
the strength life's-joy

Bald wird ein bunt Gewimmel
soon is   a   gay   throng

In allen Tiefen laut,
in all   deeps about

Und plätschert durch   den Himmel,
and splashes through the sky

Der   sich   im   Wasser baut.
which himself in the water   rests

Soon a gay and lively throng is swarming down below, splashing in the sky that lies mirrored in the water.

Doch wer   ein Netz will   stellen,
but   whoever a   net   wants to lay

Braucht Augen klar   und gut,
needs   eyes   clear and good

Muss heiter gleich den Wellen
must lively like   the waves

Und frei   sein wie die Flut.
and free be   as   the stream

Anyone who casts a net needs a good, clear eye; he must be lively as the waves, and carefree as the stream.

Dort angelt auf der Brücke
there angles on   the bridge

Die Hirtin,   schlauer Wicht!
the shepherdess sly   creature

Gib' auf nur deine Tücke,
give up just your trick

Den Fisch betrügst du   nicht!
the fish   deceive you not

There on the bridge the shepherdess is fishing. You can stop your tricks, sly creature, for the fish won't be deceived!

68. IM   FRÜHLING
IN THE SPRING

68. IN THE SPRING

Ernst Schulze

Still sitz' ich an des   Hügels Hang,
still sit   I   on of the hill   slope

Der Himmel ist so klar,
the sky   is so clear

Quietly I sit on the hill-side, the heavens are so clear. A breeze plays in the green valley, where in the first spring radiance I was once, oh, so happy!

Das Lüftchen   spielt im   grünen Tal,
the little breeze plays in the green valley

Wo   ich beim   ersten Frühlingsstrahl
where I   at the first   spring's-ray

Einst, ach so glücklich war;
once oh so happy   was

Wo   ich an ihrer Seite ging
where I   at her side walked

So traulich   und so nah',
so intimately and so close

Und tief   im   dunkeln Felsenquell
and deep in the dark   rock-spring

Den schönen Himmel blau und hell,
the lovely   sky   blue and clear

Und sie im   Himmel sah.
and her in the sky   saw

There I walked at her side, so
fondly, and so close; and deep in
the dark rocky spring I saw the
sky, clear blue and fair, and in the
sky her image.

Sieh, wie der bunte   Frühling schon
see   how the brightly-coloured spring   already

Aus Knosp' und Blüte   blickt!
from bud   and blossom looks

Nicht alle Blüten   sind mir   gleich,
not   all blossoms are to me equal

Am   liebsten   pflückt'   ich von   dem Zweig,
at the most agreeable would pluck I   from the twig

Von welchem sie gepflückt!
from which   she plucked

See, how the spring already peeps
from bud and blossom! But not all
of these have equal charm for me –
I would most like to pluck from
the branch from which she
plucked.

Denn alles   ist wie damals noch,
for   everything is as then   still

Die Blumen, das Gefild;
the flowers the fields

Die Sonne scheint nicht minder hell,
the sun   shines not less   brightly

Nicht minder freundlich schwimmt im   Quell
not less   friendly   floats   in the spring

Das blaue Himmelsbild.
the blue sky's image

For everything is as it was then;
the flowers, and the fields. And no
less brightly shines the sun, or the
sky's blue image, that floats in the
spring.

Es wandeln nur sich   Will' und Wahn,
(it) change only themselves wish and fancy

Es wechseln Lust und Streit;
(it) change joy and strife

Vorüber flieht der   Liebe Glück,
away   flees of the love joy

Und nur die Liebe bleibt   zurück,
and only the love remains behind

Die Lieb' und ach, das Leid!
the love and ah   the grief

O wär' ich doch ein Vöglein   nur
O were I but a   little bird only

Dort an dem Wiesenhang,
there on the meadow-slope

Dann blieb'   ich auf den Zweigen hier,
then would stay I   on the twigs   here

Und säng'   ein süsses Lied von ihr
and would sing a   sweet song of   her

Den ganzen Sommer lang.
the whole summer long

Only desires and fancies change, only joy and strife; all love's joys flee away, and love alone remains – and alas, the pain.

O if I were but a little bird, there on the meadow slope, then I would stay here on this twig, and sing of her the sweetest song the whole summer long.

69. STÄNDCHEN
SERENADE

Translated into German by
August Wilhelm von Schlegel

Horch, horch, die Lerch im   Ätherblau!
hark   hark the lark   in the sky-blue

Und Phöbus, neu   erweckt,
and Phoebus newly awakened

Tränkt seine Rosse mit dem Tau,
waters his   steeds with the dew

Der Blumenkelche deckt.
that flower-chalice covers

Der   Ringelblume Knospe schleusst
of the marigold   bud   opens

69. SERENADE

From *Cymbeline* by
William Shakespeare
(original text)

Hark! hark! the lark at heaven's
    gate sings,
And Phoebus 'gins arise,
His steeds to water at those
    springs
On chalic'd flowers that lies;
And winking Mary-buds begin
To ope their golden eyes:
With everything that pretty is,
My lady sweet, arise:
Arise, arise!

Die goldnen Äuglein   auf;
the golden (little) eyes –

Mit allem,   was da   reizend ist,
with everything that there charming is

Du süsse Maid, steh auf!
you sweet maiden arise –

Weil   du doch   gar so reizend   bist;
because you indeed very so charming are

Du süsse Maid, steh auf!
you sweet maiden arise –

70. DER WANDERER AN DEN MOND
THE WANDERER TO THE MOON

70. THE WANDERER
TO THE MOON

Johann Gabriel Seidl

Ich auf der Erd', am   Himmel du,
I   on the earth in the sky   you

Wir wandern beide rüstig zu:
we wander both briskly –

Ich ernst und trüb,   du mild und rein,
I   grave and melancholy you gentle and pure

Was mag der Unterschied wohl   sein?
what may the difference I wonder be

Ich wandre fremd   von Land zu Land,
I   wander unknown from land to land

So heimatlos, so unbekannt;
so homeless so unknown

Berg   auf, Berg   ab,   Wald ein, Wald aus,
mountain up mountain down wood in   wood out

Doch bin ich nirgend, ach! zu Haus.
but am I   nowhere alas at home

Du aber wanderst auf und ab
you but wander up and down

Aus Westerns Wieg' in   Ostens Grab,
from west's   cradle into east's grave

Wallst Länder ein und Länder aus,
travel lands in and lands out

I on earth, you in the heavens, we
are both hardy travellers. I am
grave and melancholy, you gentle
and pure; I wonder, in what do we
differ? A stranger, I wander from
land to land, homeless and
unknown; up mountains and
down, in and out of the woods,
but alas, nowhere am I at home.
But you travel near and far, from
your cradle in the west to your
eastern grave; out of one land, into
another – yet wherever you are,
you are at home. The sky,
spanning infinity, is your beloved
homeland. O happy is he, who
wherever he goes, is yet on his
native earth!

Und bist doch, wo   du bist, zu Haus.
and are yet   where you are at home

Der Himmel, endlos   ausgespannt,
the sky   endlessly stretched out

Ist dein geliebtes Heimatland:
is your beloved homeland

O glücklich, wer, wohin   er geht,
O happy   who whither he goes

Doch auf der   Heimat Boden   steht!
yet   on of the home   ground stands

71. *JÄGERS   LIEBESLIED* HUNTER'S LOVE-SONG

71. HUNTER'S LOVE-SONG

Franz Schober

Ich schiess den Hirsch im   grünen Forst,
I   shoot the stag   in the green forest

Im   stillen Tal   das Reh,
in the quiet valley the deer

Den Adler auf dem Klippenhorst,
the eagle on the rocky-eyrie

Die Ente auf dem See.
the duck on the lake

Kein Ort, der Schutz gewähren kann,
no   place the refuge vouchsafe can

Wenn meine Flinte zielt;
when my   gun   aims

Und dennoch hab ich harter Mann
and yet   have I harsh man

Die Liebe auch gefühlt!
the love also felt

Hab oft   hantiert in rauher Zeit,
have often operated in harsh time

In Sturm und Winternacht,
in storm and winter-night

Und übereist   und eingeschneit,
and covered with ice and snowed up

I shoot the stags in the green forest, the deer in the quiet valley; the eagles in their craggy eyries, the ducks on the lake. No refuge, no place that's safe from the aim of my gun – yet even I, a ruthless man, have felt love!

Often I've plied my skill in harsh weather on stormy winter nights, and covered with snow and ice, I've made the rocks my bed. I slept on thorns as if on down, untouched by the north wind, and yet gentle dreams of love have stirred my rugged breast.

Zum   Bett den Stein gemacht.
into the bed the rock made

Auf Dornen schlief ich wie auf Flaum,
on thorns slept I   as on down

Vom   Nordwind   ungerührt,
from the north-wind untouched

Doch hat der   Liebe zarten Traum
yet   has of the love gentle dream

Die rauhe   Brust   gespürt.
the rugged breast felt

Der wilde   Falk   war mein Gesell,
the savage hawk was my   companion

Der Wolf mein Kampfgespann;
the wolf my   fighting-team

Mir   fing   der Tag mit   Hundgebell,
to me began the day with hounds-baying

Die Nacht mit   Hussah! an.
the night with halloo   —

Ein Tannreis war die Blumenzier
a   fir-sprig was the flower-adornment

Auf schweissbeflecktem Hut,
on   sweat-stained   hat

Und dennoch schlug die Liebe mir
and yet   beat   the love   to me

Ins   wilde Jägerblut.
into the wild hunter's-blood

O Schäfer   auf dem weichen Moos,
O shepherd on the   soft   moss

Der du   mit   Blumen spielst,
who you with flowers play

Wer weiss, ob du   so heiss, so gross,
who knows if you so hotly so greatly

Wie ich, die Liebe fühlst.
as I   the love feels

Allnächtlich übern   schwarzen Wald,
every night over the black   wood

Vom   Mondenschein umstrahlt,
by the moonlight   bathed in light

The savage hawk was my companion, for the fight I harnessed wolves; my day began with the baying of hounds, the night with cries of halloo! A sprig of fir was the flower adorning my sweat-stained hat – and yet love came and beat in my wild hunter's blood.

O shepherd there on the soft moss, playing with flowers, who knows if your passion burns as fiercely, as mightily as mine? Each night in the dark forest, bathed in the light of the moon, a vision of brightness that no Master could paint hovers majestic and sublime.

Schwebt königshehr   die Lichtgestalt,
hovers   kingly sublime the light-vision

Wie sie   kein Meister malt.
as   her no   master paints

Wenn sie   dann auf mich niedersieht,
when she then on me   looks down

Wenn mich ihr Blick   durchglüht,
when me   her glance inflames

Da   weiss ich, wie   dem   Wild geschieht,
then know I   what to the game happens

Das vor   dem Rohre flieht.
that before the barrel flees

Und doch! mit   allem Glück   vereint,
and yet   with all   happiness united

Das nur   auf Erden ist,
that only on earth is

Als wenn der allerbeste   Freund
as if   the best of all friend

Mich in die Arme schliesst!
me   in the arms clasps

And when she looks down at me, I am inflamed by her glance. I know then how the hunted feel as they flee from the gun. And yet how I am at one with all the joys on earth – as if I were held in a warm embrace by my dearest friend.

72. *WINTERREISE*
WINTER-JOURNEY

Wilhelm Müller

   i. Gute Nacht
   good night

Fremd   bin ich eingezogen,
unknown am I   entered

Fremd   zieh ich wieder aus.
unknown set I   again out

Der Mai war mir   gewogen
the May was to me well-disposed

Mit manchem Blumenstauss.
with many a   nosegay

Das Mädchen sprach von Liebe,
the girl   spoke of love

Die Mutter gar   von Eh;
the mother even of   marriage

72. WINTER'S
JOURNEY

i. Good-night

I came here a stranger, a stranger I depart. In May I was favoured with many a nosegay of flowers. The girl spoke of love, her mother even of marriage. Now the world is overcast; my way covered in snow.

Nun ist die Welt   so trübe,
now is the world so overcast

Der Weg gehüllt   in Schnee.
the way covered in snow

Ich kann zu meiner Reisen
I   can for my   journey

Nicht wählen mit   der Zeit,
not   choose with the time

Muss selbst   den Weg mir   weisen
must myself the way to me show

In dieser Dunkelheit.
in this   darkness

Es zieht ein Mondenschatten
(it) goes a   moon-shadow

Als mein Gefährte   mit,
as my   companion with (me)

Und auf den weissen Matten
and on the white   meadows

Such' ich des   Wildes Tritt.
seek I of the deer   footprint

Was soll   ich länger weilen,
why shall I   longer to stay

Dass man mich trieb   hinaus?
that one me   drove out

Lass irre   Hunde heulen
let   wandering dogs howl

Vor   ihres Herren   Haus!
in front of their master's house

Die Liebe liebt das Wandern –
the love loves the wandering

Gott hat sie so gemacht –
God has her so made

Von einem zu dem andern.
from one   to the other

Fein Liebchen,   gute Nacht!
fine sweetheart good night

Will dich im   Traum nicht stören,
want you in the dream not   to disturb

Wär schad um deine Ruh.
were pity for your sleep

I cannot choose the time for my journey; I must find my way in the darkness. A shadow cast by the moon is my companion; in the white fields I seek the tracks of deer.

Why should I linger here, only to be driven away? Let straying dogs howl in front of their master's house! Love ever wanders from one to another – God has made it so. And now good-night, my sweetheart fair!

I would not disturb your dreams – why should I spoil your rest. You shall not hear my footsteps – softly, softly close the door! In

Sollst meinen Tritt nicht hören –
shall my   step not hear

Sacht, sacht die Türe zu!
softly softly the door close

Schreib im   Vorübergehen
write   in the passing by

Ans   Tor dir: gute Nacht,
on the gate to you good night

Damit du   mögest sehen,
so that you may   see

An dich hab ich gedacht.
of you have I   thought

passing write on your gate, 'Good-night' – so you may see I thought of you.

ii. *Die Wetterfahne*
    the weather-vane

ii. The weather-vane

Der Wind spielt mit der Wetterfahne
the wind plays with the weather-vane

Auf meines schönen Liebchens   Haus.
on my   fair   sweetheart's house

Da dacht ich schon in meinem Wahne,
then thought I   already in my   folly

Sie pfiff   den armen Flüohtling aus.
she hissed the poor   fugitive   away

The wind plays with the weather-vane on my fair sweetheart's house. In my folly, I thought it was this poor fugitive, that it was hissing away.

Er hätt* es eher   bemerken sollen,
he (have) it sooner (noticed) (should)

Des   Hauses aufgestecktes Schild,
of the house put up   sign

So hätt er nimmer suchen wollen
so had he never   to seek (wanted)

Im   Haus ein treues Frauenbild.
in the house a   true   woman

He should have noticed sooner the sign up there on the house; then he would never have thought of seeking a faithful woman there.

Der Wind spielt drinnen mit den Herzen
the wind plays within with the hearts

Wie auf dem Dach, nur nicht so laut.
as on the roof   only not so loudly

Was fragen sie   nach meinen Schmerzen?
what ask   they after my   sorrows

Ihr   Kind ist eine reiche Braut.
their child is a   rich bride

The wind plays within the heart as it plays on the roof, but not so loud. What do they care about my grief? Their child is a wealthy bride.

* (hätt bemerken sollen)
  – should have noticed –

iii. *Gefrorne Tränen*
   frozen   tears

Gefrorne Tropfen fallen
frozen   drops   fall

Von meinen Wangen ab:
from my   cheeks   off

Ob   es mir   denn entgangen,
(I wonder) if it to me then escaped

Dass ich geweinet hab'?
that I   wept   have

Ei Tränen, meine Tränen,
Oh tears   my   tears

Und seid ihr gar so lau,
and are you even so tepid

Dass ihr erstarrt zu Eise,
that you freeze to ice

Wie kühler Morgentau?
like cool   morning-dew

Und dringt doch aus der Quelle
and urge   yet from the spring

Der   Brust so glühend heiss,
of the breast so glowing hot

Als wolltet ihr zerschmelzen
as wanted you to melt

Des ganzen Winters Eis!
the whole winter's ice

iii. Frozen tears

Frozen drops fall from my cheeks.
Did I not know that I had wept?

O tears, my tears, are you so cool
you can turn to ice like chill
morning dew?

And yet you spring from my heart
so burning hot, as if you would
melt the whole of winter's ice!

iv. *Erstarrung*
   numbness

Ich such' im   Schnee vergebens
I   search in the snow   in vain

Nach ihrer Tritte   Spur,
for   her footprints trace

Wo   sie an meinem Arme
where she on my   arm

Durchstrich   die grüne Flur.
roamed through the green meadow

Ich will   den Boden küssen,
I   want the ground to kiss

Durchdringen Eis und Schnee
to pierce   ice and snow

iv. Numbness

In vain I search for her footprints
in the snow, there where we
roamed in a green meadow, arm in
arm.

I long to kiss the ground, to pierce
snow and ice with my hot tears,
until I see the earth beneath.

Mit meinen heissen Tränen,
with my   hot   tears

Bis ich die Erde seh.
until I   the earth see

Wo   find ich eine Blüte,
where find I   a   blossom

Where can I find a blossom? Where can I find green grass? The flowers are withered, the grass without colour.

Wo   find ich grünes Gras?
where find I   green grass

Die Blumen sind erstorben,
the flowers are faded away

Der Rasen sieht so blass.
the grass looks so pale

Soll denn kein Angedenken
shall then no   keepsake

Is there no keepsake then, that I may take from here? When my sorrows are stilled, who will speak to me of her?

Ich nehmen mit   von hier?
I take   with (me) from here

Wenn meine Schmerzen schweigen,
when my   sorrows   are still

Wer sagt   mir   dann von ihr?
who speaks to me then of   her

Mein Herz ist wie erstorben,
my   heart is as dead

My heart seems dead, her image rigid and cold within. If ever my heart should thaw, her image would melt away.

Kalt starrt ihr Bild   darin:
cold stares her image within

Schmilzt je   das Herz mir   wieder,
melts   ever the heart to me again

Fliesst auch ihr Bild   dahin.
melts also her image away

    v. Der Lindenbaum
     the linden-tree

v. The linden tree

Am   Brunnen vor   dem Tore
by the fountain before the gate

By the fountain at the gate stands a linden tree; in its shade I have dreamt many a sweet dream.

Da   steht ein Lindenbaum;
there stands a   linden-tree

Ich träumt' in seinem Schatten
I   dreamt in his   shade

So manchen süssen Traum.
so many a   sweet dream

Ich schnitt in seine Rinde
I cut   in his bark

So manches liebe Wort;
so many a dear word

Es zog   in Freud und Leide
it drew in joy   and sorrow

Zu ihm mich immer fort.
to him me   always forth

Ich musst' auch heute wandern
I   had to also today wander

Vorbei in tiefer Nacht,
past   in deep night

Da   hab ich noch im   Dunkel
then have I   even in the darkness

Die Augen zugemacht.
the eyes   closed

Und seine Zweige   rauschten,
and his   branches rustled

Als riefen sie   mir   zu:
as   called they to me –

'Komm her   zu mir, Geselle,
come here to me brother

Hier findst du   deine Ruh!'
here find you your rest

Die kalten Winde bliesen
the cold   winds blew

Mir grad   ins   Angesicht,
to me straight into the face

Der Hut flog mir vom   Kopfe,
the hat flew me from the head

Ich wendete   mich   nicht.
I   turned round myself not

Nun bin ich manche Stunde
now am I   many an hour

Entfernt von jenem Ort,
far away from that   place

In its bark I have carved many
words of love; I was drawn to it
always, in both joy and sorrow.

Now I have had to pass it again, at
dead of night; even in the darkness
I closed my eyes.

And its branches rustled as if they
called, 'Come here to me, friend,
here you will find rest!'

The cold wind blew straight into
my face; my hat flew from my
head, but I did not turn back.

Now I am many hours' journey
from that place. Yet still I hear a
rustling, 'There you would find
rest!'

Und immer hör ich's rauschen:
and ever   hear I it   rustle

Du fändest   Ruhe dort!
you would find rest   there

    vi. Wasserflut
      water-torrent

vi. Torrent

Manche Trän' aus   meinen Augen
many a tear   from my   eyes

My eyes have shed many a tear
into the snow; thirstily the cold
flakes drink in my burning pain.

Ist gefallen in den Schnee;
is fallen   in the snow

Seine kalten Flocken saugen
his   cold   flakes   suck

Durstig ein das heisse Weh.
thirstily in the hot   pain

Wenn die Gräser sprossen   wollen,
when the grasses to sprout want

When the grass begins to shoot, a
mild breeze will blow; the ice will
break and the soft snow melt.

Weht daher ein lauer Wind,
blows along a   tepid wind

Und das Eis zerspringt in Schollen
and the ice breaks   in lumps

Und der weiche Schnee zerrinnt.
and the soft   snow   melts

Schnee, du weisst von meinem Sehnen,
snow   you know of   my   longing

Snow, you know of my longing –
tell me, whither will you flow? The
little stream will engulf you, if you
follow my tears.

Sag, wohin   doch geht dein Lauf?
say   whither then goes your course

Folge   nach nur meinen Tränen,
follow after just my   tears

Nimmt dich bald das Bächlein   auf.
takes   you soon the little stream up

Wirst mit ihm die Stadt durchziehen,
will   with it   the town go through

Together you will flow through the
town, in and around busy streets.
And when you feel the burn of my
tears, there is my beloved's house.

Muntre Strassen ein und aus;
gay   streets   in and out

Fühlst du meine Tränen glühen,
feel   you my   tears   burn

Da   ist meiner Liebsten Haus.
there is of my beloved house

vii. Auf dem Flusse
    on the stream

Der du so lustig rauschtest,
who you so gaily rushed

Du heller, wilder Fluss,
you bright wild   river

Wie still bist du geworden,
how silent are you become

Gibst keinen Scheidegruss.
give no   farewell-greeting

Mit harter, starrer Rinde
with hard stiff   crust

Hast du dich   überdeckt,
have you yourself covered over

Liegst kalt und unbeweglich
lie   cold and motionless

Im   Sande ausgestreckt.
in the sand outstretched

In deine Decke grab' ich
in your cover carve I

Mit einem spitzen Stein
with a   sharp stone

Den Namen meiner Liebsten
the name of my dearest

Und Stund und Tag hinein:
and hour and day therein

Den Tag des   ersten Grusses,
the day of the first greeting

Den Tag, an dem ich ging:
the day on which I   went away

Um   Nam' und Zahlen windet
round name and figures winds

Sich ein zerbrochner Ring.
itself a broken   ring

Mein Herz, in diesem Bache
my   heart in this   brook

Erkennst du nun dein Bild?
recognise you now your image

vii. On the stream

You clear wild stream, that rushed so merrily along – how silent you are; you bid me no parting words!

You have covered yourself with a hard, stiff crust, and lie cold and rigid, stretched out in the sand.

Now on your icy crust I cut with a sharp stone the name of my beloved, the hour and the day;

the day of our first greeting, and the day I went away. And around the name and numbers, a broken ring.

O my heart, do you not see your own image in this brook? Is there beneath its icy crust a raging torrent too?

Ob's   unter seiner Rinde
whether it under his   crust

Wohl   auch so reissend schwillt?
perhaps also so tearing heaves

  viii. Rückblick
      backward-glance

Es brennt mir unter beiden Sohlen,
it burns me under both   soles

Tret ich auch schon   auf Eis und Schnee,
tread I   even though on ice and snow

Ich möcht   nicht wieder Atem   holen,
I   should like not   again breath to draw

Bis   ich nicht mehr die Türme seh.
until I   not   more the towers see

Hab mich   an jeden Stein gestossen,
have myself on every stone knocked

So eilt'   ich zu der Stadt hinaus;
so hastened I   to the town out

Die Krähen warfen Bäll' und Schlossen
the crows   threw balls and hailstones

Auf   meinen Hut von   jedem Haus.
on to my   hat from every house

Wie anders   hast du mich empfangen,
how differently have you me   welcomed

Du Stadt der   Unbeständigkeit!
you town of the inconstancy

An deinen blanken Fenstern sangen
at your   bright   windows sang

Die Lerch' und Nachtigall im   Streit.
the larks and nightingale in the contest

Die runden Lindenbäume blühten,
the round linden-trees blossomed

Die klaren Rinnen rauschten hell,
the clear rills   rushed   clear

Und ach, zwei Mädchenaugen glühten!
and ah   two maiden's-eyes glowed

Da   war's geschehn   um dich, Gesell!
then was it happened to you brother

viii. Backward glance

The soles of my feet are burning,
though I walk on ice and snow.
Until I can see no more steeples or
towers, I would draw no further
breath.

I bruised myself on every stone in
my haste to leave the town; the
crows flung snow and hail on my
hat from the top of every house.

How different was your welcome
to me, you town of inconstancy!
Before your bright windows vied
with each other nightingales and
larks.

The rounded linden trees were in
flower, the clear little streams
rushed and sparkled. And two
maiden's eyes were glowing, and
then you were lost, my friend!

Kommt mir   der Tag in   die Gedanken,
comes to me the day into the thoughts

Möcht   ich noch einmal rückwärts sehn,
would like I   more once back   to look

Möcht   ich zurücke wieder wanken,
would like I   back   again stagger

Vor   ihrem Hause stille   stehn.
before her   house silently to stand

Whenever that day comes into my mind, I long to look back once more; and stumbling return to her house once more, and before it silently stand.

ix. *Irrlicht*
   will-o'-the-wisp

ix. Will-o'-the-wisp

In die tiefsten Felsengründe
in the deepest rock-ravines

Lockte mich ein Irrlicht   hin:
enticed me   a   will-o'-the-wisp thither

Wie ich einen Ausgang finde,
how I   a   way-out find

Liegt nicht schwer mir   in dem Sinn.
lies   not   heavily to me on the mind

A will-o'-the-wisp lured me deep into rocky ravines. But how I shall find a way out does not trouble my mind.

Bin gewohnt das Irregehen,
am used to the astray-going

's führt ja   jeder Weg zum   Ziel:
it leads truly every way to the goal

Unsre Freuden, unsre Leiden,
our   joys   our sorrows

Alles eines Irrlichts   Spiel!
all   of a will-o'-the-wisp play

I am used to losing my way – every path leads to some goal: all our joys and griefs a will-o'-the-wisp's game!

Durch   des   Bergstroms   trockne Rinnen
through of the mountain-stream dry   watercourse

Wind' ich ruhig   mich hinab;
wind I   quietly me   downwards

Jeder Strom wird's Meer gewinnen,
each stream will the sea   gain

Jedes Leiden auch sein Grab.
each sorrow also its grave

Along the dry bed of a mountain stream I wind my quiet way; every stream will reach the sea, all suffering its grave.

x. *Rast*
   rest

x. Resting place

Nun merk   ich erst, wie müd ich bin,
now perceive I   only how tired I   am

Da ich zur   Ruh mich   lege;
as I   to the sleep myself lie down

Only now as I lie down to sleep, do I see how tired I am. Wandering along inhospitable paths kept me awake.

Das Wandern   hielt mich munter hin
the wandering kept me   awake –

Auf unwirtbarem Wege.
on   inhospitable paths

Die Füsse frugen nicht nach   Rast,
the feet   asked not   about rest

My feet asked no rest, it was too cold to stand; my back felt no burden – for the storm helped to drive me on.

Es war zu kalt zum   Stehen;
it was too cold for (the) standing

Der Rücken fühlte keine Last,
the back   felt   no   burden

Der Sturm half   fort   mich wehen.
the storm helped onward me   to blow

In eines Köhlers   engem Haus
in of a charcoal-burner narrow house

In a charcoal-burner's narrow hut I have found shelter. But my limbs with their aching bruises cannot rest.

Hab Obdach ich gefunden;
have shelter I   found

Doch meine Glieder ruhn nicht aus,
yet   my   limbs rest not –

So brennen ihre Wunden.
so burn   their bruises

Auch du, mein Herz, in Kampf und Sturm
too   you my   heart in struggle and storm

You too, my heart, so savage and bold midst struggle and storm, can feel in its stillness the serpent stir with its hot sting!

So wild und so verwegen,
so wild and so bold

Fühlst in der Still'   erst deinen Wurm
feel   in the stillness only your   serpent

Mit heissem Stich sich   regen!
with hot   sting itself stir

xi. *Frühlingstraum*
    spring's-dream

xi. Dream of spring

Ich träumte von bunten   Blumen,
I   dreamt of   gay-coloured flowers

I dreamt of brightly coloured flowers as they blossom in May; I dreamt of green meadows and the merry call of birds.

So   wie sie wohl   blühen im   Mai;
such as   they perhaps blossom in the May

Ich träumte von grünen Wiesen,
I   dreamt of green meadows

Von lustigem Vogelgeschrei.
of   merry   bird-clamour

Und als die Hähne krähten,
and as the cocks crowed

Da   ward mein Auge wach;
then was my eye   awake

Da   war es kalt und finster,
then was it cold and dark

Es schrieen   die Raben vom   Dach.
(it) screamed the ravens from the roof

Doch an den Fensterscheiben,
but   on the window-panes

Wer malte   die Blätter da?
who painted the leaves there

Ihr lacht wohl   über den Träumer,
you laugh perhaps over the dreamer

Der Blumen im   Winter sah?
who flowers in the winter saw

Ich träumte von Lieb um Liebe,
I   dreamt of love for love

Von einer schönen   Maid,
of   one beautiful girl

Von Herzen und von Küssen,
of   hearts and of kisses

Von Wonne und Seligkeit.
of   joy   and bliss.

Und als die Hähne krähten,
and as the cocks crowed

Da   ward mein Herze wach;
then was my heart awake

Nun sitz ich hier alleine
now sit I   here alone

Und denke dem Traume nach.
and think the dream about

Die Augen schliess ich wieder,
the eyes   shut   I again

Noch schlägt das Herz so warm.
still beats the heart so warmly

And as the cocks crowed I opened
my eyes; it was cold and dark and
ravens were croaking on the roof.

But who painted those leaves on
the window-pane? Do you laugh at
the dreamer who sees flowers in
winter?

I dreamt of love for love, of a
beautiful girl; of kisses and hearts,
and of joy and ecstasy.

And as the cocks crowed my heart
awoke. Now I sit here alone and
think on my dream.

Again I close my eyes, and still my
heart throbs warm. Leaves on the
window, when will you become
green? When shall I hold my
sweetheart in my arms?

Wann grünt   ihr Blätter am   Fenster?
when become green you leaves at the window

Wann halt ich mein Liebchen   im   Arm?
when hold I   my   sweetheart in the arm

    xii. Einsamkeit   xii. Solitude
      solitude

Wie eine trübe Wolke   As a dark cloud drifts in clear
like a   dark cloud   skies, when a faint breeze blows
                                                       through the tops of the firs –
Durch   heitre Lüfte geht,
through clear air(s) goes

Wenn in der   Tanne Wipfel
when in of the fir   (tree-)top

Ein mattes Lüftchen weht:
a   faint breeze blows

So zieh ich meine Strasse   so do I go on my way with
so go I   my   road   dragging steps, ungreeted and
                                                       alone through bright and joyful
Dahin mit trägem Fuss,   life.
thither with sluggish foot

Durch   helles, frohes Leben
through bright joyous life

Einsam und ohne   Gruss.
lonely and without greeting

Ach, dass die Luft so ruhig!   Alas, the air is so calm, and the
ah   that the air   so calm   world so full of light! When storms
                                                       were raging, I was not so wretched
Ach, dass die Welt so licht!   as this.
ah   that the world so light

Als   noch die Stürme tobten,
when still the storms raged

War ich so elend   nicht.
was I   so wretched not

    xiii. Die Post   xiii. The mail-coach
      the post

Von der Strasse   her ein Posthorn klingt.   A posthorn sounds from the
from the highway here a   posthorn sounds   highway. What is it that makes
                                                       you leap so suddenly, my heart?
Was hat es, dass es so hoch aufspringt,
what has it   that it so high leaps up

Mein Herz?
my   heart

Die Post   bringt keinen Brief für dich.
the mail-coach brings no   letter for you

Was drängst du denn so wunderlich,
what is urging you then so strangely

Mein Herz?
my   heart

Nun ja, die Post   kommt aus der Stadt,
well yes the mail-coach comes from the town

Wo   ich ein liebes Liebchen   hatt',
where I   a   dear sweetheart had

Mein Herz?
my   heart

Willst wohl   einmal hinüberseh'n
will   perhaps once   look over there

Und fragen, wie es dort   mag geh'n,
and ask   how it there may go

Mein Herz?
my   heart

The mail-coach brings you no
letter. Then why do you throb so
strangely, my heart?

Well yes, the mail-coach comes
from the town where I once had a
sweetheart so dear, my heart!

Do you want perhaps once to look
back, and ask how everything is,
back there, my heart?

    xiv. Der greise Kopf
      the hoary head

xiv. The hoary head

Der Reif   hat einen weissen Schein
the hoar-frost has a   white   sheen

Mir übers   Haar gestreuet;
to me over the hair scattered

Da glaubt' ich schon ein Greis   zu sein
then believed I   already an old man to be

Und hab mich   sehr gefreuet.
and have myself very been glad

The hoar-frost has scattered a
shining white on my hair; I
thought I had already grown old –
and rejoiced.

Doch bald ist er hinweggetaut,
but soon is he thawed away

Hab wieder schwarze Haare,
have again black   hairs

Dass mir's   vor meiner Jugend graut –
that to me it at my   youth shudders

Wie weit noch bis   zur   Bahre!
how far still (right) to the bier

But soon it had thawed, and my
hair was again black. And I
shudder at my youth – how far it is
yet to the grave!

Von Abendrot zum Morgenlicht
from sunset   to the morning-light

Ward   mancher Kopf zum Greise.
became many a head to the old man

Between dusk and dawn many a
head has turned white, and old.
Who would believe – that mine
has not on this whole journey.

Wer glaubt's?   und meiner ward   es nicht
who believes it and mine   became it not

Auf dieser ganzen Reise.
on this   whole journey

xv. Die Krähe
the crow

xv. The crow

Eine Krähe war mit   mir
a   crow was with me

Aus   der Stadt gezogen,
from the town set forth

A crow was with me as I left the
town. Still it flies over my head to
and fro.

Ist bis heute für und für
is till today – for ever –

Um   mein Haupt geflogen.
about my   head   flown

Krähe, wunderliches Tier,
crow   strange   creature

Crow, you strange creature, will
you not forsake me? Do you mean
to seize my body soon as your
prey?

Willst mich nicht verlassen?
will   me   not   forsake

Meinst wohl   bald als Beute hier
think   perhaps soon as prey here

Meinen Leib zu fassen?
my   body to seize

Nun, es wird nicht weit mehr gehn
well it is   not far more to go

Well, now it is not far for me to go
on my staff. Let constancy be with
me now, O crow, to the grave!

An dem Wanderstabe.
on my staff

Krähe, lass mich endlich sehn
crow   let me   at last see

Treue   bis   zum   Grabe.
constancy right to the grave

xvi. Letzte Hoffnung
last   hope

xvi. Last hope

Hie und da   ist an den Bäumen
here and there is on the trees

Manches bunte   Blatt zu sehn,
some   gay-coloured leaf to see

Here and there on the trees a
bright leaf may still be seen. I
often stand beneath the trees, lost
in thought.

Und ich bleibe   vor   den Bäumen
and I   remain before the trees

Oftmals in Gedanken stehn.
often   in thoughts to stand

Schaue nach dem einen Blatte,
look   at   the one leaf

Hänge meine Hoffnung dran;
hang my   hope   on it

Spielt der Wind mit   meinem Blatte,
plays the wind with my   leaf

Zittr'   ich, was ich zittern   kann.
tremble I   how I   tremble can

Ach, und fällt das Blatt zu Boden,
ah   and falls the leaf to ground

Fällt mit   ihm die Hoffnung ab,
falls with him the hope   off

Fall ich selber   mit   zu Boden,
fall I   myself with (it) to ground

Wein' auf meiner Hoffnung Grab.
weep on of my hope   grave

I gaze at a single leaf, and on it
hang my hopes. If the wind plays
with my leaf, I tremble in my
whole being.

And if the leaf falls to the ground,
ah, then my hope falls with it; and
I myself fall to the ground, and
weep on the grave of my hope.

    xvii. Im   Dorfe
      in the village

Es bellen die Hunde, es rasseln die Ketten;
(it) barks the dogs   (it) clank the chains

Es schlafen die Menschen in ihren Betten,
(it) sleep   the people   in their beds

Träumen sie manches,   was sie nicht haben,
dream   they many things what they not   have

Tun sich   im   Guten und Argen erlaben;
—   themselves in the good and bad   give comfort to

Und morgen   früh   ist alles zerflossen,
and tomorrow morning is all   melted away

Je   nun, sie haben ihr Teil genossen,
well now they have their share enjoyed

xvii. In the village

Dogs are barking, and rattling
their chains, and people are
sleeping in their beds. They dream
many things they do not have,
finding pleasure in the good and
the bad.

And next day all has vanished, but
they have enjoyed their share, and
hope to find on their pillows all
that still remains.

Und hoffen, was sie noch übrig   liessen,
and hope   what they still remaining left

Doch wieder zu finden auf ihren Kissen.
yet   again to find   on their pillows

Bellt mich nur fort, ihr wachen   Hunde,
bark me   just away you watchful dogs

Lasst mich nicht ruhn in der Schlummerstunde!
let   me not rest in the slumber-hour

Ich bin zu   Ende mit   allen Träumen,
I   am at (an) end with all   dreams

Was will   ich unter   den Schläfern säumen?
what want I   among the sleepers to linger

Send me away with your barking, you watch-dogs, give me no rest in the hours of sleep! I am done with all dreaming, so why should I linger amongst those who are slumbering still?

xviii. Der stürmische Morgen
      the stormy   morning

xviii. The stormy morning

Wie hat der Sturm zerrissen
how has the storm rent

How the storm has rent the sky's grey robe! Tattered clouds flutter in weary strife.

Des   Himmels graues Kleid!
of the sky   grey dress

Die Wolkenfetzen flattern
the cloud-tatters flutter

Umher   in mattem Streit.
all round in spent   strife

Und rote Feuerflammen
and red fire-flames

Around them it blazes a fiery red. I call this a morning just right for my mind!

Zieh'n zwischen ihnen hin:
move between them along

Das nenn' ich einen Morgen
that call I a   morning

So recht nach meinem Sinn!
so right after my   mind

Mein Herz sieht an dem Himmel
my   heart sees in the sky

My heart sees its own image painted there in the sky. It is nothing but winter – winter, cold and savage!

Gemalt sein eig'nes Bild –
painted its own   image

Es ist nichts   als der Winter,
it is nothing but the winter

Der Winter kalt und wild!
the winter cold and savage

xix. Täuschung
delusion

Ein Licht tanzt freundlich   vor   mir her,
a   light dances in a friendly way before me hither

Ich folg' ihm nach die   Kreuz und Quer;
I   follow it   after (the) – criss-cross –

Ich folg' ihm gern, und seh's ihm an,
I   follow it   readily and see it (of it) –

Dass es verlockt den Wandersmann.
that it entices the traveller

Ach! wer wie ich so elend   ist,
ah   who as I   so wretched is

Gibt gern sich   hin der   bunten List,
gives readily (himself) in to the fine   cunning

Die hinter Eis und Nacht und Graus
that behind ice and night and terror

Ihm   weist ein helles, warmes Haus.
to him shows a   bright warm house

Und eine Liebe Seele drin:
and a   dear soul within

Nur Täuschung ist für mich Gewinn!
only delusion   is for me gain

xix. Delusion

A friendly light dances before me, I follow it hither and thither. I follow it gladly, although I can see that it lures me from my way.

Oh, anyone who is as wretched as I, is glad to give in to such dazzling guile, that shows beyond the ice, the darkness and terror, a warm, bright house, and a dear one within – but all I have gained is delusion!

xx. Der Wegweiser
the sign-post

Was vermeid' ich denn die Wege,
why avoid   I   then the ways

Wo   die andern Wandrer gehn,
where the other   wanderers go

Suche mir   versteckte Stege
seek to me hidden   footpaths

Durch verschneite Felsenhöhn?
through snow-covered rocky-heights

Habe ja   doch   nichts begangen,
have certainly however nothing done

Dass ich Menschen sollte   scheu'n,
that I people   should shun

xx. The sign-post

Why do I avoid the ways that other wanderers go, and seek hidden paths on high, snowy rocks?

No wrongs have I done, that I should shun mankind, so what is this foolish yearning that drives me into desert wastes?

Welch ein törichtes Verlangen
what a   foolish longing

Treibt mich in   die Wüsteneien?
drives me   into the deserts

Weiser   stehen auf den Strassen,
signposts stand in the roads

Signposts stand by the roadside pointing towards the towns, but senselessly I wander; unresting, but seeking rest.

Weisen auf die Städte zu,
point   to the towns (to)

Und ich wandre sonder   Massen,
and I   wander without measure

Ohne   Ruh', und suche Ruh'.
without rest   and seek rest

Einen Weiser   seh' ich stehen
a   signpost see I   standing

I see a signpost before me, steady before my gaze – the road that I must travel, on which no one ever returned.

Unverrückt vor   meinem Blick;
steady   before my   glance

Eine Strasse muss ich gehen,
a   road   must I go

Die noch keiner ging zurück.
that yet   no one went back

xxi. Das Wirtshaus
the inn

xxi. The inn

Auf   einen Totenacker   hat mich mein Weg gebracht;
towards a   burial-ground has me   my   way led

My way led me to a graveyard. Here, I thought, I can spend the night. You burial wreaths could be inn-signs, that ask tired wayfarers into the inn.

Allhier will ich einkehren, hab' ich bei mir   gedacht.
here will I   turn in   have I   to myself thought

Ihr grünen Totenkränze   könnt wohl die Zeichen sein,
you green funeral wreaths could well the signs   be

Die müde Wand'rer laden ins   kühle Wirtshaus ein.
that weary wanderers invite into the cool inn   –

Sind denn in diesem Hause die Kammern all besetzt?
are then in this   house the chambers all occupied

Are all the rooms here already taken? I am weary, and grievously bruised. O cruel inn, do you then turn me away? So trusty staff, we must now wander on!

Bin matt zum Niedersinken, bin tödlich   schwer
am faint to the sinking down am mortally gravely
  verletzt.
  hurt

O unbarmherz'ge Schenke, doch weisest du mich ab?
O unmerciful   inn   yet send you me away

Nun weiter   denn, nur weiter,   mein treuer
just on and on then just on and on my   true
   Wanderstab!
   staff

xxii. Mut
   courage

Fliegt der Schnee mir   ins   Gesicht,
flies the snow to me into the face

Schüttl' ich ihn herunter.
shake off I   him down

Wenn mein Herz im   Busen spricht,
when my   heart in the breast speaks

Sing ich hell   und munter;
sing I   brightly and merrily

Höre nicht, was es mir   sagt,
hear not   what it to me says

Habe keine Ohren,
have no   ears

Fühle nicht, was es mir   klagt,
feel   not   what it to me laments

Klagen   ist für Toren.
lamenting is for fools

Lustig in   die Welt hinein
gaily into the world (into)

Gegen   Wind und Wetter!
against wind and weather

Will kein Gott auf Erden sein,
will no   god on earth be

Sind wir selber   Götter!
are we ourselves gods

xxiii. Die Nebensonnen
   the mock-suns

Drei Sonnen sah ich am   Himmel steh'n,
three suns   saw I   in the sky   (standing)

Hab' lang und fest   sie   angeseh'n;
have long and steadily them looked at

xxii. Courage

When the snow flies in my face I shake it off. When my heart cries out within, I gaily sing.

Close your ears to what the heart is saying! Do not feel its laments – for only fools lament.

Stride gaily into the world against wind and weather! If there is no God on earth, we ourselves are gods!

xxiii. Phantom suns

I saw three suns in the sky, and stared at them steadily and long. And they stayed so still, as though they would not leave me.

Und sie   auch standen da   so stier,
and they also stood   there so fixedly

Als wollten sie   nicht weg   von mir.
as wanted they not   away from me

Ach, meine Sonnen seid ihr nicht!
ah   my   suns   are you not

But you are not my suns – look
others in the face! Not long ago I
too had three; the two best of
them have gone – I'd be better in
the dark, if the third would but
follow!

Schaut ander'n doch ins   Angesicht!
look   others just in the face

Ja, neulich hatt' ich auch wohl   drei;
yes recently had I   also indeed three

Nun sind hinab die besten zwei.
now are down the best   two

Ging nur die dritt' erst   hinterdrein!
went –   the third only after

Im   Dunkeln wird mir   wohler sein.
in the dark   will to me better be

xxiv. Der Leiermann
the organ-grinder

xxiv. The organ-grinder

Drüben   hinterm   Dorfe steht   ein Leiermann,
over there behind the village stands an organ-grinder

There beyond the village an
organ-grinder stands, and with
numb fingers he is grinding, as
best he can. He stumbles barefoot
to and fro on the ice, and always
his little plate stays empty.

Und mit   starren Fingern dreht er, was   er kann.
and with numb fingers turns he what he can

Barfuss auf dem Eise wankt er hin   und her,
barefoot on the ice staggers he this way and that

Und sein kleiner Teller bleibt   ihm   immer leer.
and his little   plate remains to him always empty

Keiner mag ihn hören, keiner sieht ihn an,
no one wants him to hear no one looks him at

No one wants to listen, and no
one looks at him, and dogs snarl
around the old man. He lets it all
go by him, just as it will, and the
organ he turns is never still.

Und die Hunde knurren um   den alten Mann.
and the dogs snarl   round the old   man

Und er lässt es gehen, alles wie es will,
and he lets it go   all   as it will

Dreht, und seine Leier steht   ihm   nimmer still.
turns and his   organ stands to him never   still

Wunderlicher Alter,   soll ich mit dir geh'n?
strange   old man shall I   with you go

Strange old man, shall I go with
you? Will you grind your organ to
my songs?

Willst du   meinen Liedern deine Leier   dreh'n?
will   you my   songs your organ turn

73. DIE STERNE
THE STARS

Karl Gottfried von Leitner

Wie blitzen die Sterne so hell   durch   die Nacht!
how sparkle the stars so brightly through the night

Bin oft   schon   darüber vom   Schlummer erwacht.
am often already over it from the slumber   awakened

Doch schelt'   ich die lichten Gebilde d'rum nicht,
but reproach I   the light   forms   for it not

Sie üben   im   Stillen   manch' heilsame Pflicht.
they practise in the stillness many a healing function

Sie wallen hoch oben   in Engelgestalt,
they float   high above in angel-form

Sie leuchten dem   Pilger   durch   Heiden und Wald.
they shine   to the pilgrim through heaths and wood

Sie schweben als Boten   der   Liebe umher,
they hover   as messengers of the love all around

Und tragen oft   Küsse weit über das Meer.
and bring often kisses far over the sea

Sie blicken dem Dulder recht mild   ins   Gesicht,
they look   the sufferer very mildly into the face

Und säumen die Tränen mit   silbernem Licht,
and edge   the tears   with silver   light

Und weisen von Gräbern gar tröstlich   und hold
and point from graves   very comfortingly and kindly

Uns hinter   das Blaue mit Fingern von Gold.
to us behind the blue with fingers of gold

So sei denn gesegnet, du   strahlige Schar!
so be then blessed you gleaming multitude

Und leuchte mir lange   noch freundlich und klar.
and light   me a long time yet kindly   and clearly

Und wenn ich einst   liebe, seid hold   dem   Verein,
and when I   one day love be gracious to the union

Und euer Geflimmer lasst Segen   uns   sein.
and your glimmering let   blessing to us be

How brightly the stars shine in the night! Often they awaken me from sleep. But I do not reproach them for their radiance, to many a one in the stillness they bring stillness.

High above us they float like angels; lighting pilgrims over heath and through woods, and they hover about us, messengers of love, bearing kisses far over the sea.

They shine gently down on the sufferer's face, edging his tears in a silvery light. And they shine upon graves so comforting and kindly, and to us from the blue with fingers of gold.

So I bless your gleaming multitude – may your light shine ever kindly on me! And when the day comes when I find love, be then gracious to our union, and in your shining let us be blessed.

SCHWANENGESANG (74–87)

SWANSONG

74. LIEBESBOTSCHAFT
LOVE'S-MESSAGE

74. LOVE'S MESSAGE

Ludwig Rellstab

Rauschendes Bächlein,   so silbern und hell,
rushing   little brook so silver and clear

Eilst   zur   Geliebten so munter und schnell?
hurry (you) to the beloved so merrily and fast

Ach, trautes Bächlein,   mein Bote   sei du;
ah   dear   little brook my   messenger be you

Bringe die Grüsse   des   Fermen   ihr   zu.
bring the greetings of the distant one to her (to)

Little brook, that rushes so silver and clear, do you go to my love in such merry haste? O dear little brook, be messenger for me – bring my greetings to her from one far away!

All ihre Blumen im   Garten gepflegt,
all her flowers in the garden tended

Die   sie so lieblich   am   Busen trägt,
which she so charmingly at the breast carries

Und ihre Rosen in purpurner Glut,
and her roses in crimson glow

Bächlein,   erquicke mit   kühlender Flut.
little brook refresh with cooling   waves

All the flowers she tends in her garden, and wears with such charm at her breast – little brook, refresh her roses of glowing crimson with your cooling waves.

Wenn sie am   Ufer, in Träume versenkt,
when she on the bank in dreams absorbed

Meiner gedenkend, das Köpfchen   hängt,
of me thinking   the little head hangs

Tröste   die Süsse   mit freundlichem Blick,
comfort the sweet one with kindly   glance

Denn der Geliebte kehrt   bald zurück.
for   the beloved comes soon back

When she on your bank is absorbed in dreams, her head droops as she thinks of me – comfort my sweetheart with a kindly glance, for her beloved will soon return.

Neigt sich   die Sonne mit rötlichem Schein,
lowers (herself) the sun   with reddish shine

Wiege   das Liebchen in Schlummer ein,
rock asleep the sweetheart into slumber   –

Rausche sie murmelnd in süsse Ruh,
rustle   her murmuring into sweet sleep

Flüstre ihr   Träume der   Liebe zu.
whisper to her dreams of the love (to)

As the sun is sinking with a reddening glow, lull my sweetheart till she sleeps. Rustle and murmur her into sweet slumber, and whisper her dreams of love.

75. *KRIEGERS AHNUNG* WARRIOR'S FOREBODING

75. WARRIOR'S FOREBODING

Ludwig Rellstab

In tiefer Ruh liegt um mich her
in deep sleep lies round me about

Der Waffenbrüder Kreis;
of the weapon-brothers circle

Mir ist das Herz so bang und schwer,
to me is the heart so uneasy and heavy

Von Sehnsucht mir so heiss.
from longing to me so burning

In heavy sleep my comrades-in-arms lie round about me. My heart is leaden and uneasy, and burns with such longing.

Wie hab ich oft so süss geträumt
how have I often so sweetly dreamt

An ihrem Busen warm!
on her breast warm

Wie freundlich schien des Herdes Glut,
how friendly seemed of the hearth glow

Lag sie in meinem Arm!
lay she in my arm

How often were my dreams so sweet on her warm breast! How friendly seemed the glowing hearth as she lay in my arms!

Hier, wo der Flammen düstrer Schein
here where of the flames dark light

Ach, nur auf Waffen spielt,
ah only on weapons plays

Hier fühlt die Brust sich ganz allein,
here feels the breast (herself) quite alone

Der Wehmut Träne quillt.
of the melancholy tear wells up

Here where the flames gleam dismally, and play only on weapons, my heart feels so alone, and melancholy tears well up.

Herz! dass der Trost dich nicht verlässt,
heart that the consolation you not forsakes

Es ruft noch manche Schlacht.
(it) calls still some battle

Bald ruh ich wohl und schlafe fest,
soon rest I well and sleep fast

Herzliebste, gute Nacht!
dearest heart good-night

O heart, may solace not forsake you! Battles still are calling. Soon will I sleep, dearest heart, good-night!

76. FRÜHLINGSSEHNSUCHT
SPRING-LONGING

76. SPRING LONGING

Ludwig Rellstab

Säuselnde   Lüfte   wehend so mild,
murmuring breezes blowing so softly

Blumiger Düfte atmend   erfüllt!
of flowery scents breathing filled

Murmuring breezes, so softly blowing, breathing your fill of flowery scents – how delightful a welcome you whisper to me! What have you done to make my heart throb, and long to follow your airy course? O whither, whither?

Wie haucht ihr mich wonnig   begrüssend an!
how breathe you me   delightfully welcoming on

Wie   habt ihr dem   pochenden Herzen getan?
whatever have you to the throbbing heart   done

Es möchte   euch folgen   auf luftiger Bahn,
it would like you to follow on airy   course

Wohin? Wohin?
whither whither

Bächlein,   so munter rauschend zumal,
little brooks so merrily rushing   specially

Little brooks, you eagerly rush your silvery way down into the valley; shimmering ripples hasten there, reflecting meadow and sky in the deeps. O yearning desire, why do you draw me down, and down?

Wollen hinunter silbern ins   Tal.
want   down   silvery into the valley

Die schwebende Welle, dort eilt   sie dahin!
the hovering   ripple there hurries she thither

Tief   spiegeln sich   Fluren   und Himmel
deeply reflect (themselves) meadows and sky
   darin.
   therein

Was ziehst du mich, sehnend verlangender Sinn,
why draw you me   longing desiring   feeling

Hinab? Hinab?
down   down

Grüssender Sonne spielendes Gold,
of greeting sun   playing   gold

Gold of playing sunlight, you graciously bring a promise of bliss in your greeting. How your joyous welcoming image delights me! It softly smiles from deep blue skies, and my eyes are filled with tears. Why, O why?

Hoffende Wonne bringest du hold!
expectant joy   bring   you graciously

Wie labt   mich dein selig   begrüssendes Bild!
how delights me   your blessed welcoming image

Es lächelt am   tiefblauen Himmel so mild
it smiles in the deep-blue sky   so mildly

Und hat mir   das Auge mit   Tränen gefüllt!
and has to me the eye   with tears   filled

Warum? Warum?
why   why

Grünend umkränzet Wälder und Höh,
greening wreathes   woods and heights

Schimmernd erglänzet   Blütenschnee!
shimmering shines forth blossom-snow

So dränget   sich   alles   zum bräutlichen
so presses forward (itself) everything to the bridal
   Licht;
   light

Es schwellen die Keime, die Knospe bricht;
(it) swell   the seeds   the bud   breaks

Sie haben gefunden, was ihnen   gebricht:
they have found   what to them lacks

Und du? Und du?
and you and you

Woods and heights are crowned with green; lustrous blossoms shine radiant as snow. All things crowd toward the bridal light; the seeds swell, and buds break! They have found their fulfilment – and you? and you?

Rastloses Sehnen! Wünschendes Herz,
restless yearning desiring   heart

Immer nur Tränen, Klage und Schmerz?
always only tears   lament and grief

Auch ich bin mir   schwellender Triebe   bewusst!
too   I   am to me of rising   impulses conscious of

Wer stillet   mir endlich die drängende Lust?
who quenches to me finally the pressing desire

Nur du befreist den Lenz in der Brust,
only you set free the spring in the breast

Nur du! nur du!
only you only you

Restless yearning, a longing heart, nothing but tears, lamenting and grief? I, too, can feel upsurging life – who will ever still this turbulent desire? Only you can set free the spring in my heart – only you, only you!

77. STÄNDCHEN
SERENADE

Ludwig Rellstab

Leise flehen meine Lieder
softly entreat my   songs

Durch   die Nacht zu dir;
through the night to you

77. SERENADE

Softly through the night my songs entreat you; come down to me, my love, in the still glade!

In   den stillen Hain hernieder,
into the still   glade down

Liebchen,   komm zu mir!
sweetheart come to me

Flüsternd   schlanke Wipfel   rauschen   Slender tree-tops rustle and
whispering slender (tree-) tops rustle   whisper in the moonlight. O fair
                                                      one, have no fear of those who
In des   Mondes Licht;   might listen and betray!
in of the moon   light

Des   Verräters feindlich Lauschen
of the betrayer hostile   listening

Fürchte, Holde,   nicht.
fear   gracious one not

Hörst die Nachtigallen schlagen?   Do you hear the singing of the
hear the nightingales sing   nightingales? Ah, how they too
                                                      implore you, with the sound of
Ach! sie flehen   dich,   their sweet lament.
ah   they implore you

Mit der   Töne süssen Klagen
with of the notes sweet lament

Flehen   sie für mich.
implore they for me

Sie verstehn   des   Busens Sehnen,   They know the yearnings of the
they understand of the breast yearning   soul, the pain of love, and touch
                                                      each gentle heart with their silvery
Kennen Liebesschmerz,   tones.
know   love's-pain

Rühren mit   den Silbertönen
touch   with the silver tones

Jedes weiche Herz.
every soft   heart

Lass auch dir   die Brust bewegen,   Then let your heart be stirred, my
let   also to you the breast stir   love, O hear me! Trembling, I
                                                      await you – come give me joy!
Liebchen,   höre mich!
sweetheart hear me

Bebend   harr'ich dir entgegen!
trembling await I you –

Komm beglücke   mich!
come   make happy me

78. *AUFENTHALT*
SOJOURN

78. SOJOURN

Ludwig Rellstab

Rauschender Strom,   brausender Wald,
rushing   (great) river blustering forest

Starrender Fels, mein Aufenthalt.
rigid   rock my   abode

Wie sich   die Welle an Welle reiht,
as   (herself) the wave on wave succeeds

Fliessen die Tränen mir   ewig   erneut.
flow   the tears   to me eternally renewed

Rushing river, blustering forest, starkest crags – my only abode! My tears flow in an endless stream, as wave follows wave unceasingly.

Hoch in den Kronen   wogend sich's   regt,
high in the (tree-) tops heaving (itself) it stirs

So unaufhörlich mein Herze schlägt.
so incessantly my   heart beats

Und wie des   Felsen uraltes Erz,
and as of the rock   ancient ore

Ewig   derselbe bleibet   mein Schmerz.
eternally the same remains my   grief

Like the restless stirring high in the trees, my heart beats incessantly. Unchanging as the rock's ancient ore, eternal is my grief.

79. *IN DER FERNE*
IN THE DISTANCE

79. FROM AFAR

Ludwig Rellstab

Wehe dem   Fliehenden, Welt hinaus ziehenden!
woe to the fugitive-one world forth   going into-one

Fremde   durchmessenden, Heimat   vergessenden,
strange places traversing-one   homeland forgetting-one

Mutterhaus   hassenden, Freunde verlassenden
mother-house hating-one friends leaving-one

Folget kein Segen,   ach! auf ihren Wegen nach!
follows no   blessing alas on their ways   after

Woe to the fugitive, driven out into the world, traversing strange places, forgetting his homeland; shunning his birthplace and forsaking his friends – no blessing will follow the traveller on such ways!

Herze, das sehnende,   Auge, das tränende,
heart the longing-one eye   the weeping-one

Sehnsucht, nie   endende,   heimwärts sich
longing   never ending-one homewards herself
    wendende!
    turning-one

Heart with its yearning, eyes filled with tears, endless longing that turns towards home; O restless heart, O dying lament, O evening-star gleaming, hopelessly sinking.

Busen, der wallende,   Klage, verhallende,
bosom the agitated-one lament dying away-one

Abendstern, blinkender, hoffnunglos sinkender!
evening-star gleaming   hopelessly sinking

Lüfte, ihr säuslnden,   Wellen, sanft kräuselnden,
breezes you rustling-ones ripples softly curling-ones

Sonnenstrahl, eilender,   nirgend verweilender:
sunbeam   hastening-one nowhere tarrying-one

Die mir   mit Schmerze, ach! dies treue Herze brach,
who to me with sorrows   ah   this true heart broke

Grüsst von dem Fliehenden, Welt hinaus ziehenden!
greets from the fugitive-one world forth   going into

Rustling breezes, soft curling ripples, hastening sunbeams that never tarry; take the one who broke my true heart – take to her greetings from the one driven out in the world.

80. ABSCHIED
FAREWELL

Ludwig Rellstab

Ade!   du muntre, du fröhliche Stadt, ade!
farewell you lively   you happy   town farewell

Schon   scharret mein Rösslein   mit lustigem Fuss;
already paws   my little horse with merry   foot

Jetzt nimm noch   den letzten, den scheidenden Gruss.
now take besides the last   the parting   greeting

Du hast mich wohl   niemals noch traurig gesehn,
you have me indeed never yet sad   seen

So kann es auch jetzt nicht beim Abschied geschehn.
so can it also now not at the farewell happen

Ade,   ihr Bäume, ihr Gärten so grün, ade!
farewell you trees   you gardens so green farewell

Nun reit ich am   silbernen Strome entlang,
now ride I   by the silver   river   along

Weit   schallend   ertönet mein Abschiedsgesang;
far off ringing out sounds my   farewell-song

Nie habt ihr ein trauriges Lied gehört,
never have you a   sad   song heard

So wird euch   auch   keines beim Scheiden beschert.
so will to you likewise none at the parting be given

80. FAREWELL

Farewell, you lively, happy town, farewell! My horse already is pawing the ground, so take your last, your final farewell! Never yet have you seen me sad, and will not now as I take my leave.

Farewell, you trees and gardens so green, farewell! As I ride along by the silvery stream, my parting song rings out far and wide. You never have heard me sing a sad song, and I'll not sing one now as I take my leave.

Ade,   ihr freundlichen Mägdlein   dort, ade!
farewell you friendly   young maidens there farewell

Was schaut ihr aus   blumenumduftetem Haus
what look you out of flower-scented   house

Mit schelmischen, lockenden Blicken heraus?
with arch   enticing looks (out)

Wie sonst, so grüss ich und schaue mich um,
as usual so greet I and look me round

Doch nimmer wend ich mein Rösslein   um.
but never turn I my little horse round

Farewell, you friendly maidens there, farewell! Why do you peer from your flower-scented houses so arch and enticing? As always I hail you, and look all around, but never will I turn my little horse back!

Ade,   liebe Sonne, so gehst du zur Ruh, ade!
farewell dear sun   so go   you to the rest farewell

Nun schimmert der   blinkenden Sterne Gold.
now glimmers of the twinkling stars gold.

Wie bin ich euch   Sternlein am   Himmel so
how am I   to you dear stars in the sky   so
   hold;
   kindly disposed

Durchziehn wir die Welt auch weit und breit,
go through we the world even far and wide

Ihr gebt überall   uns das treue   Geleit.
you give everywhere to us the faithful escort

Farewell, dear sun, now go to your rest, farewell! The twinkling stars now glimmer with gold. Dear stars, how I love you, up there in the sky, for you follow us faithfully as we travel the world.

Ade!   du schimmerndes Fensterlein   hell, ade!
farewell you gleaming   little window bright farewell

Du glänzest so traulich   mit dämmerndem Schein,
you gleam so familiarly with growing dusk shine

Und ladest so freundlich ins   Hüttchen   uns ein.
and invite so kindly   into the little cottage us (in)

Vorüber, ach, ritt ich so manches Mal,
past   oh rode I so many a time

Und wär es denn heute zum   letzten Mal?
and were it then today for the last   time

Farewell, you bright, shining window there, farewell! Your gleam is so friendly in the growing dusk, as it asks us into the small abode. How often I rode there in times gone by – is it really the last time today?

Ade,   ihr Sterne, verhüllet euch   grau! Ade!
farewell you stars   veil   yourselves grey farewell

Des Fensterlein   trübes,   verschimmerndes Licht
of the little window melancholy foding away   light

Ersetzt ihr unzähligen Sterne mir   nicht.
replace you innumerable stars (for) me not

Farewell, you stars veil yourselves in grey: farewell! All you stars cannot make up for that sad window's glimmer. Here I cannot linger – I must go on. But what comfort is your company, however true!

Darf ich hier nicht weilen, muss hier vorbei,
may I here not linger must here (pass) by

Was hilft es, folgt ihr mir noch so treu!
what helps it follow you me yet so truly

81. *DER ATLAS*
THE ATLAS

81. ATLAS

Heinrich Heine

Ich unglückselger Atlas! Eine Welt,
I miserable   Atlas a   world

Die ganze Welt der   Schmerzen muss ich tragen.
the whole world of the sorrows   must I bear

Ich trage Unerträgliches,   und brechen
I bear (the) intolerable and to break

Will mir das Herz im   Leibe.
wants to me the heart in the body

I, wretched Atlas, must bear the
world, a whole world of sorrows. I
bear the unbearable, and within
my body my heart would break.

Du stolzes Herz, du hast es ja   gewollt!
you arrogant heart you have it indeed wanted

Du wolltest glücklich sein, unendlich glücklich,
you wanted happy to be infinitely happy

Oder unendlich elend,   stolzes Herz,
or   infinitely wretched arrogant heart

Und jetzo bist du elend!
and now are you wretched

O arrogant heart, this was your
desire! You wanted happiness,
infinite happiness – or infinite
misery; and now, proud heart, you
have misery!

82. *IHR BILD*
HER PICTURE

82. HER PORTRAIT

Heinrich Heine

Ich stand in dunklen Träumen
I stood in dark   dreams

Und starrt' ihr Bildnis an,
and stared her portrait at

Und das geliebte Antlitz
and the loved face

Heimlich zu leben begann.
secretly to live began

In a dark mysterous dream I stood
and gazed at her portrait, and her
beloved face came secretly to life.

Um   ihre Lippen zog   sich
about her lips   stretched itself

Ein Lächeln wunderbar,
a   smile   wonderfully

Und wie von   Wehmutstränen
and as from melancholy-tears

Erglänzte ihr Augenpaar.
shone   her eye-pair

Auch meine Tränen flossen
also my   tears   flowed

Mir   von   den Wangen herab –
to me from the cheeks down

Und ach, ich kann es nicht glauben,
and oh I   can it not believe

Dass ich dich verloren hab!
that I   you lost   have

A wondrous smile played about
her lips, and her eyes glistened as
if with melancholy tears.

And my tears too flowed down my
cheeks. Oh, I cannot believe that I
have lost you!

83. DAS FISCHERMÄDCHEN
THE FISHER-MAIDEN

83. THE FISHER-MAIDEN

Heinrich Heine

Du schönes   Fischermädchen,
you beautiful fisher-maiden

Treibe   den Kahn ans   Land;
urge on the boat to the land

Komm zu mir und setze dich   nieder,
come to me and sit   (yourself) down

Wir kosen   Hand in Hand.
we talk fondly hand in hand

Leg an mein Herz dein Köpfchen
lay on my   heart your little head

Und fürchte   dich   nicht zu sehr;
and be afraid (yourself) not too much

Vertraust du dich   doch sorglos
entrust   you yourself do   carefree

Täglich dem   wilden Meer!
daily   to the wild   ocean

O beautiful fisher-maiden, bring
your small boat to the shore.
Come here to me, and sit with me
lovingly hand in hand.

Lay your dear head upon my
breast; and do not be too afraid:
you who entrust yourself each day
to the sea so free of care!

Mein Herz gleicht ganz dem   Meere,
my   heart is like (just) to the ocean

Hat Sturm und Ebb und Flut,
has storm and ebb and flow

Und manche schöne   Perle
and many a beautiful pearl

In seiner Tiefe ruht.
in its   deeps rests

My heart is just like the ocean, with its storms and ebbs and flows; and in its depths is resting many a beautiful pearl.

84. *DIE STADT*
THE TOWN

84. THE TOWN

Heinrich Heine

Am   fernen Horizonte
on the far   horizon

Erscheint, wie ein Nebelbild,
appears like a mist-apparition

Die Stadt mit ihren Türmen,
the town with her steeples

In Abenddämmrung gehüllt.
in evening-twilight veiled

On the far horizon, like a misty vision, the town appears with its steeples veiled in the twilight.

Ein feuchter Windzug   kräuselt
a   damp   current of air ruffles

Die graue Wasserbahn;
the grey water-course

Mit traurigem Takte   rudert
with sad   measure rows

Der Schiffer in meinem Kahn.
the sailor in my   boat

A damp current of air ruffles the grey stretch of water; with dreary measure the boatman rows my little boat.

Die Sonne hebt sich   noch einmal
the sun   rises (herself) again once

Leuchtend vom   Boden empor,
shining   from the ground upwards

Und zeigt mir   jene Stelle,
and shows to me that place

Wo   ich das Liebste   verlor.
where I   the dearest one lost

From the earth the gleaming sun rises once more, and shows me the place where I lost my dear love.

85. AM MEER
BY THE SEA

Heinrich Heine

Das Meer erglänzte weit hinaus
the sea   sparkled far out

Im   letzten Abendscheine;
in the last   evening-light

Wir sassen am   einsamen Fischerhaus,
we sat   by the solitary fisherman's-house

Wir sassen stumm und alleine.
we sat   silent and alone

Der Nebel stieg, das Wesser schwoll,
the mist rose the water swelled

Die Möwe   flog hin und wieder;
the sea-gull flew to and fro

Aus deinen Augen liebevoll
from your eyes   lovingly

Fielen die Tränen nieder.
fell   the tears   down

Ich sah sie   fallen auf deine Hand
I   saw them fall   on your hand

Und bin aufs   Knie gesunken;
and am upon the knee sunk

Ich hab von deiner weissen Hand
I   have from your white hand

Die Tränen fortgetrunken.
the tears   drunk away

Seit jener Stunde verzehrt   sich   mein Leib,
since that hour   consumes (himself) my   body

Die Seele stirbt vor Sehnen;
the soul dies with longing

Mich hat das unglücksel'ge Weib
me   has the miserable   woman

Vergiftet mit ihren Tränen.
poisoned with her   tears

85. BY THE SEA

The sea was shimmering far out in the last evening light. We sat by the solitary fisherman's hut, silent and alone.

The mist was rising, the waters surged; a sea-gull was flying to and fro. And tears full of love fell from your eyes.

I saw them fall on your hand, and sank to my knees; from your white hand I drank away the tears.

From that hour my body is wasting away, and my soul dies with longing; for she, the miserable woman, has poisoned me with her tears.

86. *DER DOPPELGÄNGER*
THE DOUBLE

Heinrich Heine

Still ist die Nacht, es ruhen die Gassen,
still is the night it sleeps the (narrow) streets

In diesem Hause wohnte mein Schatz;
in this   house lived   my   sweetheart

Sie hat schon   längst   die Stadt verlassen,
she has already long ago the town left

Doch steht   noch das Haus auf demselben Platz.
yet   stands still the house in the same place

Da   steht   auch ein Mensch und starrt in die Höhe,
there stands also a   man   and stares – upwards –

Und ringt   die Hände vor   Schmerzensgewalt;
and wrings the hands from pain's-violence

Mir   graust   es, wenn ich sein Antlitz sehe –
to me shudders it when I   his   face   see

Der Mond zeigt   mir meine eigne Gestalt.
the moon shows me my   own   form

Du Doppelgänger, du   bleicher Geselle!
you double   you pallid   companion

Was äffst   du   nach mein Liebesleid,
why mimic you –   my   love's-suffering

Das mich gequält   auf dieser Stelle
that me   tormented in this place

So manche Nacht, in alter Zeit?
so many a night   in old   times

The night is still, the narrow streets are sleeping. In this house lived my sweetheart who left the town long ago. But the house is still in the same place.

A man stands there, staring up at it, wringing his hands in silent grief; I shudder as I see his face – for the moon reveals my own image.

You counterfeit, pallid companion of mine! Why do you mimic the suffering of love, which tormented me here on many a night, in times gone by?

87. *DIE TAUBENPOST*
THE PIGEON-POST

Johann Gabriel Seidl

Ich hab eine Brieftaub   in meinem Sold,
I   have a   carrier-pigeon in my   pay

Die ist gar ergeben und treu:
she is very loyal   and true

I have a carrier-pigeon in my pay, who is so loyal and true; he never fails to reach his goal, and never flies too far.

Sie nimmt mir   nie   das Ziel zu kurz,
she takes (for me) never the goal too short

Und fliegt auch nie   vorbei.
and flies also never past

Ich sende sie viel   tausendmal
I   send her many thousand times

Auf Kundschaft täglich hinaus,
on look-out   daily   out

Vorbei an manchem lieben Ort,
past – many a dear place

Bis   zu der   Liebsten Haus.
right to of the dearest house

I send him out a thousand times each day, past many a well-loved place to my sweetheart's house.

Dort schaut sie zum Fenster heimlich hinein
there looks she at the window secretly in

Belauscht ihren Blick   und Schritt,
spies out her   glance and step

Gibt   meine Grüsse   scherzend ab
delivers my   greetings playfully up

Und nimmt die ihren mit.
and takes the hers with (her)

Unseen he peeps through the window, and notes each glance and step. Merrily he gives her my greetings, and brings me back hers in return.

Kein Briefchen brauch ich zu schreiben mehr,
no note   need I to write   more

Die Träne selbst geb' ich ihr:
the tear   itself give I   to her

O sie verträgt   sie   sicher   nicht,
O she mis-carries them certainly not

Gar eifrig   dient sie mir.
very zealously serves she me

No longer do I need to write messages, I give him my very tears. He certainly will never lose them, for he serves me with such zeal.

Bei Tag, bei Nacht, im   Wachen, im   Traum,
by day by night   in the waking in the dream

Ihr   gilt   das alles gleich:
to her is worth this all   (the) same

Wann sie nur wandern, wandern kann,
when she just roam   roam   can

Dann ist sie überreich!
then is she over-rich

By day or by night, awake or asleep, it is all one to him. If he is only free to roam, he has his rich reward.

Sie wird   nicht müd', sie wird   nicht matt,
she becomes not tired she becomes not faint

Der Weg ist stets   ihr   neu;
the way is always to her new

He never tires, and is never weary; his way is always new. He needs no enticing, and no reward, and to me he is always true.

Sie braucht nicht Lockung,   braucht nicht Lohn,
she needs   not   enticement needs   not   reward

Die Taub' ist so mir   treu.
the dove   is so to me true

Drum   heg'   ich sie auch so treu an der Brust,
therefore cherish I   her really so truly in the (breast)

And so I cherish him in my heart,
assured of the greatest favours.His
name is longing – do you know
him? – the messenger of fidelity?

Versichert des   schönsten Gewinns;
assured   of the fairest   gain

Sie heisst: die Sehnsucht – kennt ihr sie?
she is called the longing   know you her

Die Botin   treuen Sinns?
the messenger of true meaning

88. DER HIRT   AUF DEM THE SHEPHERD ON   THE FELSEN ROCK

88. THE SHEPHERD ON THE ROCK

Wilhelm Müller

Wenn auf dem höchsten Fels ich steh',
when on the highest rock I   stand

When I stand on the highest rock,
looking down into the deep valley,
I sing – and the echo rises up from
the ravine.

In's   tiefe Tal   herniederseh',
into the deep valley look down

Und singe,
and sing

Ferm   aus   dem tiefen, dunklen Tal
distantly from the deep dark   valley

Schwingt sich   empor   der Widerhall
soars   itself upwards the echo

Der   Klüfte.
of the ravine

Je weiter   meine Stimme dringt,
the further my   voice   penetrates

As my voice carries further, the
clearer it echoes back from below.
My beloved lives so far away, and
I long with such passion for her
there.

Je heller sie mir   widerklingt
the clearer she to me sounds back

Von unten.
from below

Mein Liebchen wohnt so weit von mir,
my   dear one lives so far from me

Drum   sehn' ich mich   so heiss   nach ihr
therefore long I   (myself) so ardently for her

Hinüber.
over there

In tiefem Gram verzehr' ich mich,
in deep grief consume I   myself

I am torn by deep sorrow, my joy
has gone. My hope on earth has
faded – I am so lonely here.

Mir   ist die Freude hin,
to me is the joy   lost

Auf Erden mir   die Hoffnung wich,
on earth to me the hope   weakened

Ich hier so einsam bin.
I   here so lonely am

So sehnend klang   im   Wald das Lied,
so yearning sounded in the wood the song

In the wood my song echoes so
full of yearning in the night; it lifts
all hearts to heaven with its
splendid power. The spring will
come, my friend, the spring – so
now I'll make ready to be gone!

So sehnend klang   es durch   die Nacht,
so yearning sounded it through the night

Die Herzen es zum   Himmel zieht
the hearts it to the heaven draws

Mit wunderbarer Macht.
with wonderful   power

Der Frühling will kommen,
the spring   will come

Der Frühling, meine Freund,
the spring   my   friend

Nun mach' ich mich   fertig
now make I   myself ready

Zum   Wandern   bereit.
for the wandering ready

Robert Schumann
(1810–1856)

1. LIEDERKREIS, Op. 24
SONG-CYCLE

1. SONG CYCLE, Op. 24

Heinrich Heine

i.

Morgens   steh' ich auf und frage:
each morning get I up and ask

Kommt Feinsliebchen heut?
comes sweetheart today

Abends   sink' ich hin und klage:
each evening sink I down and lament

Aus blieb sie auch heut'.
away stayed she also today

In der Nacht mit meinem Kummer
in the night with my   sorrow

Lieg' ich schlaflos, wach;
lie   I sleepless awake

Träumend, wie im   halben Schlummer,
dreaming as in the half   slumber

Wandle ich bei Tag.
wander I by day

i.

Each morning I rise and ask: Will my sweetheart come today? Each evening I sink into bed downcast: today, too, she stayed away.

All night I lie awake, sleepless with sorrow. All day I wander in a dream, half in sleep.

ii.

Es treibt mich hin, es treibt mich her!
it drives me there it drives me here

Noch wenige Stunden, dann soll ich sie schauen,
still a few hours   then shall I her see

Sie selber, die schönste der   schönen Jungfrauen.
she herself the fairest of the fair   maidens

Du armes Herz, was pochst du schwer?
you poor heart what throb you heavily

ii.

I am driven here, driven there – in a few hours I will see her, the fairest of the fair! Poor heart, how violently you throb!

Die Stunden sind aber ein faules Volk!
the hours   are but a   lazy   folk

Schleppen   sich   behaglich   träge,
move slowly themselves comfortably idle

Schleichen gähnend ihre Wege;
creep   yawning their ways

Tummle dich,   du faules Volk!
hurry   yourselves you lazy   folk

Tobende Eile   mich treibend   erfasst!
raging   haste me   urging on seizes

Aber wohl   niemals liebten die Horen;
but   perhaps never   loved the hours

Heimlich im   grausamen Bunde verschworen,
secretly in the cruel   band   forsworn

Spotten sie tückisch der   Liebenden Hast.
mock   they spitefully of the loving ones haste

The hours are such a lazy crowd;
dawdling in their comfortable and
idle way, they creep along
yawning. Hurry yourselves, you
laggards!

I am seized by a raging haste –
perhaps the Hours were never in
love; in cruel and secret
conspiracy, they mock with spite
at men's haste.

iii.

Ich wandelte   unter den Bäumen
I   wandered under the trees

Mit meinem Gram allein,
with my   grief alone

Da   kam das alte Träumen
when came the old dreams

Und schlich mir in's   Herz hinein.
and stole   to me into the heart thither

Wer hat euch dies Wörtlein   gelehret,
who has you this little word taught

Ihr Vöglein   in luftiger Höh'?
you little birds in airy   height

Schweigt still, wenn mein Herz es höret,
is silent still when my   heart it hears

Dann tut   es noch einmal so weh.
then does it more once   so hurt

'Es kam   ein Jungfräulein gegangen,
it happened a   maiden   walked

Die sang es immerfort,
who sang it continually

iii.

I was wandering beneath the trees,
alone with my grief, when my old
dreams came back, and stole right
into my heart.

Who was it taught you that little
word, you birds up high in the air?
Be still, for when I hear it, I feel in
my heart such pain.

'A young girl once came walking
here, and sang it again and again.
And then we little birds caught it,
that beautiful, golden word!'

Da haben wir Vöglein gefangen
then have we little birds caught

Das hübsche, goldene Wort.'
the pretty golden word

Das sollt ihr mir nicht erzählen,
that must you me not tell

Ihr Vöglein wunderschlau,
you (little) birds very crafty

Ihr wollt meinen Kummer mir stehlen,
you want my grief (to me) to steal

Ich aber niemandem trau'.
I but no one trust

That you should not have told me, you crafty little birds. You wish to steal away my grief, but no one do I trust.

iv.

Lieb' Liebchen, leg's Händchen aufs Herze mein;
dear sweetheart lay the little hand on the heart mine

Ach, hörst du, wie's pochet im Kämmerlein?
ah hear you how it throbs in the little room

Da hauset ein Zimmermann schlimm und arg,
there dwells a carpenter bad and wicked

Der zimmert mir einen Totensarg.
who makes to me a coffin

iv.

Lay your hand on my heart, dear love – do you hear how it throbs in its little cell? Inside dwells a carpenter, wicked and bad, who is making a coffin for me.

Es hämmert und klopfet bei Tag und bei Nacht,
it hammers and taps by day and by night

Es hat mich schon längst um den Schlaf gebracht.
it has me – ago long – of the sleep deprived

Ach, sputet euch, Meister Zimmermann,
oh hurry yourself master carpenter

Damit ich balde schlafen kann.
so that I soon sleep can

There's a hammering and tapping night and day, and I can no longer sleep. Make haste, O Master Carpenter, that I soon may rest!

v.

Schöne Wiege meiner Leiden,
lovely cradle of my sorrows

Schönes Grabmal meiner Ruh,
lovely tomb of my rest

Schöne Stadt, wir müssen scheiden –
lovely town we must part

Lebe wohl, ruf' ich dir zu.
fare-well call I you (to)

v.

Sweet cradle of my sorrows, sweet tomb of my repose; sweet city, we must part, and so I call to you farewell!

Lebe wohl, du heil'ge   Schwelle,
fare-well   you hallowed threshold

Wo   da   wandelt Liebchen   traut;
where there wanders sweetheart dear

Lebe wohl, du heil'ge   Stelle,
fare-well   you hallowed place

Wo   ich sie   zuerst geschaut.
where I   her first   saw

Farewell, you hallowed threshold,
where my dear sweetheart passed
by; farewell, you hallowed place,
where I first saw her.

Hätt' ich dich doch   nie   geseh'n,
had I   you indeed never seen

Schöne Herzenskönigin!
fair   heart's-queen

Nimmer wär   es dann geschehen,
never   would be it then happened

Dass ich jetzt so elend   bin.
that I   now so wretched am

Had I but never seen you, fair
queen of my heart! Never would it
have happened then, that I am so
wretched now.

Nie   wollt' ich dein Herze rühren,
never wanted I   your heart to move

Liebe hab' ich nie   erfleht;
love have I   never begged for

Nur ein stilles   Leben führen
only a   peaceful life   to lead

Wollt' ich, wo   dein Odem weht.
wanted I   where your breath blows

I never sought to touch your heart;
I never begged for love. I only
desired to live at peace, breathing
the air you breathe.

Doch du   drängst mich selbst von   hinnen,
but you urge   me   even from here away

Bitt're Worte spricht dein Mund;
bitter words speaks your mouth

Wahnsinn wühlt   in meinen Sinnen,
frenzy   stirs up in my   thoughts

Und mein Herz ist krank und wund.
and my   heart is sick and sore

But even from here you drive me
away, and your lips speak bitter
words. My mind is stirred to a
frenzy, and my heart is sick and
sore.

Und die Glieder matt   und träge,
and the limbs   feeble and inert

Schlepp' ich fort   am   Wanderstab,
drag   I   onward on the wanderer's staff

Bis mein müdes Haupt ich lege
till my   weary head I   lay

Ferne   in ein kühles Grab.
far away in a   cool   grave

My limbs are feeble and spent, as I
drag myself on with my staff, until
I can lay my weary head in a cool
grave far away.

vi.

Warte, warte, wilder Schiffsmann,
wait   wait   wild   boatman

Gleich folg' ich zum Hafen dir;
soon   follow I   to the harbour you

Von zwei Jungfrau'n nehm' ich Abschied,
from two maidens   bid   I   farewell

Von Europa und von ihr.
from Europe and from her

Blutquell,   rinn' aus   meinen Augen,
blood-spring flow from my   eyes

Blutquell,   brich aus   meinem Leib,
blood-spring burst from my   body

Dass ich mit dem heissen Blute
that I   with the hot   blood

Meine Schmerzen niederschreib'.
my   griefs   write down

Ei, mein Lieb, warum just heute
ah, my   dear why   just today

Schaudert dich, mein Blut zu seh'n?
shudder you   my   blood to see

Sahst mich bleich und herzeblutend
saw me   pale and heart-bleeding

Lange Jahre vor   dir steh'n!
long   years before you stand

Kennst du noch das alte Liedchen
know you still the old ditty

Von der Schlang' im   Paradies,
of   the serpent in the Paradise

Die durch   schlimme Apfelgabe
that through evil   apple-gift

Unsern Ahn'   ins   Elend stiess?
our   forefathers in the misery threw

Alles Unheil   brachten Äpfel,
all   calamity brought apples

Eva bracht' damit   den Tod,
Eva brought therewith the death

vi.

Wait, wait, wild boatman, to the
harbour I'll follow you soon; I
must say farewell to my two loves,
to Europe and to her.

May a stream of blood flow from
my eyes, may a stream pour forth
from my body, that I may write in
the scalding blood of all my griefs.

Ah, my love, why do you shudder
today, at the sight of my blood?
You have seen me pale, with a
bleeding heart, for many a long
year.

Do you remember the old tale of
the serpent in Paradise, that
brought our forebears such misery,
through the evil gift of an apple?

All ills have been caused by the gift
of apples: with them Eve brought
death. It was Paris who brought
flames to Troy – now you have
brought both flames and death!

Eris brachte Trojas Flammen
Paris brought Troy's flames

Du bracht'st beides, Flamm' und Tod.
you brought both   flames   and death

vii.

Berg'   und Burgen schau'n herunter
mountains and castles look   down

In   den spiegelhellen   Rhein,
into the mirror-bright Rhine

Und mein Schiffchen segelt munter,
and my   little boat sails   merrily

Rings   umglänzt von Sonnenschein.
around shone   by   sunshine

Ruhig   seh' ich zu dem Spiele
quietly look I   at the playing

Gold'ner Wellen, kraus   bewegt,
of golden waves ruffled moved

Still   erwachen die Gefühle,
softly awaken   the feelings

Die ich tief   im   Busen hegt'.
that I   deep in the bosom cherished

Freundlich   grüssend und verheissend
in a friendly way greeting and promising

Lockt   hinab des   Stromes Pracht;
entices down of the river   splendour

Doch ich kenn' ihn; oben   gleissend,
but   I   know him above glistening

Birgt sein Inn'res Tod   und Nacht.
hides his interior death and night

Oben   Lust, im   Busen Tücken,
above joy   in the breast malice

Strom, du bist der   Liebsten Bild!
river   you are of the beloved image

Die kann auch so freundlich   nicken,
she can   also so in a friendly way nod

Lächelt auch so fromm   und mild.
smiles too   so piously and tenderly

vii.

Mountains and castles peer into the mirror-bright Rhine. My little boat sails merrily along, sunshine dancing all around it.

Quietly I watch the golden waves ripple and play. Softly the feelings I once cherished reawaken in my heart.

The river in its splendour, friendly and welcoming, is tempting in its depths; but I know, that beneath the gleaming surface, its soul hides death and night.

Joyful without, a treacherous heart within; river, you are the very image of my beloved! She, too, gives a friendly nod, and a smile, so tender and pure.

viii.

Anfangs wollt' ich fast   verzagen,
at first   wanted I   almost to despair

Und ich glaubt', ich trüg'   es nie;
and I   believed I   would bear it never

Und ich hab' es doch getragen –
and I   have it yet borne

Aber fragt mich nur nicht: wie?
but   ask   me   only not   how

ix.

Mit Myrten und Rosen, lieblich und hold,
with myrtles and roses   lovely and charming

Mit duft'gen Cypressen und Flittergold
with fragrant cypresses and gold-leaf

Möcht'   ich zieren   dies Buch wie 'nen Totenschrein,
would like I   to adorn this book like a   shrine

Und sargen   meine Lieder hinein.
and put in a coffin my   songs inside

O könnt' ich die Liebe sargen   hinzu!
O could I   the love put in a coffin besides

Auf dem Grabe der   Liebe wächst Blümlein   der
on the grave of the love grows little flower of the
    Ruh',
    peace

Da   blüht   es hervor, da   pflückt man es ab,
there blooms it forth   there plucks one it off

Doch mir   blüht's   nur, wenn ich selber im   Grab.
but   to me blooms it only when I   myself in the grave

Hier sind die Lieder, die einst so wild,
here are the songs that once as furious

Wie ein Lavastrom, der dem   Ätna entquillt,
as a   lava-stream that to the Etna flows forth

Hervorgestürzt aus   dem tiefsten Gemüt,
hurls forth   from the deepest soul

Und rings   viel   blitzende Funken versprüht.
and around many flashing sparks sprays.

viii.

At first I was near despair, and
thought I could never bear it; and
yet I have endured it – but never
ask me how?

ix.

With myrtles and roses, charming
and fair, with gold and sweet
cypress, would I adorn this book
like a shrine, and bury my songs
within.

O, if I could but bury my love
there too! For there on love's
grave grows the flower of peace for
someone to pluck. But for me it
will only bloom when I too am in
my grave.

Here are the songs that once
poured forth from the depths of
my soul, as wildly as Etna's lava
stream hurled forth and showering
fiery sparks.

Nun liegen sie   stumm und totengleich,
now lie   they silent   and death-like

Nun starren sie   kalt und nebelbleich.
now stare   they cold and mist-pale

Doch auf's neu' die alte Glut sie   belebt,
yet   – anew – the old glow them quickens

Wenn der   Liebe Geist einst   über sie   schwebt.
when of the love spirit some day over them hovers

Und es wird   mir   im   Herzen viel   Ahnung
and it becomes to me in the heart   much presentiment
   laut:
   known

Der   Liebe Geist einst   über sie   taut;
of the love spirit one day over them thaws

Einst   kommt dies Buch in   deine Hand,
some day comes this book into your hand

Du süsses Lieb, im   fernen Land.
you sweet love in the far-off land

Dann löst   sich des   Liedes Zauberbann,
then breaks itself of the song   magic-spell

Die blassen Buchstaben schau'n dich an,
the pale   letters   look   you at

Sie schauen dir   flehend   ins   schöne Aug',
they look   to you imploring in the lovely eye

Und flüstern mit Wehmut   und Liebeshauch.
and whisper with melancholy and love's-breath

Now they lie silent as death,
staring cold and pale as the mist;
yet the old fire would quicken, if a
loving soul but hovered near.

And in my heart I already know
that the spirit of love will rekindle
them; for one day this book will
come into your hands, my sweet
love, in that far-off land.

Then the spell that binds my songs
will break, pale letters will look up
at you – will gaze imploringly into
your lovely eyes, whispering with
the melancholy breath of love.

From *MYRTEN*
MYRTLES

from MYRTLES

2. *WIDMUNG*
DEDICATION

2. DEDICATION

Friedrich Rückert

Du meine Seele, du mein Herz,
you my   soul   you my   heart

Du meine Wonn', o du   mein Schmerz,
you my   joy   O you my   sorrow

You, my soul, you, my heart! You,
my joy, O you, my grief! You, the
world in which I live! You, the
heaven to which I aspire! O you,

Du meine Welt, in der   ich lebe,
you my   world in which I   live

Mein Himmel du, darein ich schwebe,
my   heaven you into it I   soar

O du mein Grab, in das   hinab
O you my   grave in which down there

Ich ewig   meinen Kummer gab!
I   for ever my   grief   gave

Du bist die Ruh', du bist der Frieden,
you are the rest   you are the peace

Du bist vom   Himmel mir   beschieden.
you are from the Heaven to me bestowed

Dass du   mich liebst, macht mich mir   wert,
that you me love   makes me   to me worthy

Dein Blick   hat mich vor mir   verklärt,
your glance has me   (to myself) transfigured

Du hebst mich liebend über   mich,
you raise me   lovingly above myself

Mein guter Geist, mein bess'res Ich!
my   good spirit my   better I

the grave where I for ever laid my
sorrow – you are rest, you are
peace; you were bestowed on me
by Heaven. Because you love me,
I find my own worth, I see myself
transfigured by your glance.
Lovingly you raise me up – you,
my good spirit, my better self.

3. FREISINN
SENSE OF FREEDOM

Johann Wolfgang von Goethe
(from the *Westöstlicher Divan*)
          west-east   collection of poems

Lasst mich nur auf meinem Sattel gelten!
let   me just on my   saddle prove worth

Bleibt in euren Hütten, euren Zelten!
stay in your huts   your tents

Und ich reite froh   in   alle Ferne,
and I   ride joyfully into all distance

Über meiner Mütze nur die Sterne.
above my   cap   only the stars

Er hat euch die Gestirne   gesetzt
he has you the constellations placed

Als Leiter zu Land und See,
as guide to land and sea

3. FREEDOM

Let me prove myself in the saddle!
Stay in your huts and tents! And
joyfully I'll ride far, far away, with
only the stars above my head.

The constellations he has placed
to guide you over land and sea; so
you can take delight in them with
a constant upward gaze.

Damit ihr euch   daran   ergötzt,
so that you (yourselves) thereon take delight

Stets   blickend in   die Höh'.
constantly looking into the high place

4. DER NUSSBAUM
THE NUT-TREE

Julius Mosen

Es grünet   ein Nussbaum vor   dem Haus,
(it) grows green a   nut-tree   in front of the house

Duftig,   luftig breitet   er blättrig die Blätter aus.
fragrantly airily spreads he leafily the leaves out

Viel   liebliche Blüten   stehen d'ran;
many lovely   blossoms stand on it

Linde Winde kommen, sie   herzlich   zu umfahn.
soft winds come   them affectionately to embrace

Es flüstern je   zwei zu zwei gepaart,
(it) whisper each two to two paired

Neigend, beugend zierlich zum   Kusse die Häuptchen
bending bowing daintily to the kiss   the (little) heads
   zart.
   delicate

Sie flüstern von einem Mägdlein,   das
they whisper of a   young maiden who

Dächte die Nächte und Tage lang, wusste, ach! selber
thought the nights and days long knew ah   herself
   nicht was.
   not what

Sie flüstern, wer mag verstehn   so gar
they whisper who may understand so very

Leise Weis'? – Flüstern von Bräut'gam   und nächstem Jahr.
soft air   whisper of bridegroom and next   year

Das Mägdlein   horchet, es rauscht im   Baum;
the young maiden listens it rustles in the tree

Sehnend, wähnend sinkt es lächelnd in   Schlaf und
yearning imagining sinks it smiling into sleep and
   Traum.
   dream

A nut-tree unfolds its green before
the house; fragrantly, airily, it
spreads its leaves.

It bears many sweet blossoms; soft
breezes come and caress them.

They whisper together in their
pairs, bowing their delicate heads
to kiss.

They whisper of a young girl, who
thinks night and day – ah, she
herself knows not what!

They whisper – but who can
understand so soft an air? –
whisper of a bridegroom and next
year.

The young girl listens, the tree
softly rustles; yearning, wondering,
she sinks smiling into sleep and
dreams.

4. THE NUT-TREE

5. *JEMAND*
SOMEONE

5. FOR THE SAKE OF
SOMEONE

German translation by W. Gerhard
(There are minor discrepancies in meaning between the
two versions)

Robert Burns
(original text)

Mein Herz ist betrübt   ich sag' es nicht,
my   heart is troubled I   tell it not

Mein Herz ist betrübt   um Jemand;
my   heart is troubled for somebody

Ich könnte wachen   die längste Nacht,
I   could be awake the longest night

Und immer träumen von Jemand.
and always dream of   somebody

O Wonne! von Jemand;
O bliss   of somebody

O Himmel! von Jemand;
O heaven of somebody

Durchstreifen   könnt' ich die ganze Welt,
roam through could I   the whole world

Aus Liebe zu Jemand.
for love for somebody

My heart is sair, I dare na tell,
My heart is sair for somebody;
I could wake a winter night,
For the sake o'somebody!
Oh-hon! for somebody!
Oh-hey! for somebody!
I could range the whole world
    around,
For the sake o'somebody.

Ihr Mächte, die ihr der   Liebe hold,
you powers who you to the love well-disposed

O lächelt freundlich auf Jemand!
O smile kindly   on somebody

Beschirmet ihn, wo   Gefahren droh'n;
protect   him where dangers threaten

Gebt sicher Geleite dem   Jemand!
give safe   escort to the somebody

O Wonne! dem   Jemand;
O bliss   to the somebody

O Himmel! dem Jemand!
O heaven to the somebody

Ich wollt', ich wollte was wollt' ich nicht
I   would I   would what would I   not

Für meinen, meinen Jemand!
for my   my   somebody

Ye powers that smile on virtuous
    love,
O, sweetly smile on somebody!
Fra ilka danger keep him free,
And send me safe my somebody.
Oh-hon! for somebody!
Oh-hey! for somebody!
I wad do – what wad I not?
For the sake o'somebody!

6. *SITZ' ICH ALLEIN*
SIT   I   ALONE

6. I SIT ALONE

Johann Wolfgang von Goethe
(from the *West-östlicher Divan*)
       west-east   collection of poems

Sitz' ich allein,
sit I alone

Wo   kann ich besser sein?
where can I better be

Meinen Wein
my   wine

Trink' ich allein;
drink I alone

Niemand setzt mir Schranken,
no one sets me limits

Ich hab' so meine eignen Gedanken.
I have so my   own thoughts

I sit alone – where could be better?
I drink my wine alone. No one sets
limits about me. I have just my
own thoughts.

7. *TRINKLIED*
DRINKING-SONG

7. DRINKING-SONG

Johann Wolfgang von Goethe
(from the *West-östlicher Divan*)
       west-east   collection of poems

Setze mir   nicht, du Grobian,
set   to me not   you boor

Mir den Krug   so derb   vor   die Nase!
to me the tankard so roughly in front of the nose

Wer mir   Wein bringt, sehe mich freundlich an,
who to me wine brings look me affably   at

Sonst   trübt sich   der Eilfer   im   Glase!
otherwise clouds himself the (special) wine in the glass

Du zierlicher Knabe, du, komm' herein,
you pretty   lad   you come in here

Was stehst du denn da   auf der Schwelle?
why stand you then there on the threshold

Du sollst mir künftig   der Schenke   sein,
you shall to me henceforth the pourer-out be

Jeder Wein ist schmackhaft und helle.
every wine is tasty   and clear

Don't set the tankard so roughly
in front of my nose, you rude
fellow! Whoever brings me my
wine must be civil, or the fine
grape will cloud in the glass.

Pretty lad, come here! Why do you
stand at the door? Hereafter you
shall pour out my wine, for every
wine should be choice and clear.

8. *DIE LOTOSBLUME*
THE LOTUS-FLOWER

Heinrich Heine

Die Lotosblume   ängstigt
the lotus-flower is afraid

Sich   vor der Sonne Pracht,
(herself) of the sun   splendour

Und mit   gesenktem Haupte
and with sunk   head

Erwartet sie träumend die Nacht.
awaits   she dreaming the night

Der Mond, der   ist ihr Buhle,
the moon who is her sweetheart

Er weckt sie mit   seinem Licht,
he wakes her with his   light

Und ihm   entschleiert sie freundlich
and to him unveils   she amiably

Ihr frommes Blumengesicht.
her innocent flower-face

Sie blüht   und glüht und leuchtet,
she blooms and glows and glimmers

Und starret stumm in   die Höh';
and stares silently into the high place

Sie duftet   und weinet und zittert
she sends forth fragrance and weeps and trembles

Vor Liebe und Liebesweh.
with love and love's-pain

8. THE LOTUS
FLOWER

The lotus-flower is afraid of the
sun's great splendour, and with
bowed head she dreamily awaits
the coming of the night.

The moon, who is her sweetheart,
awakens her with his light;
smiling, she unveils for him her
innocent flower face.

She blooms and glows and
glimmers, and silently gazing up,
breathes forth her fragrance, and
weeps and trembles with love, and
love's pain.

9. *TALISMANE*
TALISMAN

Johann Wolfgang von Goethe
(from the *West-östlicher Divan*)
            west-east   collection of poems

Gottes   ist der Orient!
of God is the Orient

Gottes   ist der Occident!
of God is the Occident

9. TALISMAN

The Orient is of God! The
Occident is of God! And North
and the South rest in the peace of
His hands.

Nord- und südliches Gelände
North and South   land

Ruht im   Frieden seiner Hände.
rests in the peace   of His hands

Er der Einzige, Gerechte,
He the only One righteous One

Will   für jedermann das Rechte.
desires for every man the justice

Sei von seinen hundert Namen
be of His   hundred names

Dieser   hochgelobet! Amen.
this one magnified   amen

Gottes   ist der Orient!
of God is the Orient

Gottes   ist der Occident!
of God is the Occident

Mich verwirren will das Irren,
me   to confuse will the erring

Doch du   weisst mich zu entwirren.
but   you know me   to extricate

Wenn ich handle, wenn ich dichte,
when I   act   when I   write poems

Gib du   meinem Weg die Richte!
give you my   way the direction

He, the only One, the righteous
One, desires justice for all
mankind. May He of a hundred
names be magnified! Amen.

The Orient is of God! The
Occident is of God!

My erring sets me in confusion,
but you know how to set me free.
Whatever I may do, whatever
poems I may write, direct me on
my way!

10. *LIED DER   SULEIKA*
SONG OF THE SULEIKA

10. SULEIKA'S SONG

Johann Wolfgang von Goethe
(from the *West-östlicher Divan*)
              west-east   collection of poems

Wie mit innigstem Behagen,
how with most deep enjoyment

Lied, empfind' ich deinen Sinn!
song sense   I   your meaning

Liebevoll du scheinst zu sagen,
lovingly you seem   to say

Dass ich ihm   zur   Seite bin.
that I   to him at the side am

With what deep contentment, O
song, do I hear your message!
Lovingly you seem to say that I am
at his side;

Dass er ewig   mein gedenket,
that he endlessly of me thinks

Seiner Liebe Seligkeit
of his love bliss

Immerdar der   Fernen   schenket,
for ever   to the distant one bestows

Die ein Leben ihm   geweiht.
who a   life   to him dedicated

that he always thinks of me, and
bestows the rapture of his love on
the one who is far away, who
dedicates her life to him.

Ja, mein Herz, es ist der Spiegel,
yes my   heart it is the mirror

Freund, worin   du dich   erblickt;
friend   wherein you yourself perceived

Diese Brust, wo   deine Siegel
this   breast where your seal

Kuss auf Kuss hereingedrückt.
kiss on kiss pressed herein

Yes, dear friend, my heart is the
mirror in which you see yourself;
this breast, the place whereon you
pressed your seal, kiss by kiss.

Süsses Dichten,   lautre   Wahrheit
sweet poetry writing undefiled truth

Fesselt   mich in Sympathie!
captivate me   in sympathy

Rein   verkörpert Liebesklarheit,
purely embodied love's-clarity

Im   Gewand der   Poesie.
in the garment of the poetry

Sweet poetry, truth undefiled,
your spirit enthrals me! Love's
bright purity, embodied in the
guise of poetry.

11. *DIE HOCHLÄNDER-WITWE*
THE HIGHLAND   WIDOW

11. THE HIGHLAND
WIDOW'S LAMENT

German translation by W. Gerhard
(There are minor discrepancies in meaning between the
two versions)

Robert Burns
(original text)

Ich bin gekommen ins   Niederland
I   am come   into the Lowlands

O weh, O weh, O weh!
O woe O woe O woe

So ausgeplündert haben sie   mich,
so plundered   have they me

Dass ich vor Hunger vergeh'!
that I   for hunger perish

Oh! I am come to the low
   countrie,
Och-on, och-on, och-rie!
Without a penny in my purse,
To buy a meal to me.

So war's in meinem Hochland   nicht;
so was it in my   Highlands not

It was nae sae in the Highland
   hills,
Och-on, och-on, och-rie!
Nae woman in the countrie wide,
Sae happy was as me.

O weh, O weh, O weh!
O woe O woe O woe

Ein hochbeglückter   Weib, als   ich,
a   more highly happy woman than I

War nicht auf Tal   und Höh'!
was not   on valley and hill

Denn damals hatt' ich zwanzig Küh';
for   then   had I   twenty cows

For then I had a score o'kye,
Och-on, och-on, och-rie!
Feeding on yon hills so high,
And giving milk to me.

O weh, O weh, O weh!
O woe O woe O woe

Die gaben Milch und Butter mir,
they gave milk and butter to me

Und weideten im   Klee.
and grazed   in the clover

Und sechzig Schafe hatt' ich dort;
and sixty   sheep had I   there

And there I had three score
   o'yowes,
Och-on, och-on, och-rie!
Skipping on yon bonnie knowes,
And casting woo' to me.

O weh, O weh, O weh!
O woe O woe O woe

Die wärmten mich mit weichem Vlies
they warmed me   with soft   fleece

Bei Frost und Winterschnee.
by frost and winter-snow

Es konnte kein'   im   ganzen Clan
(it) could no one in the whole clan

I was the happiest of the clan,
Sair, sair, may I repine.
For Donald was the bravest lad,
And Donald he was mine.

Sich   grössern Glückes   freu'n;
(himself) of greater happiness rejoice

Denn Donald war der schönste Mann,
for   Donald was the finest   man

Und Donald, der war mein!
and Donald he was mine

So blieb's,   so blieb's,   bis Charlie Stuart kam,
so remained it so remained it till Charlie Stuart came

Till Charlie Stuart cam at last,
Sae for to set us free,
My Donald's arm was wanted
   then
For Scotland and for me.

Alt-Schottland zu befrei'n;
old Scotland to set free

Da musste Donald seinen Arm
then had to Donald his   arm

Ihm und dem Lande leih'n.
him and the land   to lend

Was sie   befiel, wer weiss   es nicht?
what them befell who knows it not

Dem Unrecht wich   das Recht,
to the wrong   yielded the right

Und auf Cullodens   blut'gem Feld
and on Culloden's bloody field

Erlagen Herr   und Knecht.
slayed   master and servant

O! dass ich kam ins   Niederland!
O   that I   came into the Lowlands

O weh, O weh, O weh!
O woe O woe O woe

Nun gibt's   kein unglücksel'ger Weib
now is there no   more wretched woman

Vom   Hochland bis   zur   See!
from the Highlands right to the sea

Their waefu' fate what need I tell?
Richt to the wrong did yield:
My Donald and his country fell
Upon Culloden field.

Oh! I am come to the low
   countrie,
Och-on, och-on, och-rie!
Nae woman in the world wide
Sae wretched now as me.

12. *LIED   DER   BRAUT I*
SONG OF THE BRIDE

12. SONG OF THE
BRIDE I

Friedrich Rückert

Mutter, Mutter! glaube nicht,
mother mother believe not

Weil   ich ihn lieb' allsosehr,
because I   him love so much

Dass nun Liebe mir   gebricht,
that now love to me is abating

Dich zu lieben, wie vorher.
you to love   as before

Mutter, Mutter! seit   ich ihn
mother mother since I   him

Liebe, lieb' ich erst   dich sehr.
love   love I more than ever you much

Lass mich an mein Herz dich zieh'n,
let   me to my heart you draw

Und dich küssen wie mich er!
and you kiss   as me he

O, mother, do not think because I
love him so, I do not love you as I
did before.

O, mother, since I have loved him,
I love you more than ever. Let me
draw you to my heart, and kiss
you, as he kisses me!

Mutter, Mutter! seit   ich ihn
mother mother since I   him

Liebe, lieb' ich erst   dich ganz,
love   love I   more than ever you completely

Dass du mir   das Sein verlieh'n
that you to me the being gave

Das mir   ward zu solchem Glanz.
that to me grew to such   splendour

O, mother, since I so loved him, my love for you is only now complete – for you gave me my being, that has grown to such splendour.

13. *LIED   DER   BRAUT II*
SONG OF THE BRIDE

Friedrich Rückert

Lass mich ihm   am   Busen hangen,
let   me   to him on the breast cling

Mutter, Mutter! lass   das Bangen.
mother mother let go from the being anxious

Frage nicht: wie soll sich's wenden?
ask   not   how shall itself it turn

Frage nicht: wie soll das enden?
ask   not   how shall that end

Enden? Enden soll sich's nie;
end   end   shall itself it never

Wenden? noch nicht weiss ich, wie!
turn   yet not know I   how

Lass mich ihm   am   Busen hangen,
let   me   to him on the bosom cling

Lass mich!
let   me

13. SONG OF THE BRIDE II

Let me cling to his breast – O mother, cease your fears! Do not ask: what turn will it take? Do not ask: how will it end? End? Never must it end! Change? Not yet do I know how! Let me cling to his breast – O let me!

14. *HOCHLÄNDERS ABSCHIED*
HIGHLANDER'S FAREWELL

German translation by W. Gerhard
(There are minor discrepancies in meaning between the two versions)

Mein Herz ist im   Hochland, mein Herz ist nicht hier;
my   heart is in the highlands my   heart is not here

Mein Herz ist im   Hochland, im   Waldesrevier;
my   heart is in the Highlands in the forest-reserve

14. MY HEART'S IN THE HIGHLANDS

Robert Burns
(original text)

My heart's in the Highlands, my heart is not here;
My heart's in the Highlands, a-chasing the deer;

Dort jagt   es den Hirsch   und verfolget das Reh;
there hunts it the red deer and follows the roe

Mein Herz ist im   Hochland, wohin ich auch geh'!
my   heart is in the Highlands where- I -ever go

Leb' wohl, mein Hochland, mein heimischer Ort!
fare-well my Highlands my native   place

Die Wiege der   Freiheit, des   Mutes ist dort.
the cradle of the freedom of the valour is there

Wohin ich auch wandre, wo   immer ich bin:
where- I -ever wander where-ever I   am

Auf die Berg'; auf die Berge, zieht es mich hin.
on the hills on the hills   draws it me   thither

Lebt wohl ihr Berge, bedecket mit   Schnee!
fare-well you mountains covered   with snow

Lebt wohl, ihr Täler   voll Blumen und Klee!
fare-well you valleys full flowers and clover

Lebt wohl, ihr Wälder, bemoostes   Gestein,
fare-well you forests moss-covered rocks

Ihr stürzenden Bächlein   im   farbigen Schein!
you rushing   (little) streams in the colourful light

Chasing the wild deer, and
    following the roe,
My heart's in the Highlands
    wherever I go.
Farewell to the Highlands,
    farewell to the North,
The birthplace of valour, the
    country of worth;
Wherever I wander, wherever I
    rove,
The hills of the Highlands for ever
    I love.
Farewell to the mountains, high
    covered with snow;
Farewell to the straths and green
    valleys below;
Farewell to the forests and wild-
    hanging woods;
Farewell to the torrents and loud-
    pouring floods.

15. *HOCHLÄNDISCHES*
HIGHLAND
WIEGENLIED
CRADLE-SONG

15. HEE BALOU

German translation by W. Gerhard
(There are minor discrepancies in meaning between the
two versions)

Robert Burns
(original text)

Schlafe, süsser kleiner Donald,
sleep   sweet little   Donald

Ebenbild des   grossen Ronald!
image   of the great Ronald

Wer ihm kleinen Dieb gebar,
who him little   thief bore

Weiss der edle   Clan aufs Haar.
knows the noble clan (to a hair)

Hee balou, my sweet wee Donald,
Picture of the great Clanronald;
Brawlie kens our wanton chief
Wha got my young Highland thief.

Schelm, hast Äuglein   schwarz wie Kohlen!
rogue   hast (little) eyes black   as   coals

Wenn du   gross bist, stiehl ein Fohlen;
when you big   are   steal a   foal

Geh' die Eb'ne ab und zu.
walk the plain fro and to

Bringe heim   'ne Carlisle-Kuh!
bring   home a   Carlisle cow

Darfst in Niederland nicht fehlen;
may   in Lowlands not   be missing

Dort, mein Bübchen, magst du   stehlen;
there my   little boy may   you steal

Stiehl dir   Geld   und stiehl dir   Glück,
steal to you money and steal to you fortune

Und ins   Hochland   komm zurück!.
and into the Highlands come back

Leeze me on thy bonnie craigie!
An' thou live, thou'll steal a naigie;
Travel the country thro' and thro',
And bring home a Carlisle cow.

Through the Lowlands o'er the
   border,
Weel, my babie, may thou furder:
Herry the louns o' the laigh
   countree,
Syne to the Highlands hame to
   me.

16. AUS   DEN HEBRÄISCHEN FROM THE HEBREW GESÄNGEN MELODIES

German translation by Julius Körner
(There are considerable discrepancies in meaning
between the two versions)

Mein Herz ist schwer! Auf! von   der Wand
my   heart is heavy arise from the wall

Die Laute, nur sie allein mag   ich noch hören;
the lute   only her alone desire I   still to hear

Entlocke   mit geschickter Hand
draw from with deft   hand

Ihr Töne, die das Herz betören!
her strains that the heart delude

Kann noch mein Herz ein Hoffen nähren,
can   still my   heart a hope   nourish

Es zaubern diese Töne   her,
it charm these sounds forth

16. MY SOUL IS DARK
(from 'Hebrew Melodies')

Lord Byron
(original text)

My soul is dark – Oh! quickly
   string
The harp I yet can brook to hear;
And let thy gentle fingers fling
Its melting murmurs o'er my ear.

If in this heart a hope be dear,
That sound shall charm it forth
   again:

Und birgt   mein trock'nes Auge Zähren,
and conceals my   dry   eye   tears

Sie fliessen, und mich brennt's nicht mehr!
they flow   and me   burns it not   more

Nur tief sei, wild der   Töne   Fluss,
only deep be wild of the strains flow

Und von   der Freude weg   gekehret!
and from the joy   away turned

Ja, Sänger, dass ich weinen muss,
yes singer   that I   weep   must

Sonst   wird das schwere Herz verzehret!
or else is   the heavy   heart consumed

Denn sieh'! Vom   Kummer ward's genähret,
for see   from the sorrow was it nursed

Mit stummen Wachen   trug es lang,
with silent   watchfulness bore it long

Und jetzt, vom   Äussersten belehret,
and now by the extremity instructed

Da   brech' es oder heil' im   Sang.
then break it or   heal in the song

If in these eyes there lurk a tear,
   'Twill flow, and cease to burn my
   brain.

But bid the strain be wild and
   deep,
Now let thy notes of joy be first:
I tell thee, minstrel, I must weep,
Or else this heavy heart will burst;

For it hath been in sorrow nurs'd,
And ach'd in sleepless silence
   long;
And now 'tis doom'd to know, to
   know the worst,
And break at once – or yield to
   song.

17. VENETIANISCHES LIED I   ## 17. VENETIAN SONG I
   VENETIAN   SONG

German translation by Ferdinand Freiligrath
(There are minor discrepancies of meaning between the
two versions)

Thomas Moore
(original text)

Leis' rudern hier, mein Gondolier, leis', leis'!
gently row   here my   gondolier softly softly

Die Flut vom   Ruder sprüh't so leise   dass,
the tide from the oar   sprays so softly that

Dass sie uns nur vernimmt, zu der   wir zieh'n!
that she us only hears   to whom we go

O, könnte, wie er schauen kann, der Himmel reden
O could   as he see   can   the heaven to speak
   traun,
   venture

Now gently here, my gondolier,
   softly, so softly wake the tide,
That not an ear on earth may
   hear, but hers to whom we
   glide.
Had heav'n but tongues to speak,
   as well as starry eyes to see,
Oh think what tales 'twould have
   to tell of wandering youths like
   me!
Hush, hush, hush, hush!

Er spräche   vieles wohl   von dem, was   nachts   die
he would say much indeed of   that which at night the
   Sterne schau'n!
   stars   see

Leis', leis',   leis',   leis'!
softly softly softly softly

Nun rasten hier, mein Gondolier, sacht, sacht!
now rest   here my   gondolier gently gently

Ins   Boot die Ruder! sacht, sacht!
into the boat the oars   gently gently

Auf zum   Balkone schwing' ich mich,   doch du   hältst
on to the balcony spring   I   myself but you keep
   unten Wacht.
   below watch

O, wollten halb so eifrig   nur dem   Himmel wir
O desired half so eagerly only to the heaven we
   uns   weih'n,
   ourselves to dedicate

Als schöner Weiber Diensten traun, wir könnten Engel
as of lovely women service to trust we could   angels
   sein!
   be

Sacht, sacht, sacht, sacht!
gently gently gently gently

Now rest thee here, my gondolier,
   rest here! for up I go,
Hush, hush,
To climb yon light balcony's
   height, while thou keeps't watch
   below.
Ah! Did we take for heav'n above
   but half the pains that we
Take day and night for woman's
   love, what angels we should be!
Hush, hush, hush, hush!

18. VENETIANISCHES LIED II
VENETIAN   SONG

German translation by Ferdinand Freiligrath
(There are minor discrepancies of
meaning between the two versions)

Wenn durch   die Piazzetta die Abendluft   weht,
when through the Piazzetta the evening-breeze blows

Dann weisst du, Ninetta, wer wartend hier steht.
then   know you Ninetta who waiting here stands

Du weisst, wer trotz   Schleier und Maske dich kennt,
you know who in spite of veil   and mask you knows

Wie Amor die Venus am   Nachtfirmament.
as   Love the Venus in the night-firmament

18. VENETIAN SONG
II

Thomas Moore
(original text)

When through the Piazzetta night
   breathes the cool air,
Then dearest Ninetta, I'll come to
   thee there.
Beneath thy mask shrouded I'll
   know thee afar,
As Love knows, though clouded,
   its own Ev'ning Star.

Ein Schifferkleid trag' ich zur   selbigen Zeit,
a   sailor's-dress wear I   at the same   time

Und zitternd   dir   sag' ich: das Boot liegt bereit!
and trembling to you say I   the boat lies ready

O komm, wo   den Mond noch Wolken umzieh'n!
O come where the moon still   clouds envelop

Lass durch   die Lagunen, mein Leben, uns flieh'n!
let   through the lagoons my life   us flee

In garb then resembling some gay
    gondolier,
I'll whisper thee, trembling, 'Our
    bark, love, is near.'
Now, now while there hover those
    clouds near the moon,
'Twill waft thee safe over yon
    silent lagoon.

19. *HAUPTMANNS WEIB*
CAPTAIN'S   WIFE

19. THE CAPTAIN'S
LADY

German translation by W. Gerhard
(There are some considerable discrepancies in meaning
between the two versions)

Robert Burns
(original text)

Hoch zu Pferd!
high to horse

Stahl auf zartem Leibe,
steel on tender body

Helm   und Schwert
helmet and sword

Ziemen Hauptmanns Weibe.
become captain's   wife

O mount and go!
Mount and make you ready:
O mount and go,
And be the Captain's Lady.

Tönet   Trommelschlag
resounds drum-beat

Unter Pulverdampf,
under powder-smoke

Siehst du   blut'gen Tag
see   you bloody day

Und dein Lieb im   Kampf.
and your love in the battle

When the drums do beat,
And the cannons rattle,
Thou shalt sit in state
And see thy love in battle.

Schlagen wir den Feind,
vanquish we the foe

Küssest du   den Gatten,
kiss   you the husband

Wohnst mit ihm vereint
live   with him united

In des   Friedens Schatten.
in of the peace   shadow

When the vanquished foe
Sues for peace and quiet,
To the shades we'll go,
And in love enjoy it.

20. *DU   BIST WIE   EINE BLUME*
YOU ARE LIKE A   FLOWER

Heinrich Heine

Du bist wie eine Blume,
you are like a   flower

So hold   und schön und rein;
so sweet and lovely and pure

Ich schau' dich an, und Wehmut
I   look   you at and melancholy

Schleicht mir   ins   Herz hinein.
steals   to me into the heart thither

Mir   ist, als ob ich die Hände
to me is as if I the hands

Aufs   Haupt dir   legen sollt',
on the head to you lay   should

Betend, dass Gott dich erhalte
praying that God you may keep

So rein und schön und hold.
so pure and lovely and sweet

20. YOU ARE LIKE A
FLOWER

You are like a flower, as sweet and
fair and pure. I look at you, and
melancholy steals into my heart.

I feel I must lay my hands upon
your head, praying that God may
keep you so pure, and fair, and
sweet.

21. *AUS   DEN 'ÖSTLICHEN ROSEN'*
FROM THE EASTERN   ROSES

Friedrich Rückert

Ich sende einen Gruss   wie Duft der   Rosen,
I   send a   greeting like scent of the roses

Ich send' ihn an ein Rosenangesicht,
I   send him to a   rose-face

Ich sende einen Gruss   wie Frühlingskosen,
I   send a   greeting like spring's-caressing

Ich send' ihn an ein Aug' voll Frühlingslicht.
I   send him to an eye full spring's-light

Aus Schmerzensstürmen, die   mein Herz durchtosen,
from grief's-storms   which my   heart rage through

Send' ich den Hauch, dich unsanft rühr'   er nicht!
send I   the breath you harshly may touch he not

21. FROM 'EASTERN
ROSES'

I send a greeting like the scent of
roses; I send it to her whose face is
lovely as a rose. I send a greeting
like the caresses of spring; I send it
to eyes that are full of the light of
spring.

From the storms of grief which
rage through my heart, I send you
a breath – may its touch not be
harsh! Should you think of the one

Wenn du   gedenkest an den Freudelosen,
when you think   of the joyless one

So wird   der Himmel meiner Nächte licht.
so becomes the sky   of my nights light

without joy, then would light enter
his dark night skies.

22. *JASMINENSTRAUCH*
    JASMINE-BUSH

22. THE JASMINE
    BUSH

Friedrich Rückert

Grün ist der Jasminenstrauch
green is the jasmine-bush

Abends eingeschlafen.
at night fallen asleep

Als   ihn mit des   Morgens Hauch
when him with of the morning breeze

Sonnenlichter trafen,
sunbeams   touched

Ist er schneeweiss aufgewacht:
is he snow-white woken up

'Wie geschah   mir   in der Nacht?'
 what happened to me in the night

Seht, so geht es Bäumen,
see   so goes it to trees

Die im   Frühling träumen.
that in the spring   dream

The jasmine bush was green as it
fell asleep last night. But this
morning, touched by sunbeams
and a morning breeze,

it was white as snow. 'What
happened to me in the night?'
Well, this is what happens to trees
that dream in the spring.

23. *VOLKSLIEDCHEN*
    (LITTLE) FOLK-SONG

23. LITTLE FOLK-
    SONG

Friedrich Rückert

Wenn ich früh in   den Garten geh' in meinem grünen
when I early into the garden go in my   green
  Hut,
  hat

Ist mein erster Gedanke, was nun mein Liebster tut?
is my first thought what now my beloved is doing

When I go into the garden early in
my little green hat, my first
thought is of my beloved, and what
he might be doing. O, I would give
my sweetheart every star in the sky
– and if I could remove it, I'd
gladly give him my heart!

Am   Himmel steht   kein Stern, den ich dem   Freund
in the sky   stands no star   that I   (to) the friend

nicht gönnte.
not   would grant

Mein Herz gäb'   ich ihm   gern, wenn ich's heraus
my   heart would give I   to him gladly if   I it   out

tun könnte.
take could.

24. DER ARME PETER
THE POOR PETER

24. POOR PETER

Heinrich Heine

i.

i.

Der Hans und die Grete tanzen herum,
the Hans and the Greta dance around

Hans and Greta are dancing around, and laughing for sheer joy. Peter stands silent and still, his face as white as chalk.

Und jauchzen vor lauter Freude.
and shout   for sheer joy

Der Peter steht   so still und stumm,
the Peter stands so still and silent

Und ist so blass wie Kreide.
and is as pale as   chalk

Der Hans und die Grete sind Bräut'gam   und Braut,
the Hans and the Greta are bridegroom and bride

Hans and Greta are bridegroom and bride, sparkling in their wedding jewels. Poor Peter chews his nails as he goes his way in workaday clothes.

Und blitzen im   Hochzeitsgeschmeide.
and sparkle in the wedding-jewels

Der arme Peter die Nägel kaut,
the poor Peter the nails chews

Und geht im   Werkeltagskleide.
and walks in the workaday clothes.

Der Peter spricht leise   vor   sich   her,
the Peter talks quietly away to himself –

Peter mutters to himself, as he sadly watches them both, 'Alas! If I'd not so much sense, I'd do myself some mischief.'

Und schauet betrübet   auf beide:
and looks   miserably at both

'Ach! wenn ich nicht gar zu vernünftig wär',
ah   if   I   not at all too sensible were

Ich täte   mir   was   zu Leide.'
I   would do myself something to harm

ii.

'In meiner Brust, da   sitzt ein Weh,
 in my   breast there sits a   pain

Das will   die Brust zersprengen;
 that wants the breast to burst

Und wo   ich steh' and wo   ich geh'
 and where I   stand and where I   go

Will's   mich von hinnen drängen.
 wants it me   from here   to urge

Es treibt mich nach der   Liebsten Näh,
 it drives me to   (of) the dearest nearness

Als könnt's die Grete heilen;
 as   could it the Greta heal

Doch wenn ich der   in's   Auge seh',
 but when I   to her in the eye   look

Muss ich von   hinnen eilen.
 must I   from here   hasten

Ich steig' hinauf des   Berges   Höh',
 I   climb up   of the mountain top

Dort ist man doch   alleine;
 there is one indeed alone

Und wenn ich still dort oben steh',
 and when I   still there up   stand

Dann steh' ich still   and weine.'
 then stand I   silently and weep

iii.

Der arme Peter wankt   vorbei,
 the poor Peter staggers past

Gar langsam, leichenblass und scheu.
 very slowly   corpse-pale and timid

Es bleiben fast,   wie sie   ihn seh'n,
 (it) remain almost as   they him see

Die Leute   auf den Strassen steh'n.
 the people on the streets   stand

Die Mädchen flüstern sich   in's   Ohr:
 the girls   whisper (themselves) into the ear

'Der stieg   wohl   aus   dem Grab hervor?'
 he climbed perhaps out of the grave forth

---

ii.

'The grief that weighs in my heart
will surely burst my breast;
wherever I am, and wherever I go,
it drives me away from here.

It drives me to my loved one's
side, as if Greta could ease my
pain. But when I look into her
eyes, I have to hasten away.

I climb right to the mountain-top,
for there I can be alone. And when
I stand up there quite still, then I
just silently weep.'

iii.

Poor Peter, he goes stumbling by,
timid and pale as death. The
people in the streets almost stop at
the sight of him.

The girls whisper to each other:
'Has he just climbed out of his
grave?' 'Oh no, dear young ladies
– he is on his way there!'

'Ach nein, ihr lieben Jungfräulein,
oh no   you dear maidens

Der steigt erst in   das Grab hinein.
he   climbs just into the grave there

Er hat verloren seinen Schatz,
he has lost   his   treasure

He has lost his sweetheart, so the
grave is the best place for him – to
lie and sleep until Judgement
Day.'

Drum   ist das Grab der beste Platz,
therefore is the grave the best place

Wo   er am   besten liegen mag
where he (at) the best   lie

Und schlafen bis zum   Jüngsten   Tag.'
and sleep   – until the – judgement day

25. DIE BEIDEN GRENADIERE
THE TWO   GRENADIERS

25. THE TWO
GRENADIERS

Heinrich Heine

Nach Frankerich zogen zwei Grenadier',
to   France   went two grenadiers

Two grenadiers, taken captive in
Russia, were making their way
back to France. And when they
came to the German side, they
hung their heads in shame.

Die waren in Russland gefangen.
who were in Russia   captured

Und als sie kamen ins   deutsche Quartier,
and as they came into the German quarter

Sie liessen die Köpfe hangen.
they let   the heads hang

Da   hörten sie beide die traurige   Mär':
there heard they both the sorrowful news

For they heard the sad news, that
France was lost, and the valiant
army vanquished; and the
Emperor, their Emperor, had been
taken prisoner!

Dass Frankreich verloren gegangen,
that France   lost   gone

Besiegt   und geschlagen das tapfere Heer –
vanquished and routed   the brave army

Und der Kaiser, der Kaiser   gefangen!
and the emperor the emperor captured

Da   weinten zusammen die Grenadier'
then wept   together   the grenadiers

At the pitiful tidings both the
grenadiers wept. 'The pain,' said
the one, 'how it burns my old
wound!'

Wohl ob der kläglichen Kunde.
indeed over the lamentable tidings

Der eine sprach: 'Wie weh   wird mir,
the one said   how painful is   to me

Wie brennt meine alte Wunde!'
how burns my   old wound

Der andre sprach: 'Das Lied ist aus,
the other said   the song is over

The other said: 'Now all is lost,
and I would gladly die with you,
but at home I have a wife and
child, without me they would
surely perish.'

Auch ich möcht'   mit dir sterben,
also I   would like with you to die

Doch hab' ich Weib und Kind zu Haus,
but have I   wife and child at home

Die ohne   mich verderben.'
who without me   perish

'Was schert   mich Weib, was schert   mich Kind,
what concerns me   wife   what concerns me   child

'What do I care for wife and child!
Mine is a nobler desire! If they are
hungry, let them beg – my
Emperor, my Emperor, has been
taken!

Ich trage weit bessres Verlangen;
I   carry far better desire

Lass sie   betteln gehn, wenn sie   hungrig sind –
let   them to beg to go if   they hungry are

Mein Kaiser,   mein Kaiser   gefangen!
my   Emperor my   Emperor captured

Gewähr' mir, Bruder, eine Bitt':
grant   me brother a   request

Grant me, brother, one last wish:
if I am to die, take my body to
France, that I might be buried in
the soil of France.

Wenn ich jetzt sterben werde,
if   I now die   will

So nimm meine Leiche nach Frankreich mit,
so take   my   corpse to   France   with (you)

Begrab' mich in Frankreichs Erde.
bury   me in France's   earth

Das Ehrenkreuz   am   roten Band.
the cross of honour on the red   ribbon

Lay my Cross of Honour and red
band on my heart; put my musket
in my hand, and buckle on my
sword.

Sollst du aufs   Herz mir   legen;
shall you on the heart to me lay

Die Flinte   gib mir in die Hand,
the musket give me in the hand

Und gürt'   mir um   den Degen.
and buckle me about me sword

So will ich liegen und horchen still,
so will I   lie   and listen   silently

And thus will I lie like a sentry in
my grave, till I hear the cannons
roar, and the neighing horses
gallop.

Wie eine Schildwach', im   Grabe,
as a   sentry   in the grave

Bis   einst   ich höre Kanonengebrüll
until one day I   hear cannon-roar

Und wiehernder Rosse   Getrabe.
and of neighing chargers trotting

Dann reitet mein Kaiser   wohl   über mein Grab,   Then over my grave my Emperor
then rides my   Emperor perhaps over my   grave   will ride, and many swords will
                                                            flash and clash. And I will rise
Viel Schwerter klirren und blitzen;   right up from the grave, to defend
many swords   clash   and flash   the Emperor, the Emperor!'

Dann steig ich gewaffnet hervor aus   dem Grab –
then rise I   armed   forth out of the grave

Den Kaiser,   den Kaiser   zu schützen!'
the Emperor the Emperor to defend

26. *LIEDERKREIS Op. 39*
SONG-CYCLE

26. SONG-CYCLE
Op. 39

Josef von Eichendorff

   i. In der Fremde I   i. In foreign parts I
    in the foreign parts

Aus der Heimat   hinter den Blitzen   rot   From beyond the lightning flashes,
from the homeland behind the lightning red   clouds come from my homeland.
                                                            Father and mother are long since
Da   kommen die Wolken her,   dead, and no one here knows me
there come   the clouds here   any more.

Aber Vater und Mutter sind lange tot,
but father and mother are long dead

Es kennt mich dort   keiner mehr.
(it) knows me   there no one more

Wie bald, ach wie bald kommt die stille Zeit,   How soon, oh, how soon will
how soon oh how soon comes the quiet time   come that quiet time when I too
                                                            shall rest! And over me in lovely
Da   ruhe ich auch, und über mir   solitude, the woods will rustle, and
when rest I   also and over me   no one here will know me any
                                                            more.
Rauscht die schöne Waldeinsamkeit,
rustles the lovely woods-solitude

Und keiner kennt mich mehr hier.
and no one knows me   more here

ii. Intermezzo
   intermezzo

ii. Intermezzo

Dein Bildnis wunderselig
your image wonderfully-blissful

In wondrous joy I hold your image
deep in my heart. It looks at me,
so happy and bright, every hour of
the day.

Hab' ich im   Herzensgrund,
have I   in the heart's-bottom

Das sieht so frisch und fröhlich
that looks so fresh and happy

Mich an zu jeder Stund'.
me   at in every hour

Mein Herz still   in sich singet
my   heart quietly to itself sings

Softly my heart sings to itself an
old and lovely song, that soars into
the air and swiftly flies to you.

Ein altes, schönes Lied,
an old   lovely song

Das in die Luft sich   schwinget
that in the air   itself soars

Und zu dir eilig   zieht.
and to you speedily goes

iii. Waldesgespräch
   wood-conversation

iii. Dialogue in the woods

'Es ist schon   spät, es ist schon   kalt,
 it is already late it is already cold

'Already it is late, already cold –
why do you ride alone through the
woods? The way through the
woods is long, and you are alone.
You lovely bride, I will carry you
home!'

Was reit'st du einsam durch   den Wald?
why ride you alone   through the wood

Der Wald ist lang, du bist allein,
the wood is long you are alone

Du schöne Braut! ich führ' dich heim!'
you lovely bride I   bring you home

'Gross ist der   Männer Trug und List,
 great is of the men   deceit and cunning

'Great is the guile and cunning of
men, my heart is broken with
grief. The straying horn sounds
here and there. O fly! You know
not who I am!'

Vor Schmerz mein Herz gebrochen ist,
for grief   my heart broken is

Wohl irrt   das Waldhorn her und hin,
indeed strays the horn   here and there

O flieh'! Du weisst nicht, wer ich bin.'
O flee   you know not   who I   am

'*So reich geschmückt ist Ross   und Weib,*
so richly adorned   is horse and woman

So wunderschön   der junge Leib;
so wondrously beautiful the young body

Jetzt kenn' ich dich – Gott steh' mir bei!
now know I   you   God stand me by

Du bist die Hexe Lorelei.'
you are the witch Lorelei

'*Du kennst mich wohl, von   hohem Stein*
 you know me   well from high   rock

Schaut still mein Schloss tief in   den Rhein.
looks still my castle deep into the Rhine

Es ist schon   spät, es ist schon   kalt,
it is already late it is already cold

Kommst nimmermehr aus   diesem Wald!'
come   nevermore out of this   wood

In fine array are horse and bride, of wondrous beauty her young form; I know you now – may God protect me! You are the siren, Lorelei!

'You know me indeed – from a high rock my castle looks still and deep down into the Rhine. Already it is late, already cold – nevermore will you leave these woods!'

iv. *Die Stille*
   the tranquillity

iv. Tranquillity

Es weiss und rät   es doch   keiner,
(it) knows and guesses it indeed no one

Wie mir so wohl ist, so wohl!
how me so happy is so happy

Ach, wüsst' er nur Einer, nur Einer,
ah   knew it just one   only one

Kein Mensch es sonst   wissen soll!
no   person it otherwise know shall

No one knows, no one can guess how happy I am, how happy! Ah, if one only knew, only the one – and no one else at all!

So still ist's nicht draussen im   Schnee,
so still is it not   outside in the snow

So stumm und verschwiegen sind
so silent and secret   are

Die Sterne nicht in der Höh',
the stars   not in the heights

Als meine Gedanken sind.
as my   thoughts are

The snow outside is not as still, and the stars in their heights are not as silent and still as my thoughts.

Ich wünscht', ich wär' ein Vöglein,
I   wished   I   were a   little bird

Und zöge über das Meer,
and went over the sea

I wish I were a little bird flying over the sea – over the sea and far beyond until I were in heaven!

Wohl   über das Meer und weiter,
indeed over the sea   and further

Bis   dass ich im   Himmel wär'!
until that I   in the heaven were

   v. Mondnacht
      moon-night

Es war, als hätt' der Himmel
it was as had the heaven

Die Erde still   geküsst,
the earth quietly kissed

Dass sie im   Blütenschimmer
that she in the blossom-splendour

Von ihm nur träumen müsst'!
of   him only dream   had to

Die Luft   ging durch   die Felder,
the breeze went through the fields

Die Ähren   wogten sacht,
the ears (of corn) rocked gently

Es rauschten leis' die Wälder,
(it) rustled   softly the woods

So sternklar   war die Nacht.
so star-bright was the night

Und meine Seele spannte
and my   soul spread

Weit ihre Flügel aus,
wide her wings out

Flog durch   die stillen Lande,
flew through the silent land

Als flöge sie nach Haus.
as flew she homeward

   vi. Schöne Fremde
      lovely foreign land

Es rauschen die Wipfel   und schauern,
(it) rustle   the tree-tops and shiver

Als machten zu dieser Stund'
as made   at this   hour

v. Moonlit night

It was as if heaven had softly kissed the earth, and earth in blossoming splendour could only dream of heaven.

A breeze passing over the fields gently swayed the ears of corn. The woods softly rustled, and the night was bright with stars.

And my soul spread wide its wings, and flew over the silent land, as if it were flying home.

vi. Lovely foreign land

The tree-tops rustle and shiver, as if at this very hour the ancient gods were making their round of the half-ruined walls.

Um   die halb versunkenen Mauern
about the half sunken   walls

Die alten Götter die Rund'.
the old   gods   the round

Hier hinter   den Myrtenbäumen
here behind the myrtle-trees

Im   heimlich dämmernder   Pracht,
in the secretly growing dusk splendour

Was sprichst du   wirr   wie in Träumen
what say   you confused as   in dreams

Zu mir, phantastische Nacht?
to me fantastic   night

Here behind the myrtles, in the secret splendour of dusk – O fantastic night, what are you saying to me, confused, as in a dream?

Es funkeln auf mich alle Sterne
(it) twinkle on me   all stars

Mit glühendem Liebesblick,
with glowing   love's-glance

Es redet   trunken   die Ferne
(it) speaks intoxicated the distant place

Wie von künftigem grossen Glück!
as   of   coming   great   happiness

All the stars look down on me, twinkling and glowing with love, and speak in ecstasy from afar of great joy to come!

vii. Auf einer Burg
     in a   castle

vii. In a castle

Eingeschlafen auf der Lauer
fallen asleep on the watch

Oben   ist der alte Ritter;
on high is the old knight

Drüben   gehen Regenschauer,
over there go   rain-showers

Und der Wald rauscht durch   das Gitter.
and the wood rustles through the iron bars

Up there keeping watch, the old knight has fallen asleep; rain showers down, and the woods rustle through the iron bars.

Eingewachsen Bart   und Haare,
grown as one beard and hair

Und versteinert   Brust und Krause,
and turned to stone breast and ruff

Sitzt er viele hundert Jahre
sits   he many hundred years

Oben   in der stillen Klause.
on high in the silent cell

With his hair and beard grown together as one, his breast and his ruff turned to stone, he has sat up there in his silent cell many hundreds of years.

Draussen ist es still und friedlich,
outside   is it still and peaceful

Alle sind ins   Tal   gezogen,
all   are into the valley moved

Waldesvögel   einsam singen
woodland-birds solitary sing

In den leeren   Fensterbogen.
in the empty window-arches

Outside it is peaceful and still, all the people gone to the valley; and solitary woodland birds sing in the empty window arches.

Eine Hochzeit fährt da   unten
a   wedding sails there below

Auf dem Rhein im Sonnenscheine,
on the Rhine in the sun-shine

Musikanten spielen munter,
musicians   play   merrily

Und die schöne Braut, die weinet.
and the lovely bride she weeps

A wedding party sails by on the sunlit Rhine below; musicians are playing merrily, and the lovely bride weeps.

viii. In der Fremde II
in the foreign land

Ich hör' die Bächlein   rauschen
I   hear the little brooks rush

Im   Walde her und hin,
in the wood here and there

Im   Walde, in dem Rauschen
in the wood in the rushing

Ich weiss nicht, wo   ich bin.
I   know not where I   am

viii. In a foreign land II

I hear little streams rushing in the woods all around; in the woods with the rushing, I hardly know where I am.

Die Nachtigallen schlagen
the nightingales sing

Hier in der Einsamkeit,
here in the solitude

Als wollten sie was   sagen
as wanted they something to say

Von der alten schönen Zeit.
of the old lovely time(s)

Here in this solitude the nightingales sing, as if they would tell of times long ago.

Die Mondeschimmer fliegen,
the moon-shimmers fly

Als säh   ich unter   mir
as (if) saw I   beneath me

In the shimmer of moon-beams, I seemed to see the castle below in the valley, yet it is far from here.

Das Schloss im   Tale   liegen,
the castle   in the valley lie

Und ist doch so weit von   hier!
and is yet so far from here

Als   müsste in dem Garten
as if must in the garden

As if in the garden full of white
and red roses, my dear love was
waiting – yet she died long ago.

Voll Rosen weiss und rot,
full roses white and red

Meine Liebste auf mich warten,
my   dearest for me   wait

Und ist doch so lange tot.
and is yet   so long dead

        ix. *Wehmut*
            melancholy

ix. Melancholy

Ich kann wohl   manchmal singen,
I   can   indeed sometimes sing

I can even sing at times, as if I
were happy; but secretly my tears
well up, and my heart is set free.

Als ob   ich fröhlich sei,
as though I   happy were

Doch heimlich Tränen dringen,
but   secretly tears   are pressing

Da   wird   das Herz mir   frei.
then becomes the heart to me free

Es   lassen Nachtigallen,
(it) let   nightingales

When a spring breeze plays, the
nightingales sing out their
yearning songs from their deep
prison.

Spielt draussen Frühlingsluft,
plays outside spring-breeze

Der   Sehnsucht Lied erschallen
of the longing   song sound

Aus ihres Kerkers Gruft.
from their prison's grave

Da   lauschen alle Herzen,
then listen   all hearts

Then all hearts listen and are
made glad, but no one feels the
grief and deep pain in the song.

Und alles   ist erfreut,
and everyone is gladdened

Doch keiner fühlt die Schmerzen,
yet   no one feels the griefs

Im   Lied das tiefe Leid.
in the song the deep suffering

x. *Zwielicht*
  twilight

x. Twilight

Dämm'rung will   die Flügel spreiten,
dusk   is about to the wings spread out

Dusk begins to spread its wings,
the trees shudder and stir; clouds
gather like heavy dreams – what
can these signs of unease portend?

Schaurig rühren sich   die Bäume,
creepily stir   themselves the trees

Wolken ziehn wie schwere Träume –
clouds move like heavy dreams

Was will   dieses Grau'n bedeuten?
what does this   dread   signify

Hast ein Reh du lieb   vor   andern,
(have) a   roe you love (for) above others

If you have a favourite deer, let it
not graze alone! Huntsmen are
blowing their horns in the woods,
here and there voices call.

Lass es nicht alleine grasen,
let   it not alone graze

Jäger   zieh'n im   Wald und blasen,
huntsmen move in the wood and blow

Stimmen hin und wieder wandern.
voices   to and fro   wander

Hast du einen Freund hienieden,
have you a   friend here below

If you have a friend on this earth,
do not trust him at this hour! His
eyes and mouth may perhaps
smile, but he schemes beneath a
mask of peace.

Trau' ihm nicht zu dieser Stunde,
trust him not at this hour

Freundlich wohl   mit Aug' und Munde,
friendly   perhaps with eye and mouth

Sinnt   er Krieg im   tück'schen Frieden.
schemes he war in the deceiving tranquillity

Was heut' geht müde   unter,
what today goes wearily down

Who today sinks wearily down,
will rise tomorrow reborn. But
many a one is lost in the night – be
wary, watchful and awake!

Hebt sich morgen   neugeboren.
rises itself tomorrow new-born

Manches   geht in Nacht verloren –
many a one goes in night lost

Hüte   dich,   sei wach   und munter!
take care yourself be watchful and awake

xi. Im   Walde
    in the wood

xi. In the woods

Es zog eine Hochzeit den Berg   entlang,
(it) went a   wedding the mountain along

A wedding party passed below the mountain slopes, I heard the birds singing. Many riders flashed by, the horn sounded – it was a merry hunt.

Ich hörte die Vögel schlagen,
I   heard the birds sing

Da   blitzten viel   Reiter, das Waldhorn klang,
then flashed many riders the horn   sounded

Das war ein lustiges Jagen!
that was a   merry hunting

Und eh'   ich's gedacht, war alles   verhallt,
and before I it   thought was everything faded away

Before I had time to think, it had all faded from sight, the company enfolded in darkness. Now only the woods rustle on the mountains, and my heart is filled with foreboding.

Die Nacht bedecket die Runde,
the night covers   the company

Nur von   den Bergen   noch rauschet der Wald,
only from the mountains still rustles the wood

Und mich schauert's im   Herzensgrunde.
and me   shudders it in the heart's-bottom

xii. Frühlingsnacht
      spring night

xii. Spring night

Über'm Garten durch   die Lüfte
over the garden through the breezes

I heard the birds of passage flying over the garden on the breeze, heralds of spring's fragrance; below already it begins to bloom.

Hört'ich Wandervögel   zieh'n,
heard I birds of passage move

Das bedeutet Frühlingsdüfte,
that means   spring-scents

Unten fängt's   schon   an zu blüh'n.
below begins it already – to blossom

Jauchzen   möcht'   ich, möchte   weinen,
to shout with joy should like I   should like to weep

I want to shout with joy, and weep – I can hardly believe it is true! Old miracles appear again in the shining splendour of the moon.

Ist mir's   doch, als könnt's nicht sein!
is to me it but   as could it not be

Alte Wunder wieder scheinen
old miracles again appear

Mit dem Mondesglanz   herein.
with the moon's-splendour in here

Und der Mond, die Sterne sagen's,
and the moon the stars   say it

Und im   Traume rauscht's der Hain,
and in the dream rustles it the wood

Und die Nachtigallen schlagen's:
and the nightingales sing   it

'Sie ist deine, sie ist dein!'
she is yours she is yours

The moon and the stars all say it,
the dreaming forest whispers it,
the nightingales are calling forth:
'She is yours, she is yours!'

27. *DICHTERLIEBE*
POET'S-LOVE

27. POET'S LOVE

Heinrich Heine

i.

i.

Im   wunderschönen   Monat Mai,
in the wondrously beautiful month May

Als   alle Knospen sprangen,
when all buds   were bursting

Da   ist in meinem Herzen
then is in my   heart

Die Liebe aufgegangen.
the love risen up

In the wondrous beauty of May-
time, when all the buds were
bursting, love sprang up in my
heart.

Im   wunderschönen   Monat Mai,
in the wondrously beautiful month May

Als   alle Vögel sangen,
when all birds were singing

Da   hab' ich ihr   gestanden
then have I   to her confessed

Mein Sehnen und Verlangen.
my   longing and desire

In the wondrous beauty of May-
time, when all the birds were
singing, I told her of my longing
and desire.

ii.

ii.

Aus   meinen Tränen spriessen
from my   tears   sprout

Viel   blühende   Blumen hervor,
many blossoming flowers forth

From my tears spring many
blossoms, and my sighs become a
choir of nightingales.

Und meine Seufzer werden
and my   sighs   become

Ein Nachtigallenchor.
a   nightingales' choir

Und wenn du   mich lieb hast, Kindchen,
and if   you me – love – (little) child

Schenk' ich dir   die Blumen all',
give   I   to you the flowers all

Und vor   deinem Fenster soll   klingen
and before your   window shall sound

Das Lied der   Nachtigall.
the song of the nightingale

And if you love me, child, I'll give you the flowers, and the nightingales shall sing at your window.

iii.

Die Rose, die Lilie, die Taube, die Sonne,
the rose the lily   the dove   the sun

Die   liebt' ich einst alle in Liebeswonne.
them loved I   once all in love's-delight

Ich lieb' sie   nicht mehr, ich liebe alleine
I   love them no   more I   love only

Die Kleine,   die Feine,   die Reine,   die Eine;
the little one the fine one the pure one the only one

Sie selber, aller Liebe Wonne
she herself of all love (in) delight

Ist Rose und Lilie und Taube und Sonne.
is rose and lily and dove and sun

iii.

The rose, the lily, the dove, the sun; I loved them all in love's delight. I love them no more – I only love the little one, the fine one, the pure one, the only one! She is all of love's delight: the rose, the lily, the dove, the sun.

iv.

Wenn ich in   deine Augen seh',
when I   into your eyes   look

So schwindet all mein Leid   und Weh;
so vanishes all my   suffering and pain

Doch wenn ich küsse deinen Mund,
but when I   kiss your   mouth

So werd' ich ganz   und gar   gesund.
so become I   wholly and completely well

Wenn ich mich   lehn'   an deine Brust,
when I   myself recline on your breast

Kommt's über mich wie Himmelslust;
comes it over me   like heaven's-delight

iv.

When I look into your eyes, my suffering and pain all vanish; but when I kiss your lips, my very being is restored.

When I lie upon your breast, I am overcome with heaven's delight; yet when you say, 'I love you!' I weep most bitterly.

Doch wenn du sprichst: ich liebe dich!
but   when you say   I   love you

So muss ich weinen bitterlich.
so must I   weep   bitterly

v.

Ich will meine Seele tauchen
I   will my   soul plunge

In den Kelch der   Lilie hinein;
in the cup   of the lily   (into)

Die Lilie soll   klingend   hauchen
the lily   shall sounding breathe

Ein Lied von der Liebsten mein.
a   song of   the beloved mine

Das Lied soll   schauern und beben,
the song shall tremble and quiver

Wie der Kuss von   ihrem Mund,
like the kiss from her   mouth

Den   sie mir   einst gegeben
which she to me once (has) given

In wunderbar   süsser Stund'.
in wonderfully sweet hour

v.

I will steep my soul in the cup of
the lily; the lily shall breathe a
song of my love.

The song will tremble and quiver
like the kiss from her lips, the kiss
she once gave me in a wonderfully
sweet hour.

vi.

Im   Rhein, im   heiligen Strome,
in the Rhine in the sacred river

Da   spiegelt sich in den Well'n,
there reflects itself in the ripples

Mit seinem grossen Dome,
with its   great   cathedral

Das grosse heilige Köln.
the great sacred Cologne

Im   Dom   da   steht   ein Bildnis,
in the cathedral there stands a   portrait

Auf goldenem Leder   gemalt;
on golden   leather painted

In meines Lebens Wildnis
in of my life   wilderness

Hat's freundlich hineingestrahlt.
has it kindly   shone into

vi.

The sacred river Rhine reflects in
its ripples mighty, Cologne with its
cathedral, great and holy.

In the cathedral there is a portrait
painted on golden leather; it has
cast a kindly gleam into my life's
wilderness.

Es schweben Blumen und Englein
(it) hovers   flowers and (little) angels

Flowers and angels hover round
Our Lady; her eyes, lips and
cheeks are like those of my dear
love.

Um   unsre liebe Frau;
round Our dear Lady

Die Augen, die Lippen, die Wänglein,
the eyes   the lips   the dear cheeks

Die gleichen der   Liebsten genau.
they resemble (of) the beloved exactly

vii.

vii.

Ich grolle   nicht, und wenn das Herz auch bricht,
I bear a grudge not   and if   the heart even breaks

I bear no grudge though my heart
breaks. Love lost for ever, but I
bear no grudge. However your
splendid diamonds might gleam,
no ray can penetrate the night in
your heart.

Ewig   verlor'nes Lieb! ich grolle   nicht.
for ever lost   love I bear a grudge not

Wie du auch strahlst in Diamentenpracht,
how-you -ever shine   in diamond-splendour

Es fällt kein Strahl in deines Herzens Nacht.
(it) falls no ray   in your heart's night

Dass weiss ich längst.   Ich sah dich ja   im   Traume,
that knew I   long ago I   saw you truly in the dream

I knew it long ago – I saw you in a
dream. I saw the night within your
soul, and saw the serpent eating at
your heart. I saw, my love, your
wretchedness.

Und sah die Nacht in deines Herzens Raume,
and saw the night in your heart's place

Und sah die Schlang', die   dir   am   Herzen frisst,
and saw the serpent   which to you at the heart   gnaws

Ich sah, mein Lieb, wie sehr du elend   bist.
I   saw my   dear how much you wretched are

viii.

viii.

Und wüssten's die Blumen, die kleinen,
and if knew it the flowers the little ones

And if the tiny flowers knew how
deep are the wounds in my heart,
they would weep with me to heal
my grief.

Wie tief   verwundet mein Herz,
how deeply wounded my   heart

Sie würden mit mir weinen,
they would with me weep

Zu heilen meinen Schmerz.
to heal   my   pain

Und wüssten's die Nachtigallen,
and if knew it the nightingales

And if the nightingales knew how
sick and sad I am, they would
gladly sing a heartening song.

Wie ich so traurig und krank,
how I   so sad   and sick

Sie liessen   fröhlich erschallen
they would let gladly   resound

Erquickenden Gesang.
refreshing   song

Und wüssten sie   mein Wehe,
and if knew they my   pain

And if the golden stars but knew of my grief, they would come down from their heights to comfort me.

Die goldenen Sternelein,
the golden   little stars

Sie kämen   aus ihrer Höhe,
they would come from their height

Und sprächen   Trost   mir   ein.
and would speak comfort to me –

Sie alle können's nicht wissen,
they all can it   not know

None of them can know of my pain, it is known by only one: for she it is who has broken it – broken my heart.

Nur Eine kennt meinen Schmerz;
only one knows my   sorrow

Sie hat ja   selbst zerrissen,
she has indeed herself broken

Zerrissen mir   das Herz.
broken   to me the heart

       ix.

ix.

Das ist ein Flöten   und Geigen,
that is a   playing-of-flutes and fiddling

There's a playing of flutes and fiddles, and resounding trumpets too. There dancing, perhaps her wedding round, is my own dearest love.

Trompeten schmettern darein;
trumpets resound   thereto

Da   tanzt wohl   den Hochzeitsreigen
there dances probably the wedding-dance

Die Herzallerliebste mein.
the dearest-heart mine

Das ist ein Klingen und Dröhnen,
that is a   ringing and droning

There's a thudding and piping on drums and shawms, and amongst them sweet cherubs sob and groan.

Ein Pauken   und ein Schalmei'n;
a   beating-of-drums and a   playing-of-shawms

Dazwischen   schluchzen und stöhnen
there between sob   and groan

Die lieblichen Engelein.
the sweet   little cherubs

x.

Hör' ich das Liedchen   klingen,
hear I   the little song sound

Das einst die Liebste   sang,
that once the dearest one sang

So will   mir   die Brust zerspringen
so wants to me the breast to burst

Von   wildem Schmerzendrang.
from wild   grief's-violence

Es treibt mich ein dunkles Sehnen,
(it) drives me a   dark   longing

Hinauf   zur   Waldeshöh',
up there to the wooded heights

Dort löst   sich auf in Tränen
there dissolves itself – in tears

Mein übergrosses Weh'.
my   immense   sorrow

If I should hear the melody that once my dearest sang, then would my heart be torn by the fierce violence of grief.

A dark longing drives me to the wooded heights; there my infinite sorrow overflows in tears.

xi.

Ein Jüngling liebt ein Mädchen,
a   lad   loves a   girl

Die hat einen andern erwählt;
who has – another – chosen

Der andre liebt eine andre,
the other loves another

Und hat sich   mit dieser   vermählt.
and has himself with this (one) wed

Das Mädchen nimmt aus   Ärger
the girl   takes out of annoyance

Den ersten besten Mann,
the first   good man

Der ihr   in den Weg gelaufen;
who to her in the way (is) run

Der Jüngling ist übel   d'ran
the lad   is badly off thereby

Es ist eine alte Geschichte,
it is an old story

Doch bleibt   sie immer neu;
yet   remains (it) always new

A lad loves a girl, who has chosen another; this other loves another, and has married her.

The girl, out of pique, takes the first man who comes along, and our lad gets the worst of it.

It is an old, old story, but stays for ever new; and he to whom it happens – his heart breaks in two.

Und wem   sie just passieret,
and to whom (it) just happened

Dem   bricht das Herz entzwei.
to him breaks the heart in two

   xii.

Am   leuchtenden Sommermorgen
on the bright   summer-morning

Geh' ich im   Garten herum.
walk I   in the garden about

Es flüstern und sprechen die Blumen,
(it) whisper and talk   the flowers

Ich aber wandle stumm.
I   but wander silently

Es flüstern und sprechen die Blumen,
(it) whisper and speak   the flowers

Und schau'n mitleidig mich an:
and look   pityingly me   at

'Sei unsrer Schwester nicht böse,
 be to our sister   not angry

Du trauriger, blasser Mann.'
you sad   pale   man

   xiii.

Ich hab' im   Traum geweinet,
I   have in the dream wept

Mir träumte, du lägest   im   Grab.
to me dreamt you were lying in the grave

Ich wachte auf, und die Träne
I   woke up and the tear

Floss   noch von der Wange herab.
flowed still from the cheek down

Ich hab' im   Traum geweinet,
I   have in the dream wept

Mir   träumt', du verliessest   mich.
to me dreamt you were forsaking me

xii.

On a bright summer morning I
wander in the garden. The flowers
speak in whispers, but silently I
pass by.

The flowers speak in whispers,
and gaze at me in pity. 'Be not
angry with our sister – you pale,
sad man.'

xiii.

In my dream I was weeping; I
dreamt you lay in your grave. I
awoke, and down my cheeks the
tears still flowed.

In my dream I was weeping; I
dreamt you were forsaking me. I
awoke, and went on weeping, long
and bitterly.

Ich wachte auf, und ich weinte
I   woke up and I wept

Noch lange bitterlich.
still long bitterly

Ich hab' im   Traum geweinet,
I   have in the dream wept

Mir   träumte, du wär'st mir   noch gut.
to me dreamt you were to me still good

Ich wachte auf, und noch   immer
I   woke up   and – still –

Strömt   meine Tränenflut.
streams my   flood of tears

In my dream I was weeping; I
dreamt you cared for me still. I
awoke, and even now my
streaming tears flood on.

xiv.

Allnächtlich im   Traume seh' ich dich,
nightly   in the dream see I   you

Und sehe dich freundlich grüssen,
and see you kindly   greeting

Und laut   aufweinend stürz' ich mich
and loudly weeping   throw I   myself

Zu deinen süssen Füssen.
at your   dear feet

xiv.

Each night in a dream I see you – I
see you kindly greet me; and
loudly sobbing, I throw myself at
your dear feet.

Du siehest mich an wehmütiglich
you look me at sadly

Und schüttelst das blonde Köpfchen;
and shake   the fair   little head

Aus deinen Augen schleichen sich
from your eyes   steal   (themselves)

Das Perlentränentröpfchen.
the little pearl tear-drops

Wistfully you look at me, and
shake your small, fair head; and
from your eyes steal drops of tears
like pearls.

Du sagst mir heimlich ein leises Wort
you tell me secretly a   gentle word

Und gibst mir den Strauss   von Zypressen.
and give me the bouquet of cypresses

Ich wache auf, und der Strauss   ist fort,
I   wake up and the bouquet is gone

Und's Wort hab' ich vergessen.
and the word have I   forgotten

You whisper a gentle word to me,
and give me a wreath of cypress. I
wake – the wreath is gone, and the
word I have forgotten.

xv.

Aus alten Märchen winkt es
from old fairy tales beckons it

Hervor mit weisser Hand,
forth with white hand

Da singt es und da klingt es
there is singing it and there is ringing it

Von einem Zauberland;
from a magic-land

Wo bunte Blumen blühen
where gay flowers bloom

Im gold'nen Abendlicht,
in the golden evening light

Und lieblich duftend glühen,
and sweetly scented glow

Mit bräutlichem Gesicht;
with bridal face

Und grüne Bäume singen
and green trees sing

Uralte Melodei'n,
ancient melodies

Die Lüfte heimlich klingen,
the breezes secretly sound

Und Vögel schmettern drein;
and birds warble thereto

Und Nebelbilder steigen
and misty figures rise

Wohl aus der Erd' hervor,
(indeed) from the earth forth

Und tanzen luft'gen Reigen,
and dance airy dances

Im wunderlichen Chor;
in the strange throng

Und blaue Funken brennen
and blue sparks burn

An jedem Blatt und Reis,
on every leaf and twig

xv.

A white hand beckons from the old fairy tales; and there is singing and ringing from a magic land.

There gay flowers bloom in the golden evening light, and, with sweet-scented bridal faces glow.

And green trees chant the ancient melodies; and breezes softly murmur to the warbling of birds.

And misty figures rise up from the earth – a strange company circling in airy dance.

And blue sparks glitter on every leaf and twig, and red lights flitter crazily around.

Und rote Lichter rennen
and red lights run

Im   irren, wirren   Kreis;
in the crazy confused circle

Und laute Quellen brechen
and loud springs gush

And riotous springs gush forth
from marble crags, with weird
reflections shining from the
streams.

Aus   wildem Marmorstein,
from rough marble-rock

Und seltsam   in den Bächen
and strangely in the streams

Strahlt fort   der Widerschein.
shines forth the reflection

Ach, könnt ich dorthin kommen,
ah   could I   thither come

Oh, if I could but go there, and
gladden my heart, take away all
my anguish, and be happy and
free!

Und dort   mein Herz erfreu'n,
and there my   heart gladden

Und aller Qual   entnommen,
and all   anguish taken away

Und frei und selig   sein!
and free and blissful be

Ach! jenes Land der   Wonne,
ah   that land of the delight

Ah, what a land of delight I see in
my dreams! But when the sun
rises, it vanishes like foam.

Das seh' ich oft   im   Traum,
that see I   often in the dream

Doch kommt die Morgensonne,
but   comes the morning sun

Zerfliesst's wie eitel   Schaum.
melts   it like mere foam

xvi.

Die alten, bösen Lieder,
the old   bad   songs

xvi.

The old hurtful songs, the evil, sad
dreams, let us fetch a great coffin,
and bury them now.

Die Träume bös' und arg,
the dreams bad and evil

Die   lasst uns jetzt begraben,
them let   us now bury

Holt   einen grossen Sarg.
fetch a   great   coffin

Hinein leg' ich gar   manches,
in it   lay I   indeed many things

Doch sag' ich noch nicht was;
but say I   yet not what

Der Sarg   muss sein noch grösser
the coffin must be still larger

Wie's   Heidelberger Fass.
than the Heidelberg tun

Und holt   eine Totenbahre,
and fetch a   bier

Und Bretter fest   und dick;
and planks firm and thick

Auch muss sie sein noch länger,
also must it be still longer

Als   wie zu Mainz die Brück'.
than as   at Mainz the bridge

Und holt   mir auch zwölf   Riesen,
and fetch me too   twelve giants

Die müssen noch stärker   sein,
they must   still · stronger be

Als   wie der starke Christoph,
than as   the strong Christopher

Im   Dom   zu Köln   am   Rhein.
in the cathedral at Colongne on the Rhine

Die sollen den Sarg   forttragen,
they shall the coffin carry away

Und senken in's   Meer hinab;
and sink   in the ocean down

Denn solchem   grossen Sarge
for   to such (a) great   coffin

Gebührt ein grosses Grab.
is due   a   great grave

Wisst ihr, warum der Sarg   wohl
know you why   the coffin indeed

So gross und schwer mag sein?
so huge and heavy may be

Ich senkt' auch   meine Liebe
I   sank indeed my   love

Und meinen Schmerz hinein.
and my   grief   in it

Many things will I lay within, but what I'll not yet say; the coffin must be greater than the Heidelberger tun.

Then fetch a bier and planks that are thick and firm – for it is longer even than the bridge at Mainz!

And fetch me twelve giants, who are stronger than Saint Christopher in Cologne cathedral on the Rhine.

They shall carry the coffin away, to sink in the ocean deeps; for so mighty a coffin deserves a mighty grave.

And do you know why the coffin must be so heavy and huge? Because there inside I sank all my love, and all my grief.

28. *DEIN ANGESICHT*
YOUR FACE

28. YOUR FACE

Heinrich Heine

Dein Angesicht, so lieb   und schön,
your face   so dear and lovely

Das hab' ich jüngst im   Traum geseh'n,
that have I   lately in the dream seen

Es ist so mild und engelgleich,
it is so mild and angelic

Und doch so bleich, so schmerzenreich.
and yet so pale   so sorrowful

Last night in a dream I saw your
sweet and lovely face; so gentle
and angelic, yet so sorrowful, so
pale.

Und nur die Lippen, die   sind rot;
and only the lips   they are red

Bald aber küsst sie   bleich der Tod.
soon but kisses them pale   the death

Erlöschen   wird das Himmelslicht,
be extinguished will the heaven's-light

Das aus   den frommen Augen bricht.
that out of the innocent eyes   breaks

Only your lips are rosy still, but
soon they will fade when kissed by
death, and the divine light that
shines in your innocent eyes will
be dimmed.

29. *FRAUENLIEBE   UND*
WOMEN'S LOVE AND
-LEBEN
WOMEN'S LIFE

29. WOMAN'S LOVE
AND LIFE

Adalbert von Chamisso

i.

Seit ich ihn gesehen,
since I   him seen

Glaub' ich blind zu sein;
believe I   blind to be

Wo   ich hin   nur blicke,
where I   towards -ever look

Seh' ich ihn allein;
see I   him only

i.

Since first I saw him I have been
as if blind; I see only him wherever
I look. His image hovers before me
as in a waking dream, and rises
from deepest darkness all the
brighter.

Wie im   wachen Traume
as   in the awake dream

Schwebt sein Bild   mir vor,
hovers   his image me before

Taucht aus   tiefstem Dunkel,
emerges out of deepest darkness

Heller   nur empor.
brighter only up

Sonst   ist licht- und farblos
besides is dark and colourless

Alles   um   mich her,
everything round me   about

Nach   der Schwestern Spiele
towards the sisters'   playing

Nicht begehr'   ich mehr,
not   hanker after I   more

Möchte   lieber weinen,
would like rather to weep

Still   im   Kämmerlein;
quietly in the little bedroom

Seit   ich ihn gesehen,
since I   him seen

Glaub' ich blind zu sein.
believe I   blind to be

Everything around me is colourless and dull; I care no longer for my sisters' frolics. I would rather weep alone in my little room; since first I saw him I have been as if blind.

ii.

Er, der Herrlichste   von allen,
he the most splendid of   all

Wie so milde, wie so gut!
how so gentle how so good

Holde Lippen, klares Auge,
sweet lips   clear eye

Heller Sinn und fester Mut.
clear mind and firm courage

So wie dort in blauer Tiefe,
– as – there in blue   depth

Hell   und herrlich, jener Stern,
bright and glorious that star

ii.

He, the most splendid of all, as gentle as he is good – with his tender lips, bright eyes, clear mind and firm courage.

Like a bright and glorious star in the lofty blue, so too is he in my firmament: exalted and remote.

Also Er in meinem Himmel,
thus he in my   firmament

Hell   und herrlich, hehr   und fern.
bright and glorious exalted and remote

Wandle, wandle, deine Bahnen,
go   go   your paths

Go, go your way; whilst I behold
your radiance, behold it in my
humility, full of joy and misery.

Nur betrachten deinen Schein,
just to behold your   shine

Nur in Demut   ihn betrachten,
just in humility it   to behold

Selig   nur und traurig sein!
blissful just and sad   to be

Höre nicht mein stilles Beten,
hear not   my   silent praying

You shall not hear my silent
prayer offered for your joy alone.
You, my high, and glorious star,
can never know a lowly maid like
me.

Deinem Glücke   nur geweiht;
to your happiness only dedicated

Darfst mich nied're Magd nicht kennen,
may me lowly maid not   know

Hoher Stern der   Herrlichkeit!
high   star of the splendour

Nur die Würdigste von allen
only the worthiest of   all

Only she, the worthiest of all can
make your choice a happy one,
and her I'll bless a thousand times
in her sublimity.

Darf beglücken   deine Wahl,
may make happy your choice

Und ich will die Hohe   segnen
and I   will the sublime one bless

Viele   tausend   Mal.
many thousand times

Will mich   freuen   dann und weinen,
will (myself) to rejoice then and weep

Then I will rejoice and weep;
blissful, blissful I will be. Even
though my heart should break –
break, O heart, what matter?

Selig, selig   bin ich dann;
blissful blissful am I   then

Sollte mir   das Herz auch brechen,
should to me the heart even break

Brich, O Herz, was   liegt daran?
break O heart what lies thereon

iii.

Ich kann's nicht fassen, nicht glauben,
I   can it not grasp not believe

Es hat ein Traum mich berückt;
(it) has a   dream me   beguiled

Wie hätt' er doch unter   allen
how had he really amongst all

Mich Arme   erhöht und beglückt?
me   poor one exalted and blessed

Mir   war's, er habe gesprochen:
to me was it he had spoken

'Ich bin auf ewig dein',
 I   am for ever yours

Mir   war's, ich träume   noch immer,
to me was it I   were dreaming – still –

Es kann ja   nimmer so sein.
it can surely never   so be

O lass im   Traume mich sterben,
O let in the dream me   die

Gewieget an   seiner Brust,
rocked   upon his   breast

Den seligen Tod   mich schlürfen,
the blessed death me   to sip

In Tränen unendlicher Lust.
in tears   of infinite joy

    iv.

Du Ring an meinem Finger,
you ring on my   finger

Mein goldenes Ringelein,
my   golden little ring

Ich drücke dich fromm   an die Lippen,
I   press you devoutly to the lips

An das Herze mein.
to the heart mine

Ich hatt' ihn ausgeträumet,
I   had it   dreamed away

Der Kindheit friedlich   schönen Traum,
of the childhood peacefully beautiful dream

---

iii.

I cannot believe, or grasp it – I've been beguiled by a dream: that he from amongst all others, has blessed and exalted me?

It seemed as if he said to me: 'I am yours for ever!' I thought I must be dreaming still, for that could never be so.

O let me die within this dream, cradled upon his breast! Let me embrace a blessed death with tears of infinite joy!

iv.

O ring upon my finger, little ring of gold, with reverence I press you to my lips, with devotion to my heart.

The serene beauty of my childhood dream was gone; I found myself lost and alone in an endless, desolate world.

Ich fand   allein mich,   verloren
I   found alone myself lost

Im   öden,   unendlichen Raum.
in the desolate endless   space

Du Ring an meinem Finger,
you ring on my   finger

O ring upon my finger, you taught me, – opened my eyes for the first time to the deep and eternal in life.

Da   hast du   mich erst   belehrt,
there have you me   for the first time instructed

Hast meinem Blick   erschlossen
have to my   glance disclosed

Des   Lebens unendlichen, tiefen Wert.
of the life   eternal   deep value

Ich will   ihm dienen, ihm   leben,
I   want him to serve (for) him to live

I want to serve him, live for him, and wholly belong to him; I want to surrender, and find myself transfigured by his splendour.

Ihm angehören   ganz,
him to belong to wholly

Hin   selber   mich geben   und finden
myself myself me   to surrender and find

Verklärt   mich   in seinem Glanz.
transfigured myself in his   splendour

    v.

v.

Helft mir, ihr Schwestern,
help me   you sisters

Help me, sisters, help me today in my joy: to adorn myself, and eagerly twine the myrtle blossom about my brow.

Freundlich mich   schmücken,
kindly   myself to adorn

Dient der Glücklichen heute mir,
serve the happy one   today me

Windet geschäftig
twine   busily

Mir   um   die Stirne
to me round the brow

Noch   der   blühenden   Myrte Zier.
besides of the blossoming myrtle decoration

Als   ich befriedigt,
when I   satisfied

Whenever my beloved held me in his arms, my heart was full of joy, and always he looked forward with such longing to this day.

Freudigen Herzens,
of joyful heart

Sonst   dem   Geliebten im   Arme   lag,
formerly to the beloved in the arm(s) lay

Immer noch rief   er,
– still –   called he

Sehnsucht im   Herzen,
longing   in the heart

Ungeduldig den heutigen Tag.
impatiently the today's day

Helft mir, ihr Schwestern,
help me you sisters

Help me, sisters, help me banish
my foolish fears, that I may receive
him, the source of my joy, with
unclouded eyes.

Helft mir verscheuchen
help me to banish

Eine törichte Bangigkeit,
a   foolish anxiety

Dass ich mit klarem
that I   with clear

Aug' ihn empfange,
eye   him may receive

Ihn, die Quelle der   Freudigkeit.
him the source of the joyfulness

Bist, mein Geliebter,
are my beloved

When you, my beloved, come for
me, will your light shine on me, O
sun? In devotion, and humility, let
me bow to my lord.

Du mir   erschienen,
you to me appeared

Gibst du mir,   Sonne, deinen Schein?
give you to me sun   your light

Lass mich in Andacht,
let me in devotion

Lass mich in Demut,
let me in humility

Lass mich verneigen dem   Herren mein.
let me bow   to the lord   mine

Streuet ihm,   Schwestern,
strew to him sisters

Strew him with flowers, dear
sisters – bring him blossoming
roses! But you I bid a sad farewell,
as I joyfully leave the flock.

Streuet ihm   Blumen
strew to him flowers

Bringet ihm   knospende Rosen dar,
bring   to him budding roses –

Aber euch, Schwestern,
but you sisters

Grüss' ich mit Wehmut
greet I   with melancholy

Freudig scheidend aus   eurer Schar.
joyfully parting   from your flock

vi.   vi.

Süsser Freund, du blickest   Dearest one, you look at me in
sweet friend   you look   wonder; you cannot understand
                                               how I can weep. But let the rare
Mich verwundert   an,   jewelled drops in my eyes tremble
me   wonderingly at   with joy.

Kannst es nicht begreifen,
can   it not understand

Wie ich weinen kann;
how I   weep   can

Lass der feuchten Perlen
let the moist   pearls

Ungewohnte   Zier
unaccustomed embellishment

Freudighell   erzittern
joyously bright tremble

In dem Auge mir.
in the eye   to me

Wie so bang   mein Busen,   How anxious is my heart, how full
how so anxious my bosom   of bliss! If only I could find the
                                               words to say it! Come, hide your
Wie so wonnevoll!   face upon my breast, so I may
how so full of delight   whisper in your ear of all my joy.

Wüsst ich nur mit Worten,
knew I   only with words

Wie ich's sagen soll;
how I it   say   shall

Komm und birg   dein Antlitz
come and conceal your face

Hier an meiner Brust,
here on my   breast

Will ins   Ohr dir   flüstern
will into the ear to you whisper

Alle meine Lust.
all   my   joy

Weisst du nun die Tränen,
know you now the tears

Die   ich weinen kann,
which I   weep can

Sollst   du nicht sie   sehen
should you not   them see

Du geliebter Mann?
you beloved husband

Bleib' an   meinem Herzen,
stay against my   heart

Fühle dessen Schlag,
feel its   beat

Dass ich fest und fester
that I   firm and firmer

Nur dich drücken mag.
only you clasp   may

Hier an meinem Bette
here by my   bed

Hat die Wiege Raum,
has the cradle place

Wo   sie still   verberge
where it quietly may hide

Meinen holden Traum;
my   lovely dream

Kommen wird der Morgen,
come   will the morning

Wo   der Traum erwacht,
when the dream awakens

Und daraus dein Bildnis
and from it your image

Mir entgegen lacht.
me towards laughs

Now you understand the tears I
weep. Should you not see them,
my beloved husband? Stay near
my heart, and feel its beat, so I
may clasp you to me ever closer.

Here beside my bed will be the
cradle, softly sheltering my lovely
dream. The morning will come
when the dream comes true, and
from it your image will smile up at
me.

vii.

An meinem Herzen, an meiner Brust,
on my   heart   at my   breast

Du meine Wonne, du meine Lust!
you my   joy   you my   delight

Das Glück   ist die Liebe, die Lieb' ist das Glück,
the happiness is the love   the love is the happiness

Ich hab's gesagt und nehm's nicht zurück.
I   have it said and take it not back

Hab' überschwenglich mich   geschätzt
have rapturous   myself considered

Bin überglücklich aber jetzt.
am overjoyed   but now

Nur die da   säugt, nur die da   liebt,
only she there suckles only she there loves

Das Kind, dem   sie die Nahrung   gibt;
the child to whom she the nourishment gives

Nur eine Mutter weiss allein
only a   mother knows alone

Was lieben heisst und glücklich sein.
what to love means and happy   to be

O, wie bedaur' ich doch   den Mann,
O how pity   I   indeed the man

Der Mutterglück   nicht fühlen kann!
who mother-happiness not feel   can

Du lieber, lieber Engel, du,
you dear dear angel you

Du schauest mich an und lächelst dazu!
you look   me at and smile   too

viii.

Nun hast du mir   den ersten Schmerz getan,
now have you to me the first   pain   caused

Der aber   traf.
which however struck

Du schläfst, du harter, unbarmherz'ger Mann,
you sleep   you cruel merciless   man

Den Todesschlaf.
the death's-sleep

vii.

Lying on my heart, at my breast,
you my delight, my joy! Joy is love,
love is joy – I have said it, and
cannot deny it! I thought I knew
rapture, but now I know perfect
bliss. Only she who loves the child
she nourishes – only a mother can
know the meaning of happiness
and love. O how I pity a man, who
cannot know a mother's joy! My
dear sweet angel, how you look at
me and smile!

viii.

Now, for the first time you have
caused me grief, and it has struck
deep. Cruel and merciless, you
sleep the sleep of death.

Es blicket die Verlass'ne   vor   sich   hin,
(it) gazes the abandoned one in front of herself there

Die Welt   ist leer.
the world is empty

Geliebet hab' ich und gelebt, ich bin
loved   have I   and lived I   am

Nicht lebend mehr.
not   living more

Ich zieh' mich   in   mein Inn'res   still   zurück,
I   draw myself into my   inner self quietly back

Der Schleier fällt,
the veil   falls

Da   hab' ich dich und mein verlor'nes Glück,
there have I   you and my   lost   happiness

Du   meiner Welt!
you my world

Abandoned, I stare before me; the world is void. I have loved and lived, but now I live no more.

Silently I withdraw into myself, the veil falls. There I hold you and my lost happiness – you, my whole world.

30. *DIE KARTENLEGERIN*
THE CARD-LAYER

30. THE FORTUNE-
TELLER

Adalbert von Chamisso

Schlief   die Mutter endlich ein
fell asleep the mother at last –

Über ihrer Hauspostille?
over her book of family devotions

Nadel, liege du nun stille,
needle lie you now still

Nähen, immer nähen, nein!
sew   always sew   no

Legen will   ich mir die Karten.
to lay want I   me the cards

Ei, was hab' ich zu erwarten?
ah what have I to expect

Ei, was wird das Ende sein?
ah what will the end be

Has mother fallen asleep at last over her prayer-book? Now, needle, you can be still. Sewing, nothing but sewing – no! I'll just read the cards. Well, what does the future hold for me? Ah, where's it all leading?

Trüget   mich die Ahnung   nicht,
deceives me   the presentiment not

Zeigt sich   Einer, den   ich meine,
shows himself one   whom I   mean

Schön, da   kommt er ja,   der Eine,
good   there comes he indeed the one

Coeur-Bub   kannte   seine Pflicht.
knave of hearts recognised his   duty

Eine reiche Witwe? Wehe!
a   rich   widow alas

Ja, er freit   sie, ich vergehe!
yes he is courting her I   am lost

O verruchter Bösewicht!
O wicked   villain

Herzeleid,   und viel   Verdruss,
heart-sorrow and much annoyance

Eine Schul' und enge   Mauern –
a   school and narrow walls

Carreau-König,   der bedauern
king of diamonds who pities

Und zuletzt   mich trösten   muss.
and in the end me   comfort must

Ein Geschenk auf   art'ge Weise –
a   present in (a) nice   way

Er entführt   mich, eine Reise –
he carries off me   a   journey

Geld   und Lust   in Überfluss!
money and pleasure in plenty

Dieser Carreau-König   da
this   king of diamonds there

Muss ein Fürst sein, oder König,
must a   prince be   or   king

Und es fehlt daran   nur wenig,
and it lacks thereon only little

If I'm not deceived, the one and only is there – *the* one, I mean. Oh good, there he comes, my own love; the knave of hearts, he knew what he must do. A rich widow? Oh dear! Yes, he's courting her, I am lost! The wicked villain!

Sorrow, and a lot of trouble. A school with high, narrow walls, but the king of diamonds is sorry for me, and in the end he comforts me with a nice present. He takes me off on a journey – wealth and pleasure in plenty!

Now, this king of diamonds must be at least a prince, or even a king, and it won't take much to make me a princess! But there's an enemy trying to spoil it all for me with his Lordship. A fair man is close at hand –

Bin ich selber Fürstin   ja.
am I   myself princess indeed

Hier ein Feind, der mich zu schaden
here an enemy who me to harm

Sich   bemüht   bei seiner Gnaden,
himself takes trouble with his   Grace

Und ein Blonder   steht   mir nah.
and a   blond person stands me near

Ein Geheimnis kommt zu Tage,
a   secret   comes to day-(light)

Und ich flüchte noch beizeiten –
and I flee   still in good time

Fahret wohl, ihr Herrlichkeiten,
fare-well   you splendours

O das war ein harter Schlag!
O that was a hard blow

Hin ist Einer – eine Menge
gone is one   a   crowd

Bilden um   mich ein Gedränge,
forms round me a   throng

Dass ich sie   kaum zählen mag.
that I   them hardly count may

Kommt das dumme Frau'ngesicht,
comes the stupid woman's-face

Kommt die Alte   da   mit Keuchen,
comes the old woman there with wheezing

Lieb' und Lust mir zu verscheuchen,
love and joy me to drive away

Eh'   die Jugend mir gebricht?
before the youth me is wanting

Ach, die Mutter ist's, die aufwacht,
ah   the mother is it who wakes up

Und den Mund zu schelten aufmacht.
and the mouth to scold   opens

Nein, die Karten lügen nicht!
no   the cards lie   not

A secret comes to light – and I get
away by the skin of my teeth.
Goodbye to all these fine things –
oh, that was a bad blow! One has
gone, now a crowd appears all
round me, more than I can
possibly count.

And here's the face of a silly old
woman. Is she coming wheezing
along to drive away all the love
and happiness of my youth? Oh,
it's mother woken up, and getting
ready to scold me. Oh no, the
cards don't lie!

31. SONNTAGS AM RHEIN
SUNDAYS BY THE RHINE

31. SUNDAY BY THE RHINE

Robert Reinick

Des Sonntags in der Morgenstund'
of the Sunday in the morning-hour

How good it is to wander by the Rhine on a Sunday morning, when all around the church bells are ringing.

Wie wandert's sich so schön
how wanders it (itself) so beautifully

Am Rhein, wenn rings in weiter Rund'
by the Rhine when around in wider circle

Die Morgenglocken geh'n!
the morning-bells go

Ein Schifflein zieht auf blauer Flut,
a little boat moves on blue tide

A little boat sails in the blue waters, and on it they sing and rejoice. To sail along merrily so, little boat, must be good?

Da singt's und jubelt's drein;
there sings it and rejoices it thereto

Du Schifflein, gelt, das fährt sich gut
you little boat isn't that so that sails (itself) well

In all die Lust hinein?
in all the pleasure away

Vom Dorfe hallet Orgelton,
from the village echoes organ-sound

From the village echo the strains of an organ; a hymn can be heard, as a procession reverently moves from the church.

Es tönt ein frommes Lied,
(it) sounds a religious song

Andächtig dort die Prozession
devoutly there the procession

Aus der Kapelle zieth.
from the chapel moves

Und ernst in all die Herrlichkeit
and solemnly in all the splendour

And a castle looks solemnly down in its splendour, telling of the good days of old when it was built on the rock.

Die Burg hernieder schaut
the castle down looks

Und spricht von alter, guter Zeit,
and speaks of old good time

Die auf den Fels gebaut.
that on the rock built

Das alles   beut   der prächt'ger Rhein
(the) everything offers the glorious   Rhine

An seinem Rebenstrand,
on his   vine-shore

Und spiegelt recht im   hellsten Schein
and reflects truly in the clearest gleam

Das ganze Vaterland;
the whole fatherland

Das fromme, treue Vaterland
the good   true fatherland

In seiner vollen Pracht,
in his   full   splendour

Mit Lust und Liedern allerhand
with joy and songs   of all kinds

Vom   lieben Gott bedacht.
by the dear   God provided

All this is offered on the vine-clad
shores of the glorious Rhine, that
reflects in its gleaming the whole
Fatherland;

our glorious country, hallowed
and true, blessed by the good
Lord with joy and with song.

32. *DER HIDALGO*
THE (SPANISH) GENTLEMAN

32. THE SPANISH
GENTLEMAN

Emanuel Geibel

Es ist so süss   zu scherzen
it is so sweet to jest

Mit Liedern und mit Herzen
with songs   and with hearts

Und mit dem ernsten Streit!
and with the stern   combat

Erglänzt des   Mondes Schimmer,
shines of the moon   glimmer

Da   treibt's mich fort vom   Zimmer,
then urges it me   away from the chamber

Durch   Platz   und Gassen weit;
through square and streets far

Da   bin zur   Lieb' ich immer
there am to the love I   always

Wie zum   Gefecht bereit.
as   to the combat ready

How sweet it is to make merry
with songs and hearts, and in stern
combat. When the moon-shine is
bright, I must leave my chamber
to roam the streets and squares,
where I'm as ready for love as for a
duel.

Die Schönen von Sevilla
the fair ones of   Seville

Mit Fächern und Mantilla
with fan   and mantilla

Blicken den Strom entlang;
glance the river along

Sie lauschen mit Gefallen,
they listen   with favour

Wenn meine Lieder schallen
when my   songs sound

Zum Mandolinenklang,
to the mandoline-sound

Und dunkle Rosen fallen
and dark   roses fall

Mir vom   Balkon zum Dank.
to me from the balcony to the reward

The fair ladies of Seville, with their fans and mantillas, gaze down the river, and listen with delight to the echo of my songs and mandoline, and from their balconies dark roses fall as my reward.

Ich trage, wenn ich singe,
I   carry when I   sing

Die Zither und die Klinge,
the zither and the sword

Vom Toledan'schen Stahl.
of the Toledan   steel

Ich sing' an manchem Gitter
I   sing at many a   lattice

Und höhne manchen Ritter
and mock many   cavaliers

Mit keckem Lied zumal,
with bold   song above all

Den Damen gilt   die Zither,
the ladies   is aimed at the zither

Die Klinge dem Rival.
the sword the rival

I carry my zither when I sing, and my sword, with its blade of Toledo steel. I sing by many a gateway, mocking all the cavaliers with the boldness of my songs. The mandoline is for the ladies, the sword for my rivals.

Auf denn zum Abenteuer,
on then to the adventure

Schon losch der Sonne Feuer
already blotted of the sun   fire

Jenseits der Berge   aus.
beyond of the mountains out

Away then, to adventure! Already the fiery sun has sunk beyond the mountains. The twilight hours of this moonlit night bring tidings of love, or deadly combat.
Tomorrow I'll return home with flowers – or wounds.

Der   Mondnacht   Dämmrungsstunden,
of the moon-lit night twilight-hours

Sie   bringen Liebeskunden,
they bring   love's-tidings

Sie   bringen blut'gen Strauss,
they bring   bloody combat

Und Blumen oder Wunden
and flowers or   wounds

Trag' morgen   ich nach Haus.
carry next day I   – home –

33. *LUST DER   STURMNACHT*
JOY   OF THE STORMY-NIGHT

33. JOY IN A STORMY
NIGHT

Justinus Kerner

Wenn durch   Berg'   und Tale   draussen
when through mountain and valley outside

Regen schauert, Stürme brausen,
rain   pours   storms rage

Schild   und Fenster   hell   erklirren,
inn-sign and windows loudly clatter

Und in Nacht die Wandrer irren,
and in night the travellers lose their way

Ruht es sich   so süss   hier innen,
rests it itself so sweetly here within

Aufgelöst   in sel'ges   Minnen;
abandoned in blissful loving

All' der gold'ne Himmelsschimmer
all   the golden heaven's-shimmer

Flieht   herein ins   stille Zimmer.
retreats in here into the quiet room

Reiches   Leben, hab' Erbarmen!
abundant life   have mercy

Halt' mich fest in linden Armen!
hold me   fast in gentle arms

Lenzesblumen   aufwärts dringen,
spring-flowers upwards penetrate

When outside the rain pours down in the mountains and valleys, and storms rage, so that inn-signs and windows clatter, and wayfarers lose their way by night – how sweet is the stillness here within, where we are lost in love's delights. All the shining gold of heaven retreats to this quiet room. O abundant life, have mercy! Hold me fast in your gentle arms! Spring flowers are thrusting upwards, clouds are racing, and little birds sing. May you never end, you wild and stormy night! Let the windows clatter and inn-signs sway! Let the woods surge, and the waves roar – for I am embraced in the radiance of Heaven!

Wölklein   ziehn und Vöglein   singen.
(little) clouds move and (little) birds sing

Ende nie,   du Sturmnacht wilde!
end   never you storm-night wild

Klirrt, ihr Fenster, schwankt, ihr Schilde,
clatter you windows sway   you (inn)-signs

Bäumt euch,   Wälder, braus', o Welle,
rear up yourselves woods roar   O wave

Mich umfängt des   Himmels Helle!
me   embraces of the Heaven brilliance

34. WANDERLIED
WANDERING-SONG

Justinus Kerner

Wohlauf! Noch   getrunken den funkelnden Wein!
come on further drunk   the sparkling wine

Ade   nun, ihr Lieben!   Geschieden muss sein.
farewell now you dear friends parted   must be

Ade   nun, ihr Berge,   du väterlich Haus!
farewell now you mountains you paternal house

Es treibt in   die Ferne   mich mächtig hinaus.
it drives into the distant place me   mightily forth

Die Sonne, sie bleibet am   Himmel nicht steh'n
the sun   she remains in the sky   not   standing still

Es treibt sie, durch   Länder und Meere zu geh'n.
it drives her through lands   and seas to go

Die Woge nicht haftet am   einsamen Strand,
the wave not clings on the lonely   shore

Die Stürme, sie   brausen mit Macht durch   das Land.
the storms they bluster with might through the land

Mit eilenden Wolken der Vogel dort zieht
with hastening clouds the bird there moves

Und singt in der Ferne   ein heimatlich Lied.
and sings in the distance a   native   song

So treibt es den Burschen durch   Wälder und Feld,
so drives it the youth   through woods and field

Zu gleichen der Mutter, der wandernden Welt.
to resemble the mother the wandering world

34. SONG OF THE
WANDERER

Come, drink one more glass of
sparkling wine! And now farewell,
dear friends, we must part.
Farewell, you mountains!
Farewell, my father's house, for I
am mightily stirred to journey afar!

The sun is never still in the sky; it
hastens on over land and sea.
Waves never cling to lonely shores;
storms rage mightily over the land.

A bird flies with the hastening
clouds, and far away sings its
native song. The young man is
driven through woods and fields,
to roam the world like Mother
Earth.

Da   grüssen ihn Vögel bekannt über'm   Meer,
there greet   him birds familiar over the sea

Sie flogen von Fluren   der   Heimat   hierher;
they flew   from meadows of the homeland here

Da   duften   die Blumen vertraulich um   ihn,
there smell sweet the flowers familiarly about him

Sie   trieben vom   Lande die Lüfte   dahin.
them drove from the land   the breezes thither

Die Vögel, die   kennen sein väterlich Haus,
the birds they know   his paternal house

Die Blumen, die pflanzt' er der   Liebe zum   Strauss,
the flowers that planted he of the love for the nosegay

Und Liebe, die folgt   ihm, sie geht ihm zur   Hand:
and love   she follows him she lends him (the) hand

So wird   ihm   zur   Heimat das ferneste
so becomes to him for the home   the most distant
    Land.
    land

Over the sea he is greeted by birds
that he knew from his homeland
fields; and breezes bring familiar
scents of flowers from his own
land.

The birds, they know his father's
house, the flowers, he once sowed,
he sowed for his sweetheart's posy.
And so love follows wherever he
goes – and the most distant land
becomes his home.

35. ERSTES GRÜN
FIRST   GREEN

35. FIRST GREEN

Justinus Kerner

Du junges Grün, du frisches Gras!
you young green you fresh   grass

Wie manches Herz durch   dich genas,
how many a heart through you recovered

Das von des   Winters Schnee erkrankt,
that from of the winter snow sickens

O wie mein Herz nach dir verlangt!
O how my   heart for   you longs

Schon wächst du aus   der Erde Nacht,
already grow   you out of the earth night

Wie dir mein Aug' entgegenlacht!
how you my eye   laughs towards

Hier in des   Waldes stillem Grund
here in of the wood quiet earth

Drück ich dich, Grün, an Herz und Mund.
press I   you green to heart and mouth

You green so new, you grass so
fresh – how many hearts you have
healed, that pined with winter's
snow! O how my heart fills with
longing for you!

Already you grow from the earth's
dark night – Oh, how my eyes
laugh to see you! Here in the earth
of the quiet wood, I press your
green to my heart and lips.

Wie treibt's mich von den Menschen fort!
how drives it me from the people away

Mein Leid das hebt kein Menschenwort;
my grief that removes no people's-word

Nur junges Grün, ans Herz gelegt,
only young green on the heart laid

Macht, dass mein Herze stiller schlägt.
causes that my heart quieter beats

I am driven away from my fellow men; no words of theirs can assuage my grief. Only you young green, that I laid on my heart, brought quietness to its beating.

36. *STILLE LIEBE*
   SILENT LOVE

Justinus Kerner

Könnt' ich dich in Liedern preisen,
could I you in songs praise

Säng' ich dir das längste Lied,
would sing I to you the longest song

Ja, ich würd' in allen Weisen
yes I would in all tunes

Dich zu singen nimmer müd'.
you to sing never weary

Doch was immer mich betrübte,
but what always me grieved

Ist, dass ich nur immer stumm
is that I only always silently

Tragen kann dich, Herzgeliebte!
carry can you beloved heart

In des Busens Heiligtum.
in of the bosom shrine

Dieser Schmerz hat mich bezwungen,
this grief has me overcome

Dass ich sang dies kleine Lied,
that I sang this little song

Doch von bitterm Leid durchdrungen,
indeed with bitter grief penetrated

Dass noch keins auf dich geriet.
that yet none to you succeeded

36. SILENT LOVE

If I could but praise you in my songs, how endless they would be, and never would I weary of singing them to you.

But it always grieves me, dear love, that I can only hold you silently in my heart's silent shrine.

My grief has overcome me, so I sing this little song. But I am filled with bitter pain that not one song that I sang to you has yet succeeded.

37. *STILLE TRÄNEN*
   SILENT TEARS

37. SILENT TEARS

Justinus Kerner

Du bist vom   Schlaf erstanden
you are from the sleep risen

You rise from sleep and wander
through the meadow; wondrous
blue of the sky spreads over the
countryside.

Und wandelst durch   die Au',
and wander through the meadow

Da   liegt ob   allen Landen,
there lies above all   countryside

Der Himmel wunderblau.
the sky   wonderfully blue

So lang du ohne   Sorgen
so long you without cares

But whilst you slumbered so free
of care, these heavens wept
unceasing tears the whole night
through.

Geschlummert schmerzenlos,
slumbered   painlessly

Der Himmel bis zum   Morgen
the sky   till to the morning

Viel   Tränen niedergoss.
many tears   poured down

In stillen Nächten weinet
in still nights weeps

In such still nights many a man
weeps away his grief. And in the
morning you would think his heart
was always glad.

Oft   mancher   aus   den Schmerz,
often many a one away the grief

Und morgens   dann ihr meinet,
and each morning then you think

Stets   fröhlich sei sein Herz.
always glad   be his heart

38. *DIE SOLDATENBRAUT*
   THE SOLDIER-BRIDE

38. THE SOLDIER'S
   BRIDE

Eduard Mörike

Ach, wenn's nur der König auch wüsst',
ah   if it   only the king also knew

Oh, if the king only knew how
brave my sweetheart is! He would
lay down his life for the king – but
for me just the same.

Wie wacker mein Schätzelein   ist!
how brave my   (little) sweetheart is

Für den König, da   liess'   er sein Blut,
for the king   then would let run he his blood

Für mich aber ebenso gut.
for me   but just as well

Mein Schatz   hat kein Band   und kein' Stern,
my   sweetheart has no ribbon and no   star

Kein Kreuz, wie die vornehmen Herrn,
no   cross like the grand   gentlemen

Mein Schatz   wird   auch kein General:
my   sweetheart will be also no general

Hätt' er nur seinen Abschied einmal!
had he only his   discharge one day

Es   scheinen drei Sternen so hell
there shine   three stars   so brightly

Dort über Marienkapell';
there over Mary's-chapel

Da   knüpft uns ein rosenrot Band,
then unites us a   rose-red ribbon

Und ein Hauskreuz ist auch bei der   Hand.
and a   home-cross is also at (the) hand

My sweetheart has no ribbons or stars, no crosses like fine gentlemen. My sweetheart will never be a general – if only he'd bid it all farewell!

Three stars are shining brightly over St. Mary's church; to unite us there'll be a rose-red ribbon – and at home there'll also be a cross at hand.

39. *ROMANZE*
   ROMANCE

39. ROMANCE

Emanuel Geibel

Flutenreicher Ebro, blühendes   Ufer,
flooding-richly Ebro of blossoming shore

All' ihr grünen Matten, Schatten des   Waldes,
all you green meadows shadows of the wood

Fraget die Geliebte, die unter   euch ruhet,
ask   the beloved who among you rests

Ob in ihrem Glücke   sie meiner gedenket.
if in her   happiness she of me   thinks

Und ihr tauigen Perlen, die ihr im   Frührot
and you dewy   pearls that you in the sunrise

Den grünenden Rasen bunt   mit Farben schmückt,
the greening grass bright with colours adorn

O richly flooding Ebro, with your blossoming shores, all you green meadows, and woodland shades – ask my beloved as there she rests, if in her joy she thinks of me?

And you dewy pearls that at sunrise adorn the green grass with bright colours – ask my beloved, as she breathes the cool air, if in her joy she thinks of me?

Fraget die Geliebte, wenn sie Kühlung atmet,
ask   the beloved when she freshness breathes

Ob in ihrem Glücke   sie meiner gedenket.
if in her   happiness she of me thinks

Ihr laubigen Pappeln, schimmernde Pfade,
you leafy   poplars shimmering paths

Wo   leichten Fusses mein Mädchen wandelt,
where light   of foot my girl   wanders

Wenn sie euch begegnet, fragt sie, fragt sie,
when she you meets   ask her ask her

Ob in ihrem Glücke   sie meiner gedenket.
if in her   happiness she of me thinks

Ihr schwärmenden Vögel, die   den Sonnenaufgang singend
you roving   birds that the sunrise   singing

Ihr begrüsset mit Flötenstimmen,
you greet   with flute-voices

Fraget die Geliebte, dieses Ufers Blume,
ask   the beloved of this shore flower

Ob in ihrem Glücke   sie meiner gedenket.
if in her   happiness she of me thinks

You leafy poplars, you shimmering paths, where light of foot my sweetheart roams – ask her when she meets you – ask her, if in her joy she thinks of me?

You flocks of birds, that greet the dawn with voices like flutes – ask my beloved, flower of these shores, if in her joy she thinks of me?

40. *SONNTAG*
   SUNDAY

40. SUNDAY

Hoffmann von Fallersleben

Der Sonntag ist gekommen, ein Sträusschen auf dem Hut;
the Sunday is come   a nosegay   on the hat

Sein Aug' ist mild   und heiter, er meint's   mit allen
his eye is gentle and serene he means it with all
   gut.
   well

Er steiget auf die Berge,   er wandelt durch   das
he climbs up the mountains he wanders through the
   Tal,
   valley

Er ladet   zum Gebete die Menschen allzumal.
he summons to the prayer the people   all together

Sunday has come with flowers in his hat. His eyes are gentle and serene, and to all he bears good-will. He climbs the mountains, and wanders through the valley, summoning everyone to prayer.

Und wie in schönen Kleidern nun pranget jung und alt,
and as in lovely clothes now look fine young and old

Hat er für sie geschmücket die Flur und auch den
has he for them bedecked the meadow and also the
Wald.
wood

Und wie er allen Freude und Frieden bringt und
and as he to everyone joy and peace brings and
Ruh',
rest
So ruf' auch du nun jedem 'Gott grüss' dich!' freundlich
so call also you now each God greet you amiably
zu.
to

And as young and old all don their Sunday best, he bedecks the meadows and the woods. He brings joy and peace to everyone; so may you, too, call 'God bless you!' to everyone around.

41. DER SANDMANN
THE SANDMAN

41. THE SANDMAN

Gustav Hermann Kletka

Zwei feine Stieflein hab' ich an,
two fine little boots have I on

Mit wunderweichen Söhlchen dran;
with very soft (little) soles on them

Ein Säcklein hab' ich hinten auf,
a (little) sack have I behind on

Husch! trippl' ich rasch die Trepp' hinauf,
quick trip I quickly the stairs up

Und wenn ich in die Stube tret',
and when I into the room go

Die Kinder beten ihr Gebet;
the children are praying their prayer

Von meinem Sand zwei Körnerlein
from my sand two little grains

Streu' ich auf ihre Äugelein,
strew I on their little eyes

Da schlafen sie die ganze Nacht
then sleep they the whole night

In Gottes und der Englein Wacht.
in God's and the little angels' watch

I wear fine little boots, with soft little soles; with a sack on my back, I trip up the stairs. The children are saying their prayers as I enter their room, and if I drop two grains of sand in their eyes, they will sleep the night through, whilst God and his angels keep watch.

Von meinem Sand zwei Körnerlein
from my   sand two little grains

Streut' ich auf ihre Äugelein:
strewed I   on their little eyes

Den frommen Kindern soll gar   schön
to the good   children shall perhaps beautifully

Ein froher Traum vorübergehn.
a   happy dream go past

Nun risch und rasch mit Sack und Stab
now 'snip' and 'snap' with sack and staff

Nur wieder jetzt die Trepp' hinab,
just again now the stairs down

Ich kann nicht länger müssig stehn,
I   can not longer idle   be

Muss heut' noch zu gar vielen gehn –
must today still to very many go

Da   nickt ihr schon und lacht im   Traum,
there nod you already and laugh in the dream

Und öffnete doch mein Sacklein   kaum.
and opened yet   my   (little) sack hardly

I dropped two little grains of sand in their eyes, for good children should have sweet dreams. Now, snip snap, with my sack and stick, I trip down the stairs again. I can be idle no more, for I have many to visit this night. Already you nod and smile in your dreams – and I hardly opened my sack at all!

42. *MARIENWÜRMCHEN*
LADYBIRD

(From *Des   Knaben Wunderhorn,*
        of the boy   magic-horn
folk poems published by
Achim von Arnim and Clemens Brentano)

Marienwürmchen, setze dich
ladybird   seat yourself

Auf meine Hand, auf meine Hand,
on my   hand on my   hand

Ich tu' dir nichts   zu Leide,
I   do you nothing to harm

Es soll   dir   nichts zu Leid' gescheh'n
it shall to you nothing to harm happen

Will   nur deine bunten Flügel seh'n
want only your bright wings to see

Bunte Flügel, meine Freude!
bright wings my   joy

42. LADYBIRD

O ladybird, come, and sit on hand, for I'll do nothing to harm or hurt you. I just want to see your bright-coloured wings, for bright-coloured wings are my joy!

Marienwürmchen, fliege weg,
ladybird   fly   away

Dein Häuschen brennt, die Kinder schrei'n
your little house burns the children cry

So sehre, wie so sehre.
so much how so much

Die böse Spinne spinnt sie   ein,
the bad spider spins them in

Marienwürmchen, flieg' hinein,
ladybird   fly   in there

Deine Kinder   schreien sehre.
your children cry   much

Marienwürmchen, fliege hin
ladybird   fly   there

Zu Nachbars   Kind', zu Nachbars   Kind',
to neighbour's children to neighbour's children

Sie tun dir nichts   zu Leide,
they do you nothing to harm

Es soll dir   da   kein Leid gescheh'n,
it shall to you there no   harm happen

Sie wollen deine bunten Flügel seh'n,
they want your bright wings to see

Und grüss' sie   alle   beide.
and greet them – both of them –

O ladybird, fly home, for your house is on fire, and your children are mightily crying. All round them a spider is spinning a web, so fly home for your children are crying!

O ladybird fly to the children next-door for they will not harm or hurt you. They just want to see your bright-coloured wings, so go there and wave to them both.

43. *DIE WANDELNDE GLOCKE*
THE WALKING   BELL

43. THE WALKING
BELL

Johann Wolfgang von Goethe

Es   war ein Kind, das wollte nie
there was a child that would never

Zur   Kirche sich bequemen,
to the church itself put up with

Und sonntags   fand es stets ein Wie,
and on Sundays found it always a how

Den Weg in's   Feld zu nehmen.
the way into the field to take

Die Mutter sprach: 'Die Glocke tönt,
the mother said   the bell   is ringing

Und so ist dir's   befohlen,
and so is to you it ordered

Once there was a child who would never go to church. And on Sundays would wander off into the fields.

His mother said: 'The bell is ringing, and telling you what you must do. And if you don't change

Und hast du dich   nicht hingewöhnt
and have you yourself not   got used to there

Sie kommt und wird dich holen.'
she comes and will you fetch

your ways, it will come along and
fetch you.'

Das Kind, es denkt: 'Die Glocke hängt
the child it thinks the bell   hangs

Da   droben   auf dem Stuhle,'
there up above on the belfry

Schon   hat's den Weg in's   Feld gelenkt,
already has it the way into the field wended

Als lief' es aus   der Schule.
as ran it out of the school

The child, he thinks: the bell
hangs in the 'belfry!' and already
he's off to the fields, as if he were
playing truant from school.

Die Glocke, Glocke, tönt nicht mehr,
the bell   bell   rings not   more

Die Mutter hat gefackelt.
the mother has fibbed

Doch welch' ein Schrecken hinterher!
but   what a   fright   afterwards

Die Glocke kommt gewackelt.
the bell   comes wobbling

The bell stops ringing, Mother
was making it up. But oh, what a
fright! there's the bell, wobbling
along!

Sie wackelt schnell, man glaubt   es kaum;
she wobbles fast   one believes it hardly

Das arme Kind im   Schrecken,
the poor child in the fright

Es läuft, es rennt als wie im   Traum;
it runs it runs as if in the dream

Die Glocke wird es decken.
the bell   will it cover

It wobbles along fast, it's hard to
believe – The poor child in his
fright runs as if in a bad dream –
that the bell will come and trap
him!

Doch nimmt es   richtig seinen Husch, –
but   – he   goes off in a real rush –

Und mit   gewandter Schnelle,
and with nimble   speed

Es eilt   durch   Anger,   Feld und Busch
it hurries through meadow field and bush

Zur   Kirche, zur   Kapelle,
to the church to the chapel

But he goes like the wind, and
nimbly speeds through the fields
and woods, rushes to the church,
and the chapel.

Und jeden Sonn- und Feiertag
and every Sun- and Feast-day

Gedenkt es an den Schaden,
thinks   it of the mischief

Now on Sundays and Feastdays
he remembers his fright; and at
the first stroke of the bell he's off –
so no one will come and fetch him!

Lässt durch   den ersten Glockenschlag
lets   through the first   bell-stroke

Nicht in Person sich   laden.
not   in person itself be summoned.

44. *MEIN SCHÖNER STERN*
MY   LOVELY   STAR

Friedrich Rückert

Mein schöner Stern! ich bitte dich,
my   lovely star   I   beg you

O lasse du dein heitres Licht
O let   you your serene light

Nicht trüben durch   den Dampf in mir,
not   darken through the mist   in me

Vielmehr den Dampf in mir zu Licht,
rather   the mist   in me to light

Mein schöner Stern, verklären   hilf!
my   lovely star   to transfigure help

Mein schöner Stern! ich bitte dich,
my   lovely star   I   beg you

Nicht senk' herab zur   Erde dich,
not   sink down to the earth yourself

Weil   du mich noch hier unten siehst,
because you me   still here below see

Heb' auf vielmehr zum   Himmel mich,
raise up rather   to the Heaven me

Mein schöner Stern, wo   du schon bist!
my   lovely star   where you already are

44. MY LOVELY STAR

O lovely star! I beg you to let not
your serene light be dimmed by
the darkness within me; rather let
that dark cloud be transfigured by
your light, O lovely star!

O lovely star! I beg you not to
descend to the earth because you
see me here below; but rather raise
me up to Heaven, where you, O
lovely star, already are!

45. *AUFTRÄGE*
MESSAGES

Christian L'Egru

Nicht so schnelle, nicht so schnelle!
not   so fast   not so fast

Wart' ein wenig, kleine Welle!
wait a little   little wave

45. MESSAGES

Not so fast, not so fast – wait a
moment, little wave! I've a
message to send my sweetheart.
As you flow past her, give her my
love!

Will dir einen Auftrag geben
want you a   message to give

An die Liebste mein.
to the beloved mine

Wirst du ihr   vorüberschweben,
will   you to her float past

Grüsse sie mir   fein!
greet her to me fine

Sag' ich wäre   mitgekommen,
say I   would (have) come along too

Auf dir selbst   herabgeschwommen:
on you yourself down swum

Für den Gruss   einen Kuss
for the greeting a   kiss

Kühn mir   zu erbitten,
boldly to me to beg for

Doch der   Zeit Dringlichkeit
but   of the time urgency

Hätt'   es nicht gelitten.
would have it not   allowed

Nicht so eilig! halt! erlaube,
not   so quick stop allow (me)

Kleine, leicht beschwingte Taube!
little   light-winged   dove

Habe dir   was   aufzutragen
have to you something to carry out

An die Liebste mein!
to the beloved mine

Sollst ihr   tausend Grüsse   sagen,
shall to her thousand greetings say

Hundert obendrein.
hundred over and above

Sag' ich wär   mit dir geflogen,
say I   would be with you flown

Über Berg'   und Strom gezogen:
over mountain and river gone

Für den Gruss   einen Kuss
for the greeting a   kiss

Kühn mir zu erbitten,
boldly me to beg for

Tell her I would have come too, swimming along beside you, to beg for a kiss in return for my greeting. But the time was too pressing, and would not have allowed it.

Not so fast – please stop, and allow me – I've something to ask you, little, light dove! Give my sweetheart a thousand greetings, then a hundred more!

I'd have flown over hills and rivers, so I could boldly beg for a kiss, but the time was much too pressing, and would not have allowed it.

Doch der Zeit Dringlichkeit
but   of the time urgency

Hätt'   es nicht gelitten.
would have it not   allowed

Warte nicht, dass ich dich treibe,
wait   not   that I   you urge on

O du träge Mondesscheibe!
O you lazy moon's-disc

O you lazy moon, don't wait for me to urge you on – you know what I asked you to do: just peep through my sweetheart's window, and give her a bright greeting.

Weisst's ja,   was ich dir befohlen
know it indeed what I you bid

Für die Liebste mein:
for the beloved mine

Durch das Fensterchen   verstohlen
through the little window secretly

Grüsse sie mir   fein!
greet   her to me fine

Sag', ich wär'   auf dich gestiegen,
say I would (have) on you climbed

Selber zu ihr hinzufliegen:
myself to her to fly

I would have climbed up and flown with you, too, to exchange a kiss for a greeting. But now it's your fault – for you were in such haste!

Für den Gruss   einen Kuss
for the greeting a   kiss

Kühn mir   zu erbitten,
boldly (to me) to ask for

Du seist Schuld, Ungeduld
you be (at) fault impatience

Hätt' mich nicht gelitten.
would have me not allowed

46. *RÖSELEIN,   RÖSELEIN!*
LITTLE ROSE, LITTLE ROSE

46. LITTLE ROSE

Wilfried von der Neun

Röselein, Röselein
little rose little rose

Müssen denn Dornen sein?
must   then thorns be

Little rose, little rose, must you have thorns? Once I fell asleep by a shady little brook, and dreamed such sweet dreams; I saw in the

Schlief   am   schatt'gen Bächelein
fell asleep by the shady   little brook

Einst zu süssem Träumen ein,
once to sweet dreaming –

Sah in goldner Sonne Schein
saw in golden sun   -shine

Dornenlos ein Röselein,
thornless a   little rose

Pflückt' es auch und küsst' es fein:
plucked it also and kissed it delicately

'Dornloses Röselein!'
thornless little rose

Ich erwacht' und schaute drein:
I   awoke   and looked therein

'Hätt ich's doch! Wo   mag   es sein?'
had   I it   indeed where might it be

Rings   im   weiten   Sonnenschein
around in the spacious sunshine

Standen nur   Dornröselein!
stood   only little thorn-roses

Und das Bächlein   lachte   mein:
and the little brook laughed of me

'Lass du   nur dein Träumen sein!
let   you just your dreaming be

Merk dir's   fein:
mark to you it well

Dornröslein   müssen sein!'
little thorn-roses must   be

golden sunlight a little rose
without thorns. I plucked it, and
gently kissed it. 'Little rose
without thorns!'

I awoke and looked about me: 'If
only it were here! Where might it
be?' All around in the sunlight
grew only roses with thorns. And
the little brook laughed at me!
'You just stop dreaming, and mark
this well; all roses need thorns!'

47. MEINE ROSE
MY   ROSE

Nikolaus Lenau

Dem   holden Lenzgeschmeide,
to the lovely spring-jewels

Der   Rose, meiner Freude,
to the rose to my joy

47. MY ROSE

To this lovely jewel of Spring, to
the rose, my joy, already pale and
bowed by the scorching rays of the
sun: I hold out this cup of water
from the dark, deep spring.

Die schon   gebeugt und blasser
that already bowed and paler

Vom   heissen Strahl der   Sonnen,
from the hot   ray   of the sun

Reich'   ich den Becher Wasser
hold out I   the cup   water

Aus dunklem, tiefem Bronnen.
from dark   deep spring

Du Rose meines Herzens!
you rose of my heart

Vom   stillen Strahl des Schmerzens
from the silent ray of the grief

Bist du gebeugt und blasser;
are you bowed and paler

Ich möchte   dir   zu   Füssen,
I   would like to you at (your) feet

Wie dieser Blume Wasser,
as   to this flower water

Still   meine Seele giessen!
silently my   soul to pour

Könnt' ich dann auch nicht sehen
could I   then also not see

Dich freudig   auferstehen.
you joyously rise up

O rose of my heart! You are pale
and bowed by the silent pangs of
grief; I would silently pour out my
soul at your feet, as I pour water
on this flower. May I not then see
you joyously revive?

48. REQUIEM
REQUIEM

Catholic poem

Ruh' von   schmerzensreichen Mühen
rest from pain-abundant   labours

Aus und heissem Liebesglühen;
–   and ardent love's-glowing

Der nach seligem Verein
he for   blissful union

Trug Verlangen,
bore yearning

48. REQUIEM

Rest in peace from the toils and
deep suffering of ardent love; he
who so long did yearn for blissful
union has entered in the dwelling
of his Saviour.

Ist gegangen
is entered

Zu des   Heilands Wohnung ein.
to of the Saviour dwelling in

Dem   Gerechten leuchten helle   Bright stars shine on the tomb of
to the righteous shine   bright   the righteous one, who himself will
                                                    appear as a star, when he beholds
Sterne in des   Grabes Zelle,   the Lord in the glory of Heaven.
stars in of the grave   cell

Ihm,   der selbst   als Stern der   Nacht
to him who himself as star of the night

Wird erscheinen,
will   appear

Wenn er seinen
when he his

Herrn erschaut in Himmelspracht.
Lord beholds in Heavens's-glory

Seid Fürsprecher, heil'ge Seelen,   Intercede for him, holy souls, let
be   intercessors holy   souls   your comfort not fail him, Holy
                                                    Spirit! Hark, triumphant psalms
Heil'ger Geist, lass Trost   nicht fehlen.   resound in solemn tones to the
Holy   Spirit let comfort not be lacking   beautiful sounds of an angel's
                                                    harp:
Hörst du? Jubelsang   erklingt,
hear you jubilation-song resounds

Feiertöne,
solemn tones

Darein die schöne
thereto the lovely

Engelsharfe singt:
angel's-harp sings

Ruh' von   schmerzensreichen Mühen . . .   Rest in peace, from the toils of
rest from pain-abundant   labours   deep suffering . . .

Richard Wagner
(1813–1883)

1. *FÜNF GEDICHTE FÜR EINE*
FIVE POEMS FOR A
FRAUENSTIMME
WOMAN'S-VOICE

1. FIVE SONGS

Mathilde Wesendonck

i. *Der Engel*
the angel

i. The angel

In der Kindheit frühen Tagen
in of the childhood early days

Hört' ich oft von Engeln sagen,
heard I often of angels tell

When I was very young, I often heard tell of angels, who left the sublime joys of heaven for the sunny earth,

Die des Himmels hehre Wonne
who of the heaven sublime joy

Tauschen mit der Erdensonne,
exchange with the earth's-sun

Dass, wo bang ein Herz in Sorgen
so that where anxiously a heart in sorrows

where hidden from the world a heart was pining in anxious grief, silently bleeding and wasting away mid floods of tears;

Schmachtet vor der Welt verborgen,
pines from the world hidden

Dass, wo still es will verbluten,
so that where silently it desires to shed blood

Und vergehn in Tränenfluten,
and to waste away in tears-floods

Dass, wo brünstig sein Gebet
that where fervently its prayer

its prayer fervently begging only for deliverance. Then an angel would descend and bear it tenderly to Heaven.

Einzig um Erlösung fleht,
only for deliverance implores

Da der Engel niederschwebt,
then the angel floats down

Und es sanft gen Himmel hebt.
and it tenderly – heavenwards – raises

Ja, es stieg auch mir   ein Engel nieder,
yes it came also to me an angel down

Yes, an angel came down to me
too, and bore my spirit on
gleaming wings far from all grief to
Heaven!

Und auf leuchtendem Gefieder
and on gleaming   plumage

Führt er, ferne jedem   Schmerz,
bears he far   to every grief

Meinen Geist nun himmelwärts!
my   spirit now heavenwards

   ii. Stehe still!
    stand still

ii. Be still!

Sausendes, brausendes Rad   der   Zeit,
blustering raging   wheel of the time

Blustering, raging wheel of time,
you who measure eternity;
gleaming spheres in the wide
universe encircling the globe; O
halt, primeval creation – enough of
evolution, let me be!

Messer   du   der   Ewigkeit;
measurer you of the eternity

Leuchtende Sphären im   weiten All,
gleaming   spheres in the wide   universe

Die   ihr   umringt den Weltenball;
who you encircle the world-globe

Urewige   Schöpfung, halte doch ein,
ancient-eternal creation   halt do –

Genug des   Werdens, lass mich sein!
enough of the evolution let me   be

Halte   an dich,   zeugende   Kraft,
hold on to yourself procreating power

Hold back, creative power –
ancient of thoughts eternally
creating! Curb your breath, stay
your impulse, be still one second
long! Throbbing pulses, restrain
your beat. End, eternal day of
desiring,

Urgedanke,   der   ewig   schafft!
ancient-thought which eternally creates

Hemmet den Atem, stillet den Drang,
curb   the breath stay the impulse

Schweigend nur eine Sekunde lang!
being silent only one second   long

Schwellende Pulse, fesselt den Schlag;
growing   pulses fetter the beat

Ende, des   Wollens ew'ger Tag!
end   of the desiring eternal day

Dass in selig   süssem Vergessen
that in blessed sweet oblivion

that in sweet blessed oblivion, I
might measure all my joys! When
eyes in eyes are blissfully
absorbed, and soul submerged in

Ich mög   alle Wonnen ermessen!
I   might all   raptures measure

Wenn Aug' in Auge wonnig   trinken,
when eye   in eye   blissfully drink

Seele ganz   in Seele versinken;
soul wholly in soul submerge(s)

Wesen in Wesen sich wiederfindet,
being in being itself again finds

Und alles Hoffens Ende sich   kündet,
and all   of hope end   itself announces

Die Lippe verstummt   in staunendem Schweigen,
the lip   grows dumb in astonished silence

Keinen Wunsch mehr will   das Inn're   zeugen:
no   desire   more wants the inner self to show

Erkennt   der Mensch Ew'gen Spur,
perceives the man   Eternal trace

Und löst   dein Rätsel, heil'ge Natur!
and solves your enigma holy   nature

soul; being rediscovers being, and the end of all hoping is revealed; lips grow dumb in astonished silence, and desire no longer betrays the heart – then man perceives the mark of the Eternal, and penetrates your mystery, holy Nature.

   iii. Im   Treibhaus
      in the greenhouse

iii. In the greenhouse

Hochgewölbte Blätterkronen,
high-arched leaves' crowns

Baldachine von Smaragd,
canopies of emerald

Kinder   ihr aus   fernen Zonen,
children you from far off zones

Saget mir, warum ihr klagt?
tell   me why   you lament

High-arching leafy crowns, canopies of emerald – you children from far off lands, tell me, why do you lament?

Schweigend neiget ihr die Zweige,
silently   bow you the branches

Malet Zeichen in   die Luft,
paint signs   into the air

Und der   Leiden   stummer Zeuge
and of the suffering silent   witness

Steiget aufwärts, süsser Duft.
rises   upwards sweet fragrance

Silently you bow your branches, make signs in the air, and in silent witness of your sorrow, a sweet fragrance rises up.

Weit in sehnendem Verlangen
wide in yearning   desire

Breitet ihr die Arme aus,
stretch you the arms out

You stretch your arms wide in yearning desire, and caught in your delusion, embrace in horror a desolate void.

Und umschlinget wahnbefangen
and embrace   delusion-caught

Öder   Leere nicht'gen Graus.
of desolate void empty   horror

Wohl, ich weiss es, arme Pflanze;   Well I know, poor plant, that we
indeed I know it poor plant   share one fate; though we are both
                                          bathed in splendour and light, our
Ein Geschicke teilen wir,   homeland is not here.
a   fate   share we

Ob   umstrahlt   von Licht und Glanze,
whether shone about by light and splendour

Unsre Heimat   ist nicht hier!
our   homeland is not here

Und wie froh   die Sonne scheidet   And as the sun is glad to leave the
and as gladly the sun   parts   empty light of day, so he who truly
                                           suffers seeks to enfold himself in
Von des   Tages leerem Schein,   silent darkness.
from of the day   empty shine

Hüllet der, der wahrhaft leidet,
wraps he who truly   suffers

Sich   in Schweigens Dunkel   ein.
himself in silence's   darkness –

Stille wird's,   ein säuselnd   Weben   It grows still, and a weaving,
still becomes it a   murmuring weaving   whispering uneasily fills the dark
                                              space. And I see heavy drops
Füllet bang   den dunklen Raum: hovering on the leaves' green edge.
fills   uneasily the dark   place

Schwere Tropfen seh' ich schweben
heavy   drops   see I hover

An der   Blätter grünem Saum.
on of the leaves green   edge

    iv. Schmerzen   iv. Sorrows
        sorrows

Sonne, weinest jeden Abend   O sun, you weep each evening till
sun   weep   each evening   your lovely eyes are red; and
                                             floating on the ocean's mirror, are
Dir   die schönen Augen rot,   overtaken by an early death.
to you the lovely eyes   red

Wenn im   Meeresspiegel   badend
when in the ocean's-mirror bathing

Dich erreicht der frühe Tod!
you reaches the early death

Doch erstehst in alter Pracht,
yet   arise   in old splendour

Glorie der   düstren Welt,
glory of the dark   world

Du am   Morgen neu   erwacht,
you in the morning newly awakened

Wie ein stolzer Siegesheld!
like a   proud victory-hero

Ach, wie   sollte   ich da   klagen,
ah   wherefore should I   then lament

Wie,   mein Herz, so schwer dich sehn,
wherefore my   heart so heavy you to see

Muss die Sonne selbst   verzagen,
must the sun   herself despair

Muss die Sonne untergehn?
must the sun   go down

Und gebieret   Tod   nur Leben,
and brings forth death only life

Geben Schmerzen Wonnen nur:
give   griefs   raptures only

O wie   dank' ich, dass gegeben
O how thank I   that given

Solche Schmerzen mir   Natur!
such   sorrows   to me nature

Yet you arise in all your
splendour, glorious in a dark
world, when you wake in the
morning, victorious and proud!

Ah, why should I then lament, to
see you, my heart, so heavy! Must
the sun herself despair, must even
she go down?

And if death brings forth only life,
and grief only rapture, O what
thanks I give that nature bestowed
on me such grief!

v. Träume
dreams

v. Dreams

Sag', welch wunderbare Träume
say   what wonderful dreams

Halten meinen Sinn umfangen,
hold   my   mind encompassed

Dass sie   nicht wie leere   Schäume
that they not   like empty bubbles

Sind in ödes Nichts   vergangen?
are in bleak nothingness lost

Träume, die in jeder Stunde,
dreams that in each hour

Jedem Tage schöner   blühn,
each   day more fair blossom

Tell me, what wondrous dreams
are these that enfold my mind, but
do not like empty bubbles vanish
into a void?

Dreams, that blossom more fair
each hour each day, and blissfully
move through my mind with their
tidings of heaven!

Und mit ihrer Himmelskunde
and with their heaven's-tidings

Selig   durchs   Gemüte ziehn!
blissfully through the soul   move

Träume, die wie hehre Strahlen
dreams that like sacred rays

Dreams, that like sacred rays
penetrate my soul and paint an
everlasting image there: a deep
oblivion, and memory.

In   die Seele sich   versenken,
into the soul themselves sink

Dort ein ewig   Bild   zu malen:
there an eternal image to paint

Allvergessen,   Eingedenken!
all-forgetfulness remembrance

Träume, wie wenn Frühlingssonne
dreams as   when spring's-sun

Dreams, that like the sun in spring
kissing blossoms in the snow, and
greeting each new day with
unsuspected joy;

Aus   dem Schnee die Blüten   küsst,
out of the snow the blossoms kisses

Dass zu nie   geahnter Wonne
that to never suspected rapture

Sie   der neue Tag begrüsst,
them the new day greets

Dass sie   wachsen, dass sie   blühen,
that they grow   that they blossom

to grow and flower, and dreaming
spread their fragrance, then slowly
fading in your breast, sink down
into their grave.

Träumend spenden ihren Duft,
dreaming bestow their fragrance

Sanft an deiner Brust verglühen,
gently on your breast cease glowing

Und dann sinken in   die Gruft.
and then sink   into the grave

Johannes Brahms
(1833–1897)

1. LIEBESTREU
LOVE'S-FIDELITY

Robert Reinick

'O versenk', o versenk' dein Leid, mein Kind,
O sink   O sink   your grief my   child

In   die See,   in   die tiefe See!'
into the ocean into the deep ocean

Ein Stein wohl   bleibt auf des   Meeres Grund,
a   stone perhaps stays on of the sea   bottom

Mein Leid kommt stets   in die Höh'.
my   grief comes always – upward –

'Und die Lieb', die du im   Herzen trägst,
and the love   that you in the heart   bear

Brich sie ab, brich sie ab, mein Kind!'
break her off break her off my   child

Ob die Blum' auch stirbt, wenn man sie bricht,
if the flower even dies when one it plucks

Treue Lieb' nicht so geschwind.
true love not so fast

'Und die Treu', und die Treu', 's war nur ein Wort,
and the fidelity and the fidelity it was only a   word

In   den Wind damit hinaus.'
into the wind with it out

O Mutter, und splittert der Fels auch im   Wind,
O mother and shatters the rock even in the wind

Meine Treue, die hält   ihn aus.
my   fidelity it endures (it) –

1. FIDELITY

'Sink, O sink your grief, my child,
in the ocean, the deep ocean!' A
stone will stay at the bottom of the
sea, but my grief will always rise
again.

'And the love that you bear in
your heart – tear it out, tear it out,
my child!' A flower that is plucked
may die, but not so soon true love.

'True love, true love, are only
words – throw them to the winds!'
O mother, a rock may shatter in
the storm, but my love, which is
true, will endure.

2. *TREUE LIEBE*
   TRUE   LOVE

2. TRUE LOVE

Eduard Ferrand

Ein Mägdlein   sass am   Meeresstrand
a   young maiden sat on the sea-shore

A maiden sat on the sea-shore –
with longing she gazed far out to
sea. 'Where do you linger so long,
my dearest? The yearning of my
heart gives me no rest. If only, my
dearest, you would come this day!'

Und blickte voll Sehnsucht in's   Weite:
and looked full longing   into the distance

'Wo   bleibst du, mein Liebster, wo   weilst du so lang?
where tarry you my dearest where linger you so long

Nicht ruhen lässt   mich des   Herzens Drang.
not   to rest leaves me of the heart   craving

Ach kämst   du, mein Liebster, doch heute!'
ah   would come you my dearest still today

Der Abend   nahte,   die Sonne sank
the evening drew near the sun   sank

Evening drew on, and the sun
went down on the edge of the sky.
'Will the waves never bring you
back to me? In vain I search far
over the sea – O where can I find
you again, my love?'

Am   Saum des   Himmels darnieder.
on the edge of the sky   down

'So trägt   dich die Welle mir   nimmer zurück?
so carries you the wave to me never   back

Vergebens späht in die Ferne   mein Blick.
in vain   peers into the distance my glance

Wo   find' ich, mein Liebster, dich wieder?'
where find I   my dearest you again

Die Wasser umspielten   ihr schmeichelnd den Fuss,
the waters played round her caressing   the foot

The caressing waves lapped
around her feet; she dreamed of
blissful hours. Its silent power
drew her into the deeps. Never
more on the strand stood the
lovely form – at last she had found
her beloved!

Wie Träume von seligen Stunden;
like dreams of blissful hours

Es zog   sie zur   Tiefe mit stiller Gewalt:
it drew her to the deep with silent power

Nie   stand mehr am   Ufer die holde Gestalt,
never stood more on the shore the lovely figure

Sie hat den Geliebten gefunden!
she has the loved one found

3. *DER SCHMIED*
THE (BLACK)SMITH

Ludwig Uhland

Ich hör' meinen Schatz,
I hear my   sweetheart

Den Hammer er schwinget,
the hammer he swings

Das rauschet, das klinget,
that thunders that rings

Das dringt   in   die Weite
that penetrates into the distance

Wie Glockengeläute
like bells-pealing

Durch   Gassen und Platz.
through alleys   and square

Am   schwarzen Kamin,
by the black   chimney

Da   sitzet mein Lieber,
there sits   my   dear one

Doch geh' ich vorüber,
but go I   past

Die Bälge   dann sausen,
the bellows then blow hard

Die Flammen aufbrausen,
the flames   flare up

Und lodern um   ihn.
and glow   round him

3. THE BLACKSMITH

I hear the sound of my
sweetheart's hammer, that clangs
as he swings it, and like pealing
bells, echoes away in the alleys and
square.

There by his black chimney sits
my love. As I pass by, the bellows
roar, and around him flames flare
up and glow.

4. *AN EINE ÄOLSHARFE*
TO AN   AEOLIAN-HARP

Eduard Mörike
(also set by Wolf)

Angelehnt an die Efeuwand
leaning   on the ivy-(clad) wall

Dieser alten Terrasse,
of this old   terrace

4. TO AN AEOLIAN HARP

Leaning against the ivy-clad wall
of this old terrace, let your
mysterious strings begin to play, O
Muse, born of the air! Begin, then
begin again your tuneful lament!

Du, einer luftgebor'nen Muse
you of an air-born   Muse

Geheimnisvolles Saitenspiel,
mysterious   strings-playing

Fang' an,
– begin –

Fange wieder an
begin again –

Deine melodische Klage!
your melodious lament

Ihr kommet, Winde, fernherüber,
you come   winds from afar here

Ach, von des Knaben,
oh   from the boy

Der mir so lieb war,
who to me so dear was

Frischgrünendem Hügel.
freshly-greening hillock

Und Frühlingsblüten unterwegs streifend,
and spring-blossoms on the way brushing

Übersättigt mit Wohlgerüchen,
satiated   with perfumes

Wie süss bedrängt ihr dies Herz!
how sweetly oppress you this heart

Und säuselt her in die Saiten,
and whisper here in the strings

Angezogen von wohllautender Wehmut,
drawn   by euphonious melancholy

Wachsend im Zug meiner Sehnsucht,
growing in the wake of my yearning

Und hinsterbend wieder.
and dying away again

Aber auf einmal,
but – all at once –

Wie der Wind heftiger herstösst,
as   the wind violently buffets

Ein holder Schrei der Harfe
a   lovely cry of the harp

You come, winds, from afar, you come from the grave of the boy – oh, so dear to me, touching lightly on your way spring blossoms, heavy with fragrance. How sweetly you oppress my heart! You whisper here in the strings, drawn by the melancholy harmony that grows in the wake of my yearning, and again dies away.

But all at once with a sudden gust of wind, a lovely cry comes from the harp; and in sweet alarm echoes the sudden stirring in my heart; and here the full-blown rose, shaken, strews all her petals at my feet.

Wiederholt mir   zu süssem Erschrecken,
repeats   to me in sweet alarm

Meiner Seele plötzliche Regung;
of my soul sudden   stirring

Und hier die volle Rose streut geschüttelt
and here the full rose strews shaken

All' ihre Blätter vor   meine Füsse!
all   her petals before my   feet

5. WIE   BIST DU,   MEINE KÖNIGIN
HOW ARE YOU MY   QUEEN

Georg Friedrich Daumer

Wie bist du, mein Königin,
how are you my   queen

Durch sanfte Güte   wonnevoll!
through gentle goodness delightful

Du lächle nur, Lenzdüfte   weh'n
you smile only spring-scents drift

Durch   mein Gemüte, wonnevoll!
through my   soul   delightfully

Frisch aufgeblühter Rosen Glanz,
freshly blossoming roses splendour

Vergleich' ich ihn dem   deinigen?
compare I   him to the yours

Ach, über alles,   was da   blüht,
ah   above everything that there blossoms

Ist deine Blüte   wonnevoll!
is your flower delightful

Durch tote Wüsten wandle hin,
through dead deserts wander along

Und grüne Schatten breiten   sich,
and green shadows spread out themselves

Ob   fürchterliche Schwüle dort
though fearful   sultriness there

Ohn   Ende brüte,   wonnevoll!
without end might brood delightfully

5. HOW DELIGHTFUL
YOU ARE, MY QUEEN

How delightful you are, my queen,
in your gentle goodness! If you but
smile, the scents of spring drift
through my soul, so sweetly.

Can the radiance of roses freshly
blooming be compared with
yours? Ah, your blossoming is
more sweet than that of any
flower!

Though you should wander in the
sultry heat that broods endlessly in
desert wastes, green shades would
spread around you sweetly there!

Lass mich vergehn   in deinem Arm!
let me waste away in your   arm

Es ist in ihm   ja   selbst der Tod,
it is in himself indeed even the death

Ob   auch die herbste   Todesqual
though even the most bitter death's-torment

Die Brust durchwüte,   wonnevoll!
the breast rages-through delightful

Let me fade away, held in your arms! However sharp the pangs of death might be that raged, tormenting me within my breast, would death itself be ecstasy!

6. *SO WILLST DU   DES*
   SO WILL   YOU OF THE
   ARMEN
   POOR ONE

6. WILL YOU SHOW
   MERCY

Ludwig Tieck
(from the cycle *Die schöne Magelone*)
                    the fair   Magelone

So willst du des   Armen
so will   you of the poor one

Dich   gnädig   erbarmen?
yourself graciously show mercy

So ist es kein Traum?
so is it no   dream

Wie rieseln die Quellen,
how ripple the springs

Wie tönen   die Wellen,
how resound the waves

Wie rauschet der Baum!
how rustles the tree

Tief lag ich in bangen
deep lay I in anxious

Gemäuern gefangen,
walls   caught

Nun grüsst mich das Licht;
now greets me   the light

Wie spielen die Strahlen!
how play   the beams

Will you show gracious mercy to this poor soul? Is this no dream? How the springs murmur, the waves crash, and the trees rustle! I lay an uneasy captive within dark walls – now I am greeted by the light. How the sun-beams play around me, dazzling me, and bringing colour to my timid face!

Sie   blenden und malen
they dazzle and paint

Mein schüchtern Gesicht.
my timid   face

Und soll   ich es glauben?
and shall I   it believe

Wird keiner   mir rauben
will   no one me rob

Den köstlichen Wahn?
the precious fancy

Doch Träume entschweben,
but dreams soar away

Nur lieben   heisst leben:
only to love means to live

Willkommene Bahn!
welcome   path

Wie frei und wie heiter!
how free and how happy

Nicht eile   nun weiter,
not   hasten now on

Den Pilgerstab   fort!
the pilgrim-staff away

Du hast überwunden,
you have conquered

Du hast ihn gefunden,
you have him found

Den seligsten   Ort!
the most blessed place

Can I then believe it? Will no one
rob me of this precious fancy? But
dreams can soar, and only in love
do we live. O welcome path! How
happy and free I am! Not to hurry
away on my pilgrim's staff! To
have conquered and found it, this
blessed place!

7. *RUHE SÜSSLIEBCHEN*
SLEEP SWEET-DARLING

7. SLEEP, MY
DARLING

Ludwig Tieck
(from the cycle *Die schöne Magelone*)
                    the fair   Magelone

Ruhe, Süssliebchen, im   Schatten
sleep sweet-darling in the shadow

Der   grünen, dämmernden Nacht,
of the green   growing dusk night

Sleep, my darling, in the shadow
of green twilight; the grass rustles
in the meadows, shadows fan and
cool you, while true love keeps

Es säuselt das Gras auf den Matten,
(it) rustles the grass in the meadows

Es fächelt und kühlt dich der Schatten,
(it) fans   and cools you the shadow

Und treue Liebe wacht.
and true love watches

Schlafe, schlaf   ein,
sleep   go to sleep –

Leiser rauscht der Hain,
softer rustles the wood

Ewig   bin ich dein.
for ever am I   yours

Schweigt, ihr versteckten Gesänge,
be silent you hidden   songs

Und stört   nicht die süsseste Ruh'!
and disturb not the sweetest rest

Es lauscht der   Vögel Gedränge,
(it) listen of the birds throng

Es ruhen die lauten Gesänge,
(it) rest   the loud   songs

Schliess, Liebchen, dein Auge zu.
close   darling   your eye –

Schlafe, schlaf   ein,
sleep   go to sleep –

Im   dämmernden Schein,
in the growing dusk light

Ich will dein Wächter   sein.
I   will your watchman be

Murmelt fort, ihr Melodien,
murmur on   you melodies

Rausche nur, du   stiller Bach.
rush   just you quiet brook

Schöne   Liebesphantasien
beautiful love's-fantasies

Sprechen in den Melodien,
speak   in the melodies

Zarte   Träume schwimmen nach.
tender dreams float   after (them)

watch. Sleep, go to sleep! The wood whispers softly, 'I am forever yours!'

Hush, all you hidden singers, do not disturb her sweet rest! Throngs of birds listen, their twittering chorus stilled. Close your eyes, my darling – sleep, go to sleep – in the gathering dusk I will keep watch.

Murmur on, you melodies; babble on, you quiet little brook! Sweet fantasies of love speak in your melodies, and tender dreams float with them. In the whispering wood golden bees fly around, and they will hum you into sleep.

Durch   den flüsternden Hain
through the whispering wood

Schwärmen goldene Bienelein
swarm   golden (little) bees

Und summen zum   Schlummer dich ein.
and hum   to the slumber   you –

8. *VON EWIGER   LIEBE*
OF   ETERNAL LOVE

Josef Wenzig

Dunkel, wie dunkel in Wald und in Feld!
dark   how dark   in forest and in field

Abend   schon   ist es, nun schweiget die Welt.
evening already is it   now is silent the world

Nirgend noch Licht und nirgend noch Rauch,
nowhere still light and nowhere still smoke

Ja, und die Lerche sie schweiget nun auch.
yes and the lark   she is silent now too

Kommt aus   dem Dorfe der Bursche heraus,
comes out of the village the youth   forth

Gibt das Geleit der   Geliebten   nach   Haus,
gives the escort to the sweetheart towards home

Führt sie am   Weidengebüsche vorbei,
leads her by the willow-bushes past

Redet so viel   und so mancherlei:
talks so much and so many things

'Leidest du Schmach   und betrübest du dich,
 suffer you humiliation and distress you yourself

Leidest du Schmach   von andern um   mich,
suffer you humiliation from others about me

Werde die Liebe getrennt   so geschwind,
let be the love separated as quickly

Schnell wie wir früher vereiniget sind.
quickly as we earlier united   are

Scheide   mit Regen und scheide   mit Wind,
let separate with rain   and let separate with wind

Schnell wie wir früher   vereiniget sind.'
quickly as we formerly united   are

8. ETERNAL LOVE

How dark it is in forest and field!
It is evening, all the earth is still.
No light, no smoke are to be seen,
and even the lark is silent.

A village lad is taking his
sweetheart home. As he leads her
past the willow copse, there are
many things he has to say:

'If you feel shame and are
distressed, if they taunt you
because of me – then let us part in
the wind and the rain – as swiftly
as once we came together.'

Spricht das Mägdelein, Mägdelein spricht:
says   the maiden   maiden   says

'Unsere Liebe sie trennet   sich   nicht!
 our   love she separates herself not

Fest ist der Stahl, und das Eisen gar sehr,
firm is the steel and the iron very much

Unsere Liebe ist fester   noch mehr.
our   love is firmer still more

Eisen und Stahl, man schmiedet sie   um,
iron and steel one recasts   them –

Unsere Liebe, wer wandelt sie um?
our   love who changes her –

Eisen und Stahl, sie   können zergehn,
iron and steel they can   melt

Unsere Liebe muss ewig   bestehn!'
our   love must for ever endure

The girl replies, and says to him:
'Our love cannot divide us! Iron is
strong, and steel stronger still, but
our love is strongest of all!

Iron and steel can be recast, but
who can change our love? Iron
and steel can be melted down –
but our love will endure for ever!'

9. *DIE MAINACHT*
   THE MAY NIGHT

9. MAY NIGHT

Ludwig Hölty

Wann der silberne Mond durch   die Gesträuche blinkt,
when the silver moon through the bushes   gleams

Und sein schlummerndes Licht über den Rasen streut,
and his slumbering   light over the sward spreads

Und die Nachtigall flötet,
and the nightingale sings

Wandl' ich traurig von Busch zu Busch.
wander I   sadly from bush to bush

Überhüllet vom   Laub   girret ein Taubenpaar
enveloped by the foliage coos a   dove-pair

Sein Entzücken mir vor;   aber ich wende   mich,
its delight   me before but I turn away myself

Suche dunklere Schatten,
seek darker shadows

Und die einsame Träne rinnt.
and the solitary tear   runs

When the silvery moon gleams
through the branches, and spreads
its slumbering light over the
sward, and the nightingale sings, I
wander sadly amongst the trees.

Two doves hidden by the leaves
are cooing to me enraptured, but I
turn away seeking darker shadows,
and a lone tear falls.

Wann, o lächelndes Bild, welches wie Morgenrot
when O smiling   image which like dawn

Durch   die Seele mir   strahlt, find ich auf Erden dich?
through the soul to me shines find I   on earth you

Und die einsame Träne
and the solitary tear

Bebt   mir   heisser   die Wang' herab!
trembles to me more hotly the cheek down

O smiling image, lighting my soul like the red of dawn, when shall I find you on this earth? And the lone tear trembles hotly on my cheek!

10. AN DIE NACHTIGALL
TO THE NIGHTINGALE

10. TO THE NIGHTINGALE

Ludwig Hölty
(also set by Schubert)

Geuss nicht so laut der   liebentflammten Lieder
pour not so loud of the love-kindled   songs

Tonreichen Schall
tone-rich sound

Vom   Blütenast   des   Apfelbaums hernieder,
from the blossoming-bough of the apple-tree down

O Nachtigall!
O nightingale

Du tönest mir   mit deiner süssen Kehle
you sound to me with your sweet throat

Die Liebe wach;
the love awake

Denn schon durchbebt   die Tiefen meiner Seele
for   already thrills through the depths of my soul

Dein schmelzend 'Ach.'
your melting   ah

O nightingale, can you not hush your love-songs, pouring forth their voluptuous melody from the blossoming boughs of the apple tree! The notes from your sweet throat awake in me feelings of love; already I feel in the depth of my soul your melting sighs.

Dann flieht der Schlaf von neuem dieses Lager,
then flees the sleep – anew – of this place

Ich starre dann,
I gaze then

Mit nassem Blick und totenbleich   und hager
with moist glance and deathly-pale and haggard

Once again you chase sleep from my bed, and I stare before me, pale and drawn, with tears in my eyes. Flee away, nightingale, into the green gloom of the forest glade! And there in your nest bestow your kisses on your own true love. Flee away, flee away!

Den Himmel an.
the heaven at

Fleuch, Nachtigall, in   grüne Finsternisse,
flee   nightingale into green glooms

Ins   Haingesträuch,
into the glade-thicket

Und spend   im   Nest der   treuen Gattin Küsse,
and bestow in the nest to the true   spouse kisses

Entfleuch, entfleuch!
flee away flee away

11. BOTSCHAFT
MESSAGE

11. MESSAGE

Georg Friedrich Daumer

Wehe, Lüftchen,   lind und lieblich
blow (little) breeze softly and sweetly

Blow sweetly, gentle breeze, about my beloved's cheek; play tenderly in her locks and do not hasten away!

Um   die Wange der   Geliebten,
about the cheek of the loved one

Spiele zart   in ihrer Locke,
play   tenderly in her   lock(s)

Eile   nicht hinwegzuflieh'n!
hasten not   to flee away

Tut sie dann vielleicht die Frage,
puts she then perhaps the question

If she should ask how I, poor wretch, am faring, then say: 'His misery is endless, his plight most critical.

Wie es um   mich Armen   stehe;
how it toward me   poor wretch might stand

Sprich: 'Unendlich war sein Wehe,
say   endless   was his misery

Höchst   bedenklich seine Lage;
most highly critical   his   condition

Aber jetzo kann er hoffen,
but now can   he hope

But now he can hope with joy to come to life again, for you, O gracious one, are thinking of him!'

Wieder herrlich   aufzuleben,
again   gloriously to come to life

Denn du, Holde,   denkst an ihn.'
for   you gracious one think of him

12. *SONNTAG*
SUNDAY

12. SUNDAY

Ludwig Uhland

So hab' ich doch   die ganze Woche
so have I   indeed the whole week

For a whole week I've not seen my
sweetheart. I saw her on Sunday
standing at her door: that
thousandfold fair maiden – would
to Heaven I were with her today!

Mein feines Liebchen   nicht geseh'n
my   fine   sweetheart not   seen

Ich sah es an einem Sonntag
I   saw it on a   Sunday

Wohl   vor   der Türe steh'n:
indeed in front of the door stand

Das tausendshöne   Jungfräulein,
the thousandfold fair young maiden

Das tausendschöne   Herzelein,
the thousandfold fair little heart

Wollte   Gott, ich wär' heute bei   ihr!
would (to) God I   were today with her

So will   mir   doch   die ganze Woche
so wants to me indeed the whole week

I haven't stopped smiling for a
week, since I saw her on Sunday
going to church: that thousandfold
fair maiden – would to Heaven I
were with her today!

Das Lachen   nicht vergeh'n,
the laughter not   to cease

Ich sah es an einem Sonntag
I   saw it on a   Sunday

Wohl in   die Kirche geh'n:
indeed into the church go

Das tausendschöne . . . etc.
the thousandfold fair

13. *O LIEBLICHE WANGEN*
O LOVELY   CHEEKS

13. O LOVELY
CHEEKS

Paul Flemming

O liebliche Wangen, ihr macht mir   Verlangen,
O lovely   cheeks   you make to me longing

O lovely cheeks, you fill me with
longing, when I gaze upon your
red and your white! And I mean
not only gaze – but touch and kiss!

Dies Rote,   dies Weisse,   zu schauen   mit Fleisse.
this redness this whiteness to gaze upon with diligence

Und dies nur alleine ist's nicht, was ich meine;
and this just alone is it not   what I   mean

Zu schauen, zu grüssen, zu rühren, zu küssen!
to gaze   to greet   to touch to kiss

O Sonne der   Wonne! O Wonne der   Sonne!
O sun   of the rapture O rapture of the sun

O Augen, so   saugen das Licht meiner Augen.
O eyes   thus imbibe the light of my eyes

O englische Sinnen! O himmlisch Beginnen!
O angelic thoughts O heavenly actions

O Himmel auf Erden, magst du mir   nicht werden!
O heaven on earth   may you to me not come to be

O sun of rapture, O rapture of
sun! O eyes, that drink the light in
my eyes! O angelic thoughts, O
heavenly deeds! O Paradise on
earth, can you not be mine?

O Schönste der   Schönen! Benimm mir   dies
O fairest of the fair   take away from me this
  Sehnen,
  longing

Komm, eile,   komm, komme, du Süsse,   du
come hasten come come   you sweet one you
  Fromme!
  innocent one

Ach, Schwester, ich sterbe,   ich sterb',   ich
oh sister   I   am dying I   am dying I
  verderbe,
  am perishing

Komm, komme, komm, eile,   benimm mir   dies
come   come   come hasten take away (from) me this
  Sehnen,
  longing

O Schönste der   Schönen!
O fairest   of the fair

O fairest of the fair, set me free
from this longing! Come hasten,
come sweet one, come innocent
one, come! Ah sister, I die – I die,
I perish! Come hasten, O fairest –
from this longing set me free!

14. *DER GANG ZUM*
   THE WAY   TO THE
   LIEBCHEN
   SWEETHEART

14. THE WAY TO MY
   SWEETHEART

Bohemian folksong

Es glänzt der Mond nieder,
(it) shines the moon down

Ich sollte   doch wieder
I   should really again

The moon is shining – I must go
to my sweetheart, and see how she
fares.

Zu meinem Liebchen,
to my   sweetheart

Wie mag es ihr   geh'n?
how may it to her go

Ach weh! sie verzaget
oh   dear she despairs

Oh dear, she despairs, and
complains that she'll never see me
again.

Und klaget,   und klaget,
and complains and complains

Dass sie mich nimmer
that she me   never

Im   Leben wird seh'n!
in the life   will see

Es ging der Mond unter,
(it) went the moon down

The moon was sinking, I hurried
quite merrily – that no one would
carry my sweetheart away!

Ich eilte   doch munter,
I   hurried but merrily

Und eilte,   dass keiner
and hurried that no one

Mein Liebchen   entführt.
my   sweetheart carries off

Ihr Täubchen, o girret,
you little doves O coo

O coo, little doves! O murmur
little breezes! – that no one carries
my sweetheart away!

Ihr Lüftchen,   o schwirret,
you little breezes O whirr

Dass keiner mein Liebchen,
that no one my   sweetheart

Mein Liebchen   entführt!
my   sweetheart carries off

15. *AM   SONNTAG MORGEN*
ON THE SUNDAY   MORNING

15. ON SUNDAY
MORNING

(from *Italienisches Liederbuch*)
      Italian   song-book
translated into German by Paul Heyse

Am   Sonntag morgen   zierlich angetan,
on (the) Sunday morning finely   clad

On Sunday morning I knew quite
well where you were going so
finely clad. And some there were
saw that saw you, and came to tell

Wohl weiss ich, wo   du da   bist hingegangen,
well   know I   where you then are gone

Und manche Leute   waren, die   dich sah'n,
and some   people were   who you saw

Und kamen dann zu mir, dich zu verklagen,
and came   then to me   you to accuse

Als sie   mir's   sagten, hab' ich laut   gelacht,
as   they to me it said   have I   loudly laughed

Und in der Kammer dann geweint zur   Nacht.
and in the bedroom then wept   at the night

Als sie   mir's   sagten, fing' ich an zu singen,
as   they to me it said   began I   – to sing

Um   einsam dann die Hände wund zu ringen.
so as alone   then the hands sore to wring

me of their suspicions. As they spoke I laughed aloud, but in my room I wept the whole night through. I sang as they began to speak, but when I was alone, I wrung my hands quite sore.

16. *AN EIN VEILCHEN*
TO A   VIOLET

Ludwig Hölty

Birg,   o Veilchen, in deinem blauen Kelche,
conceal O violet   in your   blue   cup

Birg   die Tränen der   Wehmut,   bis mein
conceal the tears   of the melancholy until my
   Liebchen
   sweetheart

Diese Quelle besucht! Entpflückt sie lächelnd
this   spring visits   plucks away she smiling

Dich dem   Rasen, die Brust mit dir zu schmücken:
you (from) the grass   the breast with you to adorn

O dann schmiege   dich   ihr   an's   Herz, und sag'
O then press close yourself to her on the heart and say
   ihr,
   to her

Dass die Tropfen in deinem blauen Kelche
that the drops   in your   blue   cup

Aus der Seele des   treu'sten Jünglings flossen,
from the soul of the truest   youth   flowed

Der sein Leben verweinet   und den Tod   wünscht.
who his life   weeps away and the death wishes

16. TO A VIOLET

Hide, O violet, hide my melancholy tears in your blue petals, till my sweetheart comes down to the stream! If she smiling plucks you from the grass to adorn her breast, then, O then press close to her heart! Tell her that the drops in your blue petals flowed from a youth's true heart. His life he weeps away, and wishes now for death.

17. WIEGENLIED
CRADLE-SONG

17. CRADLE SONG

Deutsches Volkslied
German folksong

Guten Abend, gut' Nacht,
good evening good night

Mit Rosen bedacht,
with roses roofed over

Mit Näg'lein besteckt,
with pinks   stuck over with

Schlupf' unter die Deck':
slip   under the coverlet

Morgen   früh,   wenn Gott will,
tomorrow-morning if   God wills

Wirst du wieder geweckt.
will be you again awakened

Good-night, good-night, slip
under your little cover, with roses
bedecked, and pinks adorned. And
tomorrow, if God wills, you will
wake again.

Guten Abend, gut' Nacht,
good evening good night

Von Eng'lein   bewacht,
by (little) angels watched over

Die zeigen im   Traum
who show in the dream

Dir   Christkindleins Baum:
to you Christ-child's tree

Schlaf' nur selig   und süss,
sleep   only blissfully and sweetly

Schau' im   Traum's Paradies.
see   in the dream the Paradise

Good-night, good-night, with
angels keeping watch. In your
dreams they'll show you the Christ
Child's tree. Sleep, just sleep,
serene and sweet, and in your
dreams you will see Paradise.

18. AUF DEM SEE
ON THE LAKE

18. ON THE LAKE

Karl Simrock

Blauer Himmel, blaue Wogen,
blue   sky   blue waves

Rebenhügel um   den See,
vine-hills   around the lake

Blue sky, blue ripples, vine-clad
hills around the lake; beyond, blue
curving mountains shimmering
with pure white snow.

Drüber blauer Berge   Bogen
above of blue mountains curve

Schimmernd weiss im   reinen Schnee.
shimmering white in the pure   snow

Wie der Kahn uns hebt und wieget,
as   the boat   us lifts and rocks

As the little boat rocks and sways,
a light mist lifts and falls. A sweet
and heavenly peace lies over a
radiant world.

Leichter Nebel steigt und fällt,
light   mist rises and falls

Süsser Himmelsfriede   lieget
sweet Heaven's-peace lies

Über der beglänzten   Welt.
over the illuminated world

Stürmend Herz, tu   auf die Augen,
raging   heart open –   the eyes

O raging heart, open your eyes,
look around you and be still –
drink in the joy and peace of this
two-fold image of Heaven!

Sieh umher und werde   mild:
look around and become gentle

Glück   und Frieden magst du   saugen
happiness and peace   may   you imbibe

Aus des   Doppelhimmels   Bild.
from of the double-Heaven's image

Spiegelnd sieh die Flut   erwidern
reflecting see the water return

See how the water mirrors hill and
tower, village and wood; and let
your songs reflect all that is fairest
on earth.

Turm   und Hügel, Busch und Stadt,
steeple and hill   bush and town

Also spiegle du in Liedern,
thus reflect you in songs

Was die Erde Schönstes   hat.
what the earth most lovely has

19. REGENLIED
RAIN-SONG

19. SONG OF THE
RAIN

Klaus Groth

Walle, Regen, walle nieder,
flow   rain   flow down

Fall, rain, fall, and bring back
those dreams I dreamed in my
childhood, when the water foamed
in the sand.

Wecke mir   die Träume wieder,
wake to me the dreams again

Die ich in der Kindheit träumte,
that I   in the childhood dreamed

Wenn das Nass   im   Sande schäumte!
when the wetness in the sand foamed

Wenn die matte   Sommerschwüle
when the languid summer-sultriness

When the languid sultriness of summer lazily wrangled with the cool freshness, and the shining leaves were covered with drops of dew, and the fields were a darker blue.

Lässig stritt   mit frischer Kühle,
lazily wrangled with fresh   coolness

Und die blanken Blätter tauten,
and the shining leaves were dew-covered

Und die Saaten   dunkler   blauten.
and the green-crops more darkly were blue

Welche Wonne, in dem Fliessen
what bliss   in the trickling down

What bliss to stand in the trickling rain, to ramble with bare feet in the grass, and grasp at the shower with outstretched hands,

Dann zu stehn mit nackten Füssen,
then to stand with bare   feet

An dem Grase hin   zu streifen,
on the grass along to ramble

Und den Schaum mit Händen greifen,
and the foam   with hands   grasp

Oder mit   den heissen Wangen
or   with the hot   cheeks

or to let the cool drops fall on hot cheeks, and freshly awakened scents fill youthful lungs!

Kalte Tropfen aufzufangen,
cold drops   catch up

Und den neuerwachten   Düften
and the newly-awakened scents

Seine Kinderbrust   zu lüften!
his   child's-breast to air

Wie die Kelche,   die da   troffen,
like the flower-cups that there dripped

Like the cup of a flower the soul stood open, and breathing in, like scent-intoxicated blossom wrapped in the dews of Heaven.

Stand die Seele atmend   offen,
stood the soul breathing open

Wie die Blumen, düftetrunken,
like the flowers scents-intoxicated

In den Himmelstau   versunken.
in the Heaven's-dew sunk

Schauernd kühlte jeder Tropfen
shivering cooled each drop

Each drop fell cool and shivering against a beating heart, and the divine stirrings of creation reached into the very secret of life.

Tief bis an des   Herzens Klopfen,
deep even to of the heart   beating

Und der   Schöpfung heilig   Weben
and of the creation   divine activity

Drang   bis   ins   verborgne Leben.
penetrated right into the secret   life

Walle, Regen, walle nieder,
flow   rain   flow down

Wecke   meine alten Lieder,
awaken my   old   songs

Die   wir in der Türe sangen,
that we   at the door sang

Wenn die Tropfen draussen klangen!
when the drops   outside   sounded

Möchte   ihnen   wieder lauschen,
would like to them again to listen to

Ihrem   süssen, feuchten Rauschen,
to their sweet damp   rushing

Meine Seele sanft betauen
my   soul softly to bedew

Mit dem frommen Kindergrauen.
with the innocent children-dread

Fall, rain, fall, and awaken those
old songs we sang in the doorways
to the sound of the raindrops
outside!

How I would love to hear again
their sweet, wet pattering, and let
my soul be gently revived with the
innocent thrill of a child.

20. DEIN BLAUES AUGE
   YOUR BLUE   EYE

20. YOUR BLUE EYES

Klaus Groth

Dein blaues Auge hält   so still,
your blue eye   keeps so still

Ich blicke bis   zum Grund.
I   look right to the bottom

Du fragst mich, was ich sehen will?
you ask   me   what I to see want

Ich sehe mich   gesund.
I   see myself restored

Es brannte mich ein glühend Paar,
(it) burned me   a   glowing pair

Noch schmerzt das Nachgefühl:
still hurts   the after-feeling

Your blue eyes are so still, I look
into their very depths. You ask me
what I would see in them? To see
myself restored.

Once I was burnt by two glowing
eyes, the pain is with me still.
Your eyes are as clear as a lake –
and as a lake so cool.

Das deine ist wie See so klar,
the yours is as lake so clear

Und wie ein See so kühl.
and as a lake so cool

21. *MEINE LIEBE IST GRÜN*
   MY   LOVE IS   GREEN

21. MY LOVE IS
   GREEN

Felix Schumann

Meine Liebe ist grün wie der Fliederbusch,
my   love is green as the lilac-bush

Und mein Lieb ist schön   wie die Sonne;
and my   love is beautiful as the sun

Die glänzt wohl   herab auf   den Fliederbusch
she shines indeed down upon the lilac-bush

Und füllt ihn mit Duft und mit Wonne.
and fills him with scent and with rapture

Meine Seele hat Schwingen der   Nachtigall,
my   soul has soaring   of the nightingale

Und wiegt sich   in blühendem Flieder,
and rocks herself in blossoming lilac

Und jauchzet und singet vom   Duft berauscht
and exults   and sings by the scent intoxicated

Viel   liebestrunkene Lieder.
many love-drunk   songs

My love is green as the lilac tree,
and my love is as lovely as the sun
that shines on it, filling it with
fragrance, and with rapture.

My soul soars like the nightingale,
and, rocked in the blossoming lilac
and bewitched by its fragrance, it
exults and sings its love-
intoxicated songs.

22. *O WÜSST ICH DOCH DEN WEG*
   O KNEW I   ONLY THE WAY
   ZURÜCK
   BACK

20. O IF I BUT KNEW
   THE WAY BACK

Klaus Groth

O wüsst' ich doch den Weg zurück,
O knew I   only the way back

Den lieben   Weg zum Kinderland!
the delightful way to the children's-land

If I but knew the way back, the
sweet way back to childhood land!
O why did I seek after happiness,
and leave my mother's hand?

O warum sucht' ich nach dem Glück
O why   sought I   after the happiness

Und liess der   Mutter Hand?
and left of the mother hand

O wie   mich   sehnet auszuruh'n,
O how myself longs to rest

How I long to rest, roused by no
striving – oh, to close my tired
eyes, gently sheltered by love!

Von keinem Streben aufgeweckt,
by no   striving aroused

Die müden Augen zuzutun,
the tired   eyes   to close

Von Liebe sanft   bedeckt!
by   love gently sheltered

Und nichts   zu forschen, nichts   zu späh'n,
and nothing to seek   nothing to watch for

No restless seeking, no anxious
watching, just dreaming lightly,
softly; not seeing time's changes,
and once again a child!

Und nur zu träumen leicht und lind;
and only to dream   lightly and softly

Der   Zeiten Wandel nicht zu seh'n,
of the times change not to see

Zum   zweiten Mal ein Kind!
for the second time a   child

O zeig mir   doch den Weg zurück,
O show to me only the way back

O show me the way, the sweet way
back to childhood land! In vain do
I seek after happiness; around me
is but a desolate shore.

Den lieben Weg zum   Kinderland!
the sweet way to the children's-land

Vergebens such' ich nach dem Glück,
in vain   seek I   after the happiness

Ringsum   ist öder   Strand!
round about is desolate shore

23. AN DEN MOND
TO THE MOON

23. TO THE MOON

Karl Simrock

Silbermond, mit   bleichen Strahlen
silver-moon with pale   rays

O silvery moon, you paint field
and woodland with your pale rays;
you give to hill and valley a sighing
air.

Pflegst   du Wald und Feld zu malen,
are accustomed you wood and field to paint

Gibst den   Bergen,   gibst den   Talen
give to the mountains give to the valleys

Der   Empfindung Seufzer ein.
of the feeling   sighs   –

Sei Vertrauter meiner Schmerzen,
be confidant of my sorrows

You who sail in the ocean of the heavens, I confide in you my sorrows. So tell the one who is always in my heart, that I am dying of grief and love.

Segler in der   Lüfte   See:
sailer in of the breezes sea

Sag' ihr,   die ich trag' im   Herzen,
say to her who I   carry in the heart

Wie mich tötet Liebesweh.
how me   kills love's-grief

Sag' ihr   über tausend   Meilen
say to her over thousand miles

Tell her my heart longs for her a thousand miles away. 'No distance can restore me – only a single loving glance from you.'

Sehne sich mein Herz nach ihr.
longs itself my   heart for   her

'Keine Ferne   kann es heilen,
no   distance can it heal

Nur ein holder   Blick von dir.'
only a   gracious glance from you

Sag' ihr,   dass zu Tod   getroffen
say to her that by death struck

Tell her that soon in death this earthly veil will fall away; for only in sweet loving hope can it ever be sustained.

Diese Hülle bald zerfällt;
this   veil   soon falls apart

Nur ein schmeichlerisches Hoffen
only a   caressing   hope

Sei's, das sie zusammenhält.
be it that it holds together

24. GEHEIMNIS
SECRET

Karl Candidus

O Frühlings Abenddämmerung
O spring   twighlight

O spring twilight! O mild and gentle breeze! Tell me, you blossoming trees – why do you stand so close?

O laues, lindes Weh'n!
O mild gentle fluttering

Ihr Blütenbäume,   sprecht,
you blossoming-trees say

Was tut ihr so zusammensteh'n?
why do you so together

Vertraut ihr das Geheimnis euch
confide you the secret   to each other

Do you confide in each other the secret of our sweet love? What do you whisper together of our sweet love?

Von uns'rer Liebe süss?
of   our   love sweet

Was flüstert ihr einander   zu
what whisper you one another to

Von uns'rer Liebe süss?
of   our   love sweet

25. MINNELIED
LOVE-SONG

25. LOVE-SONG

Ludwig Hölty
(also set by Schubert and Mendelssohn)

Holder klingt   der Vogelsang,
lovelier sounds the bird-song

Wenn die Engelreine,
when the angel's purity

Lovelier is the song of the birds when that pure angel, who conquered my young heart, passes through the wood.

Die mein Jünglingsherz bezwang,
who my   youth's-heart conquered

Wandelt durch   die Haine.
wanders through the woods

Röter   blühen   Tal   und Au,
redder blossom valley and pasture

Brighter red are the flowers in field and valley, brighter green is the grass, where my lady's fingers gathered the wild lilies.

Grüner wird   der Wasen,
greener becomes the grass

Wo   die Finger meiner Frau
where the fingers of my lady

Maienblumen lasen.
May-flowers gathered

Ohne   sie ist alles   tot,
without her is everything dead

Without her everything is dead; flowers and leaves all fade, and now the spring sunset seems no longer bright and fair.

Welk sind Blüt'   und Kräuter:
faded are blossoms and plants

Und kein Frühlingsabendrot
and no   spring-sunset

Dünkt mir   schön und heiter.
seems to me lovely and serene

Traute, minnigliche Frau,
dear   charming woman

Wollest   nimmer fliehen,
may you never   flee

Dass main Herz, gleich dieser Au,
that my heart like   this   pasture

Mög' in Wonne blühen!
may in ecstasy bloom

O dear, sweet lady, never leave my
side; that my heart like this
meadow may bloom in ecstasy!

26. *DER KRANZ*
THE GARLAND

26. THE GARLAND

Hans Schmidt

Mutter, hilf mir armen Tochter,
mother help me poor   daughter

Sieh' nur, was ein Knabe tat:
see just what a boy   did

Einen Kranz   von Rosen flocht er,
a   garland of roses wove he

Den er mich zu tragen bat!
that he me to wear begged

O mother, help your poor
daughter! Just see what that boy
has done – he has made a chain of
roses for me and begged me to
wear it!

'Ei, sei deshalb   unerschrocken,
oh be because of that undismayed

Helfen lässt sich   dir   gewiss!
help   allows (itself) (for) you surely

Nimm den Kranz nur aus   den Locken,
take   the garland just from the locks

Und den Knaben, den vergiss!'
and the boy   him forget

'Oh, don't let that bother you –
surely there's something can be
done. Just take the garland from
your hair, and then forget the lad!'

Dornen hat der Kranz, o Mutter,
thorns has the garland O mother

Und die   halten fest das Haar!
and they hold   fast the hair

But there are thorns in the garland
that catch in my hair! And the
words the boy spoke to me,
mother, I'll remember them for
ever!

Worte sprach der Knabe, Mutter,
words spoke the boy   mother

An die   denk' ich immerdar!
of them think I   for ever

27. *VERGEBLICHES STÄNDCHEN*   27. VAIN SERENADE
VAIN   SERENADE

Folksong (from the lower Rhine)

   (Er)   (He)
    he

Guten Abend, mein Schatz,
good evening my   sweetheart

Guten Abend, mein Kind!
good evening my   child

Ich komm' aus   Lieb' zu dir,
I   come out of love to you

Ach, mach mir   auf die Tür,
oh   open to me –   the door

Mach mir   auf die Tür!
open to me –   the door

'Good evening, my sweetheart, good evening, my child! I come because I love you – so open the door, please open the door!'

   (Sie)   (She)
    she

'Mein' Tür ist verschlossen,
my   door is locked

Ich lass' dich nicht ein,
I   let   you not   in

Mutter, die rät   mir klug,
mother she advises me wisely

Wärst   du herein mit Fug,
Would be you in here with right

Wär's   mit mir vorbei!
would be it with me over

'My door is closed, and I won't let you in! Mother has given me good advice: if you were allowed to come in here, it would be all over for me!'

(Er)
he

So kalt ist die Nacht,
so cold is the night

So eisig der Wind,
so icy the wind

Dass mir das Herz erfriert,
that to me the heart is freezing

Mein Lieb erlöschen wird,
my love expire will

Öffne mir, mein Kind!'
open to me my child

(Sie)
she

Löschet dein Lieb,
expires your love

Lass sie löschen nur,
let her expire just

Löschet sie immerzu,
let expire her always

Geh heim zu Bett, zur Ruh!
go home to bed to the rest

Gute Nacht, mein Knab'!
good night my lad

(He)

'The night is so cold, and the wind is like ice, that even my heart is freezing. My love will grow cold – so open up for me, dear child!'

(She)

'If your love will perish, then just let it perish – just let it fade right away! Go home to bed, and go to sleep: good night, my lad, good-night!'

28. IN WALDESEINSAMKEIT IN WOOD-SOLITUDE

28. IN THE SOLITUDE OF THE WOODS

Karl von Lemcke

Ich sass zu deinen Füssen
I sat at your feet

In Waldeseinsamkeit;
in wood-solitude

I sat at your feet in the lonely wood; the wind's sighs, and a yearning, went through the tops of the trees.

Windesatmen,   Sehnen
wind's breathing yearning

Ging durch   die Wipfel   breit.
went through the (tree)-tops wide

In stummem Ringen   senkt' ich
in silent   struggling sank I

In silent care, I laid my head in your lap, and clasped you to me with trembling hands.

Das Haupt in   deinen Schoss,
the head   into your   lap

Und meine bebenden   Hände
and my   trembling hands

Um deine   Knie ich schloss.
around your knees I   clasped

Die Sonne ging   hinunter,
the sun   went down

The sun went down, and the day-light faded; Far, far away a nightingale sang.

Der Tag verglühte   all.
the day ceased glowing wholly

Ferne, ferne, ferne
far off far off far off

Sang eine Nachtigall.
sang a   nightingale

29. THERESE
   TERESA

29. TERESA

Gottfried Keller
(also set by Wolf)

Du milchjunger Knabe,
you milk-young boy

Why do you look at me like that, you half-weaned boy? What a question there is in your eyes!

Wie schaust   du mich an?
how are looking you me   at

Was haben deine Augen
what have   your eyes

Für eine Frage   getan!
for a   question put

Alle Ratsherrn in der Stadt
all   aldermen in the town

All the elders of the town, all the sages in the world keep silent on the question your eyes are asking!

Und alle Weisen der   Welt
and all sages   of the world

Bleiben stumm auf die Frage,
remain silent on the question

Die   deine Augen gestellt!
which your eyes   put

Eine Meermuschel liegt
a   sea-shell   lies

Auf dem Schrank   meiner Bas':
on the cupboard of my cousin

Da   halte dein Ohr d'ran,
when hold your ear to it

Dann hörst du   etwas!
then hear you something

A sea-shell lies on my cousin's
closet; hold it to your ear – and
you'll hear something!

30. *FELDEINSAMKEIT* FIELD-SOLITUDE

30. SOLITUDE IN THE FIELDS

Hermann Almers

Ich ruhe still im   hohen grünen Gras
I   rest still in the tall   green grass

Und sende lange meinen Blick nach oben,
and send long my   glance – upwards –

Von Grillen rings   umschwirrt   ohn'Unterlass,
from crickets around whirred about without ceasing

Von Himmelsbläue wundersam umwoben.
from sky's-blue   wonderfully moving around

Motionless I lie in the tall green
grass, gazing upward, with the
unceasing chirp of crickets all
around; and moving over me the
wondrous tapestry of the blue sky.

Die schönen   weissen Wolken zieh'n dahin
the beautiful white   clouds move along

Durchs   tiefe Blau, wie schöne stille Träume;
through the deep blue like lovely calm dreams

Mir ist, als ob ich längst   gestorben bin
to me is as if I   long since died   am

Und ziehe   selig   mit   durch ew'ge
and moved along blissfully with (them) through endless
   Räume.
   spaces

Beautiful white clouds float
through the deep blue, like calm
and beautiful dreams; it is as if I
had long since died, and moved
blissfully with them in endless
space.

31. NACHTWANDLER
NIGHT-WANDERER

31. NIGHT WANDERER

Max Kalbeck

Störe nicht den leisen Schlummer
trouble not   the gentle slumber

Dess,   den lind   ein Traum umfangen!
of him who softly a   dream embraces

Trouble not the gentle slumber
that softly enfolds him in a dream.
Leave him to his sweet sorrow, to
his yearning grief!

Lass ihm seinen süssen Kummer,
leave him his   sweet sorrow

Ihm sein schmerzliches Verlangen!
him his sorrowful   yearning

Sorgen und Gefahren drohen,
cares   and dangers threaten

Cares and dangers are close at
hand, but none will trouble him, if
you do not come and wake the
glad sleeper with harsh words.

Aber keine   wird ihn schrecken,
but no one will him frighten

Kommst du nicht, den Schlafesfrohen
come   you not   the sleep-happy one

Durch ein hartes Wort zu wecken.
through a   harsh word to wake

Still   in seinen Traum versunken,
tranquilly in his   dream sunk

Deep in his tranquil dreams, he
steps across deep chasms, drunk
with the light of the full moon.
Woe to the one whose lips should
call him!

Geht er über Abgrundtiefen,
walks he over abyss-deeps

Wie vom   Licht des   Vollmonds trunken,
as   from the light of the full-moon drunk

Weh' den   Lippen, die ihn riefen!
woe to the lips   that him called

32. SAPPHISCHE ODE
SAPPHIC   ODE

32. SAPPHIC ODE

Hans Schmidt

Rosen brach   ich nachts mir   am   dunklen Hage;
roses plucked I   at night to me on the dark   hedge

Süsser   hauchten Duft   sie als je   am Tage;
sweeter exhaled fragrance they than ever by day

I plucked roses at night from the
dark hedgerow, and their
fragrance was sweeter than ever by
day; but the shaken boughs

Doch verstreuten reich   die bewegten Äste
but   scattered   abundantly the moving   boughs

Tau, der   mich nässte.
dew that me   moistened

Auch der   Küsse Duft   mich wie nie   berückte,
also   of the kisses fragrance me   as never beguiled

Die ich nachts   vom   Strauch deiner   Lippen pflückte:
that I   at night from the bush   of your lips   plucked

Doch auch dir,   bewegt im   Gemüt gleich jenen,
but   also to you   stirred in the soul   like   those

Tauten   die Tränen.
fell as dew the tears

scattered wet dew luxuriantly
upon me.

And the fragrance of kisses
beguiled me as never before, as I
plucked them like roses at night
from your lips; but like the rose,
your soul was stirred, and you
shed tears like the dew.

33. *BEI   DIR SIND MEINE* WITH YOU ARE   MY *GEDANKEN* THOUGHTS

33. MY THOUGHTS ARE WITH YOU

Friedrich Halm

Bei   dir sind meine Gedanken
with you are my   thoughts

Und flattern um   dich her;
and float   around you (here)

Sie sagen, sie   hätten   Heimweh,
they say   they would have home-sickness

Hier litt'   es sie   nicht mehr.
here suffered it they not   more

Bei   dir sind meine Gedanken
with you are my   thoughts

Und wollen von   dir nicht fort;
and want from you not away

Sie sagen, das wär'   auf Erden
they say   that would be on earth

Der allerschönste   Ort.
the loveliest of all places

All my thoughts are with you,
floating around you. They say they
are full of longing, and can stay no
longer here.

My thoughts are with you, and do
not want to leave you; they say
they are in the loveliest place on
earth.

Sie sagen, unlösbar   hielte
they say   indissolubly held

Dein Zauber sie   festgebannt;
your magic them spell-bound

Sie hätten   an deinen Blicken
they would have by your   glances

Die Flügel sich   verbrannt.
the wings themselves scorched

They say that your magic holds
them fast in a spell – but your
glances could well scorch their
wings.

34. DER JÄGER
   THE HUNTER

Friedrich Halm

Mein Lieb ist ein Jäger,
my   love is a   hunter

Und grün   ist sein Kleid,
and green is his dress

Und blau ist sein Auge,
and blue is his eye

Nur sein Herz ist zu weit.
only his heart is too wide

Mein Lieb ist ein Jäger,
my   love is a   hunter

Trifft immer ins   Ziel,
hits   always into the target

Und Mädchen berückt   er,
and girls   ensnares he

So viel   er nur will.
as many he just wants

Mein Lieb ist ein Jäger,
my   love is a   hunter

Kennt Wege und Spur,
knows ways and track

Zu mir aber kommt er
to me but comes he

Durch   die Kirchtüre   nur.
through the church-door only

34. THE HUNTER

My love is a hunter, and his garb
is green. His eyes are blue – but
his heart is too wide!

My love is a hunter, and he always
hits the mark. He ensnares the
girls – just as many as he chooses.

My love is a hunter, and he knows
tracks and trails. But his only way
to me is through the church door!

35. *MÄDCHENLIED*
MAIDEN-SONG

Paul Heyse

Am jüngsten Tag ich aufersteh'
on (the) Judgement Day I rise from the dead

Und gleich nach meinem Liebsten seh'.
and at once for my beloved look

Und wenn ich ihn nicht finden kann,
and if I him not find can

Leg' wieder mich zum Schlafen dann.
lie down again (myself) to the sleeping then

O Herzeleid, Ewigkeit!
O good grief eternity

Selbander nur ist Seligkeit!
with another only is bliss

Und kommt mein Liebster nicht hinein,
and comes my beloved not there-into

Mag nicht im Paradiese sein!
like not in the Paradise to be

35. MAIDEN'S SONG

On Judgement Day I'll rise from the grave, and look at once for my sweetheart. And if I don't find him, then I'll lie down again, and go off to sleep.

Dear heart – eternity! Only with each other could it be bliss. And if my beloved doesn't come there, then I don't want to be in Paradise!

36. *DER TOD, DAS IST DIE KÜHLE NACHT*
THE DEATH THAT IS THE COOL NIGHT

Heinrich Heine

Der Tod, das ist die kühle Nacht,
the death that is the cool night

Das Leben ist der schwüle Tag.
the life is the sultry day

Es dunkelt schon, mich schläfert,
it grows dark already (I) am sleepy

Der Tag hat mich müd' gemacht.
the day has me weary made

36. DEATH IS COOL NIGHT

Death is cool night – life is sultry day. It grows dark already, and I am drowsy, for the day has wearied me.

Über mein Bett erhebt   sich   ein Baum,
over my bed springs up (himself) a   tree

D'rin singt die junge Nachtigall;
in it   sings the young nightingale

Sie singt von lauter Liebe,
she sings of   sheer love

Ich hör' es sogar im   Traum.
I   hear it even in the dream

High grows the tree above my bed, and there a young nightingale sings of pure love; I hear it even in my dreams.

37. *WIR WANDELTEN*
   WE WANDERED

37. WE WANDERED
   TOGETHER

Georg Friedrich Daumer

Wir wandelten, wir zwei zusammen,
we wandered we two together

Ich war so still, und du so stille;
I   was so still and you so still

Ich gäbe   viel,   um zu erfahren,
I   would give much so as to find out

Was du gedacht, in jenem Fall.
what you thought in that   instance

Was ich gedacht, unausgesprochen
what I   thought unspoken

Verbleibe das! Nur Eines   sag' ich:
let rest   that only one thing say I

So schön war alles,   was ich dachte,
so lovely was everything that I   thought

So himmlisch   heiter war es all'!
so beautifully serene was it all

In meinem Haupte die Gedanken,
in my   head   the thoughts

Sie läuteten wie gold'ne Glöckchen;
they rang   like golden little bells

So wundersüss,   so wunderlieblich
so wondrously sweet so wondrously lovely

Ist in der Welt kein and'rer Hall.
is in the world no   other sound

We wandered together, we two; I so still, and you so still. I would give much to know what you were thinking in that moment. What I was thinking, let it remain unsaid. Only one thing will I say: it was all so lovely what I thought, all so gloriously serene! In my head the thoughts were ringing like golden bells – so wondrously sweet and lovely is no other sound in the whole world!

38. *NACHTIGALL*
NIGHTINGALE

38. NIGHTINGALE

C. Reinhold

O Nachtigall,
O nightingale

Dein süsser Schall,
your sweet sound

Er dringet   mir durch   Mark   und Bein.
he penetrates me through marrow and bone

Nein, trauter   Vogel, nein!
no   beloved bird   no

Was in mir schafft so   süsse Pein,
what in me brings such sweet pain

Das ist nicht dein,
that is not yours

Das ist von andern, himmelschönen,
that is of   others heavenly beautiful

Nun längst   für mich verklungenen Tönen,
now long ago for me   died away   tones

In deinem Lied ein leiser Widerhall!
In your   song a   gentle echo

O nightingale, your sweet song penetrates my very soul. But no, beloved bird, no! What brings me such sweet sorrow is not your melody, but others of heavenly beauty, for me long faded away – in your song but a gentle echo!

39. *KOMM BALD*
COME SOON

39. COME SOON

Klaus Groth

Warum denn warten
why   then wait

Von Tag zu Tag?
from day to day

Es blüht   im   Garten
it flowers in the garden

Was blühen mag.
what flower may

Why do I wait from day to day? In the garden every flower is in bloom.

Wer kommt und zählt   es,
who comes and counts it

Was blüht   so schön?
what blossoms so beautifully

An Augen fehlt   es,
in eyes   is lacking it

Es anzuseh'n.
it to look at

Die meinen wandern
the mine   wander

Vom Strauch zum   Baum;
from bush   to the tree

Mir   scheint, auch andern
to me seems   also to others

Wär's wie ein Traum.
were it like a   dream

Und von den Lieben,
and of   the loved ones

Die mir   getreu,
who to me true

Und mir   geblieben,
and to me stayed

Wär'st du   dabei!
were   you thereby

But who comes to enjoy this fair blossoming? No eyes are there to see it.

My gaze wanders over bush and tree; to others it must seem like a dream.

And of those I loved, who remained true to me, how I wish that you were one!

40. TRENNUNG
PARTING

40. PARTING

Swabian folksong
(in dialect)

Da   unten im   Tale
there below in the valley

Läuft's Wasser so trüb,
runs the water   so turbid

Und i kann dir's   nit sagen,
and I can   to you it not say

I hab' di   so lieb.
I have you so dear

Down there in the valley the waters are troubled, and I can't tell you how much I love you.

Sprichst allweil von Lieb',
talk   always of love

Sprichst allweil von Treu',
talk   always of fidelity

Und a bissele   Falschheit
and a little bit falsehood

Is au   wohl   dabei!
is also perhaps thereby

You always talk of love, and being for ever true, but a little bit of falsehood is there as well!

Und wenn i dir's   zehnmal sag',
and when I to you it ten times say

Dass i di   lieb',
that I you love

Und du willst nit verstehn,
and you will not understand

Muss i halt weiter gehn.
must I just further go

If I tell you ten times over that I love you and want you, and you still won't understand, then I'll have to go away.

Für die Zeit, wo   du g'liebt mi hast,
for the time when you loved me have

Dank i dir schön.
thank I you beautifully

Und i wünsch', dass dir's   anderswo
and I wish   that you it elsewhere

Besser mag gehn.
better may go

For the time when you loved me, I thank you from my heart, and I hope it'll go better for you in some other place.

41. ZIGEUNERLIEDER GIPSY-SONGS

41. GIPSY SONGS

German translation from the original Hungarian attributed to Hugo Conrad

i.

He, Zigeuner, greife in die Saiten ein!
hey gipsy   strike into the strings in

Spiel das Lied vom ungetreuen Mägdelein!
play the song of the untrue   maiden

Lass die Saiten weinen, klagen, traurig bange,
let the strings weep lament sadly uneasy

Bis die heisse Träne netzet   diese Wange!
till the hot   tear moistens this cheek

i.

Hey, gipsy, strike up on your strings! Play the song of the girl who was untrue! Let your sad, uneasy strings weep and lament, until the hot tears flow down my cheeks!

ii.

Hochgetürmte Rimaflut,   wie bist du so trübt';
high-risen   Rima-flood how are you so troubled

An dem Ufer klag' ich laut   nach dir, mein Lieb!
on the bank lament I   loudly for you my love

Wellen fliehen,   Wellen strömen, rauschen an dem Strand
waves flee away waves gush   rush   to the beach
  heran zu mir.
  hither to me

An dem Rimaufer   lasst mich ewig   weinen nach ihr!
on the Rima-bank let me for ever weep for her

ii.

How troubled are your high flooding waters, O river Rima! On these banks I lament aloud for you, my love! The waves rush and surge towards me on the shore. Here on the banks of the Rima, O let me for ever weep for her!

iii.

Wisst ihr, wann mein Kindchen am   allerschönsten ist?
know you when my little one at the fairest of all is

Wenn ihr süsses Mündchen   scherzt und lacht und
when her sweet (little) mouth jests   and laughs and
  küsst.
  kisses

Mägdelein, du bist mein, inniglich küss' ich dich,
maiden   you are mine fervently kiss I you

Dich erschuf der liebe Himmel einzig nur für mich!
you created the good heaven solely just for me

Wisst ihr, wann mein Liebster am   besten mir gefällt?
know you when my beloved (at) the best me pleases

Wenn in seinen Armen er mich umschlungen hält.
when in his arms he me clasped   holds

Schätzelein, du bist mein, inniglich küss ich dich,
little treasure you are mine fervently kiss I   you

Dich erschuf der liebe Himmel einzig nur für mich!
you created the good heaven solely just for me

iii.

Do you know when my sweetheart is most fair? When her sweet lips jest, and laugh and kiss. You are mine, sweet maid! I kiss you with all my heart – heaven made you for me alone!

Do you know when my beloved best pleases me? When he holds me clasped in his arms! My treasure you are mine! I kiss you with all my heart – heaven made you for me alone!

iv.

Lieber Gott, du weisst, wie oft   bereut ich hab',
dear God you know how often rued I have

Dass ich meinem Liebsten einst ein Küsschen gab.
that I my   beloved once a (little) kiss gave

iv.

Dear God, you know how often I've rued the day I gave my love a sweet kiss – it was my heart that bade me. As long as I live I'll remember that first kiss!

Herz gebot, dass ich ihn küssen muss,
heart bade that I him kiss   must

Denk', so lang ich leb', an diesen ersten Kuss.
think so long I live of this first kiss

Lieber Gott, du weisst, wie oft   in stiller Nacht
dear God you know how often in still night

Dear God, you know how often in the still of night, I've thought with joy and pain of my treasure. To love is sweet, to rue is bitter – my poor heart will be for ever true!

Ich in Lust und Leid an meinen Schatz   gedacht.
I in joy and pain of my   sweetheart thought

Lieb' ist süss, wenn bitter auch die Reu',
love is sweet if   bitter also the regret

Armes Herze bleibt   ihm   ewig, ewig   treu.
poor heart remains to him for ever for ever true

v.

Brauner Bursche führt zum   Tanze sein blauäugig schönes
brown lad   leads to the dance his blue-eyed fair
   Kind,
   child

The swarthy lad leads his fair, blue-eyed love to the dance; he clashes his spurs boldly together as the tune of the Czardas begins. He hugs and kisses his sweet little dove, twirling as he leads her, and shouting with joy. And he throws three shining guilders on the dulcimer, so it rings.

Schlägt die Sporen keck   zusammen, Csardasmelodie
beats the spurs boldly together Czardas-melody
   beginnt,
   begins

Küsst und herzt   sein süsses Täubchen,
kisses and embraces his sweet little dove

Dreht sie, führt sie, jauchzt   und springt;
turns her leads her shouts for joy and leaps

Wirft drei blanke Silbergulden
throws three shining silver-guilders

Auf das Zimbal,   dass es klingt.
on the dulcimer that it sounds

vi.

Röslein   dreie in der Reihe blüh'n   so rot,
little roses three in the row   blossom so red

Three little red roses bloom in a row – no one keeps a lad from his lass. Dear God, if they could, the fair wide world would be no more – and to be single would be a sin!

Dass der Bursch zum   Mädel gehe, ist kein
that the lad   to the girl   goes is no
   Verbot!
   forbidden thing

Lieber Gott, wenn das verboten   wär'.
dear God when that forbidden were

Ständ'   die schöne weite Welt schon längst   nicht
would be the lovely wide world already long since not
    mehr;
    more

Ledig bleiben Sünde wär'!
single to stay sin   would be

Schönstes Städtchen in Alföld ist Ketschkemet,
fairest   little town in Alföld is Kecskemet,

Dort gibt es   gar viele Mädchen schmuck und nett!
there (are there) very many girls   pretty   and neat

Freunde, sucht euch dort ein Bräutchen   aus,
friends   seek you there a   (little) bride out

Freit um ihre Hand und gründet euer Haus,
woo for her hand and found your house

Freudenbecher leeret   aus!
cup of joy   empty out

Kecskemet is the fairest little town in Alföld, and it's full of sweet pretty girls. My friend, go there and choose a bride; woo her, found your family – and drink the cup of joy!

    vii.

Kommt dir   manchmal in den Sinn, mein süsses Lieb,
comes to you sometimes in the mind my   sweet love

Was du einst mit heil'gem Eide mir   gelobt?
what you once with sacred   oath to me vowed

Täusch mich nicht, verlass mich nicht,
deceive me   not   leave me not

Du weisst nicht, wie lieb ich dich hab'.
you know not how love I   you –

Lieb du mich, wie ich dich,
love you me   as I you

Dann strömt Gottes Huld auf dich herab!
then flows God's grace on you down

vii.

Do you ever remember, sweet love, what once you vowed with a sacred oath? Don't deceive me, don't forsake me – you can't know how much I love you! If you love me as I love you, on you will God's grace flow.

    viii.

Rote Abendwolken zieh'n am   Firmament,
red evening-clouds drift in the firmament

Sehnsuchtsvoll nach dir,
full of longing for   you

Mein Lieb, das Herze brennt,
my   love the heart is burning

viii.

The red clouds of evening drift across the sky, filled with my longing for you. Dear love, my heart burns; the heavens shine in flaming glory, and day and night I dream only of my sweet love.

Himmel strahlt in glüh'nder Pracht,
sky   shines in glowing splendour

Und ich träum' bei Tag und Nacht
and I   dream by day and night

Nur allein von dem süssen Liebchen   mein.
but only of the sweet sweetheart mine

42. *WIE MELODIEN ZIEHT ES* LIKE MELODIES MOVES IT

42. LIKE A MELODY

Klaus Groth

Wie Melodien zieht   es
like melodies moves it

Mir leise   durch   den Sinn,
to me gently through the mind

Wie Frühlingsblumen blüht   es
like spring-flowers blossoms it

Und schwebt wie Duft   dahin.
and floats   like fragrance away

Like a melody it softly pervades
my mind. Like spring flowers it
blossoms and its fragrance drifts
away.

Doch kommt das Wort und fasst   es
but   comes the word and grasps it

Und führt es vor   das Aug',
and leads it before the eye

Wie Nebelgrau erblasst es
like misty-grey fades it

Und schwindet wie ein Hauch.
and vanishes like a   breath

But if the word comes, and grasps
it, then brings it before the eyes, it
fades as a grey mist, and vanishes
as a breath.

Und dennoch ruht im   Reime
and yet   rests in the rhyme

Verborgen wohl   ein Duft,
hidden   perhaps a   fragrance

Den mild aus stillem Keime
that gently from tranquil germ

Ein feuchtes Auge ruft.
a   moist eye summons

And yet the rhyme conceals a
hidden fragrance, that gently from
its tranquil source brings tears to
the eyes.

43. *IMMER LEISER   WIRD*
EVER   QUIETER BECOMES
MEIN SCHLUMMER
MY   SLUMBER

43. EVER QUIETER IS MY SLUMBER

Hermann Lingg

Immer leiser   wird   mein Schlummer,
ever   quieter becomes my   slumber

Nur wie Schleier liegt mein Kummer
only as   veil   lies my   grief

Zitternd   über mir.
trembling over me

Oft   im   Traume hör' ich dich
often in the dream   hear I   you

Rufen drauss vor   meiner Tür,
call   outside before my   door

Niemand wacht   und öffnet dir,
no one   is awake and opens to you

Ich erwach' und weine bitterlich.
I   awake and weep bitterly

Ever lighter grows my slumber; only my grief lies over me like a veil. Often in a dream I hear you calling before my door. No one wakes and lets you in. I awake, and bitterly I weep.

Ja, ich werde sterben müssen,
yes I   shall die   must

Eine andre   wirst du küssen,
– another – will   you kiss

Wenn ich bleich und kalt.
when I   pale   and cold

Eh'   die Maienlüfte   weh'n,
before the May-breezes blow

Eh'   die Drossel singt im   Wald:
before the thrush sings in the wood

Willst du mich noch einmal seh'n,
want you me   again once   to see

Komm', o komme bald!
come   O come soon

I know that I must die, that you will kiss another when I lie pale and cold. Before the breezes blow in May, and the thrush sings in the wood, if you would see me once again – come, come soon!

44. *AUF DEM KIRCHHOFE*
IN   THE CHURCHYARD

Detlev von Liliencron

Der Tag ging regenschwer und sturmbewegt,
the day went rain-heavy and storm-stirred

Ich war an manch' vergess'nem Grab gewesen,
I   was by many a forgotten   grave been

Verwittert Stein und Kreuz, die Kränze alt,
weathered stone and cross   the wreaths old

Die Namen überwachsen, kaum zu lesen.
the names overgrown   hardly to read

Der Tag ging sturmbewegt   und regenschwer,
the day went storm-stirred and rain-heavy

Auf allen Gräbern fror   das Wort: Gewesen.
on all   graves   froze the word been

Wie sturmestot   die Särge schlummerten,
how storm-dead the coffins slumbered

Auf allen Gräbern taute   still: Genesen.
on all   graves   thawed softly made well

44. IN A
CHURCHYARD

The day was heavy with rain and
swept with storms. I wandered by
some forgotten graves: weathered
stone and cross, old wreaths, the
names all overgrown, and hard to
read.

The day was swept by storms and
heavy with rain. On all the graves
the words froze: no more. The
storm was silent, the coffins
slumbered. On all the graves it
thawed: redeemed.

45. *STÄNDCHEN*
SERENADE

Franz Kugler

Der Mond steht über dem Berge,
the moon is   over the mountain

So recht für verliebte Leut';
so right for in love people

Im   Garten rieselt   ein Brunnen,
in the garden trickles a   fountain

Sonst   Stille   weit und breit.
otherwise stillness far and wide

45. SERENADE

The moon shines over the
mountains, just right for those in
love; a fountain plays gently in the
garden – all around it is still.

Neben der   Mauer im   Schatten,
near   to the wall   in the shadow

Da   steh'n der   Studenten drei,
there stand of the students three

Mit Flöt' und Geig' und Zither,
with flute and fiddle and zither

Und singen und spielen dabei.
and sing   and play   therewith

Die Klänge schleichen der   Schönsten
the sounds steal   to the most beautiful one

Sacht in   den Traum hinein,
softly into the dream thither

Sie schaut den blonden Geliebten
she sees   the fair   lover

Und lispelt: 'Vergiss nicht mein!'
and murmurs softly forget   not   me

In the shadows beneath the wall stand three students, singing and playing on fiddle, flute and zither.

The sounds steal softly into the dreams of the most beautiful one: who gazes upon her fair lover, and murmurs, 'Forget me not!'

46. SALAMANDER

Karl Lemcke

Es   sass ein Salamander
there sat a   salamander

Auf einem kühlen Stein,
on a   cool   stone

Da   warf ein böses   Mädchen
then threw a   wicked girl

Ins   Feuer ihn hinein.
Into the fire   him thither

Sie meint', er soll   verbrennen,
she thought he must burn

Ihm   ward erst wohl   zu Mut,
to him was   just happy in mood –

Wohl   wie mir kühlem Teufel
happy like me cool   devil

Die heisse Liebe tut.
the hot   love   makes

46. SALAMANDER

A salamander was sitting on a cold stone, when a wicked girl threw him into the fire.

She thought he would burn, but he was quite happy, just as I, cool devil that I am, flourish in the passions of love.

47. *DAS MÄDCHEN SPRICHT*
THE MAIDEN   SPEAKS

Otto Friedrich Gruppe

Schwalbe, sag' mir an,
swallow   tell me –

Ist's dein alter Mann,
Is it your old husband

Mit dem   du's   Nest gebaut,
with whom you the nest built

Oder hast du jüngst
Or   have you lately

Erst dich   ihm   vertraut?
just yourself to him entrusted

Sag' was   zwitschert ihr,
say   what twitter   you

Sag' was flüstert ihr
say   what whisper you

Des   Morgens so vertraut?
of the morning so intimately

Gelt,   du bist wohl   auch
isn't it so you are perhaps also

Noch nicht lange Braut?
yet   not   long bride

47. THE MAIDEN
SPEAKS

Swallow, tell me, is that the
husband with whom you first built
your nest? Or are you just lately
betrothed?

Tell me, what is it you secretly
twitter and whisper each morning?
Is it, perhaps, that you've not long
been a bride?

48. *MÄDCHENLIED*
MAIDEN-SONG

Paul Heyse

Auf die Nacht in der Spinnstub'n,
at (the) night in the spinning-room

Da   singen die Mädchen,
there sing   the maidens

Da   lachen die Dorfbub'n,
there laugh the village-lads

Wie flink   geh'n die Rädchen!
how nimbly go   the little wheels

48. MAIDEN'S SONG

At night in the spinning-room the
maidens are singing, and the
village lads laughing. How nimbly
the little wheels whirr!

Spinnt Jedes   am   Brautschatz,
spins each one at the trousseau

Dass der Liebste sich   freut.
that the beloved himself rejoices

Nicht lange, so gibt es
not   long   so (is there)

Ein Hochzeitsgeläut.
a   wedding-peal

Kein Mensch, der mir   gut ist,
no   person who to me good is

Will nach mir fragen;
will after me ask

Wie bang   mir zu Mut ist,
how anxious me in mood is

Wem   soll ich's klagen?
to whom shall I it lament

Die Tränen rinnen mir   übers   Gesicht –
the tears   run   (to me) over the face

Wofür   soll ich spinnen?
for what shall I   spin

Ich weiss es nicht!
I   know it not

Each is spinning her trousseau to
please her beloved; before long
wedding bells will ring.

But for me no one cares, no one
asks for me. My heart is heavy, but
who will hear my lament?

Tears run down my face – for
what am I spinning? I do not
know.

49. *VIER ERNSTE GESÄNGE*
FOUR SERIOUS SONGS

Martin Luther (translated from the Bible)

i.

Denn es gehet dem   Menschen wie dem   Vieh; wie
for   it is to (the) man   as to the beast as

dies   stirbt, so stirbt er auch; und haben alle
this one dies   so dies he also and have all

einerlei   Odem; und der   Mensch hat nichts
one and the same breath and (the) man   has nothing

mehr denn das Vieh: denn es ist alles eitel.
more than the beast for it is all   vain

49. FOUR SERIOUS
SONGS

(Authorised Version)

i. (Eccl. III 19–22)

For that which befalleth the sons
of men befalleth beasts; as the one
dieth, so dieth the other; yea, they
have all one breath; so that a man
hath no preeminence above a
beast: for all is vanity.

Es fährt alles   *an einen Ort; es ist alles*
it goes everything to one   place it is all

von Staub gemacht und wird   *wieder zu Staub.*
of dust made   and becomes again to dust

Wer weiss, ob der Geist des   *Menschen aufwärts*
who knows if the spirit of (the) man   upwards

fahre, und der Odem des   *Viehes unterwärts*
may go and the breath of the beast downwards

unter die Erde fahre?
under the earth may go

Darum   *sahe ich, dass nichts*   *Bessers ist, denn*
therefore saw I   that nothing better is   than

dass der Mensch fröhlich sei in seiner Arbeit; denn
that the man   joyful be in his   work   for

das ist sein Teil. Denn wer will ihn dahin bringen,
that is his part for   who will him there bring

dass er sehe   *was nach ihm geschehen wird?*
that he might see what after him happen   will

All go unto one place; all are of the dust, and all turn to dust again.

Who knoweth the spirit of man that goeth upward, and the spirit of the beast that goeth downward to the earth?

Wherefore I perceive that there is nothing better, than that a man should rejoice in his own works; for that is his portion: for who shall bring him to see what shall be after him?

ii.

Ich wandte   *mich und sahe*   *an alle, die*
I   turned round myself and looked at all   who

Unrecht leiden unter der Sonne; und siehe, da
injustice suffer under the sun   and see   there

waren Tränen, derer,   *die Unrecht litten,*   *und*
were tears   of those who injustice suffered and

hatten keinen Tröster,   *und die*   *ihnen*   *Unrecht*
had   no   comforter and who to them injustice

täten,   *waren zu mächtig, dass sie*   *keinen*
would do were too powerful that they no

Tröster   *haben*   *konnten.*
comforter to have were able

Da lobte   *ich die Toten, die schon*   *gestorben*
then praised I the dead   who already dead

waren, mehr als   *die Lebendigen, die*   *noch das Leben*
were   more than the living   who still the life

   hatten;
   had

ii. (Eccl. IV 1–3)

So I returned, and considered all those oppressions that are done under the sun: and behold the tears of such as were oppressed, and they had no comforter; and on the side of their oppressors there was power; but they had no comforter.

Wherefore I praised the dead which are already dead more than the living which are yet alive.

Und der   noch nicht ist, ist besser, als   alle
and who yet   not   is is better than them

Yea, better is he than both they,
which hath not yet been, who hath
not seen the evil work that is done
under the sun.

beide, und des   Bösen nicht inne   wird,   das
both and of the evil   not   aware becomes that

unter der Sonne geschieht.
under the sun   is done

    iii.

    iii. (Ecclesiasticus XLI 1–2, from
        the Apocrypha)

O Tod, wie bitter bist du, wenn an dich gedenket
O death how bitter are you when of you thinks

O death, how bitter is the
remembrance of thee to a man
that liveth at rest in his
possessions, unto the man that
hath nothing to vex him, and that
hath prosperity in all things: yea,
unto him that is yet able to receive
meat! O death, acceptable is thy
sentence unto the needy, and unto
him whose strength faileth, that is
now in the last age, and is vexed
with all things, and to him that
despaireth, and hath lost patience

ein Mensch, der gute Tage und genug   hat und ohne
a   man   who good days and enough has and without

Sorge lebet; und dem   es wohl geht in allen
care lives and to whom it well goes in all

Dingen und noch wohl essen mag! O Tod, wie bitter bist
things and still well eat   may O death how bitter are
  du O Tod, wie wohl
  you O death how comforting

tust du dem Dürftigen, der da   schwach
(are) you to the needy one who there weak

und alt ist, der in allen Sorgen   steckt,   und
and old is who in all   troubles is stuck and

nichts   Bessers zu hoffen noch zu erwarten hat!
nothing better to hope nor to expect   has

O Tod, wie wohl   tust du,
O death how comforting (are) you

    iv.

    iv. (I Cor. XIII 1–3, 12–13)

Wenn ich mit Menschen- und mit Engelszungen
if   I   with men's   and with angels' tongues

Though I speak with the tongues
of men and of angels, and have
not charity, I am become as
sounding brass, or a tinkling
cymbal.

redete, und hätte der   Liebe   nicht, so wär'
spoke and had of the charity not   so would be

ich ein tönend   Erz   oder eine klingende Schelle.
I   a sounding brass or a   tinkling cymbal

Und wenn ich weissagen könnte, und wüsste
and if   I   prophesy could and understood

And though I have the gift of
prophecy, and understand all
mysteries, and all knowledge; and
though I have all faith, so that I

alle Geheimnisse und alle Erkenntnis und
all mysteries   and all knowledge and

hätte allen Glauben, also, dass ich Berge
had all faith so that I mountains

versetzte; und hätte der Liebe nicht, so
removed and had of the love not so

wäre ich nichts.
should be I nothing

could remove mountains, and
have not charity, I am nothing.

Und wenn ich alle meine Habe den Armen gäbe,
and if I all my goods to the poor gave

und liesse meinen Leib brennen und hätte der
and let my body burn and had of the

Liebe nicht, so wäre mir's nichts nütze.
charity not so would be to me it nothing of use

And though I bestow all my goods
to feed the poor, and though I give
my body to be burned, and have
not charity, it profiteth me
nothing.

Wir sehen jetzt durch einen Spiegel in einem
we see now through a glass in a

dunkeln Worte; dann aber von Angesicht zu
dark word then but from face to

Angesichte. Jetzt erkenne ich's stückweise; dann
face now know I it piecemeal then

aber werd ich's erkennen, gleich wie ich erkennet bin.
but shall I it know even as I known am

For now we see through a glass,
darkly; but then face to face: now I
know in part; but then shall I
know even as also I am known.

Nun aber bleibet Glaube, Hoffnung, Liebe diese
now but remains faith hope charity these

drei: aber die Liebe ist die grösseste unter
three but the charity is the greatest amongst

ihnen.
them

And now abideth faith, hope,
charity, these three; but the
greatest of these is charity.

Hugo Wolf
(1860–1903)

1. ÜBER NACHT **OVER-NIGHT**	**1. AT NIGHT**

Julius Sturm

Über Nacht, über Nacht kommt still   das Leid,
over-night   over-night comes silently the grief

Und bist du   erwacht,   o traurige Zeit,
and are you awakened O sad   time

Du grüssest den dämmernden Morgen
you greet   the dawning   morning

Mit Weinen und mit Sorgen.
with weeping and with cares

At night, at night, grief steals silently in, and if you wake, O my sorrow, you will greet the dawn with weeping and with care.

Über Nacht, über Nacht kommt still   das Glück,
over-night over-night comes silently the happiness

Und bist du   erwacht, o selig   Geschick,
and are you awakened O blessed destiny

Der düstre   Traum ist zerronnen,
the melancholy dream is melted

Und Freude ist gewonnen.
and joy   is won

At night, at night joy steals silently in, and if you wake, O blessed destiny, the dark dream is banished and joy is triumphant.

Über Nacht, über Nacht kommt Freud und Leid,
over-night over-night comes joy   and sorrow

Und eh   du's gedacht, verlassen dich beid
and before you it thought leave   you both

Und gehen dem   Herrn zu sagen,
and go   to the Lord to say

Wie du sie   getragen.
how you them bore

At night, at night joy and sorrow both steal in, and quick as thought, they leave you, and go to the Lord to tell Him how you have borne them.

2. *BESCHEIDENE LIEBE*
MODEST LOVE

2. UNDEMANDING LOVE

Poet unknown

Ich bin wie andre Mädchen nicht,
I am like other girls not

Die, wenn sie lieben, schweigen
who when they love are silent

Und ihr Geheimnis hütend stumm,
and their secret keeping dumb

Das kranke Köpfchen neigen.
the sick little head bow

Ja, meine Liebe ist nicht stumm,
yes my love is not silent

Mein Plaudern geb ich nicht darum;
my chattering give I not for that

Ich liebe doch ganz eigen.
I love indeed quite specially

Ich bin wie andre Mädchen nicht,
I am as other girls not

Die, wenn sie lieben, hoffen.
who when they love hope

Ich trage meine Lieb zur Schau
I bear my love for show

Vor aller Welt ganz offen.
before all world quite open

Oft hat mich schon lieb Mütterlein
often has me already dear (little)mother

Mit dem Herzallerliebsten mein
with the – dearest of my heart –

Beim Kosen angetroffen.
by the caressing come across

Ich bin wie andre Mädchen nicht,
I am as other girls not

Doch glücklich, wie ich glaube,
but lucky as I believe

Denn meine Liebe richtet sich
for my love prepares (herself)

I'm not like other girls, who when they are in love are silent, keeping their secret in their love-sick little heads. No, my love's not dumb, and I'll not exchange it for my chattering. I have to love in my quite special way.

I'm not like other girls in love, with all their hopes. I carry my love quite openly, for all the world to see. Often my dear good mother catches me kissing my sweetheart.

I'm not like other girls – I know how lucky I am, for my love is not intent on a ring and wedding-veil. He is my own true bridegroom, so tame and sweet when he coos: my darling, who is my dove.

Auf Trauring   nicht und Haube.
for wedding-ring not   and (marriage)

Er bleibt   mein trauter Bräutigam,
he remains my   dear   bridegroom

Er girrt so süss,   er ist so zahm,
he coos so sweetly he is so tame

Mein Lieb ist meine Taube.
my   love is my   dove

3. MORGENTAU
MORNING-DEW

(Aus   einem alten Liederbuch)
 from an   old   song-book

Der Frühhauch   hat gefächelt
the early-breeze has fanned

Hinweg die schwüle Nacht,
away   the sultry   night

Die Flur   holdselig   lächelt
the meadow most charmingly smiles

In ihrer Lenzespracht;
in her   spring-splendour

Mild singt vom   dunklen Baume
softly sings from the dark   tree

Ein Vöglein   in der Früh,
a   little bird in the early morning

Es singt noch halb im   Traume
it sings still half in the dream

Gar süsse Melodie.
very sweet melody

Die Rosenknospe hebet
the rose-bud   raises

Empor ihr Köpfchen bang,
up   her little head timidly

Denn wundersam durchbebet
for   exquisitely thrilled through

Hat sie der süsse Sang;
has her the sweet song

3. MORNING-DEW

An early breeze has fanned away
the sultry night; the meadow
smiles, charming in her spring
splendour.

From the dark tree a little bird
softly sings its early morning song;
half in dream, it sings so sweet a
melody.

The rose-bud timidly raises on
high her little head, as the sweet,
exquisite song thrills within her.

Und mehr und mehr enthüllet
and more and more discloses

Sich ihrer Blätter Füll',
itself of her petals profusion

Und eine Träne quillet
and a tear springs

Hervor so heimlich still.
forth so secretly silent

Gradually her petals unclose in
their glory, and a tear wells up,
secret and still.

4. WIEGENLIED (IM CRADLE-SONG IN THE SOMMER) SUMMER

Robert Reinick

Vom Berg hinabgestiegen
from the hill descended

Ist nun des Tages Rest;
is now of the day remainder

Mein Kind liegt in der Wiegen,
my child lies in the cradle

Die Vögel all im Nest.
the birds all in the nest

Nur ein ganz klein Singvögelein
only one quite small little song-bird

Ruft weit daher im Dämmerschein:
calls far away in the twilight

'Gut' Nacht! Gut' Nacht!
good night good night

Lieb' Kindlein, gute Nacht!'
dear little child good night

Die Wiege geht im Gleise,
the cradle moves in the rail

Die Uhr tickt hin und her,
the clock ticks to and fro

Die Fliegen nur ganz leise
the flies only quite softly

4. SUMMER CRADLE-SONG

The last light of day has sunk
behind the hills. My child lies in
the cradle, the birds all in their
nests. Just one small song-bird
calls from afar in the twilight,
'Good-night! Good-night, dear
little one, good-night!'

The cradle rocks, the clock ticks to
and fro, and insects around still
softly hum. Little creatures, leave
my child in peace! What is it you
secretly hum to him? 'Good-night!
Good-night, dear little one, good-
night!'

Sie   summen noch daher.
they hum   still around

Ihr Fliegen, lasst mein Kind in Ruh!
you flies   leave my   child in peace

Was summt ihr ihm   so heimlich zu?
what hum   you (to) it so secretly to

'Gut' Nacht! Gut' Nacht!
 good night   good night

Lieb' Kindlein, gute Nacht!'
dear little child good night

Der Vogel und die Sterne
the bird and the stars

Und alle rings umher,
and all round about

Sie haben mein Kind so gerne,
they –   my   child so (love*)

Die Engel noch viel   mehr.
the angels still much more

Sie decken's mit den Flügeln zu
they cover it with the wings up

Und singen leise: 'Schlaf in Ruh!
and sing   quietly sleep in peace

Gut' Nacht! Gut' Nacht!
good night   good night

Lieb Kindlein, gute Nacht!'
dear little child good night

The bird and the stars, and all things about have such love for my child – and still more the angels who cover him with their wings, as they quietly sing: 'Sleep peacefully, good-night! Good-night dear little one, good-night!'

5. *MAUSFALLEN-SPRÜCHLEIN*
MOUSE-TRAP LITTLE SAYING

5. MAGIC CHANT TO
CATCH A MOUSE

Eduard Mörike

(Das Kind geht dreimal   um   die Falle und spricht:)
 the child goes three times round the trap and says

Kleine Gäste, kleines Haus,
little   guests little   house

Liebe Mäusin,   oder Maus,
dear (female) mouse or   (male) mouse

(The child walks three times round the trap saying:)

Tiny guests, tiny house; dear Mr. Mouse or Mrs. Mouse, just come boldly along tonight, by moonlight! But shut the door nicely behind you, do you hear? And mind your little tail! After

   * (gerne haben – to love)

Stelle   dich   nur kecklich ein
present yourself just boldly   –

Heute Nacht bei Mondenschein,
today night by moonlight

Mach' aber die Tür fein   hinter dir zu,
shut   but the door nicely behind you –

Hörst du?
hear you

Dabei   hüte   dein Schwänzchen!
at the same time watch your little tail

Nach Tische singen wir,
after meal   sing   we

Nach Tische springen wir,
after meal   skip   we

Und machen ein Tänzchen:
and do   a   little dance

Witt! Witt!
Psst! Psst!

Meine alte Katze tanzt   wahrscheinlich mit.
my   old cat   dances probably   with (us)

Hörst du?
hear you

supper we will sing and skip, and
do a little dance. Psst! Psst! My
old cat will probably join in!

6. *ZUR   RUH, ZUR   RUH*
TO THE REST TO THE REST

6. GO TO YOUR REST

Justinus Kerner

Zur   Ruh, zur   Ruh, ihr müden Glieder!
to the rest to the rest you weary limbs

Schliesst fest euch   zu, ihr Augenlider!
shut   tight yourselves – you eyelids

Ich bin allein, fort ist die Erde;
I   am alone gone is the earth

Nacht muss es sein, dass Licht mir   werde,
night must it be   that light to me may grow

O führt mich ganz, ihr innern Mächte!
O lead me   wholly you inner powers

Go to your rest, weary limbs; and
eyelids, close! I am alone, the
world left behind; night must
come, that I may receive light. O
lead me, inner powers, to the
splendours of deepest night. Take
me far from earth's sorrows,
through night and dreams home to
the mother's breast!

Hin   zu dem Glanz   der   tiefsten Nächte.
thither to the splendour of the deepest nights

Fort aus   dem Raum der   Erdenschmerzen
away from the place of the earth-sorrows

Durch   Nacht und Traum zum   Mutterherzen!
through night and dream to the mother's-heart

7. *DER GENESENE   AN DIE*   7. TO HOPE
THE CONVALESCENT TO THE   (from one who is
HOFFNUNG   recovering)
HOPE

Eduard Mörike

Tödlich graute   mir   der Morgen:
deadly dawned to me the morning

Doch schon   lag mein Haupt, wie süss!
but   already lay my   head   how sweetly

Hoffnung, dir   im   Schoss verborgen,
hope   to you in the lap   concealed

Bis der Sieg   gewonnen hiess.
till the victory won   was called

Opfer   bracht' ich allen Göttern,
sacrifice brought I   to all gods

Doch vergessen warest du;
but forgotten were you

Seitwärts von   den ew'gen Rettern
sideways from the eternal saviours

Sahest   du dem Feste   zu.
watched you the festival –

O vergib, du   Vielgetreue!
O forgive you very faithful one

Tritt aus   deinem Dämmerlicht,
step from your   twilight

Dass ich dir ins   ewig   neue,
that I   to you into the eternally new

Mondenhelle Angesicht
moon-bright face

Deathly grey dawned the morning, but already my head lay at your breast, O hope, sweetly sheltering until the victory was won. I had sacrificed to all the gods, but had forgotten you. As you watched the rites, you stood apart from the eternal saviours.

O forgive me, you who were ever faithful! Leave your twilight, that I may gaze into your face as clear and ageless as the moon; that my very soul may see you, as a child sees, without grief. And just once free from pain, enfold me in your arms!

Einmal schaue, recht von   Herzen,
once   see   right from heart

Wie ein Kind und sonder   Harm;
as   a   child and without sorrow

Ach, nur einmal ohne   Schmerzen
oh   just once   without pains

Schliesse mich in deinen Arm!
enfold   me   in your   arm

8. DER TAMBOUR
THE DRUMMER

Eduard Mörike

Wenn meine Mutter hexen   könnt',
if   my   mother practise witchcraft could

Da müsst'   sie mit dem Regiment
then would have to she with the regiment

Nach Frankreich, überall   mit hin,
to   France   everywhere with thither

Und wär'   die Marketenderin.
and would be the canteen keeper

Im   Lager, wohl   um Mitternacht,
in the camp perhaps at   midnight

Wenn niemand auf ist als die Wacht,
when no one   up is but the watch

Und alles   schnarchet, Ross und Mann,
and everybody snores   horse and man

Vor   meiner Trommel säss'   ich dann:
in front of my   drum   would sit I   then

Die Trommel müsst'   eine Schüssel sein
the drum   would have to a   bowl   be

Ein warmes Sauerkraut   darein,
a   warm   pickled cabbage in it

Die Schlegel   Messer und Gabel,
the drum-sticks knife and fork

Ein' lange Wurst   mein Sabel;
a   long sausage my   sabre

8. THE DRUMMER-
BOY

If my mother were a witch, then
she could go everywhere in France
with my regiment, and be in
charge of the food. In the camp at
midnight, when no one but the
watch was about, and all the
horses and men were snoring, I'd
sit in front of my drum, as if it
were a bowl of hot pickled
cabbage. I'd use my drum sticks as
knife and fork, and my sabre could
be a long sausage. My cap would
make a fine tankard that I'd fill
with Burgundy blood. And as
there'd be no light, the moon
would shine into my tent in
French style, and I'd think of my
sweetheart. Oh dear, now the fun
is over! If only my mother were a
witch!

Mein Tschako wär'   ein Humpen gut,
my shako   would be a   tankard good

Den füll'   ich mit Burgunderblut.
that would fill I   with Burgundy-blood

Und weil   es mir   an Lichte fehlt,
and because it to me of light   lacks

Da   scheint der Mond in   mein Gezelt;
there shines the moon into my   tent

Scheint er auch auf französ'sch herein,
shines he also in French   in here

Mir   fällt   doch meine Liebste ein:
to me comes to mind   my   beloved –

Ach weh! Jetzt hat der Spass ein End!
oh   dear now has the fun   an end

– Wenn nur meine Mutter hexen   könnt!
   if   only my   mother cast spells could

9. *ER IST'S*
HE IS IT

Eduard Mörike
(also set by Schumann)

Frühling lässt sein blaues Band
spring   lets his blue ribbon

Wieder flattern durch   die Lüfte;
again flutter through the breezes

Süsse, wohlbekannte Düfte
sweet familiar   scents

Streifen ahnungsvoll   das Land.
rove   full of expectation the countryside

Veilchen träumen schon,
violets dream already

Wollen balde kommen.
want soon to come

Horch, von fern ein leiser Harfenton!
listen from afar a   quiet harp-tone

9. IT'S HERE!

Spring once again floats her blue
ribbons on the breezes; sweet
familiar scents drift full of promise
through the country-side. Already
violets are dreaming; soon they
will appear. Listen, a harp sounds
softly from afar! Spring, it is you
indeed – it is you I have heard!

Frühling, ja   du bist's!
spring   indeed you are it

Dich hab ich vernommen!
you have I   heard

10. *DAS VERLASSENE MÄGDLEIN* | ## 10. THE FORSAKEN
THE FORSAKEN   GIRL | GIRL

Eduard Mörike
(also set by Schumann)

Früh, wann die Hähne krähn,
early when the cocks   crow

Eh'   die Sternlein schwinden,
before the little stars vanish

Muss ich am   Herde   stehn,
must I   at the kitchen range stand

Muss Feuer zünden.
must fire   kindle

Early at cock crow, before the stars fade, I must stand at the hearth and kindle the fire.

Schön   ist der   Flammen Schein,
beautiful is of the flames   shine

Es springen die Funken;
(it) leap   the sparks

Ich schaue so   darein,
I   look   thus into it

In Leid versunken.
in grief sunk

Beautiful is the glow of flames; sparks spring up. I gaze at them sunk in grief.

Plötzlich, da   kommt es mir,
suddenly there comes it to me

Treuloser Knabe,
unfaithful youth

Dass ich die Nacht von dir
that I the night of you

Geträumet habe.
dreamt   have

Suddenly it comes to me, that last night I dreamt of you, my unfaithful love.

Träne auf Träne dann
tear   on tear   then

Stürzet hernieder;
gushes down

Tear after tear runs down my face. Another day begins – would it were ended!

So kommt der Tag heran –
so comes the day near

O ging'   er wieder!
O would go he again

11. BEGEGNUNG
ENCOUNTER

11. ENCOUNTER

Eduard Mörike

Was doch   heut Nacht ein Sturm gewesen,
what indeed – tonight – a   storm (has) been

What a storm there was last night,
that raged until the break of day!
Look how the unbidden broom
swept the chimneys and alleyways!

Bis   erst der Morgen sich geregt!
until just the morning itself stirred

Wie hat der ungebetne Besen
how has the unbidden broom

Kamin   und Gassen ausgefegt!
chimney and alleys   swept out

Da   kommt ein Mädchen schon   die Strassen,
there comes a   girl   already the streets

A girl is coming along the street,
looking timidly about her; her
little face blushing like a
windblown rose.

Das halb verschüchtert um   sich   sieht;
that half scared   about herself looks

Wie Rosen, die der Wind zerblasen,
like roses   that the wind blew apart

So unstet   ihr Gesichtchen glüht.
so unsettled her little face   glows

Ein schöner   Bursch tritt   ihr entgegen,
a   handsome lad   comes her towards

A handsome lad goes eagerly to
meet her. How joyfully, how
awkwardly they look at one
another, these unaccustomed
rogues!

Er will   ihr voll   Entzücken nahn:
he is about to her full (of) delight   approach

Wie sehn sich   freudig und verlegen
how look themselves joyfully and confused

Die ungewohnten   Schelme an!
the unaccustomed rogues at

Er scheint zu fragen, ob das Liebchen
he seems to ask   if the sweetheart

He seems to be asking if his
sweetheart has yet found time to
rebraid her hair, that last night in
the open room was ruffled by the
storm.

Die Zöpfe schon   zurecht gemacht,
the plaits already to rights put

Die heute Nacht im offnen Stübchen
that – tonight – in the open little room

Ein Sturm in Unordnung gebracht.
a storm in disorder brought

Der Bursche träumt noch von den Küssen,
the youth dreams still of the kisses

The youth still dreams of the kisses he exchanged with the sweet girl. He stands there overcome by her charm, whilst she, with a rustle, slips round the corner.

Die ihm das süsse Kind getauscht,
that to him the sweet child exchanged

Er steht, von Anmut hingerissen,
he stands by charm overcome

Derweil sie um die Ecke rauscht.
whilst she round the corner swishes

12. NIMMERSATTE LIEBE
INSATIABLE LOVE

12. LOVE NEVER SATISFIED

Eduard Mörike

So ist die Lieb'! So ist die Lieb'!
thus is the love thus is the love

Such is love, such is love – not to be quenched with kisses. What fool is there would try to fill a sieve with water? And if it were drawn for a thousand years, or you kissed for ever and ever – never would love be satisfied.

Mit Küssen nicht zu stillen:
with kisses not to satisfy

Wer ist der Tor und will ein Sieb
who is the fool and wants a sieve

Mit eitel Wasser füllen?
with mere water to fill

Und schöpfst du an die tausend Jahr',
and draw you about the thousand years

Und küssest ewig, ewig gar,
and kiss for ever for ever even

Du tust ihr nie zu Willen.
you do to her never as (she) wishes

Die Lieb', die Lieb' hat alle Stund'
the love the love has every hour

Each hour of the day love has new, strange desires. Today as we kissed our lips were quite sore. Like a lamb beneath a knife my sweetheart was still, and her eyes said, 'Keep on, keep on – the more it hurts the better!'

Neu wunderlich Gelüsten;
new strange desires

Wir bissen uns die Lippen wund,
we bit (ourselves) the lips sore

Da wir uns heute küssten.
as we (ourselves) today kissed

Das Mädchen hielt in guter Ruh,
the girl   kept in good stillness

Wie's Lämmlein unterm   Messer;
like the little lamb under the knife

Ihr Auge bat: 'Nur immer zu,
her eye   bade only always on

Je weher desto besser!'
the sorer the   better

So ist die Lieb' und war auch so,
thus is the love and was also thus

Wie lang es   Liebe gibt,
as   long there love is

Und anders   war Herr Salomo,
and otherwise was Lord Solomon

Der Weise, nicht verliebt.
the sage   not in love

Such is love, and it was ever thus
as long as there was love. And no
different was wise King Solomon,
when he was in love.

13. FUSSREISE
FOOT-JOURNEY

Eduard Mörike

Am   frischgeschnittnen Wanderstab,
with the freshly-cut   walking-staff

Wenn ich in der Frühe
when I   in the early morning

So durch   Wälder ziehe,
so through woods go

Hügel auf und ab:
hill   up and down

Dann, wie's Vöglein   im   Laube
then   as the little bird in the foliage

Singet und sich rührt,
sings and itself stirs

Oder wie die gold'ne Traube
or   as the golden grape

Wonnegeister   spürt
spirits of ecstasy senses

In der ersten Morgensonne:
in the first   morning-sunshine

13. JOURNEY ON
FOOT

Early in the morning, a fresh-cut
staff in my hand, I stride through
the woods, up hills and down. For
like a small bird that flutters and
sings amongst the leaves, or the
golden grape in the first morning
sun – so an autumn and spring
fever seizes my old Adam: a new-
born god-like courage, and a never
to be lost delight in Paradise.

So fühlt auch mein alter, lieber
so feels also my old   dear

Adam Herbst- und Frühlingsfieber,
Adam autumn and spring-fever

Gottbeherzte,
divinely emboldened

Nie   verscherzte
never trifled away

Erstlings-Paradieseswonne.
first-born Paradise delight

Also bist du nicht so schlimm, o alter
so are you not so bad   O old

Adam, wie die strengen Lehrer sagen;
Adam as the stern   sages say

Liebst und lobst   du immer doch,
love   and praise you still   indeed

Singst und preisest immer noch,
sing   and glorify – still –

Wie an ewig   neuen Schöpfungstagen,
as   on eternally new creation's-days

Deinen lieben Schöpfer und Erhalter.
your   dear Creator and Saviour

Möcht' es dieser geben,
would it this   grant

Und mein ganzes Leben
and my   whole life

Wär'   im   leichten Wanderschweisse
would be in the easy   walking-sweat

Eine solche Morgenreise!
a   such morning's journey

And so you, old Adam, are not so
bad, as the stern sages say; you
can still love, still praise, still
glorify and sing to your beloved
Saviour, and His ever-renewing
Creation. And if this is so, then
my whole life could be as the easy
toil of such a morning's journey!

14. *VERBORGENHEIT*
SECLUSION

Eduard Mörike

Lass, o Welt, o lass mich sein!
leave O world O let me be (alone)

Locket nicht mit Liebesgaben,
tempt not   with love's-gifts

14. WORLD WITHIN

Leave me in peace, O world –
tempt me not with bribes of love!
Leave my heart alone with its own
rapture, its own pain!

Lasst dies Herz alleine haben
leave this heart alone have

Seine Wonne, seine Pein!
its   rapture its   pain

Was ich traure, weiss ich nicht,
what I   mourn know I   not

Es ist unbekanntes Wehe;
it is unknown   misery

Immerdar durch   Tränen sehe
always   through tears   see

Ich der   Sonne liebes Licht.
I of the sun   dear light

Oft   bin ich mir   kaum bewusst,
often am I   to me hardly conscious

Und die helle Freude zücket
and the clear joy   quivers

Durch   die Schwere, so   mich drücket,
through the heaviness (that) so me   weighs down

Wonniglich in meiner Brust.
delightfully in my   breast

Lass, o Welt, etc.

I know not why I grieve. It is a
strange new misery; only through
tears do I see the sweet light of the
sun.

Often I am in a daze, and then
through the weight of my despair,
I feel pure joy and ecstasy
quivering within my breast.

15. IM   *FRÜHLING*
IN THE SPRING

15. IN SPRING

Eduard Mörike

Hier lieg' ich auf dem Frühlingshügel:
here lie I   on the spring's-hill

Die Wolke wird   mein Flügel,
the cloud becomes my   wing

Ein Vogel fliegt mir voraus.
a   bird flies me before

Ach, sag' mir, alleinzige Liebe,
alas tell me unique   love

Wo   du bleibst,   dass ich bei dir bliebe!
where you are staying that I   with you might stay

Doch du und die Lüfte, ihr habt kein Haus.
but   you and the breezes you have no home

Here I lie on this hill in
springtime; clouds are my wings, a
bird flies before me. O tell me
where you are, my one and only
love, that I might be with you! But
you, like the breezes, you have no
home.

Der Sonnenblume gleich steht mein Gemüte offen,
to the sunflower like stands my heart open

Sehnend,
yearning

Sich dehnend
itself stretching

In Lieben und Hoffen.
in love and hope

Frühling, was bist du gewillt?
spring what are you wanting

Wann werd' ich gestillt?
when will be I satisfied

Die Wolke seh' ich wandeln und den Fluss,
the cloud see I wander and the river

Es dringt der Sonne gold'ner Kuss
(it) penetrates of the sun golden kiss

Mir tief bis ins Geblüt hinein;
to me deep (right) into the blood in there

Die Augen, wunderbar berauschet,
the eyes wounderfully enchanted

Tun, als schliefen sie ein,
do as went to sleep they –

Nur noch das Ohr dem Ton der Biene lauschet.
only still the ear to the sound of the bee hearkens

Ich denke dies und denke das,
I think this and think that

Ich sehne mich, und weiss nicht recht nach
I am longing (myself) and know not rightly for
was:
what

Halb ist es Lust, halb ist es Klage;
half is it joy half is it lament

Mein Herz, o sage,
my heart O say

Was webst du für Erinnerung
what weave you for memory

In golden grüner Zweige Dämmerung?
in golden of green twigs twilight

– Alte unnennbare Tage!
old ineffable days

Like a sunflower my heart is open, and yearning – stretching out in hope and love. What is it you desire, O Spring? When will my longing be stilled?

I see the drifting clouds, and the river; the golden kiss of the sun passes deep into my blood. My eyes, in wondrous enchantment, feign sleep, and only my ear hears the sound of the bees.

I think of this and think of that, and am filled with longing – I know not for what; half is joy, and half is lament. O my heart, will you tell me what memories you weave in the golden-green twighlight branches? Ineffable ancient of days!

16. *AUF EINER WANDERUNG*
ON A   WALKING-TRIP

Eduard Mörike

In ein freundliches Städtchen tret ich ein,
in a friendly   little town enter I –

In den Strassen liegt roter Abendschein,
in the streets lies red evening-light

Aus einem offnen Fenster eben,
from an   open window just

Über den reichsten Blumenflor
over the richest   show of flowers

Hinweg, hört man Goldglockentöne   schweben,
away   hears one golden-bells'-tones float

Und eine Stimme scheint ein Nachtigallenchor,
and a   voice   seems a   nightingale-choir

Dass die Blüten   beben,
that the blossoms tremble

Dass die Lüfte   leben,
that the breezes live

Dass in höherem Rot die Rosen leuchten vor.
that in deeper   red the roses glow   forth

Lang hielt   ich staunend, lustbeklommen.
long stopped I astonished delight-seized

Wie ich hinaus vors   Tor   gekommen,
how I   outside in front of the gateway come

Ich weiss es wahrlich selber   nicht.
I   know it truly   myself not

Ach hier, wie liegt die Welt so licht!
ah   here how lies the world so bright

Der Himmel wogt   in purpurnem Gewühle,
the sky   rocked in crimson   tumult

Rückwärts die Stadt in goldnem Rauch,
back   the town in golden haze

Wie rauscht   der Erlenbach,   wie rauscht im
how murmurs the alders-brook how roars   in the
      Grund die Mühle,
      ground the mill

I entered a friendly little town; the streets were filled with red evening light. From an open window full of flowers, I heard a sound floating like golden bells; and a voice like a nightingale chorus, that made the blossoms tremble and the breezes stir, and the roses glow a deeper red.

For a long time I stood there entranced. How I found my way through the gateway I truly cannot say. Ah, here lies the world so bright and clear; the skies crimson in a tumult, and the town in a golden haze. How the mill-stream rushes past the alders! I am confused, as if drunk – for you have touched my heart, O Muse, with a breath of love!

Ich bin wie trunken,   irrgeführt –
I   am as intoxicated confused

O Muse, du hast mein Herz berührt
O Muse you have my   heart touched

Mit einem Liebeshauch!
with a   love's-breath

17. ELFENLIED
ELF-SONG

Eduard Mörike

Bei Nacht im   Dorf   der Wächter   rief: 'Elfe'!
at night in the village the watchman called eleven/elf

Ein ganz kleines Elfchen im   Walde schlief –
a quite small little elf in the wood was sleeping

wohl   um die   Elfe! –
indeed at (the) eleven

Und meint, es rief   ihm aus dem Tal
and thinks it called him from the valley

Bei seinem Namen die Nachtigall,
by his   name   the nightingale

Oder Silpelit hätt ihm gerufen.
or   Silpelit had him called

Reibt sich   der Elf die Augen aus,
rubs (himself) the elf the eyes   –

Begibt sich   vor   sein Schneckenhaus
proceeds (himself) in front of his snail-shell

Und ist als wie ein trunken Mann,
and is as if   a   drunken man

Sein Schläflein war nicht voll getan,
his nap   was not fully done

Und humpelt also, tippe, tapp,
and hobbles so   tip   tap

Durchs   Haselholz ins   Tal   hinab,
through the hazel-wood into the valley down

Schlupft an der Mauer hin   so dicht,
slips   to the wall   thither so close

17. SONG OF THE ELF

One night in the village the
nightwatchman called, 'Eleven!' A
tiny little elf is sleeping in the
wood – at eleven, and he thinks a
nightingale in the valley has called
him – or Silpelit maybe? The elf
rubs his eyes, and stumbles from
his snail-shell house like a drunken
man. Half asleep, he staggers, tip-
a-tap, through the hazel wood
down to the valley. He creeps
close to a wall that is glowing with
glow-worm lights. 'What are those
bright little windows? There must
be a wedding in there, and they'll
all be sitting at the feast, making
merry in the hall. I'll just peep in.'
Ouch! His head hits hard stone!
That's enough, little elf? Cuckoo!

Da   sitzt der Glühwurm Licht an Licht.
there sits the glow-worm light to light

'Was sind das helle   Fensterlein?
what are the bright little window(s)

Da   drin   wird eine Hochzeit sein:
there in there will a   wedding be

Die Kleinen   sitzen beim Mahle,
the little ones sit   at the banquet

Und treiben's   in dem Saale.
and carry on it in the   hall

Da   guck' ich wohl   ein wenig 'nein!'
there peep I   perhaps a   little in there

– Pfui, stösst den Kopf an harten Stein!
  ouch hits the head on hard   stone

Elfe, gelt,   du hast genug?
elf   isn't it you have enough

Gukuk! Gukuk!
cuckoo cuckoo

18. DER GÄRTNER
THE GARDENER

Eduard Mörike
(also set by Schumann)

Auf ihrem Leibrösslein,
on her   favourite little horse

So weiss wie der Schnee,
as white as   the snow

Die schönste   Prinzessin,
the most beautiful princess

Reit't durch   die Allee.
rides through the avenue

Der Weg, den   das Rösslein
the road which the little horse

Hintanzet   so hold,
dances along so gracefully

18. THE GARDENER

On her favourite little horse, as
white as snow, the most beautiful
princess rides down the avenue.

On the path where her little horse
gracefully prances, the sand that I
strewed sparkles like gold.

Der Sand, den   ich streute,
the sand which I   strewed

Er blinket   wie Gold!
it sparkles like gold

Du rosenfarb's   Hütlein
you rose-coloured little hat

Little rose-coloured hat, that bobs
up and down – O throw me a
feather, secretly!

Wohl   auf und wohl   ab,
(right) up and (right) down

O wirf   eine Feder,
O throw a   feather

Verstohlen herab!
secretly   down

Und willst du   dagegen
and want you in return

And if in return you would like a
bloom from me, take a thousand
for your one – for your one, take
them all!

Eine Blüte   von   mir,
a   bloom from me

Nimm tausend   für eine,
take   thousand for one

Nimm alle dafür!
take   all for it

19. *UM MITTERNACHT*
AT MIDNIGHT

19. AT MIDNIGHT

Eduard Mörike

Gelassen stieg   die Nacht ans   Land,
calmly   climbed the night along the land

Lehnt träumend an der   Berge   Wand,
leans dreaming on of the mountain wall

Ihr Auge sieht die goldne   Waage nun
her eye   sees the golden scales   now

Der   Zeit in gleichen Schalen   stille   ruhn;
of the time in equal   measures quietly rest

Und kecker rauschen die Quellen hervor,
and bolder rush   the springs forth

Night rose calmly over the land,
and now leans dreaming on the
mountain-side. She sees the
golden scales of Time quietly at
rest in equal measure. And the
springs gush boldly forth, and sing
to the night, their mother, of the
day, the day that is gone.

Sie singen der   Mutter, der   Nacht, ins   Ohr
they sing   to the mother of the night   into the ear

Vom   Tage,
of the day

Vom   heute gewesenen Tage.
of the today has been day

Das uralt   alte Schlummerlied,
the age-old old slumber-song

Sie achtet's nicht, sie ist es   müd;
she heeds it not   she is (of) it weary

Ihr   klingt des   Himmels Bläue süsser   noch,
to her sounds of the sky   azure sweeter still

Der   flücht'gen Stunden gleichgeschwung'nes Joch.
of the fleeting   hours   evenly-slung   yoke

Doch immer behalten   die Quellen das Wort,
but   always remember the springs the word

Es singen die Wasser im   Schlafe noch fort
(it) sing   the waters in the sleep   still on

Vom   Tage,
of the day

Vom   heute gewesenen Tage.
of the today has been day

She pays no heed to the age-old lullaby; she is weary of it. To her the dark blue sky, and the balanced yoke of the fleeting hours hold greater charms. But the springs remember the word, and sing on in their sleep of the day, the day that is gone.

20. SEUFZER
SIGH

Eduard Mörike

Dein Liebesfeuer,
Thy love's-fire

Ach Herr! Wie teuer
oh Lord how dearly

Wollt' ich es hegen,
desired I   it to cherish

Wollt' ich es pflegen!
desired I   it to tend

20. SIGH OF REGRET

The fire of Thy love, O Lord – how dearly I desired to tend it, and to cherish it! I have failed to tend it, I have failed to cherish it; my heart is dead, and I feel the torments of Hell!

Hab's   nicht geheget
have it not   cherished

Und nicht gepfleget,
and not   tended

Bin tot   im   Herzen,
am dead in the heart

O Höllenschmerzen!
O hell's-pains

21. *AUF EIN ALTES BILD*
   ON AN OLD   PICTURE

21. ON AN OLD
   PAINTING

Eduard Mörike

In grüner   Landschaft Sommerflor,
in of green landscape summer-blossoming

Bei kühlem Wasser, Schilf und Rohr,
by cool   water rush and reed

Schau, wie   das Knäblein sündelos
look   how the little boy sinless

Frei   spielet auf der   Jungfrau Schoss!
freely plays on of the Virgin   lap

Und dort im   Walde wonnesam,
and there in the wood delightfully

Ach, grünet   schon   des   Kreuzes Stamm!
ah   turns green already of the cross   trunk

Summer blossoms in a green
landscape, by cool water, rush and
reed; see how the little boy in
happy innocence is playing on the
Virgin's lap! And in the wood, ah,
there already a radiant green
unfolds on the trunk marked for
the cross.

22. *IN DER FRÜHE*
   IN THE EARLY MORNING

22. IN THE EARLY
   MORNING

Eduard Mörike

Kein Schlaf noch kühlt das Auge mir,
no   sleep yet cools the eye   to me

Dort gehet schon   der Tag herfür
there goes already the day forth

My eyes are not yet cooled by
sleep; already day breaks at my
window. My troubled mind is
stirred by doubts, and conjures up
dark phantoms. Be no longer

An meinem Kammerfenster.
at my   bedroom-window

Es wühlet   mein verstörter Sinn
(it) agitates my   troubled mind

Noch zwischen Zweifeln her und hin
still   amongst doubts   to   and fro

Und schaffet Nachtgespenster.
and creates night-phantoms

Ängst'ge,   quäle
make anxious torment

Dich   nicht länger, meine Seele!
yourself not   longer my   soul

Freu' dich!   Schon sind da   und dorten
rejoice (yourself) already are   here and there

Morgenglocken wach   geworden.
morning-bells awake become.

afraid, torment yourself no more! O my soul, rejoice! Already all around the morning bells are waking.

23. SCHLAFENDES JESUSKIND
SLEEPING   JESUS-CHILD

23. SLEEPING
CHRIST CHILD

Eduard Mörike

Sohn der   Jungfrau, Himmelskind!   am   Boden
son   of the Virgin   Heaven's-Child on the floor

Auf dem Holz der   Schmerzen eingeschlafen,
on   the   wood of the griefs   gone to sleep

Das der fromme Meister sinnvoll   spielend
that the devout master meaningfully playing

Deinen leichten Träumen unterlegte;
your   gentle dreams   put beneath

Blume du, noch in der Knospe dämmernd
flower you still in the bud   dawning

Eingehüllt die Herrlichkeit des   Vaters!
wrapped in the glory   of the Father

O wer sehen könnte, welche Bilder
O who see   could   which images

Hinter dieser Stirne, diesen schwarzen
behind this   brow   these black

Son of the Virgin, Child of Heaven, sleeping on the bare boards of grief, that the devout Master so meaningfully placed beneath you as you softly dream. O you flower, even in this bud wrapped in a half-light, you are the very glory of the Father! If we could but see the gently charging images flickering below that brow, and those dark lashes!

Wimpern, sich   in sanftem Wechsel
eyelashes (themselves) in gentle succession
  malen!
  are portraying

24. *GEBET*
PRAYER

Eduard Mörike

Herr! schicke was du   willt,
Lord send   what Thou wilt

Ein Liebes oder Leides;
a joy or sorrow

Ich bin vergnügt, dass beides
I   am content   that both

Aus deinen Händen quillt.
from Thy hands   flow

Wollest   mit Freuden
may (Thou) with joy

Und wollest   mit Leiden
and may (Thou) with sorrow

Mich nicht überschütten!
me   not overwhelm

Doch in der Mitten
surely in the middle

Liegt holdes Bescheiden.
lies pure humility

24. PRAYER

Lord, send me what Thou wilt, joy
or sorrow; I am content, for both
flow from Thy Hands.

But may Thou not pour on me too
great a sorrow or joy – for it is
surely between these that lies pure
humility.

25. *LEBE WOHL*
FARE-WELL

Eduard Mörike

'Lebe wohl': – Du fühlest   nicht,
fare-well   you are aware not

Was es heisst, dies Wort der   Schmerzen;
what it means this word of the sorrows

25. FAREWELL

'Farewell!' You do not know what
it means, this word of grief. You
say it with cheerful face and a light
heart.

Mit getrostem Angesicht
with hopeful face

Sagtest du's   und   leichtem Herzen.
said   you it and (with) light   heart

'Lebe wohl!' – Ach tausendmal
 fare-well   ah   thousand-times

Hab' ich mir   es vorgesprochen,
have I   to me it said aloud

Und in nimmersatter Qual
and in insatiable   torment

Mir   das Herz damit   gebrochen!
to me the heart with that broken

'Farewell!' Oh, I have said it aloud
a thousand times, and its never-
ending torment has broken my
heart!

26. *HEIMWEH*
HOMESICKNESS

Eduard Mörike

Anders   wird   die Welt mit jedem Schritt,
different becomes the world with every step

Den ich weiter   von der Liebsten mache;
that I   further from the beloved make

Mein Herz, das will   nicht weiter mit,
my   heart that wants not further with (me)

Hier scheint die Sonne kalt   ins   Land,
here shines the sun   coldly into the land

Hier deucht mir   alles   unbekannt,
here seems to me everything unknown

Sogar die Blumen am   Bache!
even the flowers by the stream

Hat jede Sache
has each thing

So fremd   eine Miene, so falsch ein Gesicht.
so strange an air   so false a face

Das Bächlein   murmelt wohl   und spricht:
the little stream murmurs indeed and says

'Armer Knabe, komm bei mir vorüber,
 poor boy   come by me along

26. HOMESICKNESS

The world changes with every step
I take away from my beloved; my
heart would go no further. Here
the sun shines coldly on the earth;
here all seems strange to me, even
the flowers by the stream.
Everything has an unfamiliar air,
so false a face. The little stream
murmurs and seems to say 'Come
here to me, poor boy, for here too
are forget-me-nots.' Oh yes, they
are fair in every place – but not as
lovely as they are there. Let me
just go on, and on. My tears
overflow.

Siehst auch hier Vergissmeinnicht!'
see   also here forget-me-nots

Ja, die sind schön an jedem Ort,
yes they are lovely in every place

Aber nicht wie dort.
but not as there

Fort, nur fort!
on   only on

Die Augen geh'n mir   über!
the eyes   run   to me over

27. DENK   ES, O SEELE
REFLECT IT O SOUL

27. CONSIDER, O MY SOUL

Eduard Mörike

Ein Tännlein   grünet   wo, wer weiss, im
a   little fir-tree becomes green where who knows in the
    Walde,
    wood

A little fir tree grows green in a wood – who knows where? And a rose bush in a garden – who knows which? Consider, O my soul, they are chosen already to take root, and grow on your grave.

Ein Rosenstrauch, wer sagt, in welchem Garten?
a   rose-bush   who says in which   garden

Sie sind erlesen schon, denk es, o Seele,
they are chosen already think it O soul

Auf deinem Grab zu wurzeln   und zu wachsen.
on your   grave to take root and to grow

Zwei schwarze Rösslein   weiden auf der Wiese,
two black   little horses graze in the meadow

Two little black horses graze in a meadow, then gaily come trotting home to the town. One day they will draw your coffin step by step – perhaps even before they cast from their hooves those flashing shoes that I now see.

Sie kehren heim zur   Stadt in muntern Sprüngen.
they return home to the town in gay   leaps

Sie werden schrittweis   gehn mit deiner Leiche;
they will   step by step go   with your dead body

Vielleicht, vielleicht noch eh' an ihren Hufen
perhaps   perhaps yet   ere on their hooves

Das Eisen   los   wird,   das ich blitzen   sehe!
the horse-shoe loose becomes that I   flash(ing) see

28. *LIED EINES VERLIEBTEN*
SONG OF AN IN-LOVE-ONE

28. LOVER'S SONG

Eduard Mörike

In aller Früh,   ach, lang vor   Tag,
in all   earliness oh   long before day

In the early hours, long before dawn, my heart awakens me to think of you, when healthy youth should sleep.

Weckt mich mein Herz, an dich zu denken,
wakes me   my   heart of you to think

Da   doch   gesunde Jugend schlafen mag.
when indeed healthy youth   sleep   may

Hell   ist mein Aug' um Mitternacht,
bright is my eye at midnight

My eyes are bright at midnight, brighter than the early morning bells – but when did you ever think of me, even by day?

Heller   als   frühe Morgenglocken:
brighter than early morning-bells

Wann hätt'st du je   am   Tage mein gedacht?
when had   you ever in the day of me thought

Wär' ich ein Fischer,   stünd'   ich auf,
were I   a   fisherman would get I   up

If I were a fisherman, I would rise, carry my nets to the river, and light of heart I would take my fish to the market.

Trüge   mein Netz hinab zum   Flusse,
would carry my   net   down to the river

Trüg'   herzlich froh die Fische zum   Verkauf.
would carry heartily glad the fish   to the selling

In der Mühle, bei Licht,   der Müllerknecht
in the mill   by (lamp)-light the miller's-boy

By the light of a lamp the miller's boy is already at work, and all around it clatters in the mill – oh, such hard toil would suit me well!

Tummelt   sich,   alle Gänge   klappern;
bustles about (himself) all workings clatter

So rüstig Treiben wär'   mir   eben recht!
such vigorous activity would be to me just right

Weh, aber ich! o armer Tropf!
alas but I   O poor wretch

But alas, I, poor wretch, lie idly grieving in my bed, with nothing in my head but a mother's unruly daughter.

Muss auf dem Lager mich   müssig grämen,
must on the bed   myself idly   grieve

Ein ungebärdig Mutterkind   im   Kopf.
an unruly   mother's-child in the head

29. *GESANG WEYLAS* SONG WEYLA'S

29. WEYLA'S SONG

Eduard Mörike

Du bist Orplid, mein Land!
you are Orplid my   land

You are my land, Orplid, gleaming far away; sea mists rise from your sunlit shores, as if to moisten the cheeks of the gods.

Das ferne   leuchtet;
that far away gleams

Vom   Meere dampfet dein besonnter Strand
from the sea   steams your sunlit   shore

Den Nebel, so der   Götter Wange feuchtet.
the mist so of the gods   cheek moistens

Uralte   Wasser steigen
ancient waters rise

Ancient waters rise renewed about your hips, my child! Before your divinity, kings bow down and serve you.

Verjüngt   um   deine Hüften, Kind!
rejuvenated about your hips   child

Vor   deiner Gottheit beugen
before your divinity bow

Sich   Könige, die deine Wärter   sind.
(themselves) kings   who your attendants are

30. *STORCHENBOTSCHAFT* STORK'S MESSAGE

30. THE STORKS' MESSAGE

Eduard Mörike

Des   Schäfers sein Haus und das steht   auf zwei
of the shepherd his house and that stands on two
    Rad,
    wheel(s)

There's a shepherd's hut, that stands on two wheels, high on the heath all day and all night. Many would be glad of such an abode – but a shepherd would never change beds with a king!

Steht   hoch auf der Heiden, so frühe wie spat;
stands high on the heath   as early as late

Und wenn nur ein mancher so'n   Nacht-quartier hätt'!
and if   only a   someone such a night-quarters had

Ein Schäfer   tauscht   nicht mit dem König sein Bett.
a   shepherd exchanges not with the king his bed

Und käm'   ihm   zur   Nacht auch was
and happened to him at the night even something
   Seltsames vor,
   strange –

Er betet sein Sprüchel und legt sich   aufs   Ohr;
he prays his little text and lays himself on the ear

Ein Geistlein,   ein Hexlein,   so luftige Wicht'
a   (little) ghost a (little) witch so airy   wights

Sie klopfen ihm   wohl,   doch er antwortet nicht.
they knock to him perhaps but he answers not

Einmal doch,   da   ward es ihm   wirklich zu
once   however then was it to him really   too
   bunt:
   colourful

Es knopert am   Laden, es winselt der Hund;
it rattles on the shutter (it) whines the dog

Nun ziehet mein Schäfer   den Riegel – ei schau!
now draws my   shepherd the bolt   oh look

Da   stehen zwei Störche, der Mann   und die Frau.
there stand two storks   the husband and the wife

Das Pärchen,   es machet ein schön   Kompliment,
the (little) pair it makes a   beautiful bow

Es möchte   gern reden,   ach wenn es nur könnt!
it would like gladly to speak oh if   it only could

Was will   mir   das Ziefer? – ist so   was erhört?
what want to me the vermin is such (a) thing heard of

Doch ist mir wohl   fröhliche Botschaft beschert?
but is me perhaps glad   tidings   bestowed upon

Ihr seid wohl   dahinten   zu Hause am   Rhein?
you are perhaps back there at home on the Rhine

Ihr habt wohl   mein Mädel gebissen ins   Bein?
you have perhaps my girl   bitten in the leg

Nun weinet das Kind und die Mutter noch mehr,
now cries the child and the mother still more

Sie wünschet den Herzallerliebsten   sich   her.
she wishes   the dearest-of-her heart herself here

Und wünschet daneben die Taufe   bestellt:
and wishes   besides the christening arranged

Ein Lämmlein, ein Würstlein,   ein Beutelein Geld?
a (little) lamb a (little) sausage a little purse gold

And even if something strange should happen in the night, he just mutters a prayer and buries his head in the pillow. Spirits, hobgoblins and misty wraiths may knock at his door – but he doesn't answer.

Once, however, things went really too far; the shutters rattle, the dog whines; the shepherd draws back the bolt – Oh look! – two storks stand there, a husband and wife.

The quaint couple solemnly curtseys and bows; they've something to say – oh, if only they could! What can these creatures want? Whoever's heard of such a thing! But perhaps it is news of a happy event?

Do you live perhaps there on the Rhine? And have paid a visit to my love? Oh, the baby's crying, and the mother still more – how she wishes that her sweetheart were there!

And she wishes, too, that the christening were fixed – with sausages, and lamb, and a little purse of gold? Just tell her I'll be

So sagt nur, ich käm'   in zwei Tag oder drei,
so say just I   might come in two days or   three

Und grüsst mir   mein Bübel   und rührt ihm
and greet to me my   little boy and stir   to him
    den Brei!
    the gruel

Doch halt! warum stellt   ihr zu   Zweien   euch
but stop why   present you in (a) twosome yourselves
    ein?
    –

Es werden doch,   hoff' ich nicht Zwillinge sein?
it will   indeed hope I   not twins   be

Da   klappern die Störche im   lustigsten Ton,
then clatter   the storks in the merriest fashion

Sie   nicken und knixen und fliegen davon.
they nod   and curtsey and fly   away

there in two or three days – and
greetings to my little boy, and give
his gruel a stir!

But wait! Just why are there two of
you here? There aren't – indeed I
hope – that it doesn't mean –
twins? The storks clap their wings
in great merriment, then curtsey
and nod, and fly right away.

31. BEI EINER TRAUUNG
AT A   WEDDING-CEREMONY

31. AT A WEDDING-CEREMONY

Eduard Mörike

Vor   lauter hochadligen Zeugen
before only aristocratic witnesses

Kopuliert man ihrer   zwei;
united   one of them two

Die Orgel hängt voll Geigen,
(the organ hangs full violins)

Der Himmel nicht, mein' Treu!
the Heaven not   my   faith

Seht doch! Sie weint ja   greulich,
see but   she weeps indeed dreadfully

Er macht ein Gesicht abscheulich!
he makes a   face   horrible

Denn leider   freilich, freilich,
for   unfortunately of course of course

Keine Lieb' ist nicht dabei.
no   love is not   there

Before witnesses of high and noble
blood, a pair of them were
married: the expectations of all
were great, those of Heaven were
not, upon my soul! Just see – *she*
weeps most dreadfully, while *he*
makes a horrible face – for of
course, of course, there was no
love at all.

32. *SELBSTGESTÄNDNIS*
SELF-CONFESSION

Eduard Mörike

Ich bin meiner Mutter einzig Kind,
I   am of my mother only   child

Und weil   die andern ausblieben sind,
and because the others absent   are

Was weiss ich wieviel,   die sechs oder sieben,
what know I   how many the six   or   seven

Ist eben   alles   an mir hängen blieben;
is certainly everything on me to hang left

Ich hab' müssen die Liebe, die Treue, die Güte
I   have had to the love   the loyalty the goodness

Für ein ganz   halb Dutzend allein aufessen,
for a   whole half dozen   alone eat up

Ich will's mein Lebtag   nicht vergessen.
I   will it my   born days not   forget

Es hätte   mir aber noch wohl   mögen
it (have) (might) me but still perhaps (might)
   frommen,
   (profited)*

Hätt' ich nur   auch Schläg für Sechse bekommen.
had   I   only also blows for six   received

I am my mother's only child, and
because the others were lacking –
who knows how many, six or
seven – I was stuck with
everything! I had to consume the
love, the devotion and the
goodness for a whole half dozen,
and I'll never forget it all the days
of my life. But I might perhaps
have profited more, if I'd also had
the cuffs for all six.

32. SELF-CONFESSION

33. *ABSCHIED*
FAREWELL

Eduard Mörike

Unangeklopft   ein Herr   tritt   abends
without knocking a   gentleman enters in the evening
   bei mir   ein:
   (my home) –

'Ich habe die Ehr'   ihr Rezensent zu sein!'
I   have the honour your critic   to be

33. FAREWELL

One evening, unannounced, a
gentleman steps into my room. 'I
have the honour to be your critic,
sir!' and he takes up a candlestick
in his hand, and moving to and
fro, looks hard at my shadow on
the wall. 'My dear young man,
please take a look at your nose

* (hätte mögen frommen – might have profited)

Sofort   nimmt er das Licht   in   die Hand,
at once takes   he the candlestick into the hand

Besieht   lang meinen Schatten an der Wand,
examines long my   shadow on the wall

Rückt nah und fern: 'Nun, lieber junger Mann,
moves near and far   now   dear young man

Sehn sie   doch gefälligst   'mal Ihre Nas' so von der
look you (do) if you please once your nose so from the
     Seite an!
     side at

Sie geben zu, dass das ein Auswuchs is.'
you agree   that it   an outgrowth is

– *'Das? Alle Wetter –   gewiss!*
   that (good heavens) undoubtedly

Ei Hasen!   Ich dachte   nicht,
(Jumping Jacks) I   thought not

All' mein Lebtage nicht,
all my   life-days not

Dass ich so   eine Weltsnase   führt im   Gesicht!!'
that I   such a   world-nose bore in the face

Der Mann sprach noch   Verschied'nes hin   und
the man   spoke besides various things thither and
     her,
     hither

Ich weiss, auf meine Ehre,   nicht mehr;
I   know on my   honour not more

Meinte vielleicht, ich sollt'   ihm   beichten.
thought perhaps I   should to him confess

Zuletzt stand er auf; ich tat   ihm   leuchten.
at last stood he up I   (made for him light)

Wie wir nun an der Treppe sind,
as   we now at the stairs are

Da   geb' ich ihm, ganz froh gesinnt,
there give I   him quite gaily disposed

Einen kleinen Tritt,
a   small   kick

Nur so von hinten aufs   Gesässe, mit –
just so from behind on the seat   with

Alle Hagel! ward das ein Gerumpel.
(all hail) was that a   rumbling

from the side. You must admit it's grotesque!' 'Indeed? Good heavens – so it is! Jumping Jacks! Never in all my days did I realise I had such a distinguished nose on my face!'

The man went on to speak of this and that – for the life of me I can't remember what. He thought perhaps I should make him some confession? But at last he stood up, and I made him some light. At the stairs, I gave him, quite playfully – a little kick on his backside. And by thunder! What a rumbling and a tumbling there was! In all my days I've never seen a man go downstairs quite so fast!

Ein Gepurzel,   ein Gehumpel!
a   somersaulting a   limping

Dergleichen hab' ich nie   gesehn,
the like   have I   never seen

All' mein Lebtage nicht gesehn,
all my   life-days not   seen

Einen Menschen so rasch   die Trepp' hinabgehn!
a   man   so quickly the stairs go down

34. DER FREUND
THE FRIEND

Joseph von Eichendorff

Wer auf den Wogen schliefe,
who on the waves would sleep

Ein sanft   gewiegtes Kind,
a   gently rocked   child

Kennt nicht des   Lebens Tiefe,
knows not   of the life   depth

Vor süssem Träumen blind.
with sweet dreaming blind

Doch wen   die Stürme fassen
but whom the storms seize

Zu wildem Tanz und Fest,
for wild   dance and feast

Wen   hoch auf dunklen Strassen
whom high on dark   streets

Die falsche Welt verlässt:
the false   world forsakes

Der lernt sich   wacker rühren,
he learns (himself) valiantly to move

Durch Nacht und Klippen hin
through night and reefs   thither

Lernt der das Steuer führen
learns he the helm to steer

Mit sichrem, ernstem Sinn.
with sure   serious feeling

34. THE FRIEND

He who would sleep on the waves
like a gently cradled child, his
vision dimmed by sweet reveries –
he cannot know life's deeps.

But he whom the storm incites to
wild dance and revelling; who
forsakes the false world for ways
high and dark –

he learns to act bravely, and with
firm, unerring touch to steer a
course through the reefs by night.

Der ist von echtem Kerne,
he is of true   core

Erprobt zu Lust und Pein,
tried   to joy and pain

Der glaubt   an Gott und Sterne,
he believes in God and stars

Der soll   mein Schiffman sein!
he shall my   ship-mate be

He who is stout of heart, well-tried in joy and pain; who believes in the stars, and in God: he shall my shipmate be!

35. *DER MUSIKANT*
THE MUSICIAN

35. THE MINSTREL

Joseph von Eichendorff

Wandern lieb ich für mein Leben,
to roam love I   for my   life

Lebe eben, wie ich kann,
live just as I can

Wollt ich mir   auch Mühe geben,
wanted I   to me even trouble to give

Passt   es mir doch gar nicht an.
would suit it me yet at all not   –

I love a life of roaming, just living as I can. Even if I took the trouble to work, it wouldn't suit me at all.

Schöne alte Lieder weiss ich;
lovely old songs know I

In der Kälte, ohne   Schuh,
in the cold   without shoe

Draussen in   die Saiten reiss' ich,
outside   into the strings pull I

Weiss nicht, wo   ich abends   ruh'!
know not   where I   in the evening rest

The songs I know are old and sweet; outside in the cold, barefoot, I pluck my strings, but do not know where I will sleep at night.

Manche Schöne   macht wohl Augen,
many a pretty one makes indeed eyes

Meinet, ich gefiel' ihr sehr,
thinks I   please her very much

Wenn ich nur was   wollte taugen,
if   I   only something wanted to be worth

So   ein armer Lump nicht wär'!
such a poor fellow not would be

Many a pretty girl makes eyes at me, thinking I might well please her, if I only would choose to prove my own worth – and wasn't such a poor fellow!

Mag dir   Gott ein'n Mann   bescheren,
may to you God a   husband give

May God give to you a husband, and provide for you a house and home! For if we two were together, my singing would be lost.

Wohl   mit Haus und Hof   verseh'n!
perhaps with house and home provide

Wenn wir zwei zusammen wären,
if   we two together   were

Möcht' mein Singen mir   vergeh'n.
might   my   singing to me vanish

36. VERSCHWIEGENE LIEBE
KEPT-SILENT   LOVE

36. SILENT LOVE

Joseph von Eichendorff

Über Wipfel   und Saaten
over (tree-)tops and corn

Over tree-tops and cornfields, drawn towards the splendour – who can guess and catch my thoughts? For thoughts are lulled and free to roam in the stillness of the night.

In   den Glanz   hinein –
into the brightness thither

Wer mag sie   erraten,
who may them guess

Wer holte   sie   ein?
who might overtake them –

Gedanken sich   wiegen,
thoughts themselves lull

Die Nacht ist verschwiegen,
the night is silent

Gedanken sind frei.
thoughts are free

Errät'   es nur Eine,
might guess it only one

If she could but guess who was thinking of her, in the rustling wood, when nothing more wakes but the drifting clouds; for my love is silent, and beautiful as the night.

Wer an   sie gedacht,
who about her thought

Beim Rauschen der   Haine,
by the rustling of the wood

Wenn niemand mehr wacht,
when no one   more is awake

Als die Wolken, die   fliegen,
but the clouds   that fly

Mein Lieb ist verschwiegen
my   love is silent

Und schön wie die Nacht.
and lovely as   the night

37. DAS STÄNDCHEN
THE SERENADE

37. SERENADE

Joseph von Eichendorff

Auf die Dächer zwischen blassen
on the roofs   between pale

Wolken schaut der Mond herfür,
clouds peers the moon forth

Ein Student dort auf der Gassen
a   student there on the street

Singt vor   seiner Liebsten Tür.
sings before of his beloved door

From pale clouds the moon peers out from the roof tops; and there in the street a student sings at his sweetheart's door.

Und die Brunnen rauschen wieder
and the springs   rush   again

Durch   die stille Einsamkeit,
through the quiet solitude

Und der Wald vom   Berge   nieder,
and the wood from the mountain down

Wie in alter, schöner Zeit.
as in old   fair   time

Springs murmur in the quiet solitude, and the woods rustle on the mountain slopes, as in fairer days of old.

So in meinen jungen Tagen
so in my   young days

Hab' ich manche Sommernacht
have I many a summer-night

Auch die Laute hier geschlagen
also the lute here struck

Und manch lust'ges Lied erdacht.
and many a jolly   song devised

Here in my youth on summer nights, I, too, sang many a lively serenade to the sound of my lute.

Aber von   der stillen Schwelle
but from the silent threshold

Trugen sie   mein Lieb zur   Ruh',
carried they my   love to the rest

But over the still threshold they carried my dear one to her rest – oh, sing on, my merry friend, sing on!

Und du, fröhlicher Geselle,
and you merry   fellow

Singe, sing' nur immerzu!
sing   sing just always

38. NACHTZAUBER
NIGHT-MAGIC

Joseph von Eichendorff

Hörst du   nicht die Quellen gehen
hear you not   the springs go

Zwischen Stein und Blumen weit
amongst stone and flowers far

Nach den stillen Waldesseen,
to   the silent forest-lakes

Wo   die Marmorbilder stehen
where the marble-statues stand

In der schönen Einsamkeit?
in the lovely   solitude

Von den Bergen   sacht hernieder,
from the mountains softly down

Weckend   die uralten Lieder,
awakening the age-old songs

Steigt   die wunderbare Nacht,
ascends the wonderful night

Und die Gründe glänzen wieder,
and the valleys gleam again

Wie du's   oft   im   Traum gedacht.
as   you it often in the dream thought

Kennst die Blume du, entsprossen
know   the flower you sprung up

In dem mondbeglänzten Grund?
in the moon-lit   valley

Aus der Knospe, halb erschlossen,
from the bud   half opened

Junge Glieder blühend   sprossen,
young limbs   blossoming sprang

38. NIGHT MAGIC

Do you not hear the streams, that flow between stones and flowers to far-off silent forest lakes, where marble statues stand in lovely solitude? Softly from the mountains, awakening age-old melodies, the wondrous night descends, and the valleys gleam as so often in your dreams.

Do you know the flower unfolding in the moon-lit valley? From the half-open bud there blossom young limbs; white arms, red lips. Nightingales sing, and all around rises, a lament of mortally wounded love, and lovely, long-lost days. Come, O come to the quiet valley!

Weisse Arme, roter Mund.
white arms red mouth

Und die Nachtigallen schlagen,
and the nightingales sing

Und rings   hebt   es an zu klagen,
and around begins it – to lament

Ach, vor Liebe todeswund,
ah   for love mortally wounded

Von versunknen schönen Tagen –
from lost   lovely days

Komm, o komm zum   stillen Grund!
come   O come to the quiet valley

39. *HEIMWEH*
   HOMESICKNESS

Joseph von Eichendorff

Wer in   die Fremde   will   wandern,
who into the unknown place wishes to wander

Der muss mit der Liebsten gehn,
he   must with the beloved go

Es jubeln und lassen die andern
(it) rejoice and leave the others

Den Fremden alleine stehn.
the stranger alone to be

Was wisset ihr, dunkle Wipfel,
what know you dark   (tree)-tops

Von der alten, schönen Zeit?
of the old   lovely time

Ach, die Heimat   hinter den Gipfeln,
oh   the homeland behind the mountain-peaks

Wie liegt sie von hier so weit!
how lies it from here so far

Am   liebsten   betracht' ich die Sterne,
(at the) most gladly look at I   the stars

Die schienen, wie ich ging zu ihr,
that shone   as I   went to her

39. HOMESICKNESS

He who journeys in far-off lands
must go with his beloved; whilst
others enjoy their own pleasuring,
and leave the stranger alone.

What do you dark tree-tops know
of the old, and lovely days? Alas,
how far is my native land beyond
the mountain peaks!

I love most of all to watch the
stars, that were shining when last I
saw her. How gladly I hear the
nightingale that was singing before
her door!

Die Nachtigall hör' ich so gerne,
the nightingale hear I   so gladly

Sie sang vor   der   Liebsten Tür.
she sang before of the dearest door

Der Morgen, das ist meine Freude!
the morning that is my   joy

Da   steig' ich in stiller Stund'
then climb I   in still   hour

Auf den höchsten Berg   in   die Weite,
on the highest mountain into the distance

Grüss dich, Deutschland, aus   Herzensgrund!
greet you Germany   from the heart's-bottom

The morning, that is my pleasure
– for then in a quiet hour, I climb
the highest peak, and great you,
Germany, with my whole heart!

40. *DER RATTENFÄNGER*
THE RAT-CATCHER

40. THE RAT-CATCHER

Johann Wolfgang von Goethe
(also set by Schubert)

Ich bin der wohlbekannte Sänger,
I   am the well-known singer

Der vielgereiste   Rattenfänger,
the much-journeyed rat-catcher

Den   diese altberühmte Stadt
whom this long-famous town

Gewiss   besonders nötig   hat.
certainly specially necessary has

Und wären's Ratten noch so viele,
and were it rats   still so many

Und wären Wiesel mit   im   Spiele,
and were weasel with (them) in the play

Von allen säub'r ich diesen Ort,
of   all   clean I this   place

Sie müssen miteinander   fort.
they must   with one another away

Dann ist der gut gelaunte Sänger
then is the good-humoured singer

Mitunter   auch ein Kinderfänger,
sometimes also a children-catcher

I'm the well-known minstrel, the
catcher of rats who goes
everywhere, and this old town
certainly needs me!

However many rats there are,
however many weasels, I'll rid the
place of all of them: they'll all be
led away!

Then is this light-hearted singer a
children-catcher too, who tames
the most unruly ones with golden
fairy-tales!

Der selbst die wildesten bezwingt,
who even the wildest   subdues

Wenn er die gold'nen Märchen   singt.
when he the golden   fairy-tales sings

Und wären Knaben noch so trutzig,
and were boys   still so defiant

Und wären Mädchen noch so stutzig,
and were girls   still so startled

In meine Saiten greif' ich ein,
in my   strings strike I   –

Sie müssen alle hinterdrein.
they must   all after (me)

However naughty the boys might
be, however stubborn the girls,
I've only to strike up in my strings,
and they all must follow me.

Dann ist der vielgewandte Sänger
then is the versatile   singer

Gelegentlich ein Mädchenfänger;
occasionally a   girl-catcher

In keinem Städtchen langt er an,
in no   little town arrives he –

Wo er's nicht mancher angetan.
where he it not   some   bewitched

Then is this many-sided minstrel –
a maiden-catcher too! There isn't
a village anywhere, where some of
them aren't bewitched.

Und wären Mädchen noch so blöde,
and were girls   still so stupid

Und wären Weiber noch so spröde,
and were women still so coy

Doch allen   wird   so liebebang
yet   each and all becomes so lovelorn

Bei Zaubersaiten und Gesang.
by magic-strings and song

The girls however bashful, and the
ladies however coy, they all are
sick with love through my magic
strings and song.

41. *KOPHTISCHES LIED I*
COPTIC   SONG

41. COPTIC SONG I

Johann Wolfgang von Goethe

Lasset Gelehrte sich   zanken und streiten,
let   scholars themselves quarrel and dispute

Streng und bedächtig   die Lehrer   auch sein!
strict and circumspect the teachers also be

Alle die Weisesten aller der   Zeiten
all   the wisest men of all of the times

Let pedants dispute and wrangle;
let scholars be astute and severe!
Wise men of old all smiled and
agreed: it is foolish to wait for
fools to grow wise! So make fools
of fools you children of sense, for
that is right and proper.

Lächeln und winken und stimmen mit   ein:
smile   and nod   and agree   with (them) –

Töricht, auf Bessrung   der   Toren zu harren!
foolish for improvement of the fools to wait for

Kinder der   Klugheit,   o habet die Narren
children of (the) intelligence O have the fools

Eben zum Narren auch, wie sich's   gehört.
just as to fools   even as (itself) it is due

Merlin der Alte,   im   leuchtenden Grabe,
Merlin the old one in the shining   grave

Wo   ich als Jüngling gesprochen   ihn habe,
where I   as youth   spoken   (to) him have

Hat mich mit   ähnlicher Antwort belehret:
has me   with similar   answer advised

Töricht, auf Bessrung   der   Toren zu harren!
foolish for improvement of the fools to wait for

Kinder der   Klugheit,   o habet die Narren
children of (the) intelligence O have the fools

Eben zum Narren auch, wie sich's   gehört.
just as to fools   even as (itself) it is due

In my youth I spoke to Old Merlin in his shining grave. And he too gave the same advice: it is foolish to wait for fools to grow wise! So make fools of fools, you children of sense, for that is right and proper.

Und auf den Höhen der   indischen Lüfte
and on the peaks of the Indian   breezes

Und in den Tiefen ägyptischer Grüfte
and in the depths of Egyptian tombs

Hab ich das heilige Wort nur gehört:
have I   the divine word only heard

Töricht, auf Bessrung   der   Toren zu harren!
foolish for improvement of the fools to wait for

Kinder der   Klugheit,   o habet die Narren
children of (the) intelligence O have the fools

Eben zum Narren auch, wie sich's   gehört.
just as to fools   even as (itself) it is due

On the wind-swept peaks of India, and deep in the Egyptian tombs, I have heard what the oracles all say: it is foolish to wait for fools to grow wise! So make fools of fools, you children of sense, for that is right and proper.

42. *KOPHTISCHES LIED II*
COPTIC   SONG II

42. COPTIC SONG II

Johann Wolfgang von Goethe

Geh! gehorche meinen Winken,
go   obey   my   suggestions

Nutze deine jungen Tage,
use   your young days

Now listen to my advice: let your youth be well-spent, and learn in due time to be wise! On the great scales of Fortune the finger is

Lerne zeitig   klüger sein:
learn in time wiser to be

Auf des   Glückes grosser Waage
on of the fortune great scales

Steht   die Zunge selten   ein;
stands still the tongue seldom –

Du musst steigen oder sinken,
you must rise   or   fall

Du musst herrschen und gewinnen,
you must rule   and win

Oder dienen und verlieren,
or   serve and lose

Leiden oder triumphieren,
suffer or   triumph

Amboss oder Hammer sein.
anvil   or   hammer be

seldom still; you must rise or must fall; you must win and be master, or lose and be a slave. You must suffer or triumph, be the anvil or the hammer.

43. *EPIPHANIAS*
   EPIPHANY

43. EPIPHANY

Johann Wolfgang von Goethe

Die heiligen drei   König' mit ihrem Stern,
the holy   three kinds with their star

Sie essen, sie trinken und bezahlen nicht gern;
they eat   they drink and pay   not gladly

Sie essen gern, sie trinken gern,
they eat   gladly they drink gladly

Sie essen, trinken und bezahlen nicht gern.
they eat   drink and pay   not gladly

Die heil'gen drei   König' sind kommen allhier,
the holy   three kings are come   all-here

Es sind ihrer   drei und sind nicht ihrer   vier:
there are of them three and are not of them four

Und wenn zu dreien   der vierte wär,
and when to threesome the fourth were

So wär   ein heil'ger Drei-König mehr.
so would be one holy   three-king more

The three Wise Men with their star like eating and drinking, but they don't like paying.

The three Wise Men are coming here: there are three of them, not four – and if a fourth one were added to the other three there'd be one Wise Man more.

Ich erster bin der weiss und auch der schön,
I   first am the white and also the handsome

Bei Tage solltet   ihr   erst mich sehn!
by day should you first me see

Doch ach, mit   allen Spezerein,
but oh with all   spices

Werd ich sein Tag   kein Mädchen mir erfrein.
will I   its day(s) no girl   me marry

I am the first, who is handsome and white of skin – you really should see me by day! But for all my many spices, no girls will marry me.

Ich aber bin der braun und bin der lang,
I   but am the brown and am the tall

Bekannt bei Weibern wohl und bei Gesang.
known   by women   well and by song

Ich bringe Gold statt   Spezerein,
I   bring gold instead of spices

Da   werd ich überall   willkommen sein.
then will I everywhere welcome   be

I am the one who is tall and dark, well-known with women and by my song. I bring gold instead of spices, so I'll be welcome everywhere.

Ich endlich bin der schwarz und bin der klein,
I   finally am the black   and am the small

Und mag auch wohl   einmal   recht lustig sein.
and like also indeed for once very merry to be

Ich esse gern,   ich trinke gern,
I   eat gladly I   drink gladly

Ich esse, trinke und bedanke   mich gern.
I   eat   drink and give thanks –   gladly

I'm the last one, black and small, and I'd like for once to be merry! For I like eating and I like drinking, and I'll gladly say thank you for them both.

Die heiligen drei   König' sind wohlgesinnt,
the holy   three kings are well-disposed

Sie   suchen die Mutter und das Kind;
they seek   the mother and the child

Der Joseph fromm   sitzt auch dabei,
the Joseph devoutly sits also there

Der Ochs und Esel liegen auf der Streu.
the ox   and ass lie   on the straw

The three Wise Men are kindly disposed: they're looking for the Mother and her Child; with Joseph sitting devoutly there, and the ox and ass in the straw.

Wir bringen Myrrhen, wir bringen Gold,
we bring myrrh   we bring gold

Dem   Weihrauch sind   die Damen hold;
(for) the frankincense (have) the ladies (liking)

Und haben wir Wein von gutem Gewächs,
and have we wine of   good vintage

So trinken wir drei so gut als ihrer   sechs.
so drink   we three so well as of you six

We're bringing myrrh, and bringing gold, and ladies always like frankincense. And if the wine we're given is good, we'll drink it like six of you!

Da wir nun hier schöne Herrn   und Fraun,
as we now here fine   gentlemen and ladies

Aber keine Ochsen und Esel schaun,
but no   oxen   and ass see

So sind wir nicht am   rechten Ort,
so are we not in the right   place

Und ziehen unseres Weges weiter   fort.
and move our   way   further on

Now, as we see here only fine
gentlefolk, and there is no ox, and
no ass – we can't have come to the
right place at all – and so we must
go on our way.

44. *GENIALISCH   TREIBEN* GIFTED WITH GENIUS DOINGS

44. DOINGS OF A GENIUS

Johann Wolfgang von Goethe

So wälz   ich ohne   Unterlass,
so trundle I   without ceasing

Wie Sankt Diogenes, mein Fass.
like Saint Diogenes my   barrel

Bald ist es Ernst,   bald ist es Spass;
now is it earnestness now is it jesting

Bald ist es Lieb, bald ist es Hass;
now is it love now is it hate

Bald ist es dies, bald ist es das;
now is it this now is it that

Es ist ein Nichts,   und ist ein Was.
it is a   nothing and is a   something

So wälz   ich ohne   Unterlass,
so trundle I   without ceasing

Wie Sankt Diogenes, mein Fass.
like Saint Diogenes my   barrel

I trundle my barrel on and on like
Saint Diogenes. Sometimes I'm
grave, sometimes I'm light-
hearted; sometimes I love, and
sometimes I hate; sometimes it's
this thing, now it's that one, now
it's something and now it's
nothing. So like Diogenes, the
Saint, I roll my barrel on.

45. *BLUMENGRUSS* FLOWER-GREETING

45. FLOWER GREETING

Johann Wolfgang von Goethe

Der Strauss, den ich gepflücket,
the nosegay that I   gathered

Grüsse   dich viel   tausendmal!
let greet you many thousand-times

With these flowers that I gathered,
I send you a thousand greetings!
Often have I bowed my head – oh,
a thousand times – and pressed

Ich habe mich oft   gebücket,
I   have myself often bent down

Ach, wohl   eintausendmal,
ah   indeed a thousand times

Und ihn ans   Herz gedrücket
and it   to the heart pressed

Wie hunderttausendmal!
as if hundred-thousand-times

them to my heart, how many
hundred thousand times!

46. *DIE SPRÖDE*
THE COY ONE

46. THE PERT
SHEPHERDESS

Johann Wolfgang von Goethe

An dem reinsten Frühlingsmorgen
on the clearest spring-morning

Ging   die Schäferin   und sang,
walked the shepherdess and sang

Jung und schön und ohne   Sorgen,
young and pretty and without cares

Dass es durch   die Felder klang,
that it through the fields rang

So la-la! le-ral-la-la!
tra-la-la le-ral-la-la

On a fair spring morning, a pretty
young shepherdess was going her
carefree way, singing through the
fields: tra-la-la, ra-la-la!

Thyrsis bot   ihr   für ein Mäulchen
Thyrsis offered to her for a   kiss

Zwei, drei Schäfchen gleich   am   Ort,
two   three lambs   instantly on the spot

Schalkhaft blickte sie ein Weilchen;
archly   looked she a   little while

Doch sie sang und lachte   fort:
but   she sang and laughed on

So la-la! le-ral-la-la!
tra-la-la le-ral-la-la

Thyrsis came and offered her a
few lambs for a kiss. Archly she
looked at him for a while, then
laughed as she sang: tra-la-la, ra-
la-la!

Und ein andrer bot   ihr Bänder,
and another offered her ribbons

Und der dritte bot   sein Herz;
and the third offered his heart

And another brought ribbons, and
a third one his heart. But to lambs,
heart and ribbons, she only just
laughed: tra-la-la, ra-la-la!

Doch sie trieb   mit Herz und Bändern
but   she made with heart and ribbons

So   wie mit den Lämmern   Scherz,
just as   with the little lambs jest

Nur la-la! le-ral-la-la!
only la-la   le-ral-la-la

47. DIE BEKEHRTE
THE CONVERT

Johann Wolfgang von Goethe

Bei dem Glanz der   Abendröte
in the glow of the sunset

Ging   ich still   den Wald entlang,
walked I   silently the wood through

Damon sass und blies die Flöte,
Damon sat and blew the flute

Dass es von   den Felsen klang,
that it from the rocks rang

So la-la! ral-la-la!
tra-la-la ral-la-la

Und er zog   mich zu sich   nieder,
and he drew me   to himself down

Küsste mich so hold,   so süss,
kissed me   so charmingly so sweetly

Und ich sagte: 'blase wieder!'
and I   said   blow again

Und der gute Junge blies,
and the dear youth played

So la-la! ral-la-la!
tra la-la ral-la-la

Meine Ruh   ist nun verloren,
my   peace is now lost

Meine Freude floh davon,
my   joy   fled away

Und ich hör vor   meinen Ohren
and I   hear before my   ears

47. THE
SHEPHERDESS
BEWITCHED

In the red glow of sunset, I passed
silently through the wood. Damon
sat playing his flute, and it echoed
from the rocks: tra-la-la, ra-la-la!

And he drew me down and kissed
me, so gently, so sweetly. And I
said, 'Play again!' and the tender
youth played: tra-la-la, ra-la-la!

Now my peace is gone, and my joy
has all fled, and all that I hear in
my ears is the old: tra-la-la, ra-la-
la!

Immer nur den alten Ton,
always just the old   sound

So la-la, ral-la-la!
tra-la-la ral-la-la

48. FRÜHLING ÜBERS   JAHR
SPRING   OVER THE YEAR

Johann Wolfgang von Goethe

Das Beet,   schon   lockert
the flower-bed already gives way

Sichs in die Höh!
itself – upwards –

Da   wanken Glöckchen,
there waver   little bells

So weiss wie Schnee;
as white as   snow

Safran entfaltet
saffron unfolds

Gewaltge Glut,
intense   glow

Smaragden keimt   es
emerald   is budding it

Und keimt wie Blut;
and stirs   like blood

Primeln   stolzieren
primroses parade

So naseweis,
so impudently

Schalkhafte Veilchen,
roguish   violets

Versteckt mit Fleiss;
hidden   with care

Was auch noch alles
ever else still all

48. SOVEREIGN
SPRING

The flower-bed is swelling up with
life! Little bells tremble, as white
as snow; saffron unfolds a glowing
radiance; emerald shoots spring
forth, and buds blood-red;
primroses flaunt their saucy heads,
and roguish violets diligently hide.
Indeed everything around is
stirring and growing – spring is at
work and alive!

Da   regt und webt,
there stirs and weaves

Genug, der Frühling,
enough the spring

Er wirkt und lebt.
it works and lives

Doch was im   Garten
yet   what in the garden

But the richest blossom in the garden is my sweet love. My heart is warmed by the glow of her glances, her gay little songs, her cheering words. An ever-open, blossoming spirit, earnest but smiling, innocent in jest. Summer may bring the lily and rose, but it vies in vain with my sweet love.

Am   reichsten blüht,
(at) the richest blossoms

Das ist des   Liebchens
that is of the beloved

Lieblich Gemüt.
sweet   disposition

Da glühen Blicke
for glow glances

Mir   immerfort,
to me continually

Erregend Liedchen,
stirring little songs

Erheiternd Wort.
cheering word

Ein immer offen,
an always open

Ein Blütenherz,
a   blossom-heart

Im   Ernste   freundlich
in the seriousness cheerful

Und rein im   Scherz.
and pure in the chaff

Wenn Ros und Lilie
when rose and lily

Der Sommer bringt,
the summer brings

Er doch vergebens
he yet   in vain

Mit Liebchen   ringt.
with sweetheart contends

49. *ANAKREONS GRAB*
   ANACREON'S GRAVE

49. ANACREON'S
   GRAVE

Johann Wolfgang von Goethe

Wo   die Rose hier blüht, wo   Reben um   Lorbeer
where the rose here blooms where vines round laurel

sich   schlingen, wo   das Turtelchen
themselves wind   where the (little) turtle-dove

lockt, wo   sich   das Grillchen   ergötzt, welch
entices where (himself) the little cricket delights what

ein Grab ist hier, das alle Götter mit Leben schön
a   grave is here that all gods with life   beautifully

bepflanzt und geziert? Es ist Anakreons Ruh.
planted   and adorned it is Anacreon's repose

Frühling, Sommer und Herbst   genoss der glückliche
spring   summer and autumn enjoyed the fortunate

Dichter; vor   dem Winter hat ihn endlich der
poet   from the winter has him finally the

Hügel geschützt.
hillock sheltered

Here where roses bloom and vines entwine the laurels, where turtle-doves call, and crickets play – whose grave is this, so adorned with such beauty and life by the gods? It is Anacreon's resting place. Spring, summer and autumn delighted this most favoured of poets, until this hillock finally gave him its shelter from winter.

50. *PROMETHEUS*
   PROMETHEUS

50. PROMETHEUS

Johann Wolfgang von Goethe
(also set by Schubert)

Bedecke deinen Himmel, Zeus,
cover   your   heavens Zeus

Mit Wolkendunst
with clouds-haze

Und übe,   dem Knaben gleich,
and practise the boy   like

Der Disteln köpft,
who thistles beheads

An Eichen dich   und Bergeshöhn;
on oaks   (yourself) and mountain-heights

Musst mir   meine Erde
must to me my   earth

Cover your heavens with a haze of clouds, O Zeus, and try your strength on oak trees and mountain peaks, like a boy beheading thistles! But leave my world untouched! Leave my dwelling, no hands of yours did build, and my hearth whose warmth you envy!

Doch lassen stehn
but let   stay

Und meine Hütte, die du nicht gebaut,
and my   hut   that you not built

Und meinen Herd,
and my   hearth

Um dessen Glut
for whose glow

Du mich beneidest.
you me   envy

Ich kenne nichts   Ärmeres
I   know nothing more wretched

Unter der Sonn', als   euch, Götter!
under the sun   than you gods

Ihr nähret kümmerlich
you feed   pityfully

Von Opfersteuern
from sacrifice-dues

Und Gebetshauch
and prayer's-breath

Eure Majestät
your majesty

Und darbtet,   wären
and would starve were

Nicht Kinder   und Bettler
not   children and beggars

Hoffnungsvolle Toren.
hopeful   fools

Da   ich ein Kind war,
when I   a   child was

Nicht wusste, wo   aus noch ein,
not   knew where out or   in

Kehrt' ich mein verirrtes   Auge
turned I   my   bewildered eye

Zur   Sonne, als wenn drüber wär'
to the sun   as if   beyond were

Ein Ohr, zu hören meine Klage,
an ear to hear my   lament

I know of nothing under the sun
so wretched as you gods! Pitifully
you feed your majesty on
sacrificial offerings and the breath
of prayers, and you would starve,
were children and beggars not
such hopeful fools.

When I was a child, not knowing
which way to turn, I gazed
bewildered towards the sun, as if
beyond someone were there to
hear my cry, a heart like mine to
pity me, the afflicted one, in my
distress.

Ein Herz wie meins,
a   heart like mine

Sich des   Bedrängten   zu erbarmen.
itself of the afflicted one to feel pity

Wer half   mir
who helped me

Who came to my aid against the arrogant Titans? Who saved me from death and slavery? Was it not my own divine fire that accomplished all this? And yet did my pure young heart not glow, deluded in its gratitude to the sleeper above for my deliverance?

Wider der   Titanen Übermut?
against of the Titans   arrogance

Wer rettete vom   Tode mich,
who saved from the death me

Von Sklaverei?
from slavery

Hast du nicht alles   selbst   vollendet,
have you not everything yourself accomplished

Heilig glühend Herz?
holy   glowing heart

Und glühtest jung   und gut,
and glowed youthfully and well

Betrogen, Rettungsdank
deceived (for) saving-thanks

Dem Schlafenden da   droben?
to the sleeping-one there above

Ich dich ehren? Wofür?
I   you honour what for

I – honour you? For what? When did you ever relieve the anguish and the burdens of men? When did you ever dry their frightened tears?

Hast du die Schmerzen gelindert
have you the pains   allayed

Je des   Beladenen?
ever of the burdened one

Hast du die Tränen gestillet
have you the tears   stayed

Je des   Geängsteten?
ever of the frightened one

Hat nicht mich zum   Manne geschmiedet
has not me to the man   forged

Was I not forged into manhood by almighty Time and everlasting Destiny – my masters, and yours?

Die allmächtige Zeit
the almighty   Time

Und das ewige   Schicksal,
and the everlasting Destiny

Meine Herrn   und deine?
my   masters and yours

Wähntest du   etwa,
thought you perhaps

Ich sollte   das Leben hassen,
I   should the life   hate

In Wüsten   fliehen,
in wildernesses flee

Weil   micht alle
because not   all

Blütenträume   reiften?
blossom-dreams matured

Hier sitz' ich, forme   Menschen
here sit   I   mould men

Nach meinem Bilde,
after my   image

Ein Geschlecht, das mir   gleich sei,
a   race   that to me similar be

Zu leiden, zu weinen,
to suffer to weep

Zu geniessen und zu freuen sich,
to enjoy   and to rejoice (itself)

Und dein   nicht zu achten,
and of you not   respect

Wie ich!
as   I

Perhaps you thought I would hate
life, and flee into the wilderness,
because not all my dreams were
fulfilled?

But here I sit, making men in my
own image; a race of men who like
me will suffer and weep, rejoice
and be happy – and be as heedless
of you as I!

51. GRENZEN   DER LIMITATIONS OF THE MENSCHHEIT MANKIND

51. LIMITATIONS OF MANKIND

Johann Wolfgang von Goethe
(also set by Schubert)

Wenn der uralte
when the age-old

Heilige Vater
Holy   Father

Mit gelassener Hand
with patient   hand

When the Eternal Father, with his
slow and patient hand, scatters his
lightning flashes from rolling
clouds in blessing over the earth, I
kiss the lowest hem of his garment
with a childlike awe, faith in my
heart.

Aus rollenden Wolken
from rolling   clouds

Segnende Blitze
beneficent lightning flashes

Über die Erde sät,
over the earth sows

Küss' ich den letzten
kiss   I   the extreme

Saum seines Kleides,
hem of his robe

Kindliche Schauer
childlike awe

Treu in der Brust.
true in the breast

Denn mit Göttern
for   with gods

Soll sich   nicht messen
shall himself not   measure

Irgendein Mensch.
any   man,

Hebt er sich   aufwärts
raises he (himself) upwards

Und berührt
and touches

Mit dem Scheitel   die Sterne,
with the crown (of his head) the stars

Nirgends haften dann
nowhere cling then

Die unsichern Sohlen,
the insecure soles

Und mit ihm spielen
and with him play

Wolken und Winde.
clouds and winds

Steht er mit festen
stands he with firm

Markigen Knochen
marrowy bones

Let no man measure himself
against the gods! If he reaches up
to touch the stars, his unsure feet
find no hold, and he becomes the
plaything of the winds and clouds.

But if he stands fast and secure on
the firm, enduring earth, his
meagre stature compares not even
with that of the oak or vine.

Auf der wohlgegründeten
on the well-established

Dauernden Erde,
enduring   earth

Reicht   er   nicht auf,
reaches he not   up

Nur   mit der Eiche
(even) with the oak

Oder der Rebe
or   the vine

Sich   zu vergleichen.
himself to compare

Was unterscheidet
what distinguishes

Götter von Menschen?
gods   from men

Dass viele   Wellen
that many waves

Vor   jenen   wandeln,
before those ones go

Ein ewiger Strom:
an   eternal stream

Uns hebt die Welle,
us   lifts the wave

Verschlingt die Welle,
devours   the wave

Und wir versinken.
and we founder

Ein kleiner Ring
a   little   ring

Begrenzt unser Leben,
bounds   our   life

Und viele Geschlechter
and many generations

Reihen sich   dauernd
follow each other continuously

An ihres   Daseins
in of their existence

Unendliche Kette.
unending   chain

What distinguishes gods from
men? Before the gods, unceasing
waves roll on in an never-ending
stream. But we are tossed by
waves that lift us up and swallow
us, and then we founder.

Our life is bound by a little ring.
And countless generations succeed
one another: links in the unending
chain of their existence.

52. From *SPANISCHES LIEDERBUCH*
SPANISH   SONGBOOK

Translations of Spanish folksongs into German by
Emmanuel Geibel and Paul Heyse

From *Geistliche Lieder*
    sacred   songs

   iii.

(Der heilige Joseph singt:)
  the holy   Joseph sings

Nun wandre, Maria,
Now go on   Mary

Nun wandre nur fort.
now go on   only onward

Schon krähen   die Hähne,
already are crowing the cocks

Und nah ist der Ort.
and near is the place

Nun wandre, Geliebte,
now go on   love

Du Kleinod mein,
you treasure my

Und balde wir werden
and soon we shall

In Bethlehem sein.
in Bethlehem be

Dann ruhest du fein
then rest   you well

Und schlummerst dort.
and slumber   there

Schon krähen   die Hähne
already are crowing the cocks

Und nah ist der Ort.
and near is the place

52. From SPANISH
SONGBOOK

From Sacred Songs

iii.

(Joseph sings:)

Keep onward, Mary, keep on.
Already the cock crows, and the
place is near.

Keep onward, my jewel, keep on.
For soon we shall be in
Bethlehem. There you will find
sweet rest and sleep. Already the
cock crows, and the place is near.

Wohl   seh ich, Herrin,
indeed see I   lady

Die Kraft   dir   schwinden;
the strength to you vanish

Kann deine Schmerzen,
can   your pains

Ach, kaum   verwinden.
ah   scarcely overcome

Getrost!   Wohl finden
take comfort surely find

Wir Herberg dort.
we shelter there

Schon krähen die Hähne
already crow   the cocks

Und nah ist der Ort.
and near is the place

I see your strength fading, dear
wife – I can hardly bear to see your
pain. Take heart, we will surely
find shelter there. Already the
cock crows, and the place is near.

Wär erst bestanden
were just endured

Dein Stündlein,   Marie,
your (little) hour Mary

Die gute Botschaft,
the good tidings

Gut lohnt   ich sie.
well would repay I   (it)

Das Eselein   hie
the (little) ass here

Gäb   ich drum   fort!
would give I   for that away

Schon krähen   die Hähne,
already are crowing the cocks

Komm! Nah ist der Ort.
come   near is the place

Would that your time were over,
Mary. I'd give much to hear good
tidings – I would gladly give this
little ass! But come, the cock
crows, and the place is near.

    iv.

Die ihr schwebet
who you hover

Um   diese Palmen
round these palm-trees

iv.

You angels, hovering around the
palm trees in the night wind –
hush the rustling leaves, for my
Child is sleeping!

In Nacht und Wind,
in night and wind

Ihr heil'gen Engel,
you holy   angels

Stillet die Wipfel!
hush the tree-tops

Es schlummert mein Kind.
(it) slumbers my child

Ihr Palmen von Bethlehem
you palms of Bethlehem

In   Windesbrausen,
in the winds-blustering

Wie mögt ihr heute
how can   you today

So zornig sausen!
so angrily sough

O rauscht nicht also!
Oh rustle   not so

Schweiget, neiget
be silent   bow

Euch   leis' und lind;
yourselves softly and gently

Stillet die Wipfel!
hush the tree-tops

Es schlummert mein Kind.
(it) slumbers my child

Der Himmelsknabe
the Heaven's-boy

Duldet Beschwerde,
bears burden

Ach, wie so müd' er ward
oh   how so weary he was

Vom Leid   der   Erde.
of the sorrow of the earth

Ach num im   Schlaf ihm
oh now in the sleep to him

Leise gesänftigt
softly mitigated

You palms of Bethlehem, why do
you sway so angrily in the
blustering wind this day. Oh,
please do not rustle! Be still, and
bow softly, gently down. Hush the
rustling leaves, for my Child is
sleeping!

The Son of Heaven has such grief
to bear. How weary he is of the
sorrowing world. But now this
pain is eased in quiet sleep – hush
the rustling leaves, for my Child is
sleeping!

Die Qual zerrint,
the pain disappears

Stillet ihr   Wipfel!
hush you tree-tops

Es   schlummert mein Kind.
(it) sleeps   my   child

Grimmige Kälte
fierce   cold

Sauset   hernieder;
blows hard down

Womit   nur   deck' ich
with what simply cover I

Des   Kindleins Glieder!
of the child   limbs

O all ihr Engel,
O all you angels

Die ihr geflügelt
who you winged

Wandelt im   Wind,
wander in the wind

Stillet die Wipfel!
hush the tree-tops

Es   schlummert mein Kind.
(it) slumbers my   child

Cold winds blow fiercely – with what can I cover my Child? O all you winged angels who soar in the wind – hush the rustling leaves, for my Child is sleeping!

vi.

Ach, des   Knaben Augen sind
oh of the boy   eyes (have)

Mir so schön und klar erschienen,
to me so lovely and clear appeared

Und ein Etwas   strahlt aus ihnen,
and a   something radiates from them

Das mein ganzes Herz gewinnt.
that my   whole heart wins

Blickt er doch mit diesen süssen
looks he but with these sweet

Augen nach den meinen hin!
eyes   to   the mine   thither

vi.

Oh, this boy's eyes, they seem so beautiful and clear, and from them something shines that wholly wins my heart.

With His sweet eyes, He looks right into mine. If He should see His image there, He would perhaps give me a loving smile.

Säh'   er dann sein Bild   darin,
would see he then his image therein

Würd' er wohl   mich liebend grüssen.
would he perhaps me   lovingly greet

Und so geb'   ich ganz   mich   hin,
and so surrender I   wholly myself –

Seinen Augen nur   zu dienen,
his   eyes   only to serve

Denn ein Etwas   strahlt aus ihnen,
for   a   something shines from them

Das mein ganzes Herz gewinnt.
that my   whole heart wins

And so I give my very soul to
follow and serve those eyes, for in
them something shines, that
wholly wins my heart.

ix.

Herr, was   trägt der Boden hier,
Lord what bears the soil   here

Den du   tränkst so bitterlich?
that you water so bitterly

'Dornen, liebes Herz für mich,
thorns   dear heart for me

Und für dich der   Blumen Zier.'
and for you of the flowers adornment

Ach, wo   solche Bäche   rinnen,
oh   where such brooks flow

Wird ein Garten da   gedeihn?
will a   garden then thrive

'Ja, und wisse! Kränzelein,
yes and know little garlands

Gar verschiedne, flicht   man drinnen.'
very different   weaves one in there

O mein Herr, zu wessen Zier
O my Lord to whose adornment

Windet man die Kränze? Sprich!
twines one the garlands say

'Die   von Dornen sind für mich,
those of thorns are for me

Die   von Blumen reich ich dir.'
those of flowers give I   to you

ix.

Lord, what is borne here within
this earth, so watered by your
bitter tears? 'Flowers for you for
your adornment – and thorns,
dear heart, for me.'

Oh, where such streams are
flowing, can a garden thrive? 'Yes,
and know they will twine there
crowns and garlands – but of very
different kinds.'

O Lord, please say, for whose
adornment they twine the garlands
and wreaths? 'Those of thorns,
they weave for me; those of
flowers I will give to you.'

From *Weltliche Lieder*
   secular   songs

From Secular Songs

i.

i.

Klinge, klinge mein Pandero,
sound sound my   tambourine

Sound, sound, my tambourine –
but the thoughts in my heart are
somewhere else.

Doch an   andres   denkt mein Herz.
but   about soemthing else thinks my   heart

Wenn du, muntres Ding,   verständest
if   you merry   creature would understand

If you, so merry and bright, could
understand my grief, each note
you played would be a sad lament.

Meine Qual   und sie empfändest,
my   torment and she would feel

Jeder Ton, den du entsendest,
every note that you send away

Würde klagen meinen Schmerz.
would lament my   sorrow

Bei des   Tanzes Drehn und Neigen
to of the dance twirling and bowing

I beat the wild rhythm of the
swaying, twirling dance to silence
the thoughts that remind me of my
grief.

Schlag ich wild   den Takt zum Reigen,
beat   I   wildly (the) time to the dance

Dass nur die Gedanken schweigen,
that only the thoughts are silent

Die mich mahnen an den Schmerz.
that me   remind of the grief

Ach, ihr Herrn,   dann will im   Schwingen
ah   you gentlemen then wants in the whirling round

Oh, you fine men, how often in
your whirling dance I felt my heart
would break, and my song
becomes an anguished cry – for
my thoughts are elsewhere.

Oftmals mir   die Brust zerspringen,
often   to me the breast burst

Und zum Angstschrei   wird   mein Singen,
and to the cry of anguish becomes my   singing

Denn an   andres   denkt mein Herz.
for   about something else thinks my   heart

ii.

ii.

In dem Schatten meiner Locken
in the shadow of my locks

In the shadow of my locks my
lover fell asleep. Shall I wake him
now? Oh, no!

Schlief   mir   mein Geliebter ein.
fell asleep to me my   lover   –

Weck' ich ihn nun auf? Ach nein!
wake I   him now up   oh no

Sorglich strählt   ich meine krausen
carefully combed I   my   curly

Locken täglich in der Frühe,
locks   daily   in the early morning

Doch umsonst   ist meine Mühe,
but   for nothing is my   trouble

Weil   die Winde sie   zersausen.
because the winds them dishevel

Lockenschatten, Windessausen
locks'-shadow wind's-blustering

Schläferten   den Liebsten ein.
lulled to sleep the dearest –

Weck' ich ihn nun auf? Ach nein!
wake I   him now up oh   no

Hören muss ich, wie ihn gräme,
hear   must I   how him grieved

Dass er schmachtet schon   so lange,
that he languishes already so long

Dass ihm   Leben geb' und nehme
that to him life   gave and took

Diese meine braune Wange,
this   my   brown cheek

Und er nennt mich seine Schlange,
and he calls me   his   serpent

Und doch schlief   er bei mir ein.
and yet   fell asleep he by me –

Weck' ich ihn nun auf? Ach nein!
wake I   him now up oh   no

Early in the morning I comb my
locks so carefully, but all in vain,
for the wind just blows them all
about. The shadow of my locks,
and the soughing of the wind have
lulled my dearest one to sleep.
Shall I wake him now? Oh, no!

I have to hear how much he pines,
how long he languished, how my
brown cheeks bring life and death
to him. And he calls me a serpent
– yet falls asleep beside me! Shall I
wake him now? Oh, no!

v.

Auf dem grünen Balkon   mein Mädchen
on   the green balcony my girl

Schaut nach mir durchs   Gitterlein.
looks at   me through the (little) trellis

Mit den Augen blinzelt sie freundlich,
with the eyes   twinkles she in a friendly way

Mit dem Finger sagt sie mir: Nein!
with the finger says she to me no

v.

From her green balcony my
sweetheart peeps out at me
through the trellis. Her twinkling
eyes encourage me, but her finger
says no!

Glück, das nimmer ohne   Wanken
fortune that never   without wavering

Fortune, that never quite favours young love here below, has given me joy – as well as some doubts. For I hear at her window both pleasantries and quarrelling. Joy tinged with pain – that's just the way with girls. Her twinkling eyes encourage me, but her finger says no!

Junger Liebe folgt   hienieden,
young love attends here below

Hat mir eine Lust beschieden,
has me one joy given

Und auch da   noch muss ich schwanken.
and also there still must I   falter

Schmeicheln hör' ich oder Zanken,
flattery   hear I   or   quarrelling

Komm' ich an ihr Fensterlädchen.
come   I   to her (little) window-shutters

Immer nach dem Brauch der   Mädchen
always after the custom of the girls

Träuft ins   Glück   ein bisschen Pein:
drops into the happiness a   little   pain

Mit den Augen blinzelt   sie freundlich,
with the eyes   twinkles she in a friendly way

Mit dem Finger sagt sie mir: Nein!
with the finger says she to me no

Wie sich   nur in ihr vertragen
how (themselves) only in her are reconciled

However can my passion and her coldness be reconciled? With her in my heaven, joy and gloom are in joint pursuit. The wind bears my sighs, that my sweetheart never held me. Yet so finely she holds me off – for her twinking eyes encourage me, but her finger tells me no!

Ihre Kälte,   meine Glut?
her coldness my   passion

Weil   in ihr mein Himmel ruht,
because in her my   heaven rests

Seh' ich Trüb und Heil   sich   jagen.
see I   gloom and happiness each other pursue

In   den Wind gehn meine Klagen,
into the wind go   my   laments

Dass noch nie   die süsse Kleine
that as yet never the sweet little one

Ihre Arme schlang um   meine;
her arms entwined about mine

Doch   sie hält   mich hin so fein –
indeed she holds me   off so well

Mit den Augen blinzelt sie freundlich,
with the eyes   twinkles she in a friendly way

Mit dem Finger sagt sie mir: Nein!
with the finger says she to me no

   vi.

Wenn du   zu den Blumen gehst,
when you to the flowers go

Pflücke die schönsten,   dich   zu schmücken.
pluck   the most beautiful yourself to adorn

Ach, wenn du in dem Gärtlein   stehst,
oh   if   you in the (little) garden were standing

Müsstest   du dich selber   pflücken.
would have to you – yourself – pluck

Alle Blumen wissen ja,
all   flowers know indeed

Dass du   hold   bist ohne   gleichen.
that you lovely are – without equal –

Und die Blume, die   dich sah –
and the flower that you saw

Farb' und Schmuck   muss ihr   erbleichen.
colour and adornment must to her grow pale

Wenn du   zu den Blumen gehst,
when you to the flowers go

Pflücke die schönsten,   dich   zu schmücken.
pluck   the most beautiful yourself to adorn

Ach, wenn du in dem Gärtlein   stehst,
oh   when you in the (little) garden are

Müsstest du dich selber   pflücken.
must   you – yourself – pluck

Lieblicher als   Rosen sind
lovelier   than roses are

Die Küsse, die dein Mund verschwendet,
the kisses that your mouth lavishes

Weil   der Reiz   der   Blumen endet,
because the charm of the flowers ends

Wo   dein Liebreiz erst beginnt.
where your charm   just begins

vi.

When you walk amongst the flowers, pluck the loveliest for your adornment. Oh, if you were in the garden, you would have to pluck yourself!

All the flowers know so well that you are lovely beyond compare; for any flower that looks at you must fade and lose her lustre. When you walk amongst the flowers . . . etc.

Lovelier than roses are the kisses lavished by your lips; because the charm of flowers ends where yours is just beginning. When you walk amongst the flowers . . . etc.

Wenn du   zu den Blumen gehst,
when you to the flowers go

Pflücke die schönsten,   dich   zu schmücken.
pluck   the most beautiful yourself to adorn

Ach, wenn du in dem Gärtlein   stehst,
oh   when you in the (little) garden are standing

Müsstest du   dich selber   pflücken.
must   you – yourself – pluck

xiii.

Mögen alle bösen   Zungen
may   all malicious tongues

Immer sprechen was   beliebt,
always say   what pleases (them)

Wer mich liebt, den lieb' ich wieder,
who me   loves him love I   in return

Und ich lieb' und bin geliebt.
and I   love and am loved

Schlimme, schlimme Reden flüstern
wicked   wicked   words whisper

Eure Zungen schonungslos,
your tongues pitilessly

Doch ich weiss es, sie   sind lüstern
but I   know it   they are lustful

Nach unschuld'gem Blute bloss.
for   innocent   blood only

Nimmer soll   es mich bekümmern,
never   shall it me   trouble

Schwatzt so viel   es euch beliebt;
gossip   as much it you pleases

Wer mich liebt, den lieb' ich wieder,
who me   loves him love I   in return

Und ich lieb' und bin geliebt.
and I   love and am loved

Zur Verleumdung sich   verstehet
to the slander   (himself) understands well

Nur, wem Lieb' und Gunst   gebrach,
only whom love and affection lacked

xiii.

All those spiteful tongues may say what they please; for he who loves me, I love in return – I can both love and be loved.

Without mercy your tongues whisper such wicked, wicked words, yet you lust after innocent blood. But gossip all you please – it won't trouble me: for he who loves me I love in return – I can both love, and be loved.

Slander only comes from those who know no love, because they lack affection, at feel they are unloved. I am proud of the love

Weil's   ihm   selber elend ·   gehet
because it to him himself wretchedly goes

Und ihn niemand minnt und mag.
and him no one loves and likes

Darum   denk' ich, dass die Liebe,
therefore think I   that the love

Drum   sie schmäh'n, mir Ehre   gibt;
around it they despise   me honour gives

Wer mich liebt, den lieb' ich wieder,
who me   loves him love I   in return

Und ich lieb' und bin geliebt.
and I   love and am loved

Wenn ich wär aus Stein und Eisen,
if   I   were of stone and iron

Möchtet ihr darauf bestehn,
might   you then   insist

Dass ich sollte   von   mir weisen
that I   should from me banish

Liebesgruss   und Liebesflehn.
love's greeting and love's-entreating

Doch mein Herzlein   ist nun leider
but   my   (little) heart is now unfortunately

Weich, wie's Gott uns   Mädchen gibt,
tender as it God to us maidens gives

Wer mich liebt, den lieb' ich wieder,
who me   loves him love I   in return

Und ich lieb' und bin geliebt.
and I   love and am loved

that they despise; for he that loves
me. I love in return – I can both
love, and be loved.

If I were made of iron and stone,
you would think I would turn
away from love's pleadings, but
my heart is tender – as God makes
maidens' hearts. And he that loves
me, I love in return – I can both
love and be loved.

xxi.

Alle gingen, Herz, zur   Ruh,
all   went   heart to the rest

Alle schlafen,   nur nicht du.
all   are sleeping only not   you

Denn der hoffnungslose Kummer
for   the hopeless   grief

Scheucht   von deinem Bett den Schlummer,
frightens away from your   bed the slumber

xxi.

All things have gone to their rest,
my heart; all are sleeping but you.

For hopeless grief drives slumber
from your bed, and your thoughts
stray in silent sorrow to your love.

Und dein Sinnen   schweift in stummer
and your thinking strays   in silent

Sorge   seiner Liebe zu.
sorrow its   love to

xxiv.

Bedeckt mich mit Blumen,
cover   me   with flowers

Ich sterbe   vor Liebe.
I   am dying of love

Dass die Luft   mit leisem Wehen
that the breeze with gentle blowing

Nicht den süssen Duft mir   entführe,
not   the sweet scent to me may carry away

Bedeckt mich!
cover   me

Ist ja   alles   doch   dasselbe,
is (yes) everything indeed the same

Liebesodem   oder Düfte
love's-breath or   scents

Von Blumen.
of   flowers

Von Jasmin und weissen Lilien
of   jasmine and white   lilies

Sollt ihr hier mein Grab bereiten,
shall you here my   grave prepare

Ich sterbe.
I   am dying

Und befragt   ihr mich: Woran?
and question you me   what of

Sag' ich: unter süssen Qualen
say I   from sweet torments

Vor Liebe.
of love

xxxiv.

Geh', Geliebter, geh' jetzt!
go   darling go now

Sieh, der Morgen   dämmert.
see   the morning dawns

xxiv.

Cover me with flowers, for I am dying of love!

So the gentle blowing breezes may not carry their sweet scent away, cover me!

Are they not indeed the same – the breath of love, the scent of flowers?

Prepare here my grave with jasmine and white lilies, for I am dying.

And if you ask, of what? I will say, of the sweet pangs of love!

xxxiv.

Go, my darling, go now – see, the day is dawning!

Leute gehn schon durch   die Gasse,
people walk already through the street

Und der Markt wird   so belebt,
and the market is becoming so busy

Dass der Morgen wohl, der blasse,
that the morning indeed the pale (one)

Schon   die weissen Flügel hebt.
already the white   wings lifts

Und vor   unsern Nachbarn   bin ich
and before our   neighbours am I

Bange, dass du Anstoss gibst;
afraid that you offence give

Denn sie   wissen nicht, wie innig
for   they know not   how fervently

Ich dich lieb' und du   mich liebst.
I   you love and you me   love

Already people are in the street, and the market begins to bustle. Pale morning already lifts white wings, and I fear the neighbours will be shocked. They cannot know how deeply we both love.

Drum,   Geliebter, geh' jetzt!
therefore beloved   go   now

Sieh, der Morgen   dämmert.
see   the morning dawns

And so, my darling go now – see, the day is dawning!

Wenn die Sonn' am   Himmel scheinend
when the sun   in the sky   shining

Scheucht   vom   Feld die Perlen klar,
shoos away from the field the pearls clear

Muss auch ich die Perle weinend
must also I   the pearl weeping

Lassen,   die mein Reichtum war.
part with that my   wealth   was

When the bright sun in the sky chases clear pearls from the fields, must I too, weeping, give up my pearl, that was my treasure.

Was als Tag den   andern funkelt,
what as day to the others sparkles

Meinen Augen dünkt es Nacht,
to my   eyes   seems it night

Da die Trennung bang   mir   dunkelt,
as the separation anxiously to me darkens

Wenn das Morgenrot erwacht.
when the dawn   awakes

What to others is bright day, to my eyes seems as night; for I feel a dark dread of our parting, when the day awakens.

Geh', Geliebter, geh' jetzt!
go   darling   go   now

Sieh, der Morgen dämmert.
see   the morning dawns

Fliehe denn aus   meinen Armen!
flee   then from my   arms

Denn versäumest du die Zeit,
for   let slip by you the time

Möchten für ein kurz Erwarmen,
would   for a   short warming

Wir ertauschen langes Leid.
we exchange long sorrow

Ist in Fegefeuersqualen
is in purgatory's-torments

Doch ein Tag schon   auszustehn,
yet   one day however surely to endure

Wenn die Hoffnung fern in Strahlen
when the hope   afar in rays

Lässt des   Himmels Glorie sehn.
lets of the heaven   glory show

Drum   Geliebter, geh' jetzt!
therefore darling   go   now

Sieh, der Morgen dämmert.
see   the morning dawns

Go my darling, go now – see, the day is dawning!

Flee then from my arms! For if you let the time slip by, we may, for one short tender hour, exchange a long time of sorrow. We can endure one single day of purgatory's pain, when hope in distant rays reveals all Heaven's glory.

Therefore, my darling, go now – see, the day is dawning!

53. *ITALIENISCHES LIEDERBUCH* ITALIAN SONG-BOOK

53. ITALIAN SONG-BOOK

(Italian poems translated into German by Paul Heyse)

i.

Auch kleine Dinge können uns entzücken,
even little things can   us delight

Auch kleine Dinge können teuer   sein.
even little things can   precious be

Bedenkt, wie gern wir uns   mit Perlen schmücken;
consider how gladly we ourselves with pearls adorn

i.

Even little things can delight us, even little things be precious. Think how gladly we adorn ourselves with pearls; their price is high, and yet they are so small. Think how small is the olive, and yet how sought for its goodness.

Sie werden schwer bezahlt und sind nur klein.
they are   heavily paid for and are only small

Bedenkt, wie klein ist die Olivenfrucht,
consider how little is the olive-fruit

Und wird um ihre Güte   doch gesucht.
and is   for her goodness yet sought

Denkt an die Rose nur, wie klein sie ist,
think of the rose just how little she is

Und duftet doch so lieblich, wie ihr wisst.
and smells yet so sweetly as you know

Just think of the rose, how small it is – and yet, as you know, its scent is so sweet.

ii.

Mir ward gesagt, du reisest in die Ferne.
to me was told   you journey into the distant place

Ach, wohin gehst du, mein geliebtes Leben?
oh   whither go you my beloved life

Den Tag, an dem du scheidest, wüsst' ich gerne;
the day on which you depart would know I gladly

Mit Tränen will ich das Geleit dir geben.
with tears will I the escort to you give

Mit Tränen will ich deinen Weg befeuchten –
with tears will I your path moisten

Gedenk' an mich, und Hoffnung wird mir leuchten!
think of me and hope will to me glimmer

Mit Tränen bin ich bei dir allerwärts –
with tears am I with you everywhere

Gedenk' an mich, vergiss es nicht, mein Herz!
think of me forget it not my heart

ii.

They told me you will journey far away. Oh, where are you going, my dearest life? If I but knew the day of your leaving, I would go with you and water your path with my tears. But think of me, and my hopes will glimmer. My tears are with you everywhere. Think of me – and do not forget, dear heart!

iii.

Ihr seid die Allerschönste weit und breit,
you are the fairest of all far and wide

Viel schöner als im Mai der Blumenflor.
much fairer than in the May the flower-blossoming

Orvietos Dom steigt so voll Herrlichkeit,
Orvieto's cathedral rises so full of splendour

Viterbos grösster Brunnen nicht empor.
Viterbo's greatest fountain not up

iii.

You are the fairest far and wide, fairer than the blossoming in May! Neither Orvieto's dome, nor Viterbo's greatest fountain can surpass such beauty, for such enchanting grace is yours alone – even Siena's cathedral must bow before you. Oh, you are so rich in grace and charm; even Siena's cathedral is not your peer.

So   hoher Reiz   und Zauber   ist dein eigen,
such lofty grace and enchantment is your own

Der Dom   von Siena muss sich   vor   dir neigen.
the cathedral of   Siena must himself before you bow

Ach, du   bist so an Reiz   und Anmut reich,
oh   you are so in charm and grace rich

Der Dom   von Siena selbst   ist dir   nicht gleich
the cathedral of   Siena himself is to you not   equal

iv

Gesegnet sei, durch   den   die Welt entstund;
Blessed be through whom the world began

Wie trefflich   schuf   er sie nach allen Seiten!
how admirably created he her on   all   sides

Er schuf   das Meer mit endlos   tiefem Grund,
he created the ocean with endlessly deep bottom

Er schuf   die Schiffe, die   hinübergleiten,
he created the ships   which glide across

Er schuf   das Paradies mit ew'gem Licht,
he created the Paradise with eternal light

Er schuf   die Schönheit und dein Angesicht.
he created the beauty   and your face

Blessed be He through whom the world began; how admirably He made it on every side! He made the ocean with its endless deeps; He made the ships which glide across it; He made Paradise with its eternal light; He made beauty – and your face.

v.

Selig   ihr Blinden,   die ihr nicht zu schauen
blessed you blind people who you not to see

Vermögt die Reize, die uns Glut   entfachen;
are able the charms that to us passion kindle

Selig   ihr Tauben,   die ihr ohne   Grauen
blessed you deaf people who you without horror

Die Klagen der   Verliebten   könnt verlachen;
the laments of the in love ones can   laugh at

Selig   ihr Stummen,   die ihr nicht den Frauen
blessed you dumb people who you not   to the women

könnt eure Herzensnot   verständlich machen;
can   your heart's-misery intelligible make

Blessed are the blind, who cannot see the charms that kindle our passion; blessed are the deaf, who can laugh without fear at lovers' laments; blessed are the dumb, who cannot speak to women of their hearts' grief; blessed are the dead in their graves, for they shall have peace from the torments of love.

Selig   ihr Toten,   die man hat begraben!
blessed you dead ones who one has buried

Ihr sollt vor Liebesqualen   Ruhe haben.
you shall from love's-torments peace have

vi.

Wer rief   dich denn? Wer hat dich herbestellt?
who called you then who has you sent for

Wer hiess dich kommen, wenn es dir zur   Last?
who bade you to come if   to you (to) the burden (is)

Geh zu dem Liebchen,   das dir mehr gefällt,
go to the sweetheart who you more pleases

Geh dahin, wo   du die Gedanken hast.
go thither where you the thoughts have

Geh nur, wohin   dein Sinnen   steht und Denken!
go just whither your brooding is   and thinking

Dass du zu mir kommst, will ich gern   dir schenken.
that you to me come   will I   willingly you excuse

Geh zu dem Liebchen,   das dir mehr gefällt!
go to the sweetheart who you more pleases

Wer rief dich denn? Wer hat dich herbestellt?
who called you   then   who has you   sent for

vi.

Who called you then? Who sent for you? Who asked you to come, if you find it such a burden? Go to the sweetheart who pleases you more – go there where your thoughts belong! Go there where your thoughts and fancies lie! I excuse you gladly from your coming here. Go to the sweetheart who pleases you more! Who called you then? Who asked you to come?

vii.

Der Mond hat eine schwere Klag'   erhoben
the moon has a   grave   complaint raised

Und vor   dem Herrn die Sache kund   gemacht;
and before the Lord the thing known made

Er wolle nicht mehr stehn   am   himmel droben,
he wants not more to stand in the sky   there above

Du habest ihn um seinen Glanz   gebracht.
you have him – his   splendour made away with

Als er zuletzt   das Sternenheer gezählt,
as he the last time the star-host   counted

Da   hab' es an der vollen Zahl gefehlt;
there has it in the full   count been missing

vii.

The moon has made a grave complaint, and made it known to the Lord; no longer will he stand up there in the sky, for you have robbed him of his splendour. When last he counted the host of stars, the number was not complete: from the loveliest you have stolen two: those two eyes there that have blinded me.

Zwei von den schönsten   habest du entwendet:
two of the most beautiful have   you stolen

Die beiden Augen dort, die   mich verblendet.
the both eyes   there that me   dazzled

viii.   viii.

Nun lass uns Frieden schliessen, liebstes Leben,   Now, my dearest life, let us make
now let us peace make   dearest life   peace – our feud has lasted far too
                                                        long. If you will not give way, then
Zu lang ist's schon,   dass wir in Fehde liegen.   I will yield to you – how could we
too long is it already that we in feud are   fight to the death? Kings and
                                                        princes, they make peace – should
Wenn du nicht willst,   will ich mich dir   ergeben;   lovers then not crave it? Princes
if   you not are willing will I   me to you yield   and soldiers, they make peace –
                                                        can then two lovers fail? Do you
Wie könnten wir uns   auf den Tod   bekriegen? think that what great men can do,
how could   we ourselves unto the death make war   two hearts that are content cannot
                                                        achieve?
Es schliessen Frieden Könige und Fürsten,
(it) make   peace   kings and princes

Und sollten Liebende nicht darnach dürsten?
and should lovers   not for it   crave

Es schliessen Frieden Fürsten und Soldaten,
(it) make   peace   princes and soldiers

Und sollt'es   zwei Verliebten wohl   missraten?
and should it two lovers   indeed fail to do

Meinst du, dass, was so   grossen   Herrn
think you that what such (for) great gentlemen
      gelingt,
      succeeds

Ein Paar zufriedner   Herzen nicht vollbringt?
a   pair of contented hearts not   achieve

ix.   ix.

Dass doch gemalt all' deine Reize   wären,   If only all your charms were
that yet painted all your charms were   painted in a portrait that a pagan
                                                        prince would find! Great gifts he
Und dann der Heidenfürst   dsas Bildnis fände.   would bestow on you, and lay his
and then the pagan-prince the portrait would find   crown in your hands. His whole
                                                        kingdom, to its farthest ends
Er würde dir   ein gross' Geschenk verehren,   would be converted to the one
he would to you a   great gift   bestow   true faith. Throughout the land it
                                                        would be proclaimed: everyone
Und legte   seine Kron' in deine Hände.
and would lay his crown in your hands

Zum rechten Glauben müsst' sich
to the right faith would have to himself
  bekehren
  be converted

Sein ganzes Reich, bis an sein fern'stes Ende.
his whole kingdom even to its furthest end

Im ganzen Lande würd' es ausgeschrieben,
in the whole land would be it proclaimed

Christ soll ein jeder werden und dich lieben.
Christian shall everyone become and you love

Ein jeder Heide flugs bekehrte sich
– every – heathen at once would convert himself

Und würd' ein guter Christ und liebte
and would become a good Christian and would love
  dich.
  you

shall be a Christian, and will adore you! Everyone at once would be converted, become good Christians, and would worship you.

x.

Du denkst mit einem Fädchen mich zu fangen,
you think with a little thread me to catch

Mit einem Blick schon mich verliebt zu machen?
with one glance even me in love to make

Ich fing schon andre, die sich höher
I caught already others who themselves higher
  schwangen,
  soared

Du darfst mir ja nicht trau'n, siehst du mich lachen.
you must me indeed not trust see you me laugh

Schon andre fing ich, glaub' es sicherlich.
already others caught I believe it certainly

Ich bin verliebt, doch eben nicht in dich.
I am in love but just not in you

x.

You think you can catch me with a tiny thread, and make me fall in love, with just one glance? Already I've caught others who aimed higher. You really shouldn't trust me, when you see me laugh! I've certainly caught others, do believe me. I am in love – but not with you!

xi.

Wie lange schon war immer mein Verlangen:
how long already was always my yearning

Ach, wäre doch ein Musikus mir gut!
ah were but a musician to me kind

Nun liess der Herr mich meinen Wunsch erlangen
now let the Lord me my wish attain

xi.

How long have I yearned to be loved by a musician! Now the Lord has granted me my wish, and has sent me one, all pink and white as milk. And here he comes with gentle mien, and bows his head and plays the violin.

Und schickt mir einen, ganz wie Milch und Blut.
and sends me one   just like milk and blood

Da   kommt er eben her   mit sanfter Miene,
there comes he just here with gentle mien

Und senkt   den Kopf und spielt die Violine.
and lowers the head and plays the violin

xii.

Nein, junger Herr, so treibt   man's nicht, fürwahr;
no   young sir   so carries on one it not   in truth

Man sorgt   dafür, sich   schicklich zu betragen.
one takes care of it   oneself properly to behave

Für alltags   bin ich gut   genug, nicht wahr?
for every day am I   good enough not   true

Doch bessre suchst du   dir   an Feiertagen.
yet   better seek you to you on festive days

Nein, junger Herr, wirst du so weiter   sünd'gen,
no   young sir   will you so further sin

Wird dir   den Dienst dein Alltagsliebchen
will to you the post   your everyday sweetheart
   künd'gen.
   give notice to

xii.

Oh no, young sir, this really won't
do – one must try and behave;
in a proper manner! I'm good
enough for weekdays, but on
Feast days you seek elsewhere.
Oh no, young sir, if you go on like
this, your everyday love'll give in
her notice!

xiii.

Hoffärtig seid Ihr, schönes Kind, und geht
haughty are you pretty child and go

Mit Euren Freiern um   auf stolzem Fuss.
with your   suitors about on proud foot

Spricht man Euch an, kaum dass Ihr Rede steht,
speaks one you to hardly that you – answer –

Als kostet'   Euch zuviel   ein holder   Gruss.
as would cost you too much a   pleasant greeting

Bist keines Alexanders   Töchterlein,
are no   Alexander's (little) daughter

Kein Königreich wird deine Mitgift sein,
no   kingdom will your dowry be

Und willst du   nicht das Gold, so nimm das Zinn;
and want you not the gold so take the tin

Willst du nicht Liebe, nimm   Verachtung hin.
want you not love   put up with contempt –

xiii.

You are so proud, my fine one, so
high and mighty with your suitors!
If one speaks to you, you hardly
answer, as if a pleasant greeting
cost too much. You're no
Alexander's daughter – you'll have
no kingdom for your dowry. If you
don't want gold, take tin instead!
If you don't want love, then take
contempt!

xiv.

Geselle, woll'n wir uns in Kutten hüllen,
brother shall we us in cowls wrap

Die Welt dem   lassen, den   sie mag ergötzen?
the world to him leave whom she may please

Dann pochen wir an Tür um   Tür im Stillen:
then knock we on door after door – on the quiet –

'Gebt einem armen Mönch um Jesu willen.'
give to a poor monk for Jesus sake

– O lieber Pater, du musst später kommen,
  O dear father you must later come

Wenn aus   dem Often wird das Brot genommen.
when out of the oven is   the bread taken

O lieber Pater, komm nur später wieder,
O dear father come just later again

Ein Töchterlein   von mir   liegt krank darnieder.
a   little daughter of mine lies ill   –

– Und ist sie krank, so lass mich zu ihr gehen,
  and is she ill   so let me to her go

Dass sie nicht etwa   sterbe   unversehen.
that she not perhaps might die unexpectedly

Und ist sie krank, so lass mich nach ihr schauen,
and is she ill   so let me at   her have a look

Dass sie mir   ihre Beichte   mag vertrauen.
that she to me her confession may confide

Schliesst Tür und Fenster, dass uns keiner   störe,
shut   door and window that us no one might disturb

Wenn ich des   armen Kindes Beichte   höre!
when I   of the poor   child   confession hear

Come, brother, let us put on monks' robes, and leave the world to those who can enjoy it! Then we will steal from door to door, and knock, 'Give alms to a poor monk for Jesus' sake!' 'O you must come later, dear father, when the bread is taken from the oven. O come back later, dear father, for my little daughter lies sick!' 'But if she is sick, let me go to her, for she may suddenly die! If she is sick, then let me see her, that she may confess to me – and close the door and window, so no one disturbs us as I hear the poor child's confession!'

xv.

Mein Liebster   ist so klein, dass ohne   Bücken
my   sweetheart is so small that without stooping

Er mir   das Zimmer fegt   mit seinen Locken.
he (for) me the room   sweeps with his   locks

Als   er ins   Gärtlein   ging, Jasmin zu
when he into the (little) garden went jasmine to
    pflücken,
    gather

My sweetheart is so small, that even without stooping he sweeps the room with his hair. When he went into the garden to gather jasmine, he was badly frightened by a snail. He went indoors, and sat down to get his breath, but a fly knocked him head over heels. And when he stepped up to my

Ist er vor einer Schnecke sehr erschrocken.
is he by a   snail   very frightened

Dann setzt' er sich   ins   Haus um   zu
then put he himself into the house in order to
    verschnaufen,
    recover breath

Da warf ihn eine Fliege übern   Haufen;
then threw him a   fly   (over in a heap)

Und als   er hintrat   an mein Fensterlein,
and when he stepped up to my (little) window

Stiess   eine Bremse ihm den Schädel ein.
knocked a   horsefly him the skull   into

Verwünscht sei'n alle Fliegen, Schnaken, Bremsen
cursed   be   all flies   gnats   horseflies

Und wer ein Schätzchen   hat aus den Maremmen!
and who a   little sweetheart has from the Maremma

Verwünscht sei'n alle Fliegen, Schnaken, Mücken
cursed   be   all flies , gnats   midges

Und wer sich,   wenn er küsst, so tief muss bücken!
and who (himself) when he kisses so deep must stoop

window, a horsefly bumped into his head. A curse on all flies and gnats, and all those with sweethearts from Maremma! A curse on all flies and midges – and all who must stoop so low to kiss!

xvi.

Ihr jungen Leute, die ihr zieht ins   Feld,
you young people who you march into the field

Auf meinen Liebsten sollt   ihr Achtung geben.
to my   dearest should you attention give

Sorgt,   dass er tapfer sich   im   Feuer hält;
take care that he bravely himself in the fire   holds

Er war noch nie   im   Kriege all sein Leben.
he was as yet never in the war   all his life

Lass nie ihn unter freiem Himmel schlafen;
let never him under open sky   sleep

Er ist so zart,   es möchte sich   bestrafen.
he is so delicate it might (itself) be punishing

Lasst mir   ihn ja   nicht schlafen unterm
let   (to me) him certainly not   sleep   under the
    Mond;
    moon

Er ginge   drauf, er ist's ja   nicht gewohnt.
he might perish then he is it really not   used

xvi.

You young lads marching off to war, take care of my sweetheart! See that he's brave under fire – he was never in his life in a battle! Don't let him sleep in the open – he's so delicate, he might catch his death! On no account let him sleep under the moon – he's not used to it, and might catch his death.

xvii.

Und willst du   deinen Liebsten sterben sehen,
and want you your   dearest die   to see

So trage nicht dein Haar gelockt, du Holde.
so wear not   your hair curled you lovely one

Lass von den Schultern frei   sie   niederwehen;
let from the shoulders freely them flow

Wie Fäden sehn sie   aus von purem Golde.
like threads look they – of pure gold

Wie goldne Fäden, die der Wind bewegt,
like golden threads that the wind moves

Shön sind die Haare, schön ist, die sie   trägt!
lovely are the hairs   lovely is who them wears

Goldfäden,   Seidenfäden   ungezählt –
gold-threads silken-threads uncounted

Schön sind die Haare, schön ist, die sie   strählt!
lovely are the hairs   lovely is who them combs

xvii.

And if you would see your sweetheart die of love, my fair one, do not bind up your hair! Let the strands about flow freely round your shoulders, like threads of pure gold, stirred by the breeze. Your hair is lovely as she whom it crowns. Threads gold and silken, threads without number – your hair is beautiful, as she who combs it!

xviii.

Heb' auf dein blondes Haupt und schlafe nicht,
lift up your fair   head and sleep not

Und lass dich   ja   vom   Schlummer nicht
and let yourself certainly from the slumber   not
betören.
be bemused

Ich sage dir   vier Worte von Gewicht,
I   say to you four sayings of weight

Von denen darfst du keines   überhören.
of   which must you not one miss

Das erste: dass um dich mein Herze bricht,
the first that for you my   heart is breaking

Das zweite: dir   nur will ich angehören,
the second to you only want I   to belong

Das dritte: dass ich dir   mein Heil   befehle,
the third that I   to you my   well-being entrust

Das letzte: dich allein liebt meine Seele.
the last   you alone loves my   soul

xviii.

Raise your fair head, and sleep no more – let not slumber bemuse you! I have four weighty things to say, and not one must you miss. The first: for you my heart is breaking; the second: to you alone do I belong; the third: to you I entrust my whole well-being; and the last: my soul loves you alone.

xix.

Wir haben beide lange Zeit geschwiegen,
we have both long time been silent

Auf   einmal kam uns   nun die Sprache wieder.
– all at once – came to us now the speech again

Die Engel, die   herab vom   Himmel fliegen,
the angels who down from the heaven fly

Sie   brachten nach dem Krieg den Frieden wieder.
they brought after the war the peace again

Die Engel Gottes   sind herabgeflogen,
the angels of God are flown down

Mit ihnen ist der Frieden eingezogen.
with them is the peace   moved in

Die Liebesengel   kamen über Nacht
the love's-angels came over-night

Und haben Frieden meiner Brust   gebracht.
and have peace   to my breast brought

xix.

For a long while we were silent,
then all at once our speech
returned. Angels flew down from
heaven and after our warfare
brought peace again. God's angels
flew down and with them came
peace. Love's angels in the night
brought peace to my heart.

xx.

Mein Liebster singt am   Hus   im   Mondenscheine,
my   dearest sings by the house in the moonlight

Und ich muss lauschend hier im   Bette liegen.
and I   much listening here in the bed lie

Weg von der Mutter wend' ich mich   und weine,
away from the mother turn I   myself and weep

Blut   sind die Tränen, die   mir   nicht versiegen.
blood are the tears   which to me not run dry

Den breiten Strom am   Bett hab' ich geweint,
the broad stream by the bed have I   wept

Weiss nicht vor Tränen, ob der Morgen   scheint.
know not   for tears   if the morning appears

Den breiten Strom am   Bett weint' ich vor Sehnen;
the broad stream by the bed wept I   for longing

Blind haben mich gemacht die blut'gen Tränen.
blind have me   made   the bloody tears

xx.

My beloved sings by the house in
the moonlight, and I must lie
listening here in my bed. I turn
away from my mother, and weep;
the tears are my blood that I
cannot stem. I have wept a broad
stream of them by my bed; I am
blinded by tears, and cannot see
if it is day. In my longing I have
wept a broad stream by my bed;
the tears of my blood have blinded
me.

xxi.

Man sagt mir, deine Mutter woll' es nicht;
one told me your mother wants it not

So bleibe weg, mein Schatz,   tu'   ihr   den
so stay away my sweetheart carry out (to her) the
     Willen.
     wish

Ach Liebster, nein! tu   ihr   den Willen nicht,
an dearest no   carry out (to her) the wish not

Besuch' mich doch,   tu's ihr zum   Trotz, im stillen!
visit   me yes (do) do it her to the spite   – secretly –

Nein, mein Geliebter, folg'   ihr nimmermehr,
no   my beloved listen to her never more

Tu's ihr zum   Trotz, komm öfter   als   bisher!
do it her to the spite   come oftener than hitherto

Nein, höre   nicht auf sie, was   sie auch sage;
no   listen not to her what she ever might say

Tu's ihr zum   Trotz, mein Leib, komm alle   Tage!
do it her to the spite   my   love come every day

They tell me your mother disapproves; so stay away, beloved, and do as she bids! Oh no, dearest, no! Do not do as she bids – defy her, and come here, but secretly! No, my beloved, don't obey her any more – to spite her come more often, whatever she may say. Just do it, my dearest, and come every day!

xxii.

Ein Ständchen Euch   zu bringen kam ich her,
a   serenade to you to bring   came I   here

Wenn es dem   Herrn   vom   Haus nicht ungelegen.
if   it to the master of the house not   unwelcome

Ihr habt ein schönes Töchterlein.   Es wär'
you have a   pretty (little) daughter it were

Wohl   gut, sie nicht zu streng im   Haus zu
perhaps good her not   too strictly in the house to
     hegen.
     enclose

Und liegt sie schon   im   Bett, so bitt' ich sehr,
and lies she already in the bed so beg I   very much

Tut es zu wissen ihr von meinetwegen,
(let) it to know her for my sake

Dass ihr Getreuer hier vorbeigekommen,
that her true love here passed by

I have come to sing you a serenade – if the master of the house does not object. You have a pretty daughter; it would be as well if you were less strict in keeping her in. And if she is now in bed, then tell her that her true love did pass by; that he thinks of her day and night, and for twenty-four hours each day, he misses her for twenty-five.

Der Tag und Nacht sie in den Sinn genommen,
who day and night her in the mind (had)

Und dass am   Tag, der   vierundzwanzig zählt,
and that in the day which twenty-four   numbers

Sie fünfundzwanzig Stunden lang mir   fehlt.
she twenty-five   hours   long to me is missing

xxiii.

Was für   ein Lied soll dir   gesungen werden,
what kind of a song shall to you sung   be

Das deiner würdig sei? Wo   find' ich's nur?
that of you worthy be wher- find I it   ever

Am liebsten   grüb' ich es tief aus   der Erden,
– preferably – would dig I   it deep out of the earth

Gesungen noch   von keiner Kreatur.
sung   as yet by no   creature

Ein Lied, das weder Mann noch Weib   bis heute
a   song that neither man   nor woman till today

Hört' oder sang, selbst nicht die ält'sten`Leute.
heard or   sang even not   the oldest people

xxiii.

What kind of song can I sing that is worthy of you? Wherever can I find it? I should most like to dig it from deep in the earth, as yet unsung by any creature; a song that no man or woman has ever heard or sung until today – not even the very oldest one.

xxiv.

Ich esse nun mein Brot   nicht trocken mehr,
I   eat now my bread not   dry   (any) more

Ein Dorn ist mir   im   Fusse stecken   blieben.
a   thorn is to me in the foot (sticking) remained

Umsonst nach rechts und links blick' ich umher,
in vain to   right and left look I   around

Und keinen find' ich, der mich möchte lieben.
and no one find I   who me   might love

Wenn's doch   auch nur ein altes Männlein wäre,
if it   indeed even only an old little man might be

Das mir erzeigt' ein wenig Lieb' und Ehre.
who me showed a   little love and respect

Ich meine nämlich, so ein wohlgestalter,
I   mean of course so a   well-built

Ehrbarer   Greis,   etwa von meinem Alter.
respectable old man about of my   age

xxiv.

Dry bread no longer is enough for me; a thorn sticks in my flesh. I look around to right and left, and find no one to love me. If there were just one little old man who showed me some love and respect! I mean, of course, an old, upstanding man about my age. I mean, to be quite frank, a little old man about fourteen.

Ich meine, um   mich   ganz zu offenbaren,
I   mean so as myself quite to reveal

Ein altes Männlein so von vierzehn Jahren.
an old little man so of   fourteen years

xxv.

Mein Liebster   hat zu Tische mich geladen
my   sweetheart has to dinner me   invited

Und hatte doch kein Haus mich zu empfangen,
and had yet no   house me   to receive

Nicht Holz noch Herd   zum   Kochen und zum
not   wood nor hearth to the cooking and to the
    Braten,
    roasting

Der Hafen   auch war längst   entzwei gegangen.
the earthen pot even was long since in two gone

An einem Fässchen   Wein gebrach es auch,
of a   (little) cask wine (of) it also

Und Gläser hat er gar nicht im   Gebrauch;
and glasses has he at all not in the use

Der Tisch war schmal, das Tafeltuch   nicht besser,
the table was narrow the table-cloth not   better

Das Brot   steinhart   und völlig   stumpf das Messer.
the bread stone-hard and completely blunt the knife

xxvi.

Ich liess mir   sagen und mir   ward erzählt,
I   let to me say and to me was told

Der schöne   Toni hungre sich   zu Tode;
the beautiful Toni starves himself to death

Seit ihn so überaus   die Liebe quält,
since him so exceedingly the love torments

Nimmt er auf einen Backzahn sieben Brote.
takes he for one   molar   seven loaves

Nach Tisch, damit er die Verdauung stählt,
after meal so that he he the digestion steels

Verspeist er eine Wurst   und sieben Brote,
consumes he a   sausage and seven loaves

xxv.

My sweetheart asked me to dine,
and yet he had no house – no
wood, no hearth to boil and bake,
and even the pot had long been in
two! There was no cask of wine,
no glasses at all to fill; the table
was mean, the cloth no better; the
bread like stone and the knife
completely blunt!

xxvi.

I asked, and they told me, that
handsome Toni starves himself to
death. Since he suffered so from
love, he eats just seven loaves per
tooth. After a meal, to strengthen
his digestion, he consumes a
sausage and seven more loaves,
and if Tonina doesn't ease his
pangs, there'll soon be famine and
inflation!

Und lindert nicht Tonina seine Pein,
and eases not Tonina his pain

Bricht nächstens Hungersnot und Teurung ein.
sets   very soon famine   and inflation in

xxvii.

Schon streckt' ich aus im   Bett die müden Glieder,
already stretched I   out in the bed the weary limbs

Da tritt   dein Bildnis vor   mich hin, du Traute.
when appears your image before me   there you beloved

Gleich spring' ich auf, fahr' in   die Schuhe wieder
at once spring I   up slip into the shoes again

Und wandre durch   die Stadt mit   meiner Laute.
and wander through the town with my   lute

Ich sing' und spiele, dass die Strasse schallt;
I   sing and play   that the street resounds

So manche   lauscht – vorüber bin ich bald.
so many a one listens   gone by am I   soon

So manches Mädchen hat mein Lied gerührt,
so many a girl   has my   song touched

Indes der Wind schon   Sang und Kland entführt.
while the wind already song and sound carries off

xxvii.

As I stretched my weary limbs in bed, your image, darling, rose before me. At once I spring up, put on my shoes again, and wander through the town with my lute. The street resounds as I sing and play; many listen, but soon I am gone. Many a girl is touched by my song, as the wind bears the singing and playing away.

xxviii.

Du sagst mir, dass ich keine Fürstin sei;
you tell me that I no   princess be

Auch du bist nicht auf Spaniens Thron entsprossen.
also you are not on Spain's throne sprung up

Nein, Bester,   stehst du auf bei Hahnenschrei,
no   my dear fellow get   you up at cock-crow

Fährst du aufs   Feld und nicht in Staatskarossen.
ride   you to the field and not   in state-coaches

Du spottest mein um meine Niedrigkeit,
you jeer at me for my   lowliness

Doch Armut tut   dem Adel   nichts zuleid.
but poverty does the nobility nothing to harm

xxviii.

You tell me I'm no princess, but neither did you spring from the Spanish throne! No, my lad, when you get up at cock-crow, you go off to the fields – and in no state coach! You jeer at my low station, but even nobles are not shamed by poverty. You jeer because I have no crown or coat of arms – but you yourself just ride Shanks's pony!

Du spottest, dass mir   Krone fehlt   und
you mock   that to me crown is wanting and
  Wappen,
   coat of arms

Und fährst doch selber   nur mit Schusters Rappen.
and ride   yet   yourself only with Shanks's pony

   xxix.   xxix.

Wohl kenn' ich Euern Stand, der   nicht gering.   I know full well your station is no
well   know I   your   station which not   inferior   mean one; you need not have
                                                       stooped so low to love one so
Ihr   brauchtet nicht so tief herabzusteigen,   humble and poor, for the fairest of
you need   not   so low desend   the fair bow down before you. You
                                                       conquer so easily the most
Zu lieben solch ein arm und niedrig Ding,   handsome men, so I know you
to love   such a   poor and humble thing   only trifle with me. You mock me
                                                       – they tried to warn me. But you
Da sich   vor   Euch die Allerschönsten neigen. are so lovely! Who could be angry
as themselves before you the fairest of all bow down   with you?

Die schönsten   Männer leicht besiegtet Ihr,
the most handsome men   easily conquer you

Drum   weiss ich wohl, Ihr treibt nur Spiel mit mir.
therefore know I   well you make only fun of me

Ihr spottet mein,   man hat mich warnen wollen,
you mock (of) me one has me to warn (wanted)

Doch ach, Ihr seid so schön! Wer kann Euch grollen?
but   ah   you are so lovely who can   you   be cross with

   xxx.   xxx.

Lass sie nur gehn, die so die Stolze   spielt,   Let her go then, if she acts so
let   her just go   who so the haughty one acts   haughtily, the fairest flower in the
                                                         field! You can see what her bright
Das Wunderkräutlein   aus   dem Blumenfeld.   eyes are seeking, for every day
the little wonder-plant from the   flower-field   another takes her fancy. She
                                                         carries on like Tuscany's river,
Man sieht, wohin   ihr blankes Auge zielt,   that every mountain stream must
one sees whither her shining eye   aims   follow. It seems to me, she carries
                                                         on like the Arno; one moment she
Da Tag um Tag ein andrer ihr gefällt.   has many suitors – the next, not
as day by day another   her pleases   one.

Sie treibt   es grade wie Toscanas   Fluss,
she carries on it just   like Tuscany's river

Dem jedes Berggewässer   folgen muss.
which any mountain-waters follow must

Sie treibt   es wie der Arno, will   mir   scheinen:
she carries on it like the Arno (does) to me seem

Bald hat sie viel   Bewerber, bald nicht einen.
now has she many suitors   now not one

xxxi.

Wie soll   ich fröhlich sein und lachen gar,
how shall I   happy be and laugh even

Da   du   mir   immer zürnest   unverhohlen?
when you to me always are angry openly

Du kommst nur einmal alle   hundert Jahr,
you come   only once every hundred years

Und dann, als hätte man dir's   anbefohlen.
and then as had one to you it ordered

Was kommst du, wenn's die Deinen ungern   sehn?
why come   you when it the yours are sorry to see

Gib frei mein Herz, dann magst du weitergehn.
set free my heart then may you move on

Daheim mit deinen Leuten leb' in Frieden,
at home with your   people live in peace

Denn was der Himmel will, geschieht   hienieden.
for   what the heaven wills comes to pass here below

Halt Frieden mit den Deinigen zu Haus,
keep peace with the yours   at home

Denn was der Himmel will,   das bleibt   nicht
for   what the heaven desires that fails to appear not
aus.
—

xxxi.

How can I be merry and laughing, when you are always so openly vexed with me? You come but once in a hundred years, and then as if it were by order. Why do you come if your family disapproves? Set my heart free, and then go your way. Live at home with your family in peace – what heaven ordains will come to pass. Keep the peace with your family at home – for what heaven ordains, will come to be.

xxxii.

Was soll   der Zorn, mein Schatz, der dich erhitzt?
what means the rage my   treasure that you inflames

Ich bin mir   keiner Sünde ja   bewusst.
I   am (to me) of no sin   indeed conscious

Ach, lieber nimm ein Messer wohlgespitzt
oh rather take a knife well-sharpened

Und tritt zu mir, durchbohre mir die Brust.
and come to me piece   (me) the breast

xxxii.

Why this rage, my love, that so inflames you? I know of no wrong that I have done. Oh, rather take a sharpened knife, and come and plunge it in my breast! And if a knife is of no avail, then take a sword, and let the fountain of my blood well up to heaven! And if a sword is no use, take a dagger of steel, and let my blood wash away all my torment!

Und taugt ein Messer nicht, so nimm ein Schwert,
and serves a knife not so take a sword

Dass meines Blutes Quell   gen Himmel fährt.
that of my blood fountain to heaven ascends

Und taugt ein Schwert nicht, nimm des   Dolches Stahl
and serves a sword not take of the dagger steel

Und wasch' in meinem Blut   all meine Qual.
and wash in my   blood all my   torment

xxxiii.

Sterb' ich, so hüllt in Blumen meine Glieder;
die I so cover in flowers my   limbs

Ich wünsche nicht, dass ihr ein Grab mir grabt.
I wish   not that you a grave me dig

Genüber jenen Mauern legt mich nieder,
opposite these walls   lay me down

Wo   ihr so manchmal mich gesehen habt.
where you so sometimes me   seen   have

Dort legt mich hin,   in Regen oder Wind;
there lay me down in rain or wind

Gern sterb' ich, ist's um dich, geliebtes Kind.
gladly die I   is it for you beloved child

Dort legt mich hin   in Sonnenschein und Regen;
there lay me down in sunshine   and rain

Ich sterbe lieblich, sterb' ich deinetwegen.
I die   sweetly die I because of you

xxxiii.

If I should die, then cover my
limbs with flowers! I do not wish
that you should dig a grave for me.
Lay me down beside those walls,
where you have so often seen me.
There let me be laid in rain and
wind, for gladly I would die for
you, dear love. There let me be
laid in sunshine and rain: dying for
me is sweet, if I am dying for you!

xxxiv.

Und steht Ihr früh am   Morgen auf vom   Bette,
and get you early in the morning up from the bed

Scheucht Ihr vom   Himmel alle Wolken fort,
scare   you from the sky   all clouds away

Die Sonne lockt Ihr auf die Berge   dort,
the sun   lure you on the mountains there

Und Engelein   erscheinen um die Wette
and little angels appear   in the rivalry

Und bringen Schuh und Kleider Euch   sofort.
and bring shoe and clothes to you at once

xxxiv.

And when you rise early from your
bed, you chase away all clouds
from the sky; you lure the sun to
the mountains, and cherubs vie
with each other to bring your
shoes and clothes. Then, when
you go to Mass, all men are drawn
to follow you, and when you
approach the sanctuary the very
lamps are kindled by your glance.
You take holy water and moisten
your brow, and you cross yourself,

Dann, wenn Ihr ausgeht in die heil'ge Mette,
then when you go out   the holy   Mass

So zieht Ihr alle Menschen mit Euch fort,
so draw you all people   with you   along

Und wenn Ihr naht der benedeiten Stätte,
and when you near the blessed   place

So zündet Euer Blick die Lampen an.
so lights your glance the lamps   up

Weihwasser nehmt Ihr, macht des   Kreuzes Zeichen
holy water take   you make of the cross   sign

Und netzet   Eure weisse Stirn sodann
and moisten your white brow then

Und neiget Euch   und beugt die Knie ingleichen –
and bow (yourself) and bend the knee also

O wie holdselig   steht   Euch alles   an!
O how most sweetly becomes you everything –

Wie hold   und selig   hat Euch Gott begabt,
how graciously and blessedly has you   God endowed

Die Ihr der   Schönheit Kron' empfangen habt!
who you of the beauty   crown received   have

Wie hold   und selig   wandelt Ihr im   Leben;
how graciously and blessedly go   you in (the) life

Der   Schönheit Palme ward an Euch gegeben.
of (the) beauty   palm was to you   given

as you bow your head and kneel. With what sweetness it all becomes you! What grace and blessings has God bestowed on you – you, who received beauty's crown! You go through life so graciously blessed – you to whom beauty's palm was given!

xxxv.

Benedeit   die sel'ge Mutter,
blessed be the blessed mother

Die so lieblich dich geboren,
who so sweetly you delivered

So an Schönheit auserkoren,
so in beauty   most favoured

Meine Sehnsucht fliegt dir zu!
my   longing   flies you to

Du so lieblich von Gebärden,
you so lovely of gesture

Du die Holdeste   der   Erden,
you the most gracious of the earth

XXXV.

Blessed be the mother, who with joy so sweetly bore you! You, so favoured with such beauty – how my longing flies to you!

You, so sweet of gesture, you, most gracious one on earth – how sweet and blessed are you!

Du mein Kleinod, meine Wonne,
you my treasure my   delight

Süsse, benedeit bist du!
sweet blessed are you

Wenn ich aus der Ferne schmachte
when I   from – afar – languish

Und betrachte deine Schöne,
and behold your beauty

Siehe wie ich beb'   und stöhne,
see   how I   quiver and groan

Dass ich kaum es bergen kann!
that I   hardly it hide   can

Und in meiner Brust gewaltsam
and in my   breast violently

Fühl' ich Flammen sich   empören,
feel I   flames   (themselves) rage

Die den Frieden mir   zerstören,
that the peace to me destroy

Ach, der Wahnsinn fasst   mich an!
ah   the madness seizes me –

When far from you I languish,
reflecting on your beauty – see
how I tremble, how I sigh, for I
hardly can conceal it!

And in my breast I feel the flames
that rage within destroy my peace,
and a madness seizes me!

xxxvi.

Wenn du, mein Liebster, steigst   zum   Himmel auf,
when you my   dearest ascend to the heaven –

Trag' ich mein Herz dir in der Hand entgegen.
carry I   my   heart you in the hand to

So liebevoll umarmst du mich darauf,
so lovingly embrace you me   thereupon

Dann woll'n wir uns dem   Herrn zu Füssen legen.
then will   we us to the Lord at feet   lay

Und sieht der Herrgott   uns're Liebesschmerzen,
and sees the Lord God our   love's-sorrows

Macht er ein Herz aus   zwei verliebten Herzen,
makes he one heart out of two in love   hearts

Zu einem Herzen fügt er zwei zusammen,
to one   heart joins he two together

Im   Paradies, umglänzt   von Himmelsflammen.
in the Paradise shone around by heaven's-flames

xxxvi.

When you, my beloved, go up to
heaven, I will meet you, my heart
in my hand. Then you will
lovingly embrace me, and we will
lay ourselves at the feet of the
Lord. And when He sees the
anguish of our love, He will make
our two loving hearts as one; the
Lord God will join our two hearts
as one in Paradise, in the glorious
radiance of Heaven.

xxxvii

Wie viele Zeit verlor ich, dich zu lieben!
how much time lost   I   you to love

Hätt' ich doch Gott geliebt in all der   Zeit.
had I   but God loved in all of the time

Ein Platz im   Paradies wär'   mir verschrieben,
a   place in the Paradise would be to me assigned

Ein Heil'ger sässe   dann an meiner Seit'.
a   saint   would sit then at my   side

Und weil   ich dich geliebt, schön frisch Gesicht,
and because I you loved lovely fresh face

Verscherzt' ich mir des   Paradieses Licht,
lost foolishly I   to me of the Paradise light

Und weil   ich dich geliebt, schön Veigelein,
and because I you loved lovely little bird

Komm' ich nun nicht ins   Paradies hinein.
come I   now not in the Paradise in there

How much time has been wasted
in loving you! If I had loved God
in all this time, a place in Heaven
would now be mine; with a saint
to sit at my side. But because I
loved you and your lovely young
face, I have foolishly lost the light
of Paradise; and because it is you I
have loved, little bird, I now shall
never enter there.

xxxviii.

Wenn du mich mit den Augen streifst und lachst,
when you me   with the eyes   brush and laugh

Sie   senkst und neigst das Kinn zum Busen dann,
them lower and bow the chin to the bosom then

Bitt' ich, dass du mir erst ein Zeichen machst,
beg I   that you me first a sign   make

Damit ich doch   mein Herz auch bänd'gen kann,
so that I   indeed my heart also subdue can

Dass ich mein Herz mag bänd'gen, zahm und still,
that I   my heart may subdue   tame and still

Wenn es vor grosser Liebe springen will,
when it for great love to leap wants

Dass ich mein Herz mag halten in der Brust,
that I   my heart may keep in the breast

Wenn es ausbrechen   will   vor grosser Lust.
when it to burst forth wants for great joy

When you caress me with a glance
and laugh, lower your eyes, and
bow your head, I beg you for a
warning sign, that I may subdue
my heart, and keep it tame and
still, when it would leap for love so
great; that I may keep my heart
within my breast, when it would
burst forth for sheer joy!

xxxix.

Gesegnet sei das Grün und wer es trägt!
blessed be the green and who it wears

Ein grünes Kleid will ich mir   machen lassen.
a   green dress will I   to me make   let

Ein grünes Kleid trägt   auch die Frühlingsaue,
a   green dress wears too the spring-meadow

Grün kleidet sich   der Liebling meiner Augen.
green dresses himself the darling of my eyes

In Grün sich   kleiden ist der   Jäger Brauch,
in green himself to dress is of the hunter custom

Ein grünes Kleid trägt   mein Geliebter auch;
a   green dress wears my   loved one too

Das Grün steht   allen Dingen lieblich   an,
the green is becoming all   things charmingly to

Aus Grün wächst jede   schöne Frucht heran.
from green grows each lovely fruit   —

Blessed be green and all who wear it! A green dress I'll have made, for the meadows in spring wear green – like the darling of my eyes. Green is the colour that hunters wear, and my beloved dresses in green. Green is becoming to everything, and from green grows every sweet fruit.

xl.

O wär' dein Haus durchsichtig wie ein Glas,
O were your house transparent as a   glass

Mein Holder, wenn ich mich   vorüberstehle!
my   darling when I   myself steal by

Dann säh'   ich drinnen dich ohn'   Unterlass,
then would see I   inside you without ceasing

Wie blickt'   ich dann nach dir mit   ganzer Seele!
how would look I   then at   you with whole soul

Wie viele   Blicke schickte   mir dein Herz,
how many glances would send me your heart

Mehr als   da   Tropfen hat der Fluss im   März!
more than there drops   has the river in the March

Wie viele   Blicke schickt'   ich dir entgegen,
how many glances would send I   you towards

Mehr als   da   Tropfen niedersprühn im   Regen!
more than there drops   shower down in the rain

If only your house were transparent as glass, my love, when I steal by! Then I would always see you within – and would gaze at you with all my soul! And the looks that your heart would send in return – would be more than a river's drops in March! How many times I would look at you – more times than there are drops of falling rain.

xli.

Heut' nacht erhob ich mich   um Mitternacht,
– tonight – rose I   myself at   midnight

Da war mein Herz mir   heimlich fortgeschlichen.
then was my   heart to me secretly stolen away

Ich frug: Herz, wohin   stürmst du so mit Macht?
I   asked heart whither rage   you so with might

Es sprach: Nur Euch zu sehn, sei es entwichen.
it said   only you to see is it escaped

Nun sieh, wie muss es um   mein Lieben stehn:
now see how must it with my   loving stand

Mein Herz entweicht der Brust, um   dich zu sehn!
my   heart escapes   the breast so as you to see

Last night I rose at midnight, and
found my heart had stolen secretly
away. I asked: Where do you rush
so mightily, heart? It said it
escaped just to see you, so see just
how it stands with my love? To see
you my heart escapes from my
breast!

xlii.

Nicht länger kann ich singen, denn der Wind
not   longer can I sing   for the wind

Weht stark   und macht dem Atem was   zu
blows strongly and gives the breath somewhat to
    schaffen.
    work

Auch fürcht' ich, dass die Zeit umsonst   verrinnt.
also fear   I   that the time to no purpose runs away

Ja wär' ich sicher, ging'   ich jetzt nicht schlafen.
yes were I   sure   would go I   now not   sleep

Ja wüsst' ich was,   würd' ich nicht heimspazieren
yes knew I   something would I   not go home

Und einsam diese schöne Zeit verlieren.
and alone   this lovely time lose

No longer can I sing, for the wind
is strong and takes my breath
away. I fear, too, that I waste my
time. If I were only sure, I would
not go off and sleep; if I had but
one sign, I would not go home and
waste this lovely night alone.

xliii.

Schweig' einmal still, du garst'ger Schwätzer dort!
be silent for once –   you detestable babbler   there

Zum   Ekel ist mir dein verwünschtes Singen.
(– makes sick – me) your cursed   singing

Und triebst du es bis morgen   früh   so fort,
and carried you it till tomorrow morning so on

Be quiet there, you garrulous
wretch! I am sick of your cursed
singing, and even if you carried on
till the break of day, you wouldn't
come out with a single pleasing
song. Be quiet at once, and go off
to bed! I'd rather have a donkey's
serenade!

Doch würde dir   kein schmuckes Lied gelingen.
yet   would to you no   pretty   song succeed

Schweig' einmal   still und lege dich   aufs   Ohr!
be silent for once –   and lay yourself (on the ear)

Das Ständchen eines Esels   zög'   ich vor.
the serenade of a donkey would prefer I   –

xliv.   xliv.

O wüsstest du, wie viel   ich deinetwegen,
O if knew you how much I   because of you

Du falsche Renegatin, litt   zur   Nacht,
you false   renegade suffered at (the) night

Indes du im   verschlossnen Haus gelegen
while you in the locked   house (were) lying

Und ich die Zeit im   Freien zugebracht.
and I   the time in the open spent

Als Rosenwasser diente mir der Regen,
as rose-water served me the rain

Der Blitz   hat Liebesbotschaft mir   gebracht;
the lightning has love's-message to me brought

Ich habe Würfel mit dem Sturm gespielt,
I   have dice   with the storm played

Als unter deinem Dach ich Wache hielt.
as under your   roof I   watch kept

Mein Bett war unter deinem Dach bereitet,
my   bed was under your   roof made ready

Der Himmel lag als Decke   drauf gebreitet,
the sky   lay as blanket on it spread out

Die Schwelle deiner Tür, das war mein Kissen –
the threshold of your door that was my   pillow

Ich Ärmster,   ach, was hab' ich aussteh'n müssen!
I   poor wretch alas what have I   – endure had to –

If you only knew how much I've suffered each night because of you, false fickle one! While you were lying in your locked house, I was outside in the open, with rain as my rosewater, and lightning signalling love; I played at dice with the storm, as I kept watch beneath your eaves. I made my bed beneath your roof; with the sky and doorstep as blanket and pillow. O miserable of men – how much I've had to endure!

xlv.   xlv.

Verschling' der Abgrund meines Liebsten Hütte,
let engulf the abyss   of my lover   hovel

An ihrer Stelle schäum' ein See zur   Stunde.
in her   place foam   a lake in the hour

May my lover's hovel be engulfed by the earth, and a lake swirl there in its place! May the heavens rain bullets, and a serpent dwell in the

Bleikugeln soll der Himmel drüber schütten,
lead-bullets shall the sky over there pour

Und eine Schlange hause dort im Grunde.
and a serpent dwell there in the ground

Drin hause eine Schlange gift'ger Art,
therein let dwell a serpent of poisonous kind

Die ihn vergifte, der mir untreu ward.
who him would poison who to me untrue was

Drin hause eine Schlange, giftgeschwollen,
therein let dwell a serpent swollen with poison

Und bring' ihm Tod, der mich verraten wollen!
and bring to him death who me — means to betray —

earth! And let the serpent be poisonous, and poison the one who was untrue! Let the serpent swell up with venom, and to him, who would betray me, bring death!

xlvi.

Ich hab' in Penna einen Liebsten wohnen,
I have in Penna a lover (living)

In der Maremmeneb'ne einen andern,
in the Maremma plain one other

Einen im schönen Hafen von Ancona,
one in the lovely harbour of Ancona

Zum vierten muss ich nach Viterbo wandern;
to the fourth must I to Viterbo go

Ein andrer wohnt in Casentino dort,
one other lives in Casentino there

Der nächste lebt mit mir am selben Ort,
the next lives with me in the same place

Und wieder einen hab' ich in Magione,
and again one have I in Magione

Vier in La Fratta, zehn in Castiglione.
four in La Fratta ten in Castiglione

xlvi.

I have a lover who lives in Penna, another in the Maremma plain; one in the lovely port of Ancona, for the fourth I must go to Viterbo; another one lives in Casentino, the next one in my own town; I've yet another one in Magione – four in La Fratta – and in Castiglione, I've ten!

54. TRETET EIN, HOHER KRIEGER ENTER PROUD WARRIOR

54. ENTER, PROUD WARRIOR

Gottfried Keller

Tretet ein, hoher Krieger,
enter – proud warrior

Der sein Herz mir ergab!
who his heart to me yielded

Enter, proud warrior! You have given your heart to me! So lay down your scarlet cloak and golden spurs.

Legt den purpurnen Mantel
lay the crimson cloak

Und die Goldsporen   ab.
and the golden-spurs down

Spannt   das Ross   in den Pflug,
harness the steed to the plough

Meinem Vater zum   Gruss!
to my   father in (the) greeting

Die Schabrack   mit   dem Wappen
the saddle-cloth with the   coat-of-arms

Gibt 'nen Teppich meinem Fuss.
give a   carpet to my   foot

Harness your steed to the plough
in homage to my father, and your
saddle-cloth with its coat of arms
can be a rug for my feet.

Euer Schwertgriff muss   lassen
your sword-hilt must part with

Für mich Gold und Stein,
(to) me   gold and stone

Und die blitzende Klinge
and the flashing blade

Wird ein Schüreisen sein.
will a   poker   be

Your sword hilt must give me its
gold and precious stones, and its
shining blade can serve as a poker.

·Und die schneeweisse Feder
and the snow-white feather

Auf dem blutroten   Hut
on the blood-red cap

Ist zu 'nem kühlenden Wedel
is as a   cooling   fan

In der Sommerszeit   gut.
in the summer-time good

And the snow-white feather on
your blood-red cap will make a fan
that can cool me in summer.

Und der Marschalk muss lernen,
and the marshall   must learn

Wie man Weizenbrot   backt,
how one wheat-bread bakes

Wie man Wurst   und Gefüllsel
how one sausage and stuffing

Um   die Weihnachtszeit hackt.
round the Christmas-time chops

The marshall must learn how to
bake wheat-bread, and at
Christmas make sausages and
stuffing.

Nun befehlt   eure Seele
now commend your soul

Dem   heiligen Christ!
to the Holy   Christ

Euer Leib ist verkauft,
your body is sold

Wo   kein Erlösen   mehr ist!
where no   redeeming more is

And now commend your soul to
Christ our Lord! For your body is
sold, and cannot be redeemed!

55. MORGENSTIMMUNG
MORNING-MOOD

55. MORNING MOOD

Robert Reinick

Bald ist der   Nacht ein End' gemacht,
soon is of the night an end made

Schon   fühl' ich Morgenlüfte   wehen.
already feel I   morning-breezes blow

Der Herr, der spricht: 'Es werde   Licht!'
the Lord he says   it   let become light

Da   muss, was dunkel ist, vergehen.
then must what dark   is vanish

Soon the night will be at an end;
already I feel the fresh morning
breeze. The Lord He says, 'Let
there be light!' – that all that is
dark must vanish!

Vom   Himmelszelt   durch   alle Welt
from the Heaven's-vault through all world

Die Engel freudejauchzend   fliegen;
the angels shouting with joy fly

Der   Sonne Strahl durchflammt   das All.
of the sun   ray   flames through the universe

Herr, lass uns kämpfen, lass uns siegen!
Lord let us strive   let us conquer

Angels from Heaven's vaults fly
over the earth, singing in
exultation; and the Universe is
flooded with fiery flames. O Lord,
let us strive, let us conquer!

Gustav Mahler
(1860–1911)

1. LIEDER EINES
SONGS OF A
FAHRENDEN GESELLEN
– WAYFARER –

Gustav Mahler

1. SONGS OF A
WAYFARER

i.

i.

Wenn mein Schatz   Hochzeit macht,
when my   sweetheart wedding celebrates

The day my sweetheart weds will
be my saddest day. I will go in my
room, my little dark room, and
weep for my treasure, my dear
treasure!

Hab' ich meinen traurigen Tag!
have I   my   sad   day

Geh' ich in   mein Kämmerlein, dunkles Kämmerlein,
go   I   into my little room   dark   little room

Weine, Wein' um meinen Schatz,   um meinen lieben
weep   weep for my   sweetheart for my   dear
    Schatz!
    sweetheart

Blümlein   blau! Verdorre nicht!
little flower blue wither   not

Little blue flower, do not wither!
Little singing bird, on the green
heath – how beautiful is the world!
Tchk!

Vöglein   süss! Du singst auf grüner Heide!
little bird sweet you sing   on green heath

Ach! Wie ist die Welt   so schön!   Ziküth!
oh   how is the world so beautiful chirrup

Singet nicht! Blühet   nicht! Lenz   ist ja   vorbei!
sing   not   blossom not   spring is indeed over

Sing no more, bloom no more –
for spring is now past – all singing
is at an end. Each night when I go
to bed, I think of my grief.

Alles Singen ist nun aus!
all   singing is now ended

Des   Abends, wenn ich schlafen geh',
in the evening when I   to sleep go

Denk' ich an mein Leid! An mein Leide!
think I   of my   grief of my   grief

Fröhliche Hochzeit macht,
gladsome wedding celebrates

ii.

Ging   heut' Morgen über's   Feld,
walked this   morning over the field

Tau noch auf den Gräsern hing;
dew still   on the grasses hung

Sprach zu mir der lust'ge Fink:
spoke to me the merry finch

'Ei, du! Gelt? Guten Morgen! Ei, gelt?   Du!
hey you isn't it good morning oh isn't it you

Wird's nicht eine schöne   Welt? schöne   Welt?
is it   not   a   beautiful world beautiful world

Zink! Zink! Schön und flink!
chink chink fair   and bright

Wie mir doch   die Welt gefällt!'
how me indeed the world pleases

Auch die Glockenblum' am   Feld
also   the harebell   in the field

Hat mir lustig,   guter   Ding',
has me merrily – in high spirits –

Mit den Glöckchen klinge, kling,
with the little bells tinkle tinkle

Ihren Morgengruss   geschellt:
her   morning-greeting rung

'Wird's nicht ein schöne   Welt? schöne   Welt?
is it   not   a   beautiful world beautiful world

Kling! Kling! Schönes Ding!
tinkle tinkle beautiful thing

Wie mir doch   die Welt gefällt! Heia!'
how me indeed the world pleases hey ho

Und da   fing   im   Sonnenschein
and then began in the sunshine

Gleich   die Welt zu funkeln an;
at once the world to sparkle –

Alles,   alles   Ton und Farbe gewann im
everything everything tone and colour gained in the
    Sonnenschein!
    sunshine

Blum' und Vogel, gross und klein!
flower and bird   great and small

ii.

This morning I walked in the fields; dew still hung on the grass. The merry chaffinch called to me, 'Hey, you there! Good morning! – well, isn't it? You there, is the world not fair? Chink! Chink! Bright and fair! How I love the world!'

The harebell too in the field, in gay and happy mood, rang out her morning greetings on her little bells: Ding! Ding! 'Is the world not fair, fair? Ding! Ding! isn't it fair! How I love the world! Hey ho!'

And in the sunshine the world at once began to shine. Everything grew bright in the sun: flowers and birds, both great and small. 'Good day, good day! Is the world not fair? Hey, you there, isn't it? A fair world!'

'*Guten Tag, Guten Tag! Ist's nicht eine schöne   Welt?*
good day good day is it not a   beautiful world

Ei, du! Gelt? Schöne   Welt!
hey you isn't it beautiful world

Nun fängt   auch mein Glück   wohl   an?
now begins also my   happiness perhaps –

Now will my own happiness begin as well? Oh no, I believe that mine can never blossom!

Nein! Nein! Das ich mein', mir   nimmer blühen   kann!
no   no   that I think to me never blossom can

iii.

Ich hab' ein glühend Messer, ein Messer in meiner Brust.
I   have a burning knife   a   knife   in my   breast

iii.

I feel a knife burning within my breast, alas, alas! It cuts so deep into every joy and delight. Oh, what an evil guest it is, never still, never at rest by day or night, even when I sleep, alas, alas!

O weh! O weh!
O woe O woe

Das schneid't so tief   in jede Freud' und jede
that cuts   so deeply into every joy   and every
   Lust,   so tief!
   delight so deeply

Ach! was ist das für ein böser Gast!
ah   what is that for an evil guest

Nimmer hält   er Ruh', nimmer hält   er Rast,
never   keeps he still   never   takes he rest

Nicht bei Tag, nicht bei Nacht, wenn ich schlief!
not by day not by night when I   slept

O weh! O weh!
O alas O alas

Wenn ich in   den Himmel seh',
when I   into the sky   look

When I look up at the sky, I see two blue eyes, alas, alas! When I walk through the yellow corn fields, I see from afar her fair hair blowing in the wind, alas, alas!

Seh' ich zwei blaue Augen steh'n!
see I   two blue eyes (being) there

O weh! O weh!
O alas O alas

Wenn ich im   gelben Felde geh',
when I   in the yellow field walk

Seh' ich von fern das blonde Haar im   Winde weh'n!
see I   from afar the fair   hair in the wind blow

O weh! O weh!
O alas O alas

Wenn ich aus   dem Traum auffahr'
when I   from the dream start up

Und höre klingen ihr silbern Lachen,
and hear sound her silvery laugh

O weh! O weh!
O alas O alas

Ich wollt', ich läg'   auf der schwarzen Bahr'
I   wished I   might lie on the black   bier

Könnt nimmer die Augen aufmachen!
could never   the eyes   open

When I start up from a dream, and hear her silvery laugh, alas, alas! I wish I were lying in a black coffin, and my eyes would never open!

iv.

Die zwei blauen Augen von meinem Schatz,
the two blue   eyes   of   my   treasure

Die haben mich in   die weite Welt geschickt.
they have me into the wide world sent

Da   musst' ich Abschied nehmen vom
then had to I   parting to take from the
    allerliebsten   Platz!
    most loved of all place

O Augen blau! Warum habt ihr mich angeblickt?
O eyes   blue why   have you me   looked at

Nun hab' ich ewig   Leid und Grämen!
now have I   for ever pain and grieving

Ich bin ausgegangen in   stiller Nacht,
I   am gone out   into still night

In   stiller Nacht wohl   über die dunkle Heide.
into still night indeed over the dark   heath

Hat mir   niemand ade   gesagt, ade!
has to me no one   farewell said   farewell

Mein Gesell'   war Lieb' und Leide!
my   companion was love and grief

Auf der Strasse stand ein Lindenbaum,
on the road   stood a linden-tree

Da   hab' ich zum   erstenmal im   Schlaf geruht!
there have I   for the first time in the sleep rested

Unter dem Lindenbaum, der hat
under the linden tree   that has

Seine Blüten   über mich geschneit,
his   blossoms over me   snowed

My sweetheart's blue eyes have driven me out into the world, and so I bid farewell to the place I love the best. O blue eyes, why did you ever look at me? Now pain and grief will be with me for ever!

In the still of night I went over the dark heath. No one said farewell; my only companions were love and grief. By the road was a linden tree, and there for the first time I found rest and sleep.

The linden tree shed blossoms on me like snow, and I forgot what life can do – all, and all was well again! All – love and grief, and world and dream!

Da   wusst' ich nicht, wie   das Leben tut,
there knew I   not   what the life   does

War alles, ach alles wieder gut!
was all   ah all   again well

Alles! Alles! Lieb' und Leid,
all   all   love and grief

Und Welt   und Traum!
and world and dream

2. WER HAT DIES LIEDLEIN
WHO HAS THIS LITTLE SONG
ERDACHT?
DEVISED

2. WHO THOUGHT
UP THIS LITTLE
SONG?

(From *Des   Knaben Wunderhorn,*
    of the boy   magic-horn
folk poems published by
Achim von Arnim and Clemens Brentano)

Dort oben am   Berg in dem hohen Haus,
there above on the hill in the tall   house

Da   gucket ein fein's, lieb's Mädel heraus.
there peeps a   fine   dear maid out

Es ist nicht dort daheime!
it is not   there at home

Es ist des   Wirts   sein Töchterlein!
it is of the inn-keeper his little daughter

Es wohnet auf grüner Heide!
it lives   on green heath

Mein Herzle   ist wund!
my   (little) heart is sore

Komm, Schätzle,   mach's g'sund!
come   (little) sweetheart make it well

Dein schwarzbraune Äuglein,   die hab'n mich
your dark brown   (little) eyes they have me
    verwund't!
    wounded

Dein rosiger Mund macht Herzen gesund,
your rosy   mouth makes hearts well

Up there on the hill, a fair pretty
maiden peeps out of a tall house.
She doesn't live there – she's the
inn-keeper's daughter, and lives
on the green heath!

My heart is sore – come,
sweetheart, make it well! Your
dark brown eyes have wounded
me. Your rosy lips mend broken
hearts, make youth wise, give life
to the dead, and health to the sick.

Macht Jugend verständig, macht Tote   lebendig,
makes youth wise   makes (the) dead alive

Macht Kranke gesund, ja gesund!
makes invalid well   yes well

Wer hat denn das schön schöne Liedlein   erdacht?
who has then the lovely lovely little song devised

Who thought up this sweet little song? Three geese brought it over the water – two greys and a white one! And whoever can't sing this little song, then they'll whistle it to him!

Es haben's drei Gäns' übers   Wasser gebracht.
(it) have it three geese over the water   brought

Zwei graue und eine weisse!
two grey and a   white

Und wer das Liedlein   nicht singen kann,
and who the little song not   sing   can

Dem   wollen sie es pfeifen! Ja.
to him will   they it whistle yes

3. RHEINLEGENDCHEN
RHINE LEGEND

3. RHINE LEGEND

(From *Des   Knaben Wunderhorn,*
        of the boy   magic-horn
folk poems published by
Achim von Arnim and Clemens Brentano)

Bald   gras'   ich am   Neckar, bald
sometimes cut grass I   by the Neckar sometimes
    gras'   ich am   Rhein,
    cut grass I   by the Rhine

Bald   hab' ich ein Schätzel, bald   bin ich
sometimes have I   a sweetheart sometimes am I
    allein!
    alone

Was hilft mir   das Grasen, wenn d'Sichel   nicht
what use to me the grazing if   the sickle not
    schneid't,
    cuts

Was hilft mir   ein Schätzel,   wenn's bei mir nicht
what use to me a   sweetheart if it   with me not
    bleibt!
    stays

Sometimes I make hay by the Neckar, and sometimes I make hay by the Rhine. Sometimes I have a dear sweetheart, and sometimes I'm alone. But what use is making hay, if the scythe is blunt: what use is a sweetheart who doesn't stay with me!

So soll   ich denn grasen am   Neckar, am   Rhein;
so must I   then graze by the Neckar by the Rhine

So werf' ich mein goldenes Ringlein   hinein!
so throw I   my   golden (little) ring right in

Es fliesset im   Neckar und fliesset im   Rhein,
it flows in the Neckar and flows in the Rhine

Soll   schwimmen hinunter ins   Meer tief hinein!
must swim   down   into the sea   deep therein

Und schwimmt es, das Ringlein,   so frisst   es ein Fisch!
and swims   it the (little) ring so devours it a   fish

Das Fischlein   soll   kommen auf's   Königs sein Tisch!
the (little) fish shall come   on to the king's his table

Der König tät   fragen, wem's   Ringlein
the king   would ask   to whom the (little) ring

  sollt'   sein?
  is supposed be

Da tät   mein Schatz   sagen: 'Das Ringlein
then would my   sweetheart say   the (little) ring

  g'hört   mein!'
  belongs to me

Mein Schätzlein tät   springen bergauf und bergein,
my   sweetheart would run   up-hill and down-hill

Tät   mir wied'rum bringen das Goldringlein   fein!
would me again   bring   the little gold ring fine

Kannst   grasen am   Neckar, kannst   grasen am
can (you) graze by the Neckar can (you) graze by the

  Rhein!
  Rhine

Wirf du mir   nur immer dein Ringlein   hinein!
throw you to me just always your (little) ring therein

So whenever I make hay by the Neckar or the Rhine, I throw my gold ring right in! It sweeps along the Neckar, and sweeps along the Rhine, and it swims deep into the sea.

And as it swims it is swallowed by a fish, and that fish must come to the king's table! The king will ask, 'Whose ring is this?' And my sweetheart will say, 'It is mine!'

Then my sweetheart will run right up-hill and down-dale to bring back my golden ring to me! So if you make hay by the Neckar, or make hay by the Rhine, all you do is to throw in your ring!

4. *KINDERTOTENLIEDER* CHILDREN'S DEATH SONGS

4. SONGS ON THE DEATH OF CHILDREN

Friedrich Rückert

  i.

  i.

Nun will die Sonn' so hell   aufgeh'n,
now will the sun   so brightly rise

Als sei   kein Unglück   die Nacht gescheh'n.
as were no misfortune the night happened

Soon the sun will rise again, as brightly as if the night had brought no sudden grief. But this grief was mine alone, and the sun shines on

Das Unglück   geschah   nur mir   allein,
the misfortune happened   just to me alone

Die Sonne, sie scheinet allgemein!
the sun   she shines   universally

Du musst nicht die Nacht in dir   verschränken,
you must not the night in you enfold

Musst sie ins   ew'ge   Licht versenken!
must her in the eternal light sink

Ein Lämplein   verlosch   in meinem Zelt,
a   little lamp went out in my   tabernacle

Heil sei dem   Freudenlicht der   Welt!
hail be to the light of joy of the world

everyone. You must not enclose
the night within yourself, but let it
merge in the Eternal Light. A tiny
lamp went out in my small
dwelling – blessed be the joyous
Light of the world!

ii.

Nun seh' ich wohl, warum so   dunkle Flammen
now see I   indeed why   such dark   flames

Ihr sprühtet mir   in manchem Augenblicke,
you flashed to me in many a   moment

O Augen!
O eyes

Gleichsam um   voll in einem Blicke
as if   in order full in a   glance

Zu drängen eure ganze Macht   zusammen.
to press   your whole strength together

Doch ahnt' ich nicht, weil   Nebel mich umschwammen,
but sensed I   not   because mist me   swam around

Gewoben vom   verblendenden Geschicke,
woven   by the deluding   Fate

Dass sich   der Strahl bereits   zur   Heimkehr
that himself the ray   already to the return home
  schicke,
  might be reconciled

Dorthin, von   wannen alle Strahlen stammen.
thither   from whence all rays   spring

Ihr wolltet mir   mit eurem Leuchten sagen:
you wanted to me with your shining   to say

Wir möchten nah dir   bleiben gerne,
we would – near to you to stay – like

Doch ist uns das vom   Schicksal abgeschlagen.
but is us that by the fate   refused

ii.

Now I understand why the flames
in your eyes that you sometimes
flashed at me were so dark, as if
you would press your whole
strength into a single glance.
Deluding Fate shrouded me in its
mists, so I did not suspect that this
bright ray was ready to return to
the Source of all light. In your
shining you wanted to say: gladly
would we stay with you, but Fate
will not allow it. Look at us now,
for soon we shall be far away!
What today you see as eyes, in
nights to come to you will just be
stars.

Sieh' uns nur an, denn bald sind wir dir   ferne!
look us just at for soon are we to you far away

Was dir   nur Augen sind in diesen Tagen,
what to you only eyes are in these days

In künft'gen Nächten sind es   dir   nur Sterne.
in coming nights are they to you only stars

iii.

Wenn dein Mütterlein
when your (little) mother

Tritt zur Tür herein,
comes at the door in

Und den Kopf ich drehe,
and the head I turn

Ihr entgegensehe,
her look towards

Fällt auf ihr Gesicht
falls on her face

Erst der Blick mir nicht,
first the glance to me not

Sondern auf die Stelle
but   on the place

Näher nach der Schwelle,
nearer to the threshold

Dort wo   würde dein
there where would your

Lieb Gesichtchen sein,
dear little face be

Wenn du freudenhelle
if   you bright with joy

Trätest mit   herein
walked with (her) in here

Wie sonst,   mein Töchterlein.
as formerly my little daughter

Wenn dein Mütterlein
when your (little) mother

Tritt zur Tür herein
walks to the door in here

Mit der Kerze Schimmer,
with the candle glimmer

iii.

When your dear mother comes in at the door, and I turn my head to look at her, my first glance falls not on her face, but on the place nearer the threshold where your small face would be, if you were at her side, bright with joy as once you were, little daughter.

When your dear mother comes in at the door with a flickering candle, it seems as if you were with her, slipping into the room as you used to do. O you of your father's seed: a light of joy – alas, extinguished, all too soon.

Ist es mir,   als immer
is it to me as always

Kämst du mit   herein,
came you with (her) in here

Huschtest hinterdrein
slipped   behind

Als wie sonst   ins   Zimmer!
– as – formerly into the room

O du, des   Vaters Zelle,
O you of the father cell

Ach, zu schnelle
ah   too quickly

Erloschner   Freudenschein!
extinguished light of joy

iv.

Oft   denk' ich, sie sind nur ausgegangen!
often think I   they are just gone out

Bald werden sie   wieder nach Hause gelangen!
soon will   they again – home – arrive

Der Tag ist schön! O sei nicht bang!
the day is fair   O be not anxious

Sie   machen nur   einen weiten Gang!
they make   only a   long walk

Jawohl,   sie   sind nur ausgegangen
yes indeed they are only gone out

Und werden jetzt nach Hause gelangen!
and will   now – home – arrive

O sei nicht bang,   der Tag ist schön!
O be not   anxious the day is fair

Sie   machen nur   den Gang zu jenen Höhn!
they make   only the walk to those hills

Sie sind uns   nur vorausgegangen
they are to us only gone ahead

Und werden nicht wieder nach Haus verlangen!
and will   not   again – home – desire

Wir holen   sie   ein auf jenen Höh'n
we overtake them –   on those hills

iv.

I sometimes think they have just
gone out, and will soon be coming
home again. It is a lovely day –
Oh, be not anxious – they have
only gone for a long walk! Yes, of
course, they have just gone out,
and will soon be coming home.
Do not be anxious, it is a lovely
day! They have only gone for a
walk to those hills. They have just
gone ahead, and without wish to
return home. We will overtake
them there on the hills in the sun.
It is a beautiful day up there in the
hills.

Im   Sonnenschein!
in the sunshine

Der Tag ist schön auf jenen Höh'n.
the day is fair   on those hills

v.

In diesem Wetter, in diesem Braus,
in this   weather in this   raging

Nie   hätt'   ich gesendet die Kinder   hinaus!
never would have I   sent   the children out

Man hat sie   hinaus getragen,
one has them out   taken

Ich durfte   nichts   dazu sagen!
I   was allowed nothing to that to say

In diesem Wetter, in diesem Saus,
in this   weather in this   storm

Nie   hätt'   ich gelassen die Kinder   hinaus,
never would have I   let   the children out

Ich fürchtete, sie   erkranken,
I   was afraid they might fall ill

Das sind nun eitle Gedanken.
they are now vain thoughts

In diesem Wetter, in diesem Graus,
in this   weather in this   horror

Nie   hätt'   ich gelassen die Kinder   hinaus,
never would have I   let   the children out

Ich sorgte,   sie stürben   morgen,
I   was anxious they might die next day

Das ist nun nicht zu besorgen.
that is now not to be anxious about

In diesem Wetter, in diesem Saus, in diesem Braus,
in this   weather in this   storm in this   tumult

Sie ruhn als wie   in der   Mutter Haus,
they sleep as though in of the mother house

Von keinem Sturme erschrecket,
by no   storm frightened

Von Gottes Hand bedecket.
by   God's hand sheltered

v.

In such weather, in such a storm, I would never have sent the children out. But they were taken out, and I could say nothing. In such weather, in such a gale, I would never have let the children go out. I was afraid they might fall ill – but these are vain thoughts. In such dreadful weather, I would never have let the children go out. I was afraid they might soon die – but now there is nothing to fear. In such weather, such a gale, in such tumult, they sleep as in their mother's house – frightened no more by storms, sheltered by God's hand.

5. *FÜNF RÜCKERT LIEDER*
FIVE RÜCKERT SONGS

5. FIVE SONGS BY RÜCKERT

Friedrich Rückert

i.

Ich atmet'   einen linden Duft.
I   breathed a   gentle fragrance

Im   Zimmer stand
in the room   was

Ein Zweig der   Linde
a   twig   of the lime-tree

Ein Angebinde
a   gift

Von lieber Hand.
from dear hand

Wie lieblich war der Lindenduft!
how lovely was the lime-scent

Wie lieblich ist der Lindenduft!
how lovely is the lime-scent

Das Lindenreis
the linden-sprig

Brachst du   gelinde;
broke   you gently

Ich atme   leis'
I   breathe softly

Im   Duft der   Linde
in the scent of the lime

Der   Liebe linden Duft.
of the love gentle fragrance

i.

I breated a gentle fragrance. In the
room was a sprig of lime, a gift
from your dear hand. How sweet
was the scent of the lime!

How sweet is the scent of the lime!
You broke the sprig so gently, and
I softly breathe the scent of the
lime, the gentle fragrance of love.

ii.

Liebst du   um Schönheit, o nicht mich liebe!
love   you for beauty   O not me love

Liebe die Sonne, sie trägt ein goldnes Haar!
love the sun   she (has) (a) golden hair

ii.

If you love beauty, then do not
love me – love the sun, with its
golden hair!

Liebst du um Jugend, o nicht mich liebe!
love you for youth O not me love

Liebe den Frühling, der jung ist jedes Jahr!
love the spring   which young is each year

Liebst du um Schätze, o nicht mich liebe!
love you for treasure O not me love

Liebe die Meerfrau, sie hat viel Perlen klar!
love the mermaid she has many pearls clear

Liebst du um Liebe, o ja – mich liebe!
love you for love O truly me love

Liebe mich immer, dich lieb ich immerdar!
love me always you love I for ever

If you love youth, then do not love me – love the spring, which is young every year!

If you love treasure, then do not love me – love the mermaid with her many shining pearls!

If it is love you love – O then love me! Love me always, as I will always love you!

iii.

Blicke mir nicht in die Lieder!
look me not at the songs

Meine Augen schlag' ich nieder,
my eyes cast I down

Wie ertappt auf böser Tat.
as if caught in bad deed

Selber darf ich nicht getrauen,
myself can I not trust

Ihrem Wachsen zuzuschauen,
their growing to watch

Deine Neugier ist Verrat.
your curiosity is betrayal

Bienen, wenn sie Zellen bauen,
bees   when they cells build

Lassen auch nicht zu sich schauen,
let   – neither – at them gaze

Schauen selber   auch nicht zu.
look   themselves – nor –

Wenn die reichen Honigwaben
when the rich   honeycombs

Sie zu Tag befördert haben,
they to daylight dispatched have

Dann vor   allen nasche du!
then above all nibble you

iii.

Do not look my songs! I lower my eyes, as though caught doing wrong. I cannot trust myself to watch their growing – but your curiosity is betrayal.

When bees build their cells, they too let no one see – they do not even watch themselves. When their rich honeycombs first see the light of day, only then may you enjoy a taste!

iv.

Ich bin der Welt abhanden gekommen,
I am to the world lost (become)

Mit der ich sonst viele Zeit verdorben;
with which I formerly much time wasted

Sie hat so lange nichts von mir vernommen,
she has so long nothing from me heard

Sie mag wohl glauben, ich sei gestorben.
she may perhaps believe I am dead

Es ist mir auch gar nichts daran gelegen,
it is to me also at all – of no consequence –

Ob sie mich für gestorben hält.
whether she me for dead takes

Ich kann auch gar nichts sagen dagegen,
I can also at all nothing say against that

Denn wirklich bin ich gestorben der Welt.
for really am I dead to the world

Ich bin gestorben dem Weltgetümmel
I am dead to the world-turmoil

Und ruh' in einem stillen Gebiet.
and rest in a quiet sphere

Ich leb' allein in meinem Himmel,
I live alone in my heaven

In meinem Lieben, in meinem Lied.
in my love in my song

iv.

I am lost to the world, where once I wasted so much time. So long has it not heard of me, it may even think me dead.

It is nothing to me if it thinks me dead; indeed I cannot deny it, for I am truly dead to the world.

I am dead to the turmoil of the world and rest in a quiet place: alone I dwell in my own heaven, within my love, within my song.

v.

Um Mitternacht
at midnight

Hab ich gewacht
have I awakened

Und aufgeblickt zum Himmel;
and looked up at the sky

Kein Stern vom Sterngewimmel
no star of the star-throng

Hat mir gelacht
has me laughed at

Um Mitternacht.
at midnight

v.

At midnight I was awake, and looked up to the heavens; not one of the starry host smiled back at midnight.

Um Mitternacht
at   midnight

Hab ich gedacht
have I thought

Hinaus in   dunkle Schranken;
out   into dark enclosures

Es hat kein Lichtgedanken
(it) has no   light-thought

Mir Trost   gebracht
to me comfort brought

Um Mitternacht
at   midnight

At midnight, my thoughts reached out in the enclosing darkness; no lightening thought brought me comfort, at midnight.

Um Mitternacht
at   midnight

Nahm ich in acht
took I – heed of –

Die Schläge meines Herzens;
the beats   of my heart

Ein einz'ger Puls des   Schmerzens
a   single   pulse of the pain

War angefacht
was kindled

Um Mitternacht
at   midnight

At midnight, I took heed of the beating of my heart; one throbbing pulse of pain was burning at midnight.

Um Mitternacht
at   midnight

Kämpft ich die Schlacht,
fought I   the battle

O Menschheit, deiner   Leiden;
O mankind   of your suffering

Nicht konnt ich sie entscheiden
not   could I   (it) resolve

Mit meiner Macht
with my   might

Um Mitternacht
at   midnight

At midnight, I fought the battle of your suffering, O mankind; with all my might I could not resolve it at midnight.

Um Mitternacht
at   midnight

Hab ich die Macht
have I   the might

In   deine Hand gegeben:
into your hand given

Herr über Tod   und Leben,
Lord over death and life

Du hältst die Wacht
you keep the watch

Um Mitternacht.
at   midnight

At midnight, I gave my whole
strength into Thy hands. O Lord:
Thou keepest watch over life and
death, at midnight!

Richard Strauss
(1864–1949)

1. ZUEIGNUNG
DEDICATION

Hermann von Gilm

Ja, du weisst es, teure Seele,
yes you know it dear soul

Dass ich fern von dir mich quäle,
that I far from you myself torment

Liebe macht die Herzen krank,
love makes the hearts sick

Habe Dank.
have thanks

Einst hielt ich, der Freiheit Zecher,
once held I of the freedom reveller

Hoch den Amethysten-Becher
high the amethyst goblet

Und du segnetest den Trank,
and you blessed the draught

Habe Dank.
have thanks

Und beschworst darin die Bösen,
and exorcised therein the evil

Bis ich, was ich nie gewesen,
until I that I never was

Heilig, heilig an's Herz dir sank,
hallowed hallowed on the heart to you sank

Habe Dank.
have thanks

1. DEDICATION

Yes, you know, dear heart, that far from you I am tormented. Love makes the heart sick – for this I give thanks!

Once, reveller of freedom, I raised high a goblet of amethyst, and you blessed the draught – for this I give thanks!

And you drove the evil away, till I was purified as never before, and sank on your breast – for this I give thanks!

2. DIE NACHT
THE NIGHT

2. NIGHT

Hermann von Gilm

Aus dem Walde tritt die Nacht,
from the wood treads the night

Night is creeping out of the wood,
stealing softly from the trees,
peering around in widening
circles. Now, take care!

Aus den Bäumen schleicht sie leise,
from the trees steals she softly

Schaut sich um in weitem Kreise,
looks her about in wide circle

Nun gib acht.
now take heed

Alle Lichter dieser Welt,
all lights of this world

She blots out light from all the
earth: all flowers, all colours; and
steals the sheaves away from the
field.

Alle Blumen, alle Farben
all flowers all colours

Löscht sie aus und stiehlt die Garben
blots she out and steals the sheaves

Weg vom Feld.
away from the field

Alles nimmt sie, was nur hold,
everything takes she what -ever lovely

All that is fair she takes away: the
silver from the stream, and from
the copper on the dome, the gold.

Nimmt das Silber weg des Stroms,
takes the silver away from the river

Nimmt vom Kupferdach des Doms
takes from the copper roof of the cathedral

Weg das Gold.
away the gold

Ausgeplündert steht der Strauch,
stripped stands the bush

Stripped stands the bush – edge
nearer, soul to soul! Oh, I am
afraid the night will steal you from
me too.

Rücke näher, Seel' an Seele;
move nearer soul to soul

O die Nacht, mir   bangt, sie stehle
O the night   (I am afraid) she might steal

Dich mir   auch.
you   (from) me too

3. ALLERSEELEN
ALL SOULS

Hermann von Gilm

Stell' auf dem Tisch die duftenden   Reseden,
lay   on the table the sweet-smelling mignonette

Die letzten roten Astern trag' herbei,
the last   red   asters carry herewith

Und lass uns wieder von der Liebe reden,
and let us again of   the love speak

Wie einst im   Mai.
as   once in the May

Gib mir die Hand, dass ich sie heimlich drücke,
give me the hand that I   her secretly may press

Und wenn man's sieht, mir   ist es einerlei,
and if   one it sees to me is it all the same

Gib mir nur einen deiner süssen Blicke,
give me only one   of your sweet glances

Wie einst im   Mai.
as   once in the May

Es blüht   und duftet   heut' auf jedem Grabe,
it blossoms and is fragrant today on each grave

Ein Tag im   Jahr ist ja   den Toten   frei,
one day in the year is indeed the dead one free

Komm an mein Herz, dass ich dich wieder habe,
come to my heart that I   you again have

Wie einst im   Mai.
as   once in the May

3. ALL SOULS

Lay on the table the fragrant
mignonette and the last red asters,
and let us speak again of love, as
once in May!

Give me your hand, that I may
press it secretly – and if anyone
should see, what then? Just give
me one sweet glance, as once in
May!

Today each grave is fragrant and
blossoms with flowers, for one day
in the year the dead are free.
Come to my heart that I may hold
you again, as once in May!

4. STÄNDCHEN
SERENADE

4. SERENADE

Adolf Friedrich von Schack

Mach' auf, mach' auf, doch leise, mein Kind,
open up open up but softly my child

Um keinen vom Schlummer zu wecken.
so as no one from the slumber to wake

Kaum murmelt der Bach, kaum zittert im Wind
hardly murmurs the brook hardly trembles in the wind

Ein Blatt an den Büschen und Hecken.
a leaf on the bushes and hedges

D'rum leise, mein Mädchen, dass nichts sich regt,
therefore softly my sweetheart that nothing (itself) stirs

Nur leise die Hand anf die Klinke gelegt.
just softly the hand on the latch laid

Open, open the door, but softly
my child, so no one wakes. The
brook barely murmurs, the leaves
hardly tremble on bush and hedge.
So softly, my love, that nothing
stirs, lay your hand, but gently on
the latch.

Mit Tritten wie Tritte der Elfen so sacht,
with footsteps like footsteps of the elves so light

Um über die Blumen zu hüpfen,
so as over the flowers to skip

Flieg' leicht hinaus in die Mondscheinnacht,
fly nimbly out into the moonlight-night

Zu mir in den Garten zu schlüpfen.
to me into the garden to slip

Rings schlummern die Blüten am rieselnden Bach
around slumber the flowers by the rippling brook

Und duften im Schlaf, nur die Liebe ist
and send forth fragrance in the sleep only the love is
wach.
awake

With steps light as elfin steps
skipping over flowers, fly nimbly
into the moonlit night, and steal
out to me in the garden. By the
rippling brook the flowers are
sleeping, fragrant in slumber. And
only love keeps watch.

Sitz' nieder, hier dämmert's geheimnisvoll
sit down here grows dusk it mysteriously

Unter den Lindenbäumen,
under the linden-trees

Die Nachtigall uns zu Häupten soll
the nightingale to us at (our) heads shall

Von uns'ren Küssen träumen
of our kisses dream

Sit here, where the dusk
mysteriously gathers beneath the
linden trees; the nightingale above
will dream of our kisses, and in the
morning when she awakens the
rose will glow with the quivering
rapture of the night.

Und die Rose, wenn sie am   Morgen erwacht,
and the rose when she in the morning awakens

Hoch glühn von den Wonneschauern der   Nacht.
highly to glow from the rapture-shivers of the night

5. *WIE SOLLTEN WIR GEHEIM SIE*   5. SECRET RAPTURE
HOW SHOULD WE SECRET HER
HALTEN
KEEP

Adolf Friedrich von Schack

Wie sollten wir geheim sie halten,   How can we keep it secret, this
how should we secret her keep   rapture with which we are filled?
                                             No, let it be revealed, all that lies
Die Seligkeit, die uns erfüllt?   in the deepest folds of our hearts!
the bliss   that us fills

Nein, bis in   seine tiefsten Falten
no   till into its   deepest folds

Sei allen unser Herz enthüllt!
be to all our   heart revealed

Wenn zwei in Liebe sich   gefunden,   The whole of nature rejoices,
when two in love themselves found   when two beings have found their
                                             love. Then the day in lengthening
Geht Jubel   hin   durch   die Natur,   hours of bliss spreads wide over
goes rejoicing thither through the nature   meadow and wood.

In längern wonnevollen Stunden
in longer blissful   hours

Legt   sich   der Tag auf Wald und Flur.
spreads (itself) the day on wood and meadow

Selbst aus der   Eiche morschem Stamme,   From the rotting trunk of the oak,
even from of the oak rotten   trunk   that endured a thousand years, a
                                             new green shoot flames high in its
Die ein Jahrtausend   überlebt,   branches, rustling and trembling
that a   thousand years survived   with youthful joy.

Steigt neu des   Wipfels   grüne Flamme
rises anew of the (tree-)top green flame

Und rauscht von Jugendlust   durchbebt.
and rustles with youthful joy trembling through

Zu höherm Glanz   und Düfte brechen
to higher splendour and scents burst

Die Knospen auf beim Glück   der Zwei,
the buds   open at the happiness of the two

Und süsser   rauscht   es in den Bächen
and sweeter murmurs it in the streams

Und reicher blüht   und reicher glänzt der Mai.
and richer blossoms and richer shines the May

Buds burst open with heightened fragrance and splendour at the lovers' joy, and even sweeter murmur the streams, even richer May blossoms and shines.

6. *ALL MEIN GEDANKEN*
ALL MY   THOUGHTS

6. ALL MY
THOUGHTS

Felix Dahn

All mein Gedanken, mein Herz und mein Sinn,
all my thoughts my heart and my mind

Da, wo   die Liebste ist, wandern sie   hin.
there where the beloved is wander they thither

Gehn ihres Weges trotz   Mauer und Tor,
go their way in spite of wall and gate

Da hält   kein Riegel, kein Graben nicht vor,
there holds no bolt no moat not out

Gehn wie die Vögelein   hoch durch   die Luft,
go like the (little) birds high through the air

Brauchen kein Brücken über Wasser und Kluft,
need no bridges over water and ravine

Finden das Städtlein   und finden das Haus,
find the (little) town and find the house

Finden ihr Fenster aus   allen heraus,
find her window out of all out

All my thoughts, my heart and mind, stray to my beloved. They go their way in spite of wall and gate; no bolt can hold them, no moat can keep them out. They soar like birds high in the air; they need no bridge over water or ravine. They find her town, they find her house, and they find her window from amongst them all.

Und klopfen und rufen:
and knock and call

Mach auf, lass uns ein,
– open – let us in

Wir kommen vom   Liebsten
we come from the beloved

Und grüssen dich fein,
and greet you fine

Mach auf, mach auf, lass uns ein.
open up open up let us in

And there they knock and call, 'Open up – let us in! We come with fine greetings from your beloved – so open up, open up – and let us in!'

7. *DU   MEINES HERZENS*
YOU OF MY   HEART
KRÖNELEIN
LITTLE CROWN

7. LITTLE JEWEL OF
MY HEART

Felix Dahn

Du meines Herzens Krönelein,
you of my heart   little crown

Du bist von lautrem Golde,
you are of   pure   gold

Wenn andere daneben sein,
when others close by be

Dann bist du   noch viel   holde.
then   are you still (very) lovely

Little jewel of my heart, you are of
pure gold. When others are near
you appear even lovelier.

Die andern tun so gern gescheit,
the others act so like clever

Du bist gar sanft   und stille,
you are very gentle and quiet

Dass jedes Herz sich   dein   erfreut,
that each heart itself (of) you delights

Dein Glück   ist's, nicht dein Wille.
your happiness is it not   your wish

Others like to put on airs, but you
are gentle and still. That every
heart delights in you is not your
will, but your joy.

Die andern suchen Lieb und Gunst
the others seek   love and favour

Mit tausend   falschen Worten,
with thousand false   words

Du ohne   Mund- und Augenkunst
you without mouth- and eyes-artifice

Bist wert   an allen Orten.
are valued in all   places

Others seek love and favour, with
a thousand spurious words, but
you, without artful speech or
glance, are beloved everywhere.

Du bist als wie die Ros' im   Wald,
you are like as the rose in the wood

Sie weiss   nichts   von ihrer Blüte,
she knows nothing of   her bloom

Doch jedem, der   vorüberwallt,
yet   to each who past wanders

Erfreut sie das Gemüte.
delights she the feelings

You are like the rose in the wood,
of its beauty unaware, but to
everyone who passes by, the heart
of each is made glad.

8. *RUHE, MEINE SEELE*
REST   MY   SOUL

8. REST, MY SOUL

Karl Henckell

Nicht ein Lüftchen   regt sich   leise,
not   a (small) breeze stirs (itself) quietly

Sanft entschlummert   ruht der Hain;
gently fallen into slumber rests the wood

Durch   der   Blätter dunkle Hülle
through of the leaves dark   covering

Stiehlt sich   lichter Sonnenschein.
steals (himself) bright sunshine

No breath of air is softly stirring;
in gentle slumber rests the wood;
through the leaves dark covering
bright sunshine steals.

Ruhe, ruhe, meine Seele,
rest   rest my   soul

Deine Stürme gingen wild,
your storms went fiercely

Hast getobt und hast gezittert,
have raged and have shuddered

Wie die Brandung, wenn sie schwillt!
like the surf   when she rises

Rest, rest my soul; fierce were
your storms, that raged and
shuddered like the heaving of
breaking waves!

Diese Zeiten sind gewaltig,
these times are violent

Bringen Herz und Hirn in   Not –
bring   heart and brain into misery

Ruhe, ruhe, meine Seele,
rest   rest my   soul

Und vergiss, was dich bedroht!
and forget what you threatens

These times are violent; they bring
distress to heart and mind. Rest,
rest my soul, and forget what
threatens you!

9. *CÄCILIE*
CECILIA

9. CECILIA

Heinrich Hart

Wenn du es wüsstest, was träumen heisst
if   you it knew   what to dream means

Von brennenden Küssen, von Wandern   und Ruhen mit
of burning   kisses of wandering and resting with
    der Geliebten,
    the beloved

If you but knew what it is to
dream of burning kisses: of
wandering with your sweetheart,
then resting – gazing into each
other's eyes, and speaking loving
words – if you but knew, your
heart would change!

Aug' in   Auge und kosend   und plaudernd,
eye   into eye   and caressing and talking

Wenn du es wüsstest, du neigtest   dein Herz!
If   you it knew   you would bow your heart

Wenn du es wüsstest, was bangen   heisst,
if   you it knew   what to be anxious means

If you but knew what it is to
spend anxious, solitary nights,
surrounded by (*shuddering*) storms,
with no gentle lips to comfort the
strife-weary soul – if you but
knew, you would come to me!

In einsamen Nächten, umschauert   vom   Sturm,
in solitary   nights   showered around by the storm

Da   niemand tröstet   milden Mundes die kampfmüde
when no one   comforts gentle of mouth the strife-weary
    Seele,
    soul

Wenn du es wüsstest, du kämest   zu mir.
if   you it knew   you would come to me

Wenn du es wüsstest, was leben heisst,
if   you it knew   what to live means

If you but knew what it is to live,
to feel God's Breath about you, to
be lightly borne and soar up to
Elysian heights – if you but knew,
you would dwell with me!

Umhaucht   von der   Gottheit weltschaffendem
breathed around by of the Deity   world-creating
    Atem,
    breath

Zu schweben empor,   lichtgetragen, zu seligen Höh'n,
to soar   upwards lightly borne to blissful heights

Wenn du es wüsstest, du lebtest   mit mir!
if   you it knew   you would dwell with me

10. *HEIMLICHE AUFFORDERUNG*
SECRET   INVITATION

10. SECRET
INVITATION

John Henry Mackay

Auf, hebe die funkelnde Schale empor zum   Mund,
up   raise the sparkling vessel up   to the mouth

Und trinke beim Freudenmahle dein Herz gesund.
and drink at the feast   your heart well

Und wenn du sie hebst, so winke mir heimlich zu,
and when du sie hebst, so wave me secretly to

Dann lächle ich und dann trinke ich still   wie du . . .
then smile I   and then drink I   silently like you

Raise the sparkling vessel to your
lips, drink and cheer your heart at
the feast! And when you raise it,
sign to me in secret, that I may
smile and silently drink like
you . . .

Und still   gleich mir betrachte um   uns das Heer
and silently like me watch   around us the host

Der   trunknen Schwätzer – verachte sie   nicht zu sehr.
of the drunken babblers   disdain them not too much

Nein, hebe die blinkende Schale, gefüllt mit Wein,
no   lift the shining vessel filled with wine

Und lass beim   lärmenden Mahle sie   glücklich sein.
and let at the noisy   banquet them happy be

Doch hast du   das Mahl genossen, den Durst gestillt,
but   have you the meal enjoyed the thirst quenched

Dann verlasse der   lauten Genossen festfreudiges Bild,
then leave   of the noisy comrades feast-merry picture

Und wandle hinaus in   den Garten zum   Rosenstrauch,
and wander out   into the garden to the rose-bush

Dort will ich dich dann erwarten nach altem Brauch,
there will I   you then await   after old   custom

Und will an die Brust dir   sinken, eh'   du's
and will on the breast to you sink   before you it

  gehofft,
  hoped

Und deine Küsse trinken, wie ehmals oft,
and your kisses drink   as of old often

Und flechten in   deine Haare der   Rose Pracht.
and entwine into your hair   of the rose splendour

O komm, du wunderbare ersehnte   Nacht!
O come you wonderful longed for night

And silently like me, you will watch this crowd of drunken babblers – only do not be too harsh in your disdain. No, raise the shining vessel filled with wine, and let them be merry at their carousing!

But when you have enjoyed the feast, and quenched your thirst, then leave these noisy comrades and their merry scene, and wander out to the garden, to the rose-bush, where I'll await you as of old.

Sooner than you dare to hope, I'll sink into your arms, and drink your kisses as I used to do, and entwine the roses in all their splendour in your hair. O come, wonderful night for which I long!

11. MORGEN
   TOMORROW

11. TOMORROW

John Henry Mackay

Und morgen   wird die Sonne wieder scheinen
and tomorrow will the sun   again shine

Und auf dem Wege, den   ich gehen werde,
and on the path which I go   will

Wird uns, die Glücklichen, sie wieder einen
will us   the happy ones she again unite

Inmitten   dieser sonnenatmenden Erde . . .
in the midst of this sun-breathing   earth

And tomorrow the sun will shine again, and on the path that I shall take, it will again unite us, the blessed ones, in the midst of this sun-breathing earth . . .

Und zu dem Strand, dem weiten, wogenblauen,
and to the shore   the wide   waves'-blue

Werden wir still   und langsam niedersteigen,
will   we quietly and slowly   descend

Stumm werden wir uns in   die Augen schauen,
silently will   we us into the eyes   look

Und auf uns sinkt des   Glückes   stummes
and on us falls of the happiness mute
    Schweigen...
    silence

And quietly and slowly we will go
down to the wide, blue-waved
shore; silently we will gaze into
each other's eyes, and upon us will
fall the still silence of joy ...

12. TRAUM DURCH   DIE DREAM THROUGH THE *DÄMMERUNG* TWILIGHT

12. DREAM IN THE TWILIGHT

Otto Julius Bierbaum

Weite   Wiesen   im   Dämmergrau;
distant meadows in the twilight-grey

Die Sonne verglomm,   die Sterne ziehn,
the sun   ceased glowing the stars advance

Nun geh ich hin   zu der schönsten Frau,
now go I   there to the fairest   woman

Weit über Wiesen   im   Dämmergrau,
far   over meadows in the twilight-grey

Tief in   den Busch von Jasmin.
deep into the bush of jasmine

Distant meadows in the twilight
grey; the sun's glowing dimmed,
and stars appeared. Now I go to
my fairest one, far over meadows
in the twilight grey, amongst the
jasmine deep;

Durch   Dämmergrau in   der   Liebe Land;
through twilight-grey into of the love land

Ich gehe nicht schnell, ich eile   nicht;
I   walk not fast   I   hasten not

Mich zieht   ein weiches samtenes Band
me   draws a soft   velvety ribbon

Durch   Dämmergrau in der   Liebe Land,
through twilight-grey in of the love land

In   ein blaues, mildes Licht.
into a blue   gentle light

through the twilight grey to the
land of love. I go not fast, I walk
without haste, drawn by a ribbon
velvety soft – through the grey
twilight to the land of love.

13. SCHLAGENDE HERZEN
BEATING HEARTS

13. BEATING HEARTS

Otto Julius Bierbaum

Über Wiesen   und Felder ein Knabe ging;
over meadows and fields a boy   walked

Kling klang, schlug ihm   das Herz,
bing bang beat to him the heart

Es glänzt ihm   am   Finger von Golde ein Ring,
it shone to him on the finger of gold a ring

Kling klang, schlug ihm   das Herz!
bing bang beat to him the heart

O Wiesen,   o Felder, wie seid ihr schön!
O meadows O fields how are you lovely

O Berge,   o Täler, wie schön!
O mountains O valleys how fair

Wie bist du gut, wie bist du schön,
how are you good how are you lovely

Du gold'ne Sonne in Himmelshöhn!
you golden sun   in heaven's heights

Kling klang, schlug ihm   das Herz.
bing bang beat to him the heart

Schnell eilte   der Knabe mit fröhlichem Schritt,
fast   hurried the boy   with merry   step

Kling klang, schlug ihm   das Herz.
bing bang beat to him the heart

Nahm manche lachende Blume mit —
took   many a laughing flower with (him)

Kling klang, schlug ihm   das Herz.
bing bang beat to him the heart

Über Wiesen   und Felder weht Frühlingswind,
over meadows and fields blows spring's-wind

Über Berge   und Wälder weht Frühlingswind.
over mountains and woods blows spring's-wind

Der treibt zu dir mich leise, lind.
that drives to you me softly gently

Kling klang, schlug ihm   das Herz.
bing bang beat to him the heart

A boy walked over the meadows and fields. (Bing bang beat his heart.) On his finger shone a golden ring. (Bing bang beat his heart.) 'O meadows, O fields, how lovely you are! O mountains, O valleys, how fair! How good you are, how lovely you are, O golden sun in the heavens!' (Bing bang beat his heart.) The boy hurried along with a merry step. (Bing bang beat his heart.) He took many a smiling flower. (Bing bang beat his heart.) 'Over meadows and fields, and mountains and woods, a breeze blew into my heart. And softly, gently it sends me to you!' (Bing bang beat his heart.) A maiden was there in the meadows and fields. (Bing bang beat his heart.) She shaded her eyes with her hand to see. (Bing bang beat her heart.) 'He hurries to me over meadows and fields, over mountains and through the woods. If only he were already with me!' (Bing bang beat her heart.)

Zwischen Wiesen   und Feldern ein Mädel stand,
among   meadows and fields   a   girl   stood

Kling klang, schlug ihr   das Herz,
bing bang beat to her the heart

Hielt über die Augen zum Schauen die Hand,
held over the eyes   – to gaze –   the hand

Kling klang, schlug ihr   das Herz.
bing bang beat to her the heart

Über Wiesen   und Felder, über Berge   und Wälder,
over meadows and fields over mountains and woods

Zu mir schnell kommt er her,
to me quickly comes he here

O wenn er bei mir nur, bei mir schon   wär.
O if   he with me only with me already were

Kling klang, schlug ihr   das Herz.
bing bang beat to her the heart

14. *FÜR FUNFZEHN PFENNIGE*
FOR FIFTEEN   PFENNIGS

(From *Des   Knaben Wunderhorn,*
        of the boy   magic-horn
folk poems published by
Achim von Arnim and Clemens Brentano)

Das Mägdlein will   ein' Freier habn,
the girl   wants a   suitor to have

Und sollt sie'n   aus   der Erde grabn,
and must she him out of the earth dig

Für funfzehn Pfennige.
for fifteen   pfennigs

Sie grub wohl   ein, sie grub wohl   aus
she dug indeed in   she dug indeed out

Und grub nur   einen Schreiber heraus
and dug only a   clerk   out

Für funfzehn Pfennige.
for fifteen   pfennigs

14. FOR FIFTEEN
PENCE

The girl wants a lover, and will
have to dig him out of the ground
– for fifteen pence.

She digs down, she digs up, and
only digs out a clerk – for fifteen
pence.

Der Schreiber hatt des Gelds zu viel, the clerk had of the money too much	The clerk has too much money, and buys the girl anything she wants – for fifteen pence.
Er kauft dem Mädchen was sie will he buys (to) the girl what she wants	
Für funfzehn Pfennige. for fifteen pfennigs	
Er kauft ihr einen Gürtel schmal, he buys her a girdle narrow	He buys her a narrow girdle all bristling over with gold – for fifteen pence.
Der starrt von Gold wohl überall, that bristles with gold indeed all over	
Für funfzehn Pfennige. for fifteen pfennigs	
Er kauft ihr einen breiten Hut, he buys her a wide hat	He buys her a broad brimmed hat, that's good for the sun – for fifteen pence.
Der wär wohl für die Sonne gut, that would be indeed for the sun good	
Für funfzehn Pfennige. for fifteen pfennigs	
Wohl für die Sonn', wohl für den Wind, indeed for the sun indeed for the wind	Good for the sun, and good for the wind; stay with me, dear love – for fifteen pence.
Bleib du bei mir, mein liebes Kind, stay you with me my dear child	
Für funfzehn Pfennige. for fifteen pfennigs	

15. *HAT GESAGT – BLEIBT'S*
    HAS SAID   ABIDES IT
    NICHT DABEI
    NOT   BY

15. PROMISES – BUT IDLE ONES

(From *Des   Knaben Wunderhorn,*
      of the boy   magic-horn
folk poems published by
Achim von Arnim and Clemens Brentano)

Mein vater hat gesagt, my father has said	My father says I must rock the baby to sleep, then this evening he'll boil me three eggs. But if he boils three for me, he'll eat two of
Ich soll das Kindlein wiegen, I must the baby rock	

Er will mir auf den Abend
he will me in the evening

Drei Gaggeleier   sieden;
three chicken's-eggs boil

Siedt er mir   drei,
boils he to me three

Isst er mir   zwei,
eats he to me two

Und ich mag nicht wiegen
and I   like not to rock

Um ein einziges Ei.
for a single egg

Mein' Mutter hat gesagt,
my   mother has said

Ich soll   die Mägdlein verraten,
I   must the maids   betray

Sie wollt   mir   auf den Abend
she would to me in   the evening

Drei Vögelein   braten, ja braten;
three (little) birds roast   yes roast

Brat sie mir   drei,
roasts she to me three

Isst sie mir   zwei,
eats she to me two

Um ein einzig Vöglein
for a   single (little) bird

Treib'   ich kein Verräterei.
carry on I   no treachery

Mein Schätzlein   hat gesagt,
my   (little) sweetheart has said

Ich soll sein   gedenken,
I   must of him think

Er wollt   mir   auf den Abend,
he would (to) me in the evening

Drei Küsslein   auch   schenken;
three (little) kisses (indeed) give

Schenkt er mir drei,
gives   he me three

Bleibt's nicht dabei,
stays it not thereat

them – and I'm not going to rock the baby for a single egg!

My mother says I must tell on the maid, then this evening she'll roast me three birds. But if she roasts three, she'll eat two of them – and for a single bird I'm not going to tell on anyone!

My sweetheart says I must think of him, then this evening he'll give me three kisses. He'll give me three, but it won't stop at that – so what do I care about birds or eggs!

Was kümmert mich's Vöglein,
what is that to me the (little) bird

Was schiert   mich das Ei.
what is that to me   the egg

16. *MEINEM KINDE*
   TO MY   CHILD

Gustav Falke

Du schläfst   und sachte neig' ich mich
you are sleeping and softly lean I   (myself)

Über dein Bettchen   und segne dich.
over your (little) bed and bless you

Jeder behutsame Atemzug
each careful   breath

Ist ein schweifender Himmelsflug,
is a roving   Heaven's-flight

Ist ein Suchen   weit umher,
is a searching far around

Ob   nicht doch   ein Sternlein   wär',
whether not   indeed a   (little) star were

Wo   aus   eitel Glanz   und Licht
which out of sheer brightness and light

Liebe sich   ein Glückskraut   bricht,
love herself a   happiness-plant plucks

Das sie geflügelt hernieder trägt
that she winged down   carries

Und dir   auf's weisse Deckchen   legt.
and to you on the white (little) coverlet lays

16. TO MY CHILD

Softly you sleep; I lean over your
cot and give you my blessing.
Each gentle breath is a soaring
flight to Heaven, a far-flung search
for a star, where, from its pure
brightness, love itself might pluck
a happy flower, and fly down with
it to lay on your white coverlet.

17. *WIEGENLIED*
   CRADLE-SONG

Richard Dehmel

Träume, träume, du mein süsses Leben,
dream   dream you my sweet life

Von dem Himmel, der die Blumen bringt.
of   the heaven that the flowers brings

17. CRADLE SONG

Dream, my sweet life, dream of
heaven that brings the flowers.
Blossoms shimmer there,

Blüten   schimmern da,   die leben
blossoms shimmer   there that live

trembling with the song your
mother sings.

Von dem Lied, das deine Mutter singt.
by the song that your mother sings

Träume, träume, Knospe meiner Sorgen,
dream   dream bud   of my sorrows

Dream, little bud of my sorrows –
dream of the day when the flower
first appeared, of the bright
blossoming day, when your little
soul opened to the world.

Von dem Tage, da   die Blume spross;
of   the day   when the flower budded

Von dem hellen Blütenmorgen,
of   the bright blossom-morning

Da   dein Seelchen sich der   Welt erschloss.
when your little soul itself to the world opened

Träume, träume, Blüte   meiner Liebe,
dream   dream blossom of my love

Dream, little blossom of my love,
dream of the silent and hallowed
night, when the flowering of his
love made this world for me into
heaven.

Von der stillen, von der heil'gen Nacht,
of   the silent of the holy   night

Da   die Blume seiner Liebe
when the flower of his love

Diese Welt zum   Himmel mir gemacht.
this   world to the heaven me made

18. *MUTTERTÄNDELEI*
MOTHER-DALLYING

18. MOTHER'S
CROONING

Gottfried August Bürger

Seht   mir   doch mein schönes Kind,
look at (for) me do   my   lovely child

Just look at my beautiful child
with her golden curls, blue eyes
and little red cheeks! Have you,
dear people, such a one! No, dear
people, you have none!

Mit den gold'nen Zottellöckchen,
with the golden   shaggy-little curls

Blauen Augen, roten Bäckchen!
blue   eyes   red   little cheeks

Leutchen,   habt ihr auch so   eins?
dear people have you also such (a) one

Leutchen,   nein, ihr habt keins!
dear people no   you have none

Seht mir doch mein süsses Kind,
look at (for) me do my sweet child

Fetter als ein fettes Schneckchen,
fatter than a fat little snail

Süsser als ein Zuckerweckchen!
sweeter than a sugar-roll

Leutchen, habt ihr auch so eins?
dear people have you also such a one

Leutchen, nein, ihr habt keins!
dear people no you have none

Seht mir doch mein holdes Kind,
look at (for) me do my lovely child

Nicht zu mürrisch, nicht zu wählig!
not too sullen not too hard to please

Immer freundlich, immer fröhlich!
always cheerful always merry

Leutchen, habt ihr auch so eins?
dear people have you also such (a) one

Leutchen, nein, ihr habt keins!
dear people no you have none

Seht mir doch mein frommes Kind,
look at (for) me do my innocent child

Keine bitterböse Sieben
no angry vixen

Würd' ihr Mütterchen so lieben.
would her dear mother so love

Leutchen, möchtet ihr so eins?
dear people would like you so one

O, ihr kriegt gewiss nicht meins!
O you get certainly not mine

Komm' einmal ein Kaufmann her!
let come once a merchant here

Hunderttausend blanke Taler,
hundred-thousand shining talers

Alles Gold der Erde zahl' er!
all gold of the earth would pay he

O, er kriegt gewiss nicht meins!
O he gets certainly not mine

Kauf' er sich woanders eins!
let buy he himself elsewhere one

Just look at my sweet child, plumper that a plump little snail, sweeter than a sugar bun! Have you, dear people, such a one! No, dear people, you have none!

Just look at my winsome child, never sulky, hard to please; always friendly, always merry. Have you, dear people, such a one! No, dear people, you have none!

Just look at my innocent child! No angry little vixen could love her mother so. Dear people would you, like one like this? Oh, you certainly won't get mine!

If a buyer came along with a thousand shining shillings, all the gold in the world – he would never get mine! Let him buy one elsewhere!

19. *FREUNDLICHE VISION*
FRIENDLY   VISION

Otto Julius Bierbaum

Nicht im   Schlafe hab ich das geträumt,
not   in the sleep   have I   it   dreamed

Hell   am   Tage sah ich's schön vor   mir:
bright in the day   saw I it lovely before me

Eine Wiese   voller Margeritten;
a   meadow full of daisies

Tief ein weisses Haus in grünen Büschen;
deep a   white house in green bushes

Götterbilder   leuchten aus   dem Laube.
god-like forms glimmer from the leaves

Und ich geh'   mit Einer, die   mich lieb hat,
and I   am walking with one   who me   – loves –

Ruhigen Gemütes in die Kühle
quiet   of spirit in the coolness

Dieses weissen Hauses, in   den Frieden,
of this white   house   into the peace

Der   voll Schönheit wartet, dass wir kommen.
which full of beauty   waits   that we come

Und ich geh'   mit Einer, die   mich lieb hat,
and I   am waling with one   who me   – loves –

In   den Frieden voll   Schönheit!
into the peace   full of beauty

19. A FRIENDLY
VISION

It was not in sleep or in dreams,
but in bright day that I saw it,
lovely before me; a meadow full of
daisies, and a white house deep in
green bushes, where god-like
figures glimmered among the
leaves. And serene in spirit I am
walking with one who loves me
into the coolness of this white
house, where peace full of beauty
awaits our coming. And I walk
with one who loves me, into the
beauty-filled peace.

20. *EINERLEI*
SAMENESS

Achim von Arnim

Ihr Mund ist stets   derselbe,
her mouth is always the same

Sein Kuss mir   immer neu,
(its) kiss to me always new

20. SWEET SAMENESS

Her lips are ever the same; its kiss
ever new. Her eyes ever the same,
her open glances ever true.

Ihr Auge noch dasselbe,
her eye   still the same

Sein freier Blick mir   treu;
(its) open glance to me true

O du liebes Einerlei,
O you dear sameness

O sweet sameness, how many
things are born of you!

Wie wird   aus   dir so mancherlei!
how becomes out of you so many things

21. SCHLECHTES WETTER
   BAD   WEATHER

21. BAD WEATHER

Heinrich Heine

Das ist ein schlechtes Wetter,
this is a   bad   weather

What terrible weather! There's a
raging storm, and rain, and snow.
I'm sitting at the window, looking
out into the darkness.

Es regnet und stürmt und schneit;
it rains and storms and snows

Ich sitze am   Fenster und schaue
I   sit at the window and look

Hinaus in   die Dunkelheit.
out   into the darkness

Da   schimmert   ein einsames Lichtchen,
there is shimmering a   solitary little light

A solitary little light is glimmering,
and moving slowly away across the
street. A motherly little woman
totters along with her lantern.

Das   wandelt langsam fort:
which goes   slowly   away

Ein Mütterchen   mit dem Laternchen
a (little) mother with the (little) lantern

Wankt über die Strasse dort.
totters over the street there

Ich glaube, Mehl und Eier
I   think flour and eggs

I think she's been buying some
flour and eggs and butter to bake a
cake for her big spoilt daughter.

Und Butter kaufte sie ein;
and butter bought she –

Sie will   einen Kuchen backen
she wants a   cake   to bake

Für's   grosse Töchterlein.
for the big   dear daughter

Die liegt   zu Haus im   Lehnstuhl
she is lying at home in the easy chair

Und blinzelt schläfrig ins   Licht;
and blinks sleepily into the light

Die goldenen Locken wallen
the golden locks flow

Über das süsse Gesicht.
over the sweet face

She's lying at home in the easy chair, blinking sleepily at the light. Her golden curls flow softly over her sweet face.

22. *VIER LETZTE LIEDER* FOUR LAST SONGS

22. FOUR LAST SONGS

i. *Beim Schlafengehen* by the going to bed

i. Whilst falling asleep

Hermann Hesse

Nun der Tag mich müd' gemacht,
now the day me   weary made

Soll mein sehnliches Verlangen
shall my   yearning desire

Freundlich die gestirnte Nacht
kindly   the starry   night

Wie ein müdes Kind empfangen.
like a   tired   child receive

Now the day has wearied me, and I yearn for the starry night to receive me gently, like a tired child.

Hände, lasst   von allem Tun,
hands let go of   all   doing

Stirn, vergiss du   alles Denken,
brow forget you all   thinking

Alle meine Sinne   nun
all   my   senses now

Wollen sich   in   Schlummer senken.
want   (themselves) into slumber   to sink

Hands, rest from all doing; brow, cease from all thinking, for now all my senses would sink into slumber.

Und die Seele unbewacht,
and the soul unguarded

Will   in freien Flügen schweben,
wants in free   flights to float

Um im   Zauberkreis der   Nacht,
so as in the magic-circle of the night

Tief   und tausendfach   zu leben.
deeply and thousandfold to live

And my unguarded soul would move in flight unfettered – to live a thousandfold more deeply in the magic circle of the night.

ii. September
September

Hermann Hesse

ii. September

Der Garten trauert,
the garden mourns

The garden mourns; the rain falls cool upon the flowers. Silently the summer shivers towards its close.

Kühl sinkt in   die Blumen der Regen.
cool sinks into the flowers the rain

Der Sommer schauert
the summer shivers

Still   seinem Ende entgegen.
quietly his   end   towards

Golden tropft Blatt um Blatt
golden drops leaf by leaf

Leaf after leaf drips golden from the tall acacia tree. Summer, astonished and spent, smiles on the dying garden dream.

Nieder vom   hohen Akazienbaum.
down from the tall   acacia-tree

Sommer lächelt erstaunt   und matt
summer smiles astonished and spent

In   den sterbenden Gartentraum.
into the dying   garden-dream

Lange noch bei den Rosen
long   still by the roses

It tarries long among the roses, yearning for rest, and slowly closes eyes grown (large and) weary.

Bleibt   er steh'n, sehnt sich   nach Ruh.
remains he standing yearns (himself) for   rest

Langsam tut   er die (grossen)*
slowly   closes he the (large)

Müdgewordnen Augen zu.
tired-become   eyes   –

iii. Frühling
Spring

Hermann Hesse

iii. Spring

In dämmrigen Grüften träumte ich lang
in dusky   vaults   dreamt I   long

As in a gloomy vault, I dreamt so long of your blue skies and trees, and of your fragrance and the songs of birds.

Von deinen Bäumen und blauen Lüften,
of   your   trees   and blue   breezes

Von deinem Duft   und Vogelgesang.
of   your   fragrance and bird-song

* omitted in the song

Nun liegst du   erschlossen in Gleiss und Zier,
now lie   you disclosed in glitter and finery

Von Licht übergossen   wie ein Wunder vor   mir.
by   light poured over like a   miracle before me

Du kennst mich wieder, du lockst mich zart.
you know me   again   you entice me   tenderly

Es zittert   durch   all meine Glieder
(it) quivers through all my   limbs

Deine selige   Gegenwart!
your blessed presence

Now you lie like a miracle before me, unfolded in lustrous adornment and flooded with light. You know me of old; you draw me to you, and tenderly your blessed presence sends a quivering through every limb!

   iv. Im   Abendrot
     in the evening glow

iv. In the evening glow

Joseph von Eichendorff

Wir sind durch   Not   und Freude
we are through misery and joy

Gegangen Hand in Hand;
gone   hand in hand

Vom   Wandern ruhen wir (beide)*
from the wandering rest   we two

Nun überm   stillen Land.
now above the still   countryside

Through joy and sorrow we have gone hand in hand; now we will rest from our wanderings, here above the silent countryside.

Rings   sich   die Täler   neigen,
around (themselves) the valleys slope

Es dunkelt   schon   die Luft,
(it) grows dark already the air

Zwei Lerchen nur noch steigen
two larks   only still rise

Nachträumend in   den Duft.
dreamily   into the scent

Around us the valleys slope away, the air grows dark and only two larks dreamily rise up in the haze.

Tritt her   und lass sie   schwirren,
step here and let them whirr

Bald ist es Schlafenszeit,
soon is it sleep-time

Come, leave them hovering; soon it will be time to sleep, and in this solitude we must not stray.

  * omitted in the song

Dass   wir uns nicht verirren
would that we us   not   go astray

In dieser Einsamkeit.
in this   solitude

O weiter, stiller Friede,   O wide, still peace! Deep in the
O wide   still   peace   twilight, how weary we are of
                                               wandering – can this be death?

So tief   im   Abendrot.
so deep in the evening glow

Wie sind wir wandermüde –
how are we wandering-weary

Ist dies etwa   der Tod?
is this perhaps the death

Index of titles and first lines

Titles of song cycles appear in italics